THE FIRST 100 YEARS

This book is dedicated to
all Bristol City fans,
past, present and future

THE FIRST 100 YEARS

THE OFFICIAL STORY OF BRISTOL CITY FOOTBALL CLUB

Leigh Edwards and David M. Woods

WITH CONTRIBUTIONS BY
David Foot, Steve Henderson,
Michael Martin, Graham Russell
and John Sansom

First published in 1997 for Bristol City Football Club by SANSOM & COMPANY
under the Redcliffe Press imprint.

© 1997 Bristol City Football Club Limited and the authors

Distributed to the trade by Halsgrove Distribution, Tiverton

British Library Cataloguing in Publication Data
A catalogue record for this book is available from The British Library

ISBN 1 900178 26 5 casebound
ISBN 1 900178 36 2 softbound
There is also a limited and numbered edition with players' signatures.

Book design by Neil Champken and Steve Henderson
Cover design by Cursor Graphics

Typesetting and origination by Bristol City Media
Printed by WBC Book Manufacturers Ltd, Bridgend

CONTENTS

Colour plates included

Acknowledgements

Bristol City Football Club and the publishers wish to acknowledge particularly the help of Michael Martin whose enthusiasm and commitment have been crucial to the publication of this centenary celebration. They are grateful, also, to Scott Davidson for the loan of his memorabilia collection, Marina Dolman, Rebecca Henderson, Neil Champken, Shaun Parker, Willie Hardie, Derek Lawton, Paul Gwatkin and Helen Lister of Cursor Graphics, Matt Gore, Thomas Hopegood and Bristol United Press, all of whom have helped in the production of this book.

Thanks go also to Kathryn Britton, Ross Burnham, R Crane, Pam Day, Elliot Feltham, John Hill, Martin Powell and Mark Watson for the use of material which they first wrote for inclusion in *Football Crazy*, published by New Words in 1995.

CHAIRMAN'S PREFACE

It is a great honour and privilege to be invited to write this preface for a book which so wonderfully celebrates the centenary of Bristol City Football Club. 'The First 100 Years' is the most detailed record of our Club's history ever published and is a great tribute to all those, both past and present, who have contributed to Bristol City's grand tradition.

While this tremendous compilation of memorabilia, facts and figures is a wonderful legacy for future generations of supporters, it is of course, our individual passions and memories that continue to fuel our dreams and aspirations of tomorrow. Whether 'your team' is from the fifties, sixties or seventies, or your all-time favourite is Wedlock, Atyeo, Merrick, Dziekanowski or Cole, this book is an absolute treasure for City supporters of all ages.

I believe our club has an exciting future and collectively we must take responsibility for encouraging the next generation of City supporters to Ashton Gate. While we can all be very proud of City's first one hundred years, together we must ensure that our past successes are long-celebrated and that those magic moments from our history serve as standards which those that follow strive to emulate.

During my twenty-five years as a supporter, I can reflect on the highs and lows, the excitement of the mid-seventies and despair of sitting 92nd and bottom of the League in the early eighties. All those experiences, win or lose, promotion or relegation had one thing in common: supporting the greatest football club in the world – BRISTOL CITY FC . . . COME ON YOU REDS!

SCOTT DAVIDSON
Chairman, BCFC
October 25th, 1997

CITY – THE CONTINUING LOVE AFFAIR

Sam Hollis was Bristol City's first manager – and he kept coming back for more. At least three times he was in charge. When the directors interfered too much or quibbled about his salary, he resigned. Then another manager would be appointed but eventually, after a year or two, Sam was persuaded to return.

He did a good job for City. When he arrived from Woolwich Arsenal, where he had been the trainer, he brought several of their players. That reflected a compelling manner and convivial personality as befitted a pub landlord. Somehow he recruited a useful side on a minimal budget. When the committee-room politics got too heated, he simply walked out: until the next time.

Hollis went back to polishing his glasses and pulling the pints. Then came the predictable plea. 'We can do with you again, Sam.' He'd stroke his bushy moustache and shake his head in a gesture of apparent helplessness – and return to a club with which he had such an odd, lingering, enigmatic relationship. And many can understand it. They have experienced that same kind of emotional association.

I grew up in a village 50 miles from Bristol. City were my nearest League club. Apart from the occasional youthful aberration – Barrow, for heaven's sake, were my favourite team until they went out of the League – I faithfully chronicled the mostly undistinguished progress of Bristol City. In the year I was born, the Cow Shed (Stand No.2) at Ashton Gate caught fire and in the same year, deep in the Depression, Alex Raisbeck resigned as manager.

Such unrelated facts were absorbed and stored in my memory as soon as I was able to read. I didn't shed any tears over the fire-damaged stand, but I never quite forgave the directors for falling out with Alex, a fine centre-half for Liverpool (I pretended I saw all my heroes play) and a Scottish international.

City have had a few dozen managers and I like to imagine I knew all of them, free to argue about their summer signings, their selective whims and the tactical styles that they cussedly pursued. Yes, there was Harry Thickett, never without his black bowler or a tale about his days as a full-back for Sheffield United and England . . . And Joe Palmer, an army sergeant not averse to a little military discipline at Ashton Gate . . . And . . . But I must come clean. They'd come and gone long before I'd begun to savour romantic names like Clarrie Bourton, Ernie Brinton and Cliff Morgan.

Let us stay with the managers for a moment. There was the amiable Geordie, Bob Hewison, with a cigarette holder that you suspected would reach from the penalty area to the corner flag; Pat Beasley, sparing of words and capable of sleeping standing-up on the team coach (some players said he was the best of them all); Jimmy Seed, just passing through in a fug of cigar smoke; Peter Doherty, a great player who found it hard to accept that some of his team were lesser mortals; Bob Houghton, who stared at you intimidatingly with the eyes of a stage hypnotist; Terry Cooper, who captivated the reporters with his acerbic one-liners . . . a long managerial line all the way through to Joe Jordan and John Ward.

Somewhere in between, in the post-war seasons, came Fred Ford and Alan Dicks. Maybe Fred lacked a little ambition, certainly not warmth. He was strong on humour and integrity and should have been No.2 to his pal Bill Shankly at Anfield. He didn't like spending, and sometimes wasting, other people's money. Ford could have bought himself out of trouble at Ashton Gate. Instead he was given the sack – despite the impassioned pleadings for him to stay, from the players. Dicks stayed longer than any other manager at the club, largely on merit. He was an astute, well-organised man who can rightly bask in the fact that he took City back into the top division after 65 years.

Why do so many of us have this especial affection for Bristol City? It can't be for the way the club has periodically been mismanaged, miraculously averting bankruptcy and extinction. Most of us continue to fidget uneasily over the ingenious manner City was restructured and players were persuaded to tear up their contracts in the process.

Our love-affair has also been severely tested by the recurrent episodes of boardroom disharmony, the FA inquiry into the club's affairs in the 1920s, chairman George Jenkins' unedifying walk-out and refusal to accept life membership, all the politicking and talk of reform groups. Such acrimony happens in a great many clubs. Human nature is no better regulated, historically, at Ashton Gate.

Deep affection for a football club, whatever its level of opulence and status, means accepting the low points and the rough edges. We try to forget them and pretend they won't recur. We do our best to squeeze them out of our memories by happier, more heart-warming images. At City, over the decades we think again of the twopenny programmes and the Georges beer ads. We think of Ashton Alf and past ages of innocence when the working-class theatre of Saturday afternoons rumbled with good humour and crowd hooliganism was unknown.

We kid ourselves we were on one of those bulging GWR trains that in 1909 took the City fans to London, where City were playing Manchester United at the Crystal Palace in the FA Cup final. It wasn't much of a game but who cares? Two years before that, City had come second in the old first division. That wonderful, under-praised goalkeeper, Harry Clay, was letting nothing past him; Billy Wedlock, small and stocky, was creating optical illusions as he outjumped every opposing centre forward.

Billy, or Fatty (he didn't much approve of that description), played 26 times for his country. In his old age, in the pub across the road from the ground, he showed me his caps. That was a cherished occasion for me. How I wish I'd seen him play, been able to glimpse his flawless timing whenever he went up to challenge. There were so many I'd have liked to watch; little 'Tot' Walsh, with his Lancashire accent and exuberant, bustling, goal-hungry style, Walter Wadsworth, a commanding centre-half who arrived from Liverpool to captain the Ashton Gate club.

When I came to Bristol to live, it was the days of Guy and Bailey – and Ernie Peacock, that symbol of fiery reliability. There was something especially vibrant about that promotion side of the Fifties. So, of course, there was about City's triumphant team of 1976. They announced their arrival among the game's elite by impishly beating Arsenal. Paul Cheesley scored the famous winning goal. Three days later, his career was wretchedly over when he injured his knee in the first home game.

City weren't strong enough to stay in the first division for long. In fact, their history hasn't been laden with too much success. They've flirted with the game's glamour. But that should not detract from their imperishable appeal. Vaunted players have come and gone, Norman Hunter and Andy Cole among them. And, of course, John Atyeo remains an ageless idol. He was a village boy, a quantity surveyor and a schoolmaster. He chose Bristol City rather than Portsmouth, although his railway-man father wished only for him to play cricket for Somerset.

Atyeo played for his country half a dozen times. He had so many natural gifts. Goalscoring was pragmatically the most important. All of us treasure reminiscences – of his body swerves and perfect balance, of the intuitive way he picked up the passes from Cyril Williams, Bobby Etheridge, Shadow and Jantzen. We saw his tears at his final match and knew he could never have left the West Country.

Close-knit family feeling is fast disappearing from modern football. But it was a significant characteristic at Ashton Gate. After Don Clark came Brian; after Arnie Rodgers came David. There was also the deep-rooted Scottish connection. We can go back to Bob Kelso and popular keeper Hugh Monteith, forward to Gerry Gow, Tom Ritchie and Gerry Sweeney, and beyond.

Local voices have also been important. That was why Cliff Morgan and his successors combed the local parks and village touchlines. Nowadays a renewed emphasis is being wisely placed on emerging West Country-based talent. Amid the dressing-room chatter of a dozen different regional accents, it's still reassuring to hear a Bristol voice as authentic as the Avon which flows past, just down the road.

Unwavering City fans have always been prepared to weep as well as cheer. They did so, long ago, when the team were obsessed with nerves in that sole appearance in the FA Cup final. Many years later, they did so as the club, seemingly in disarray though holding the bailiffs at bay, plummeted out of control or obvious means of support, from the first to the fourth division.

Harry Dolman, dogmatic, wholehearted and such an undeniable influence on the club, was an incorrigible fan. In moments of Saturday-night confidence, he used to say: 'We'll be up there with the very best one day.' Those who zestfully run Bristol City today, with their new resolves and ideas, are fired by the same shafts of optimism.

Success at a high level must be a beacon-like ambition. But there is another side to every club – about its spirit and its soul. In an odd way, famous glitzy clubs, laden with silverware and acclaim, are not always great ones.

This centenary history, so lovingly researched, is about the humanity and quirks of Bristol City. From the Bedminster and St John's Lane days to the all-seater grandeur of Ashton Gate in the Nineties, there has persisted a potent south-of-the-river tribal fervour about City. It's impossible, on the big match occasions, not to be caught up in it. That was what Harry Dolman had in mind. It was what caused old bewhiskered Sam Hollis to keep coming back.

DAVID FOOT

THE FIRST
ONE HUNDRED YEARS

CHAPTER ONE

EARLY DAYS

This book celebrates the hundred years during which the proud name of Bristol City Football Club has appeared on the sports pages of the local and national press. But the story goes back some years before that crucial day of August 7th, 1897 on which the Football Association finally authorised a change of name from Bristol South End to Bristol City.

Bristol South End was the somewhat parochial title adopted at an inaugural meeting held in a house in Milford Road, Southville, in April 1894. The new club was spawned from two events: the decision of Bristol South AFC to disband and the growing dissent in the ranks of the rival Bedminster club which had been founded some seven years earlier. Among the eighteen association enthusiasts who assembled were J.A. Stevens (Secretary of the Bristol & District League), Bill Hodgkinson, the one-time secretary of Eastville Rovers, two notable local players in Arthur Jones and Hamer Clements and two erstwhile Bedminster members, Fred Keenan and John Durant.

After the princely sum of £6.8.6d had been pledged towards setting up costs, a subsequent meeting at Rock Lodge in Southville, the home of John Durant, appointed the first officials. W.R. Nurse became chairman, Bill Hodgkinson was the first secretary, assisted by Fred Keenan, while the brothers Harry and Ted Locke shared the treasurer's role. Colonel Plant was elected President, with John Durant as his deputy. The club's name had been suggested by J.A. Stevens, a self-confessed admirer of Preston North End.

The fledgling Bristol South End, ambitious from the outset, had no interest in filling the niche left by Bristol South who had been the very first champions of the South Bristol & District League. They set their sights instead on competing with clubs like Warmley, St George, Clifton Association, Eastville Rovers and Bedminster, who dominated the Bristol & District League (about to become the Western League). Their application to join the league, though, met with an early rebuff when, on April 25th, they were told that "the League cannot entertain a club without any history". Undaunted, they set about compiling a fixture list of friendlies, attracting to the St John's Lane ground such notable teams as (appropriately) Preston North End, along with Swindon Town, Tottenham Hotspur, 1st Scots Guards and the London Welsh Regiment. All this raised the public profile of the club, but did little to impress league officials.

Responding to that first rejection, the South End members decided by a large majority at a meeting in April, 1895 not to seek election to the League for 1895/96. Their statement

A crowd gather to watch Bristol South End at the St. John's Lane ground prior to the transfer to Ashton Gate.

declared that "This meeting desires to add its appreciation of the good work done by the Bristol & District League . . . and is in no way antagonistic to that body. This Club will always be glad to work and cordially co-operate with the League for the advancement of football in the district."

Another round of friendlies followed, but when Cardiff was expelled from what was now called the Western League at the turn of the year, the club offered to take over the Welsh side's fixtures. This time, they were turned down by nine votes to seven, with the Byzantine explanation that "The Western League thank the South End Club for their offer, but regret that they cannot see their way clear, owing to the question of points and other various difficulties of this case, to accept it, but the League trust that [the club] will renew its application next season, and the South End Club is further assured that this resolution has nothing to do with any personal matter between the League and the South End Club."

Undeterred, the Garibaldians – as South End were popularly known because of their red shirts – tried again in the summer and at a League meeting at the Conservative Club, Old Market Street, Bristol, on June 3rd, 1896, they were at last successful.

THE PROFESSIONAL GAME

South End quickly justified their new status, winning their opening four games. They were, though, no match for the eventual champions, Warmley, losing 4-0 on the Tennis Court Ground in front of 4,464 spectators in December and 3-0 at St John's Lane at the end of April, 1897. Even so, the Garibaldians ended their first League campaign as runners-up, six points behind Warmley and four ahead of Bedminster.

By now the club was determined to embrace professionalism and gain admission to the Southern League. A heavy 10-0 home defeat by the Old Carthusians in the first round proper of the FA Amateur Cup on January 30th, 1897 confirmed that they had progressed as far as they could with local amateur players. A meeting of South End members at the Albert Hall, Bedminster in April voted in favour of professionalism after the Southern League Secretary, Nat Whittaker, had assured them that the club would be successful in securing election to the Southern League's First Division.

Those present agreed to become guarantors at ten shillings each, and the meeting was

OGDEN'S CIGARETTES

BRISTOL CITY

adjourned, pending a further report from an investigation committee who had been looking into the question of professionalism. Another meeting, on May 19th – two days after Southern League status had been achieved – saw the Albert Hall overflowing with enthusiastic supporters, who duly elected a management committee to get things moving. Two of the Southern League representatives who attended were presented with silver cigarette boxes in appreciation of their assistance.

The proposed guarantee system was seen to be unworkable and the next meeting of members, on June 4th, approved the proposed conversion of the club to limited liability status. The meeting elected Albert Denby as chairman of the board, his fellow directors being James Crompton, H.C. Ewens, F.H. Hawksby and Walter Tozer. These were later joined by three more directors: James Barnes, William Kingston and Joseph Daveridge. The company was capitalised at £2,500 in £1 shares, of which 1,500 were to be offered to the public.

A NEW NAME – AT LAST

The investigation committee had decided early in their deliberations that the club's new status demanded a new identity, and that it might as well go for the best. Their application to adopt the name of Bristol City Football Club was considered by the Gloucestershire Football Association at their meeting at the Full Moon, Stokes Croft on April 27th, 1897. The initial response was not encouraging, with the association ruling that "it would be detrimental to the interests of the clubs in the city and neighbourhood if any one club was allowed to take the name of Bristol City". The *Bristol Times & Mirror* weighed in, commenting the following day that "this ruling should put a stopper on any club calling itself by this name and even had they not taken this action, surely Bristol Rugby Club would have the right to protest".

Undeterred, the Garibaldians continued to press their case. The *Times & Mirror* had accurately predicted the response of the local rugby club, who complained to the rugby union authorities. The argument dragged on throughout the summer, but after Walter Tozer had appealed directly to the Football Association, the Gloucestershire FA eventually gave its approval on August 7th, 1897.

The good news, though, was somewhat tempered by the realisation that the delay may have prejudiced the outcome of the share issue. When the subscription list eventually opened on September 1st, only 531 of the 1,500 shares offered to the public were taken up and the board had to make good the poor response.

The Bristol " Magpie," September 30th, 1897.

DAVEY. HOLLIS (trainer). MONTEITH. [*Photo, G. H. Wicks.*

MANN. HIGGINS (capt.) SINCLAIR. HAMILTON.

WYLLIE. CARNELLY. CAIE. O'BRIEN. RUSSELL.

THE UNBEATEN "BRISTOL CITY" TEAM.

Sam Hollis

SAM HOLLIS BECOMES MANAGER

In going professional, the club needed a professional manager, and one name stood out among the applicants for the job. Stan Hollis had been Woolwich Arsenal's trainer for three years, and was to prove arguably the most influential manager in City's history. But he faced an uphill task, as the Club had little money and no professional players. Immediately on returning to London after meeting with prominent City members on April 21st, 1897, he sounded out a number of Woolwich Arsenal players who proved willing to sample West Country life provided the money was good enough.

A week later, chairman Albert Denby and H.C. Ewens were in Southampton to meet Hollis at the Hampshire Cricket Club ground where his Arsenal side beat Southampton St Mary's 5-1 in a friendly match. After the game, the Saints' secretary offered the Bristol representatives not only support for their Southern League application, but also some of their surplus players. The first offer was gratefully accepted, but the second was politely rejected. "If they are not good enough for you, they are not good enough for us," commented Stan Hollis. "We want players that you want." Straight talk indeed, especially as the Bristol manager still did not know how much money was available for bargaining.

Hollis insisted on knowing the financial score before he left for London. "What time does your train go?" asked Denby. "6.05pm," responded Hollis. "How much do you want?" "£20 or £30 – £30, I should say." "All right, I will be at the station with it." It was three minutes past the hour when the club chairman dashed up in a hansom cab and thrust a cheque for £30 into the manager's hands with the words: "Do your best for us."

It was a less-than-princely budget, but Hollis proved equal to the task. On the journey back to London he persuaded four Arsenal players – Alex Caie, Paddy O'Brien, Jock Russell and Finlay Sinclair – that it would be such an honour to play for City that they agreed to join without a signing-on fee. After this brilliant coup, Hollis set his sights a little higher, and with a further £10 from Denby he secured the services of Loughborough trio Jack Hamilton, Billy Jones and Hugh Monteith, Leicester Fosse pair Albert Carnelly and Harry Davy, as well as Billy Higgins (who would be City's first captain) from Grimsby Town, Tom Wyllie from Bury and George Mann from Manchester City.

Hollis had achieved a minor miracle. The side he assembled for £40 proved almost good enough to win the Southern League Championship and for many years was fondly regarded as City's finest ever team. The new players were introduced to supporters at a club concert at Bedminster Town Hall on August 11th, 1897, and a crowd of almost 800 was present when the team started ball practice at St John's Lane the following day. Similarly well attended practice sessions were held every Tuesday and Thursday evening throughout the rest of the month.

The first opponents of the Bristol Babe, City's popular nickname, were fellow Southern Leaguers Southampton, who had just dropped 'St Mary's' from their title, in a friendly at St John's Lane on September 1st. City's 3-1 victory in torrential rain on a half-flooded pitch was marred by tragedy when a little girl drowned in the swollen waters of the brook running alongside the ground. Further friendly home wins over Swindon Town and Lancashire League champions Chorley followed before the club's first Southern League fixture on September 11th, 1897.

SOUTHERN LEAGUE

The visitors to St John's Lane for this historic match were Wolverton, and a crowd of 6,000 cheered a rampaging first-half which saw City 6-1 ahead at the interval. The visitors fought back to within two goals before City clinched a 7-4 win. Jock Russell netted City's first Southern League goal and the other scorers were Alex Caie (3), Albert Carnelly (2) and Billy Higgins.

The following Saturday City travelled to face Millwall on their East Ferry Road ground. Runners-up the previous season and champions the year before that, Millwall were expected to be formidable opponents, but the newcomers swept to a tremendous 6-2 victory to thrill their many fans who had travelled on a special GWR excursion. It was a performance to astound the soccer world. City were clearly a force to be reckoned with. It was not until New Year's Day that they suffered their first Southern League defeat, going down 4-0 at Southampton. Revenge came two weeks later when the Saints were humbled 5-2 at St John's Lane in front of a new record Southern League crowd of 12,170. Southampton went on to win the title, with City runners-up.

In the Professional Section of the Western League though, City were not to be denied and their championship-winning side was described by League Secretary J.A. Stevens as "the best team ever seen in the competition". Further accolades followed when City defeated Eastville Rovers and Bristol St George in the Gloucestershire Senior Cup, before overcoming the renowned Warmley club 2-1 in the final to avenge defeat in the 2nd Round of the Bristol Charity Cup. In the FA Cup, City lost 2-0 at Southampton in the 3rd Qualifying Round. It was in this competition that City helped hasten the demise of Clifton Association, beating them 9-1 in the opening round; two months later the third oldest local club (founded in 1883) had disbanded. This marked the start of a rationalisation process that saw the end of Warmley and St George, both formed in 1882, as well as the amalgamation of Bedminster with Bristol City. Only Eastville Rovers, who had been formed as the Black Arabs in 1883, remained unchanged, though in February 1899 they adopted their present title of Bristol Rovers.

On January 26th, 1898 City stormed to a record victory as goals by Billy Jones (4), Albert Carnelly (2), Billy Higgins (2), Tom Wyllie (2), Alex Caie, Jack Hamilton, Jock Russell and Brocklehurst o.g. gave them a 14-1 Western League home win over Eastleigh. Only six weeks earlier Eastleigh had lost 10-3 to City in the 1st Round of the Bristol Charity Cup, and not surprisingly they scratched from their return Western League match in March.

BID FOR FOOTBALL LEAGUE MEMBERSHIP

Bristol City's first campaign as a professional club not only realised an operating profit of £66.5s.9d but it encouraged the board to make a bid for Football League status. At the Football League's AGM at Manchester on May 20th, 1898, City entered the ballot along with three Second Division clubs seeking re-election – Lincoln City, Darwen and Loughborough Town – as well as non-League Burslem Port Vale, Nelson and New Brighton Tower. The delegates were apparently not impressed, as City finished bottom of the poll with only one vote.

During the three years before their next, and successful, bid for Football League status,

City's Southern League title ambitions were twice thwarted by all-conquering Southampton. The 1898/99 season saw Sam Hollis make further notable signings, including Billy Stewart from Everton, who took over as captain, Pat Finnerhan (Liverpool), John McLean (Grimsby Town), Billy Langham, John Murphy and Billy Potter, all from Notts County, as well as George Barker, an international trialist, described as the best full-back in the Southern League. City were top of the table when Southampton came to Bristol for the final match of the campaign on April 29th, 1899. With a 2-0 lead at half-time, a record crowd of 13,000 must have been thinking that City's time had come, but the visitors finished strongly to win 4-3 and retain the championship.

In the FA Cup (then commonly known as the English Cup) Bristol City became the first local club to win through to the 1st Round Proper, losing 4-2 to Sunderland at St John's Lane in front of 16,945 spectators on January 28th, 1899. City's cup run had earlier seen tragedy when a spectator fell from a tree and died during a tie at Bristol St George's Bell Hill ground. The City directors contributed £10 in opening a relief fund for his widow and six children.

NEW MANAGER AND NEW PARTNER

In March, 1899 Sam Hollis announced his intention of leaving at the end of the season. He objected to increasing interference by the directors and to the conditions they attached to the offer of a new £200 a year contract. City now cultivated links they had made during Sunderland's FA Cup visit a few months earlier, and persuaded the northern club's secretary-manager, Bob Campbell, to take over in a similar capacity at St John's Lane. It meant paying £70 a year more than they had offered Hollis, but the new man recruited what appeared to be a very good set of players, including Alex Downie from Third Lanark, Adam Godsman (St Bernards), Fred Molyneux (Stoke) and Alex Crawford and Alex McDonald, both from Clyde, as well as re-signing Talbot-Lewis from Everton.

Despite this infusion of talent and the engagement of the renowned Jim Blessington from Derby County in October, City had a poor season, struggling to finish in ninth place, above Bristol Rovers only on goal average. Indeed, the team was performing so badly that the directors had called a crisis meeting with the players at the Angel Hotel, Redcliffe Street, in December, but their strictures did nothing to improve the season's performance. Meanwhile, local honours were taken by Bedminster who finished sixth, and also beat City in the Gloucestershire Senior Cup Final. Ironically, Sam Hollis had taken over as the Minster's secretary-manager, but any elation on his part was doubtless tempered by the amalgamation of the two clubs at the end of the season.

It was more a takeover by Bristol City, as they provide the ground, colours and manager, while Bedminster provided only players, as well as half the new board. Quite why the combined club retained City's St John's Lane ground rather than Bedminster's superior Ashton Gate venue, where Bristol's first international match took place on March 20th, 1899 when England beat Wales 4-0, is unclear. Easier access for fans was perhaps the reason, although it was thought expedient – to retain erstwhile Bedminster supporters – to share home matches between the two grounds to start with, and fourteen games were played at Ashton Gate in 1900/01.

THE MINSTER

Bedminster AFC had moved to Ashton Gate at the start of the 1896/97 season, with the first match there taking place on September 12th, 1896 when Staple Hill were defeated 4-2 in a friendly.

Before this, the Minster had played on the Bedminster Cricket Ground, having joined forces with the cricket club in 1889. Their ground was then on the strip of land on Greenway Bush Lane where later stood the tobacco factories which were demolished in 1994. It was this link with the cricket club that brought about the change of name from Southville, used since their formation in 1887 when their home ground was in Greville Smyth Park. The Ashton Gate ground was shared by the cricket club for 15 years until they moved to the Clanage in 1912.

The cricket link enabled Bedminster AFC to establish themselves as one of the top local sides. After winning the Gloucestershire Senior Cup for the first time in 1891, when they beat Warmley 2-0 on the old St George ground, they became a founder member of the Western League in 1892. They went on to become champions of the Amateur Section of the Western League in 1897/98, before embracing the professional code the following season, when they won the Bristol Charity Cup. This final was played on the Bristol City ground at St John's Lane on April 24th, 1899 when Bedminster surprised Reading by recovering from a 2-0 deficit in the second half to gain a notable 3-2 victory watched by only 500 spectators.

This 1898/99 season was Bedminster's first in the Southern League and after an opening 1-1 draw with Tottenham Hotspur at Northumberland Park they performed well enough, under the guidance of manager Harry Smith, to hold eighth place at the campaign's conclusion. Bedminster's final season, 1899/1900, saw them finish as runners-up in the Professional Section of the Western League, as well as sixth in the Southern League. Further honours followed when they retained the Charity Cup. After beating City 6-0 in a replayed semi-final at St John's Lane, they accounted for Bristol Rovers 4-1 at the same venue in the final. The Minister's final match on April 30th saw them win the Gloucestershire Cup with a 2-1 victory over Bristol City.

So passed into history this pioneer of local football and the hopes of south Bristol were now to rest solely with Bristol City, whose achievements over the amazing decade to come would underline the foresight of Bedminster chairman, A.W. Francis and financial secretary, Billy Burland in resolutely pressing for amalgamation.

MOUNTING LOSSES

The 1900/01 season saw City move their headquarters from the Angel Hotel to Bank Chambers, East Street, Bedminster. Bob Campbell strengthened his squad with the addition of Phil Bach and Billy Fulton from Sunderland, David McDougall (Partick Thistle), Billy Michael (Heart of Midlothian), David Nichol (Millwall Athletic) and Jim Stevenson from Newcastle United, as well as Billy Wedlock from local club Arlington Rovers, whom City had beaten 4-0 in a pre-season trial match at Ashton Gate.

For the third time in four seasons, City had to suffer the bitter-sweet disappointment of finishing Southern League runners-up as well as incurring a loss of £974 which, with the deficit brought forward from the previous year, meant that accumulated losses now exceeded £2,000. Instead of cutting back, the board made a further bid for Football League membership.

This time they were successful, largely due to Bob Campbell's contacts, and they finished joint top of the poll at the Football League AGM in Manchester on May 17th, 1901, when the votes were cast as follows: Bristol City 23 (elected), Burton Swifts (re-elected and name changed to Burton United on amalgamation with Burton Wanderers), Doncaster Rovers 16, Stockport County 16, Stalybridge Rovers 7, Walsall 7, Crewe Alexandra 5 and Darwen 0.

Ironically, the main architect of Bristol City's successful bid was not involved with their Football League debut. After major disagreements with board policy, Bob Campbell resigned his three-year contract. City again turned to Sam Hollis, who had been concentrating on his hotel business, but who now agreed to step into the breach on the clear understanding he would have a free hand.

Again Hollis was faced with the task of building a side with little money. He introduced economies, including a reduction in his own salary, and called on benefactors for financial assistance. His appeal raised an impressive £345 which was enough for him to set off on a player-signing mission. Eleven new players joined from other clubs around the country. These, along with those retained from the previous campaign – Robert Davies, Billy Jones, Peter Chambers, Paddy O'Brien and John McLean – helped City finish their inaugural Football League season holding sixth position in the Second Division. Notable among those released was Billy Wedlock, later to rejoin the club under Thickett in 1905 and destined to become one of the best centre-halves ever to turn out for England.

The menu for the Bristol City Second Annual Complimentary Dinner held at the Prince Hotel, Totterdown on Saturday, May 13th, 1899.

Chapter Two

EDWARDIAN HOLIDAY

Bristol City kicked off its Football League career on September 7th, 1901 when two goals from Paddy O'Brien brought a 2-0 win against Blackpool at Bloomfield Road. After a defeat at Burslem Port Vale, 7,000 spectators cheered a 3-0 success against Stockport County in City's first home game on September 14th. All home matches were now played at St John's Lane until a permanent move to Ashton Gate for the 1904-05 campaign.

The faithful Sam Hollis remained in charge during this time, but even though he recruited well, the promotion prize remained beyond his grasp as City finished fourth in three successive seasons. Notable successes in the FA Cup offered some compensation, with impressive wins over First Division Bolton Wanderers (5-0) at Burnden Park in February, 1903 and Woolwich Arsenal (1-0) in a replay at Ashton Gate two years later – a game in which City first played in green shirts. At this time, the longer-established club had the option of playing in their own colours at all times and although most teams did not insist on this when playing away, Arsenal caused much local annoyance by doing so on this when facing City.

RECORD CROWD AND THE MOVE TO ASHTON GATE

A record St John's Lane crowd of 17,909 saw the home side go down 3-1 to Sheffield United in the First Round Proper of the FA Cup on February 6th, 1904 – an attendance which brought home to the directors the need to develop the ground or find an alternative venue. The club opted to move to Ashton Gate, and the last Football League match was played at St John's Lane on April 23rd, 1904 when Burslem Port Vale were beaten 2-1.

In 1903/04, Bristol City started up a competitive reserve team for the first time since the South End days, although they had fielded a second team for friendlies in the last season of the old century. The championship of both the Second Division of the Western League and the Bristol Charity League was secured, and a special match to close the St John's Lane ground on April 30th saw the First Team beat the Reserves by the odd goal in five.

Spectators' first view of the new Ashton Gate was at the public trial match in August, 1904, and the changes since the last match played there – back in 1901 – were impressive. £2,500 had been spent on building the Number 1 Grandstand on the south-western side of the pitch, erecting cover at the south-eastern end and relocating the old grandstand (called Number 2). The pitch was moved from the south-east corner to its new central position.

Bolton Wanderers spoilt the official opening on September 3rd, 1904 when they scored

Manager Harry Thickett's Football League Division Two Champions Medal.

twice in the dying minutes of the game to win an exciting Second Division game 4-3 in front of 14,000 fans. Special guests present included F.J. Wall, Secretary of the Football Association, J.A. Tayler and J.R. Riddell, President and Chairman respectively of the Gloucestershire FA and G. Humphreys, chairman of Bristol Rovers.

The new ground was chosen to stage an international trial match in February, 1905 when a 7,500 crowd saw the South lose 3-1 against the North. Bristol City supplied two South players – Peter Chambers and Billy Jones – along with Bristol Rovers' goalkeeper Arthur Cartlidge, while their opponents included Bristolian Freddy Wilcox, who played for Small Heath.

RECORD BREAKERS

For the new season, former Sheffield United right-back, Harry Thickett replaced Sam Hollis who wanted, again, to spend more time on his hotel business. The new manager made an immediate impression, taking City to promotion in 1905/06. In the process, they became the first club to win thirty League games in a season, created a new points record and equalled the run of fourteen consecutive League wins set by Manchester United the previous season. This run is still a record, although shared with Preston North End since 1950/51.

The first match of the season had given no hint of the success to follow, as City went down 5-1 at Manchester United. Bouncing back, however, the club embarked on a remarkable 24-match unbeaten run, and did not lose another League match until February 17th when visitors Leicester Fosse pulled off a surprise 2-1 win. These two were the only League defeats of the season, although in the FA Cup City fell victim to giant-killing Brentford, losing 2-1 after leading at the interval.

The opening match in the First Division brought promotion partners Manchester United to the West Country on September lst, 1906 in the middle of a heatwave. A fifth minute penalty by Walter Bennett gave City an early lead, but United came back to win 2-1. City soon found their feet, though, and by the end of the year looked strong contenders for Championship honours. The title eluded them, after three successive defeats over the Easter period, and City finished runners-up, three points behind Newcastle United. Even so, this was a remarkable achievement, and was to remain

The 1907/08 line-up, back row l to r: Batten (Trainer); T. Gale, W. Rippon, R. Young, W. Demmery, A. Spear, Mr. Bacon (Director), Mr Thickett (Manager). Front row: R. Marr, F.W. Staniforth, W.P. Maxwell, S. Gilligan, F. Connolly, P. Hanlin, J. Cottle, Mr Deveridge (Director). Sitting: W. Wedlock, F. Hilton.

the highest first-season position attained by a debutant club in the First Division until it was equalled by Charlton Athletic in 1936/37 and eventually eclipsed by Ipswich Town in 1960/61.

ENGLAND CAPS

On February 16th, 1907 centre-half Billy Wedlock became the second Bristol City player to win an England cap, following in the footsteps of Billy Jones who had made his sole international appearance in a 3-0 win over Ireland six years earlier at Southampton. Unlike Jones, Wedlock was Bristol-born, but even so was not the first Bristolian to represent his country, as leading amateur, C. Wreford Brown (Clifton Association, Oxford University, Corinthians and Old Carthusians) had won the first of four caps in 1889 when turning out against Ireland.

Another Bristol-born player joined this illustrious group on February 13th, 1909 when City's Joe Cottle played alongside Wedlock in the England team that beat Ireland 4-0 at Bradford Park Avenue.

Pre-season optimism that City would go one better in 1907/08 and clinch the Championship seemed well founded with an opening 3-2 home win over Everton and a 4-0 outing at Woolwich Arsenal, but form faded and just one win in sixteen games after Christmas found City in the relegation zone with four matches left to play. Victory by two goals to nil over Bolton Wanderers at home restored flagging hopes just enough for City to finish a roller-coaster season with an unbeaten run that hoisted them to tenth place.

CUP FINALISTS

The following season is best remembered for an FA Cup run that saw City reach the Final – played at the Crystal Palace on April 24th, 1909 – for the first and only time to date. They got there the hard way, with replays in every round except the Third. In the Semi-Final match against Derby County at Stamford Bridge on March 27th, City were saved by a last-gasp penalty by Willis Rippon, and another Rippon penalty helped them to a 2-1 victory in the replay at St Andrews four days later.

City's opponents in the Final, old rivals

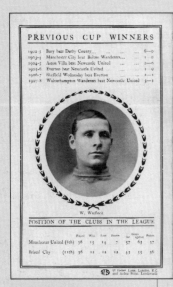

The programme for the 1908/09 English Cup Final, played at the Crystal Palace between Bristol City and Manchester United.

Manchester United, were favourites after their Championship success the previous year, and Bristol City had lost two key players in Reuben Marr and Rippon because of injury. The only goal of the match was scored by United's Sandy Turnbull, and although City wasted opportunities to equalise, the consensus was that the Northerners deserved to win the Cup for the first time.

The Cup run brought a welcome profit of more than £3,000, which enabled the Club to pay shareholders a dividend and funded ground improvements, with the Number 1 Grandstand extended towards the Covered End during the summer of 1909.

With the previous season's excitements whetting appetites for more cup glory, the 1909/1910 campaign proved to be an anti-climax. After a first round win over Liverpool, City lost 4-2 in a replay at West Bromwich Albion. In the league, relegation was avoided with a crucial 1-0 home success over Chelsea in the closing weeks of the season, and the club's best performance was reserved for the final game, when John Cowell scored all four goals to beat Nottingham Forest at Ashton Gate.

RELEGATION

There was to be no such salvation in 1910/11, even though City kicked off with a 1-0 victory at Newcastle United. By October, the club was in bottom place, after going down by two goals to nil at Notts County. Manager Harry Thickett was dismissed two days later and director Frank Bacon assumed temporary control. His brief tenure saw some improvement, but following a shock 3-0 FA Cup defeat at home to non-League Crewe Alexandra, he stood down when Sam Hollis was yet again persuaded to return.

Hollis started promisingly with a win over Middlesbrough, but just one victory in the following twelve games left City propping up the table with only three matches remaining. A 5-1 home triumph over Nottingham Forest, followed by a battling 2-1 win at Manchester City raised hopes of escape when the club met Everton at home in the season's final match. City went down 1-0, and relegation brought about boardroom changes, with Ernest Murdock replacing William Panes Kingston as chairman that summer.

F.W. Staniforth's 1908/09 FA Cup Runners-up medal.

Billy Wedlock's 1909/10 GFA Senior Cup winners medal.

CHAPTER THREE
THE LONG EXILE

Few expected City to do well back in the Second Division, and true to expectation they struggled to keep above the re-election zone that 1911/12 season. Eleven points from the final seven games, however, enabled them to finish thirteenth in the table. This escape prompted many spectators to predict promotion next season, and indeed a seven-match unbeaten run augured well for success. It was not until mid-October that City suffered their first defeat, at Glossop – this, despite Wedlock scoring a rare goal – but after winning their next game at home to Clapton Orient, they failed to win again for another two months.

In January 1913, Stockport County were beaten 7-2 at Ashton Gate, with Ginger Owers scoring four times. The last-but-one game of the season, a 3-0 defeat at Grimsby, was the last with Sam Hollis in charge. Four days later, he was replaced by George Hedley as City finished a disappointing sixteenth.

One highlight was the staging of another international at Ashton Gate, when a crowd of 9,000 saw England beat Wales by the odd goal in seven on March 17th, 1913. The disappointment was that Billy Wedlock, by now England's regular centre-half, had to withdraw because of injury.

THE HOWARTH AFFAIR

The sensation of the 1913/14 season concerned City's new centre-forward, Tommy Howarth, who was signed after impressing in a trial match while visiting Bristol on Christmas leave from the Army. After the normal period of notice, Bristol City arranged for him to purchase his discharge and found him suitable employment. However, the Football Association then stepped in, and Howarth was suspended for twelve months. City were fined £50 for involvement in a practice the FA were determined to stamp out.

The outbreak of war in August 1914 gave the 1914/15 round of league and cup matches an unreal feel. Many felt that football should have shut down, and there was bad feeling towards players who had not answered the country's call to arms. Critics were partly mollified when the authorities responded by arranging recruitment campaigns at football matches. Four wins, including a 4-0 home success over Preston North End, in their opening five games put Bristol City in second spot, and despite fluctuating form they were still well in the running for honours when they beat Grimsby Town by an emphatic seven (first half) goals to nil on Boxing Day. They finished no higher than thirteenth, though, after falling away in the new year.

WAR-TIME FOOTBALL

Four difficult war seasons followed. Bristol City competed in the South West Combination in 1915/16 against Bristol Rovers, Cardiff City, Newport County, Portsmouth, Southampton and Swindon Town. This League folded the following season when Portsmouth and Southampton joined the London Combination and City then played a succession of friendlies until midway through 1917/18, when the formation of the Bristol County Combination restored a measure of competition. City pipped Bristol Rovers for the inaugural championship, although the roles were reversed the following year. The statistical highlight of the war years was City's record win, in a friendly match in April, 1916, when they overwhelmed the Army Service Corps by 20 goals to one, with Albert Chapman scoring eight times and Dickie Reader five. Hat-tricks for Bert Neesam and C. Slade, and a goal by W. Cross, completed the score line. In the Bristol County Combination, City also heavily beat the R.A.F. (Filton) side 14-2, whilst a 4-0 victory over Southampton was their best win in the South West Combination.

The most signficant development, though, was the purchase of Ashton Gate when the lease expired on March 21st, 1917. It was a bold move, as the club had lost almost £1,350 over the previous two seasons, and also had suffered financially when gales damaged the Covered End, which finally had to be demolished. The directors' foresight at a difficult time would stand City in good stead, as it was ultimately to provide the platform for the very survival of the club in the crises of 1933 and 1982.

BOOM AND BUST

The pleasure of football returning to normal for the 1919/20 season was more than tinged with sadness by the death in action of two City players, goalkeeper Tommy Ware, who died on the Western Front in June, 1915, and Edwin Burton who was killed in action fourteen months later. Former City player, Albert Edwards, also perished in the carnage. Of several club players and officials who served in the armed forces, Arthur Moss was decorated in 1917. Club Secretary Frank Hill was called up that year, and thankfully survived to resume his duties at the end of hostilities.

Joe Palmer now took over as manager from popular Jack Hamilton, who had been in charge since George Hedley was called to the colours in January 1917. For Palmer, who had risen to the rank of Sergeant-Major during his army career, this was a happy return to Ashton Gate, where he had been trainer under Hedley before the war.

The Football League programme got underway on August 30th, 1919 when Bury were beaten in front of 10,000 spectators at Ashton Gate. Jack Howarth scored the opening goal of the season, which was enough to win the match.

As expected, post-war crowds were high, and the £1,000 barrier for home receipts was broken for the first time in October, when a crowd of more than 20,000 paid £1,150 to watch the Fulham match. This record take was comfortably beaten on January 31st, when an attendance of 25,900 at the FA Cup visit by Arsenal yielded receipts of £2,031 – a figure to be dwarfed by the £3,551 raised just three weeks later when Cardiff City were the cup visitors in front of a crowd of 32,432.

Although City had a satisfactory League campaign, finishing eighth in the Second

Division, it was their FA Cup exploits which excited the Bristol fans. Starting with a 2-1 win at Grimsby Town, Palmer's team brushed aside First Division Arsenal and Southern League Cardiff City to draw First Division Bradford City at home in the Quarter-finals. Two goals from Joe Harris put City only one step away from their second Final.

UNLUCKY STAMFORD BRIDGE

City were lucky to avoid First Division sides Aston Villa and Chelsea and to find themselves paired with Second Division rivals Huddersfield Town in the Semi-Final at neutral Stamford Bridge on March 27th, 1920. Watched by a crowd of 35,863, City became one of the early victims of Huddersfield's remarkable rise to greatness. Threatened with closure only four months previously, the Yorkshire side became the first club to win the League Championship three times in a row.

The 1920/21 season saw Bristol City mount a strong promotion bid, eventually finishing a creditable third behind champions Birmingham and newly-elected Cardiff City. Much credit went to the defence which conceded just 29 goals – a club record low – in their 42 League outings. In a dramatic turn around the following season, City conceded twice as many goals to suffer relegation to the Third Division (South).

So poor was City's form that their cause was hopeless by Christmas and there was no real expectation of Alex Raisbeck being able to save them following his appointment as secretary-manager in late-December.

Joe Palmer had gone two months previously, in somewhat controversial circumstances. After attending a board meeting on the evening of October 18th, 1921, he was reported to be surprised to receive a letter the following morning asking for his resignation. Palmer refused and asked to discuss the matter, but the board's position was that they had no option but to terminate his engagement with immediate effect. Archie Annan took over on a temporary basis, assisted by trainer Dick Batten.

Bristol City were much too strong for the lower division and they stormed to a championship win in 1922/23, heading the table from mid-December. The euphoria was short-lived, as in the following season City's first win didn't come until the seventh game – at Derby – and in the return match a week later, they were humbled 8-0 at Ashton Gate. Seemingly anchored in the bottom two positions, City were doomed to relegation well before the campaign's end and so found themselves back in the Third Division (South) for 1924/25.

Bristol City Football Team – Season 1923-24.

This yo-yo existence had its repercussions in the board room as early as March 1921, with Major Ernest Murdock being replaced as chairman by E. Gwynne Vevers. Disharmony marred the whole of the relegation season of 1921/22, despite a mid-season 'healing meeting' at the Grand Hotel, and amid recriminations at a subsequent special meeting at the Ford Memorial Hall, Bedminster in June 1922, the directors agreed to resign, with a new board to be elected fourteen days later. At the next meeting, 185 shareholders voted on the fifteen nominations for the ten places. Among those standing was Sam Hollis, who was chairman of the Shareholders Association, but he and Major Murdock were among those defeated. George Jenkins was narrowly elected and played a major role in City's history following an FA Inquiry into the dealings of the club.

FA INQUIRY

The inquiry, held in camera in June, cut short the promotion celebrations in 1923 as six directors – E. Gwynne Vevers, W. Pont, G.H. Bacon, H. Pruett, F.H. Thomas and W. Weeks – were suspended for life from any involvement in running a football club. Secretary-manager Alex Raisbeck was fined £50 and the club £250. The bans remained in force for almost three years until, following strenuous campaigning by Alex Raisbeck, they were eventually lifted in January, 1926. Only three directors – Harry Drewett (the new chairman), former secretary Frank Hill and George Jenkins – survived the AGM on July 19th, 1923. Seven more directors, including Percy Daniell, who became vice-chairman, were elected at this meeting.

Relegation in 1924 brought a three-season spell back in the Third Division (South) before the championship was secured in 1926/27. Bristol City scaled new heights that season, setting a new points record for the Division with 62, as well as eclipsing previous City records in the Football League by beating Gillingham 9-4 in January, 1927, when Tot Walsh scored six times, and netting a season's total of 104 goals.

COVERED END

This outstanding form continued in the higher division and, in winning their opening five games in the 1927/28 season, City looked intent on regaining First Division status. But they could not sustain this performance, and finished the campaign in twelfth place, some twenty points behind champions

Bristol City AFC, 1927/28. At rear: R. Batten (Groundsman), A. Annan (Scout), L. Southway (Assistant Trainer). Back row: F.J. Widgery (Director), D.J. Murray, J. Pugsley, H. Neesam, A.E. Keating, C. Blakemore, W. Coggins, J. Geddes, T. Walsh, W. Holbrook, A. Smailes, A.R.P. Bray (Director), J.A. Hooper (Director). Middle row: F. Drewett (Director), J. Paul, C. Gilhespy, J. Foster, J. Walsh, B. Williams, P. Callaghan, G. Newland, H. Good, C. Bourton, E. Glenn, W.H. Roberts (Director) J. Matthews (Director). Front row: P.O. Daniell (Vice-chairman), G. Garland, F. Searle, A. Torrance, J. Taylor, J. Martin, G. Jenkins (Chairman), W. Wadsworth (Captain), A. Rankin, P. Cherrett, R. Hughes, J. Brain, A.G. Raisbeck (Secretary/Manager). On ground: J. Nicholson (Trainer), C.H. Hancock (Assistant Secretary). Trophies: Glos. Senior Cup, Third Division Shield and the Western League Cup.

Manchester City. Many Bristol fans were outraged when Clarrie Bourton and Albert Keating were transferred to Blackburn Rovers for a combined fee of £3,650 immediately following the last game of the season. The money was used to pay for the erection of cover to replace that pulled down almost eleven years earlier. Euphemistically christened the Keating Stand, it was later known as the Covered End for many years until the construction of the Atyeo Stand at the other end of the ground in 1994. Two years after this, it was renamed the Wedlock Stand in honour of City's most renowned player.

Bristol City AFC, 1932/33. At rear: T.A. Pickett, L. Southway (Assistant Trainer), W. Young. Back row: E. Mellors (Trainer), A. Sharp, W.Jennings, J.S. Taylor, E.H. Coombs, A. Turner, E. Bowen, E.J. Brinton, R. Hewison (Manager), C.H. Hancock (Secretary. Middle row: A.P.R. Bray (Director), F.J. Humphries (Director), B. Hall, G. Reed, T.A. Parker, J. Donaldson, E.Dunn, J.A. Heale, F. Drewett (Director), G. Jenkins (Chairman). Front row: F. Joyce, W.P. Cainey, T. Wren, C.Bridge, S. Homer, J.T. Wilson (Captain), E. Scriven, J.L. Loftus, W. Knox, C.I. Morgan, F.E. Farr.

Three seasons of struggle now led to City's worst ever campaign, in 1931/32. They were under the management of Joe Bradshaw, who had taken charge at Ashton Gate in August, 1929, seven weeks after the surprise resignation of Alex Raisbeck. His first season in charge was not without incident. The campaign started with part of Number 2 Stand burning down and ended with City securing twelve points from their last nine games to dramatically avoid relegation. There was no such escape in 1931/32, though, and with only three League wins from the first 26 games, Bradshaw resigned in February, to be succeeded by Bob Hewison eleven weeks later.

FINANCIAL CRISIS

In 1932/33, Bristol City fielded a virtually new line-up after seven players were transferred. The fees received kept an impending financial crisis at bay for a while, and at the club's AGM in June, 1932 chairman George Jenkins was able to declare a profit of £1,093. Despite a bright start, City struggled to keep clear of the re-election zone and finished in fifteenth place. The decimation of the playing strength had manifested itself, and the consequent fall-off in support brought to a head the financial problems that threatened the club's very survival the following season.

With an overdraft standing at £16,517, a public meeting was held at the appropriately named Provident Hall, Redcliffe on May 5th, 1933 when George Jenkins made an appeal for the £10,000 share capital which remained available to be taken up. Gifts totalling £227 were pledged, adding to that raised by the Knowle Stadium Company which came to City's

The programme for the Second Division match between Bristol City and Port Vale on September 6th, 1930. The programme cover design remained much the same for nearly thirty years.

aid by putting on a special benefit greyhound meeting. A loss of £4,351 was declared at City's AGM six weeks later, but the financial position was already beginning to improve.

Four more seasons of League struggle followed, only relieved by City's cup performances. In 1933/34 the Welsh Cup was won – City defeating Cardiff City, New Brighton and Port Vale en route to the first all-English final against Tranmere Rovers at Wrexham. After a 1-1 draw, City won the replay at Chester by three goals to nil.

The following season brought further Cup glory, when City progressed to the Fifth Round of the FA Cup. This proved to be the club's salvation, as such was the interest that Ashton Gate attendance records were twice broken, first for the Fourth Round Replay visit of Portsmouth on January 30th, 1935. The official attendance for this game, which City won 2-0, was 42,885 with takings of £2,570, although with the gates being rushed, at least 50,000 were estimated to be in the ground. These official records were surpassed in the Fifth Round, a goal-less draw with Preston North End being watched by 43,335 paying £3,209. Unfortunately, City went down 5-0 in the replay at Deepdale.

ALFIE ROWLES – TRIUMPH AND TRAGEDY

The 1937/38 season brought an upturn in the club's League fortunes. An exciting five-way tussle with Millwall, Queen's Park Rangers, Watford and Brighton ended with Millwall pipping City by a single point for the Third Division (South) title. This improvement boosted attendances, and a remarkable crowd of 38,953 at the Cardiff match in March saw the visitors win 1-0.

The season was notable for the goal-scoring exploits of Alfie Rowles. After netting a hat-trick on his League debut as City beat Exeter 4-1 in January, he went on to create a Football League record for consecutive scoring by a debutant, hitting the target in the next five games, adding a further nine goals in the process, before his run ended with three goals in City's record 8-2 away win at Walsall at the end of February. This promising career was tragically cut short after an injury in the home game with Notts County in September, 1938. Despite attempted comebacks, Rowles was eventually forced to retire and a player of great potential was lost to the club just as, almost forty years later, City were to lose the services of Paul Cheesley.

City's decline in form in 1938/39 was due, in no small measure, to another investigation into the club's affairs. Following a joint Football Association and Football League inquiry into illegal payments to amateurs, City's directors and secretary were censured, while manager Bob Hewison was suspended from October 3rd, 1938 for the rest of the season. Captain Clarrie Bourton, who took over as player-manager, did well to steer the side into a respectable position in the top half of the table. The end of the campaign saw Hewison, who had continued working for City as chief scout, take over the managerial reins again. Unfortunately, City fans were never to know whether the side put together for 1939/40 would have made a serious challenge for promotion.

WAR-TIME FOOTBALL

Despite gathering war clouds, the new season started as normal, but after three games the competition was abandoned when war was declared on Germany on September 3rd. This marked the end of normal League football for the duration although, after seven weeks of friendlies, various League and Cup competitions were organised under the auspices of the Football League. The composition of City's team varied greatly from week to week, and they frequently needed to field members of the Colts side.

Clubs maintained a retained list of players throughout the war, but paid them only on a match-by-match basis. Many were engaged in war work – whether in the armed forces or in industry – and consequently could be based anywhere. The ruling that players could turn out for any club in their locality gave Ashton Gate fans the chance to see the likes of Ronnie Dix of Tottenham Hotspur, Jack Hargreaves (Leeds United), Jack Preece (Wolves), Bob Shankly (Falkirk), Alec Stock (Queen's Park Rangers) and George Tadman (Charlton Athletic) guest for the Bristol club. Occasionally things were so bad that players were borrowed from the ranks of the opposition, and when City played at Southampton on Christmas Day 1941 only two players, Bourton and Preece, had arrived by kick-off. City's depleted resources were supplemented by six Saints players, including trainer Gallagher – who scored one of City's goals in a 5-2 defeat – and three spectators.

Highlights of war-time football for Bristol City included reaching the Third Round of the War League Cup in 1942/43 when they lost 2-1 on aggregate against Aston Villa and an amazing Second Round, Second Leg match at Cardiff City on April 14th, 1945. City's 2-1 win, to claim the League points also at stake, led to extra-time as Cardiff had won the first leg by the same score at Ashton Gate a week earlier. After extra-time, the tie went to sudden death and many spectators went home for tea before returning to witness the conclusion when Cardiff's Billy Rees summoned enough energy to put the ball in the net after the match had been in progress for a record 3 hours 22 minutes.

The Number 1 Stand at Ashton Gate was a casualty of war, being hit twice by enemy bombers. Work started on a replacement in 1951 and was completed two years later.

A page showing the League table from the programme of the Third Division match between Bristol City and Millwall on February 2nd, 1935.

CHAPTER FOUR

THE POST-WAR YEARS

When Football League action resumed in 1946/47, a free-scoring forward line saw Don Clark score 36 goals to head the Third Division (South) scoring chart and help Bristol City to finish third behind champions Cardiff City and Queen's Park Rangers. The fixtures for the campaign were the same as for the aborted 1939/40 season, so City again started at Aldershot where they had won 1-0 previously. This time, though, they suffered an unexpected 4-3 reverse, but went on to go thirteen League games without defeat, including the home match against Bournemouth on October 12th, when 22,336 fans turned up for Cliff Morgan's second benefit. Ten of the 21 home League games attracted attendances of more than 20,000 and the top-of-the-table clash with Cardiff City in April was watched by 32,535 fans. These high attendances contributed towards a record profit of £5,450. The return fixture with Aldershot on December 28th, 1946 brought Bristol City their record 9-0 Football League victory in front of 17,690 spectators.

Expectations were high for another promotion challenge in 1947/48, especially after City had started the season by beating Southend United 6-0 at home and won ten of their first 13 fixtures. Defeat at home by Watford in late-October heralded a decline and the following seven League matches produced just one win, although scoring form returned in the FA Cup when non-League Dartford were heavily defeated in a First Round replay. Despite a sweet 5-2 home victory over Bristol Rovers in mid-February, there was not much improvement and City finished a disappointing seventh, even though they boasted the Division's leading marksman again as Len Townsend scored 31 goals. Despite the poor performances, attendances remained high. Eleven of the twenty-one home games each attracted over 20,000 spectators, with the January visit of Tommy Lawton's Notts County being watched by more than 35,000 who saw City win 1-0.

The slide continued into 1948/49, and public dissatisfaction led to the appointment of four new directors in February. Matters came to a head at the AGM at the Grand Hotel on March 15th, 1949, just seven days after the resignation of manager Bob Hewison following a boardroom row over team selection. Chairman George Jenkins, together with Arthur Sperring, offered himself for re-election but was voted off the board by a show of hands. He had been the only director who refused to lend the club £1,000. As the major shareholder, he could have demanded a poll which would have been likely to guarantee his re-election, but a vote of no-confidence was

The programme for the Division Three (South) game between City and Queen's Park Rangers on March 20th, 1948.

called, and responding to the hostility of many of the 140 shareholders present, he withdrew his nomination and left the board, declining the offer of life membership. It was a sad end for a man who had given much to the club and guided it through many difficult years.

THE COMING OF HARRY DOLMAN

Harry Dolman, who succeeded George Jenkins, was destined to have a similar lengthy reign as chairman. The intention was that he would hold office for twelve months, with Arthur Sperring taking over the following year, but Sperring's sudden death prompted Dolman's unanimous re-election in 1950. This heralded what many considered to be a benevolent dictatorship at Ashton Gate. The new chairman's first task was to select a manager and when his preferred choice, Irish international Peter Doherty, became player-manager of Doncaster Rovers, Dolman was forced to look elsewhere. After abortive approaches to Bill Dodgin at Southampton and Arthur Rowe at Chelmsford City, Bob Wright (assistant to Jimmy Seed at Charlton Athletic) was appointed in April 1949 at a salary of £850 a year. His reign was short, however, as he resigned fourteen months later, despite the offer of a new three-year contract, on the grounds that he had not been given the free hand promised.

Pat Beasley took over as player-manager in July 1950 and his five-year contract was the longest awarded by the club. His appointment set Bristol City on course for better things, and the team improved slightly to finish tenth in 1950/51. The return of Cyril Williams from West Bromwich Albion together with the signings of Jimmy Rogers from Wolves, Jack Boxley from Stourbridge and, most notably, John Atyeo took City to fifth place in 1952/53, and third the following season before the Third Division (South) title was won for a record third time in 1954/55. Atyeo scored 28 goals that season to underline what a good day's work chairman Harry Dolman had accomplished when he persuaded the England Youth international to join City after playing two First Division games as an amateur for Portsmouth.

CHAMPIONSHIP HONOURS

It was an outstanding team that took the Third Division (South) Championship. City started the 1954/55 season with an unbeaten run of 13 League games, leading from mid-September after beating Colchester United 4-0 at Ashton Gate. Apart from the pre-Christmas week and

Bristol City v Gillingham, December 19th, 1954. A John Atyeo shot beats the Gillingham goalkeeper. Although City went on to lose this match 1-4, it didn't stop them gaining promotion to the Second Division at the end of the season.

a six-match spell early in the new year, Beasley's side headed the table for the rest of the campaign, equalling the Division's record both for points (70) and for wins (30) set by Nottingham Forest four years earlier.

Back in the Second Division after a 22-year absence, Bristol City looked on target for further championship honours when they led the table for five weeks up to Christmas Eve. This form could not be sustained, however, and a final placing of eleventh left them some ten points behind champions Sheffield Wednesday. Even so, the goals flowed throughout the season, with a 6-0 home win over Plymouth Argyle and five at home to Rotherham United, Hull City and Lincoln City as well as an outstanding 6-4 success at Blackburn Rovers.

The 1956/57 season saw the familiar pattern of struggle after a good initial season in higher company and relegation was averted only after a dramatic improvement in form from the turn of the year. Competitive matches under floodlights were eventually sanctioned during this season, and City's first Football League game wholly under lights was staged at Ashton Gate on February 20th, 1957 when Notts County were beaten 3-0 in front of 19,288 fans.

City's first experience under floodlights had been in a friendly at Swindon Town six years earlier, and this had led to Harry Dolman's designing and manufacturing floodlights for Ashton Gate. These cost £3,500 and by present-day standards were very primitive – consisting of a series of metal poles with a cluster of three lights on top – but they did a magnificent job, enabling the club to reap the benefits of being an early pioneer of floodlit football. Harry Dolman's floodlights were first used at Ashton Gate on January 27th, 1953 when 23,866 fans saw Wolves win a friendly 4-1. The success of this venture encouraged many more well-supported floodlit friendlies.

Ashton Gate was selected to host an Under-23 international against France in October, 1956. Four more Under-23 internationals have since been staged at Ashton Gate and the ground has also been used for two Under-21 internationals as well as a Football League representative fixture.

Further struggle in 1957/58 brought about the dismissal of manager Pat Beasley in January 1958. Physio Les Bardsley then briefly ran the team with Harry Dolman, before Jimmy Seed, who had been assisting Pat Beasley in an advisory capacity, took over as caretaker manager for nine days before joining Milwall. This time Dolman secured the services of the man he had wanted nine years earlier, and Peter Doherty signed a three-year contract at the end of the month. Doherty's first match in charge was a 2-1 defeat at his old club, Doncaster Rovers but he quickly improved City's fortunes. The signing of Bert Tindill from Doncaster for £6,400 was the catalyst that produced seven wins and two draws in the final third of the campain that secured safety for the club.

City started the following season in brilliant style, creating a new post-war Football League record with thirteen goals in their first two matches – a 6-1 home success over Rotherham United and an amazing 7-4 victory at Barnsley. Attendances at Ashton Gate were high, with 42,594 turning out for the FA Cup visit of Blackpool in January and a new ground midweek attendance record for a League match was set in September when just under 30,000 witnessed City's 2-1 win against Huddersfield Town. Though they finally finished a disappointing tenth, City were involved in the promotion race for much of the season.

Bristol City FC, 1957/58: Back row: Cyril Williams, Jack Bailey, Ernie Peacock, Bob Anderson, John Atyeo, John Watkins, Bobby Etheridge. Front row: Dermot Curtis, Mike Thresher, Jackie White, Wally Hinshelwood, Alec Eisentrager.

THE SPLIT-CAMP AFFAIR

The 1959/60 season opened with City tipped as a promotion favourite, especially as Doherty pulled off what many thought the best deal of the summer when he signed Barnsley's Johnny McCann and Malcolm Graham. The left-wing pair were purchased in a club record deal valued at £20,000 – £14,500 in cash, plus the transfer of popular Bert Tindill to Oakwell. However, things did not turn out as hoped, and far from heading the table City were relegated after a dismal campaign left them bottom of the Second Division with only 27 points.

Problems at Ashton Gate first came to public notice in the 1959 close season when John Atyeo, Tommy Burden and Mike Thresher refused to re-sign. Manager Doherty had wanted to improve first-team competition by reducing the wages of those demoted to the Reserves. This trio insisted that the club should honour the agreement made when promotion was achieved four years earlier: a maximum of £20 a week in the season and £17 in summer, whether or not they were holding down a first-team place. This dispute, which Harry Dolman resolved in the players' favour, was only the tip of the iceberg.

Although Atyeo was to be on friendly terms with Doherty later in life, he had been less than happy with his appointment as City's manager. They had come to blows in the Ashton Gate tunnel back in April 1956 following Doncaster's 4-0 defeat in a Second Division fixture. An uneasy peace reigned through Doherty's early career at Ashton Gate, but relations deteriorated, partly, it seems, following the high-profile signing of Irish international Tommy Casey from Portsmouth in March 1958, followed by the arrival of Graham and McCann. Doherty's standing was not helped by the release of popular left-winger Johnny Watkins, who went on to star in Cardiff City's successful promotion campaign.

Possibly the trigger for the Split-Camp Affair was the £2,500 signing of Tommy Cavanagh from Doncaster Rovers in July 1959. Cavanagh's highly combative nature did not sit at ease with the more laid-back approach of many established City players, and it was not long before the club became divided into pro- and anti-Doherty factions. This was reflected even on the field of play, to the extent that a City scorer might receive the congratulations only of the faction to which he belonged. This was especially noticeable during the FA Cup Third Round defeat at home to Charlton Athletic after a 2-0 half-time lead was squandered.

Despite all the problems, there were some good performances to cheer, the best being a 1-0 home success over Liverpool and a 3-1 win at Stoke when Graham notched two goals on his much delayed debut. But the club's overall form was so poor that Doherty relinquished his position in charge of the Northern Ireland side, which he had taken to the 1958 World Cup Quarter-finals, to concentrate on City's plight. Results though, did not improve and with reports of players fighting in training it was no surprise when he was dismissed in March, 1960.

Team affairs were taken over by a committee comprising Les Bardsley, Harry Dolman, vice-chairman Bill Kew, director Rev. F.C. Vyvyan Jones and the re-instated captain Tommy Burden, but although there were some good performances at the end of the season, relegation was inevitable.

Fred Ford oversees a schoolboy training session with the help of the first team squad.

CHAPTER FIVE

THE WAY TO THE TOP

The sixty applicants for the vacant manager's job at Ashton Gate did not include the man that Harry Dolman wanted. Bristol Rovers' coach Fred Ford had been sounded out without much success, but while on a course at Lilleshall, he met up with City coach Bill Harvey and Les Bardsley who made it clear that the job was his for the asking. A telephone call to Harry Dolman led to his appointment as City manager in July 1960 on a three-year contract worth £2,750 a year.

Fred Ford took charge of a club that had its debts wiped out after Harry Dolman donated enough shareholding stock in his company, Brecknell, Dolman & Rogers to clear the £55,000 deficit. There was a proviso, however, and the chairman demanded, for reasons never made public, the resignation of fellow-directors George Jones and the Rev Vyvyan Jones.

The factions that had developed under Peter Doherty's regime had given City something of a reputation for an unhappy dressing-room. Ford's first task was to sort out some of the older professionals – a job he did so well that he also succeeded in winning over the many fans who initially did not take kindly to his coming from arch-rivals, Bristol Rovers. His period in charge was characterised by the entertaining football that was played.

The following five seasons saw City in the Third Division, formed at the end of the 1957/58 season when the top halves of the North and South sections joined together. During this period, City's attack never scored fewer than 50 League goals at home in any season, although in 1960/61 poor away performances almost brought relegation. Only a significant improvement from mid-January brought a final placing of fourteenth.

City gained their record FA Cup victory, beating non-League Chichester 11-0 in a Guy Fawkes' Day spectacular in the First Round at Ashton Gate, when John Atyeo scored five goals. In the new Football League Cup, City received a First Round bye and their opening game was a 1-1 draw at Aldershot. A 3-0 win in the replay was to be their sole win in the competition for eight years.

Promotion was a real possibility in 1961/62, until City were twice beaten by eventual champions Portsmouth and finished sixth. High scoring was a feature of many games, Ashton Gate fans treated to wins of 6-0 over Notts County and 6-1 over Bradford Park Avenue, as well as seeing five goals put past both Reading and Swindon Town. City completed the double over Swindon by winning 4-0 at the County Ground. Other inspiring away performances brought

Bristol City FC, 1964/65: Back row: Alec Briggs, Gordon Parr, Jack Connor, Mike Gibson, Tony Ford, Gordon Low, Chuck Drury. Middle row: B. Bush (Secretary), Gerry Sharpe, Jantzen Derrick, Peter Hooper, John Atyeo (Captain), Fred Ford (Manager), Terry Bush, Brian Clark, Lou Peters, Ray Savino, Les Bardsley (Trainer). Front row: G.W. Young (Director), G. Whittock (Director), A.J. Amor (Director), L. Smart (Vice-Chairman), H.J. Dolman (Chairman), N.B. Jones (Director), W.G. Garland (Director), S.F. Kew (Director), R.T. Poeton (Director).

victories at Peterborough, Halifax and Crystal Palace. In contrast, City went down by 7-3 to a Barnsley side avenging their heavy reverse of three years earlier.

Goals also flowed in the FA Cup as City defeated Dartford 8-2 in the Second Round at Ashton Gate after disposing of Hereford United in a replay at Edgar Street. Chairman Harry Dolman had visions of his team in European competition, and the club entered the Welsh Cup for the first time since before the war. It was then announced that only Welsh sides would qualify for the European Cup Winners' Cup. City honoured their commitment, though, beating Merthyr Tydfil 4-2 to earn a plum home tie against First Division Cardiff City which attracted a crowd of 13,579 spectators. The venture was a financial success even though the tie was lost.

THE BIG FREEZE

Bristol City scored exactly 100 goals in League games in 1962/63, but finished fourteenth after conceding 92. This gave the Club a League record of sorts, as this was the lowest placing of any side scoring a hundred goals or more. Southend were beaten 6-3 at Ashton Gate in mid-April when footballing cricketer Barrie Meyer grabbed a hat-trick on his final first-team appearance. Notable victories were achieved at Bradford Park Avenue, Carlisle United and Halifax Town as well as at home to Barnsley. The severe winter badly disrupted the football programme and precipitated the first appearance of the Pools Panel. City reached the Third Round of the FA Cup, drawing a twice postponed home match with Aston Villa after beating Wellington Town and Wimbledon. There were nine more postponements before City lost 3-2 in the Villa Park replay.

The defence was strengthened the following season by the arrival of goalkeeper Mike Gibson from Shrewsbury Town. This completed City's strong backbone, the skills of John Atyeo and ability of Gibson supplemented by the whole-hearted displays of Jack Connor in central defence. City conceded 64 goals in their League programme, while a still prolific attack exceeded this by 20 goals to finish fifth, just five points off promotion. City suffered their worst FA Cup defeat, 6-1 to an impressive Sunderland side at Roker Park in the Fourth Round.

PROMOTION

Confident of promotion in 1964/65, optimistic supporters were shocked when City's season opened with a 5-2 defeat at newly relegated Scunthorpe United, although their faith was to be rewarded when City clinched the second promotion place with a slightly better goal average than Mansfield Town. They showed such brilliant early form that few anticipated such a tight finish. City went top of the table in mid-September before a slump all but destroyed their hopes and by the time new leaders Bristol Rovers visited Ashton Gate in mid-February, Fred Ford's team looked well out of the picture in ninth place.

Goals from Brian Clark and Terry Bush enabled City to come from behind to beat Rovers 2-1 and provide the impetus for an amazing run of success. Only one defeat in the final 15 games secured promotion and a 2-0 home win over Oldham Athletic in front of 28,248 fans on April 24th, 1965 kept City just in front of Mansfield.

The 1965/66 campaign almost brought further success, only the dropping of three points to Southampton over Easter preventing promotion to the First Division. A final placing of fifth was a highly creditable performance for a season when the team's play away from home was often outstanding. At Ashton Gate, though, City struggled to score, and remarkably it was not until the final League game, when Ipswich Town were beaten 4-1, that the two-goal barrier was breached. This game saw the end of John Atyeo's illustrious career, and it was fitting that the former England international could mark his farewell by scoring two goals to reach the grand total of 350 City goals in League and Cup.

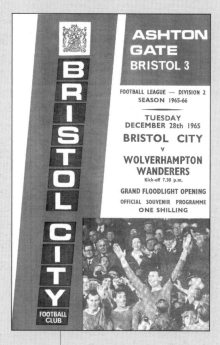

Atyeo's departure brought a slump in form, and after his appearance in his benefit match against Leeds on October 10th, 1966, Chairman Dolman tried to persuade him to return. The game produced receipts of £3,930 from a crowd of 17,425 who were disappointed that the renowned Atyeo goal touch was missing in City's 4-2 defeat, though few doubted that he would still have been an asset to City's struggling Second Division team. Atyeo was not to be persuaded, though, and Fred Ford had to look elsewhere to strengthen his ailing side.

Ford struck gold by signing John Quigley from Huddersfield Town towards the end of October and followed this later in the season with the capture of ex-England international Chris Crowe from Nottingham Forest and Hugh McIlmoyle from Wolves for a record £27,000 fee. These signings had an electrifying effect on the team and with City reaching the Fifth Round of the FA Cup, it is doubtful if the optimism generated among fans has ever been bettered. It was this Cup run that introduced a new club song, the popular melody by Adge Cutler and the Wurzels called 'Drink Up Thee Cider'.

FALSE HOPES

League safety was assured with a placing of fifteenth and there was a not unreasonable aspiration for promotion the following season. After a dream start to 1967/68, with Crowe scoring the quickest goal of the opening day, these hopes were to be cruelly dashed. That opening game with Huddersfield Town, at home, was lost 3-2 and a further three straight League defeats led to Fred Ford's leaving the club as early as September 19th. Alan Dicks, who had been Jimmy Hill's assistant at Coventry City during the 'Sky Blue Revolution' was appointed in his place.

'A.D.'s first match was against Portsmouth at Fratton Park and produced a defence-orientated display from City that ended in a 2-0 defeat. As the season progressed, more adventurous policies were adopted, and the £35,000 signing of John Galley from Rotherham United, even with a leg in plaster and unable to take the field for a month, was a master stroke. A hat-trick in his first game, in which Huddersfield were beaten 3-0 in mid-December, demonstrated his worth; and his 16 league goals were a major factor in City's relegation escape, a fate to which his previous club succumbed.

In the FA Cup, Bristol City defeated Bristol Rovers and Middlesbrough after replays to reach the Fifth Round for the second successive season. The 2-0 defeat at Leeds United is unfortunately remembered most for the ill feeling engendered as both Chris Garland and Leeds keeper Gary Sprake were sent off for fighting.

FOOTBALL LEAGUE CUP

Disappointing League form in 1968/69 was partly offset by the first success in the League Cup for eight years. Wins over Newport County and Middlesbrough earned another trip to Elland Road in the Third Round. This time City put up a much better performance, with Chris Garland scoring in a 2-1 defeat by the holders and eventual League champions. The following campaign brought a tremendous tussle with Leicester in the League Cup Second Round, which City eventually lost 3-1 in a second replay at Filbert Street.

City's find of the 1969/70 season was Brian Drysdale whom Alan Dicks signed from Hartlepool for a bargain £10,000. A largely unsung player, Drysdale went on to give sterling service to Bristol City and formed an excellent full-back pairing with Gerry Sweeney who came from Morton for £22,000 in August 1971. Key mid-fielder Bobby Kellard, City's record £36,300 signing from Portsmouth in 1968, departed for Leicester City for £49,000 in August 1970, giving Gerry Gow a chance to make his mark. Though he looked raw in his early games, Gow became a key player over the following ten years.

In yet another struggle to avoid the drop, Alan Dicks' job was saved when City reached the semi-finals of the League Cup for the first time in 1970/71, beating Rotherham United, Blackpool, Leicester City and Fulham in the process. Alan Skirton's goal was cancelled by Alan Gilzean as City drew 1-1 at home to Spurs in December 1970. The second leg went to extra time before Spurs finally dashed City's hopes of their first major Cup Final appearance in 62 years.

The 1971/72 season brought a marked improvement in the club's League fortunes and they were early Second Division leaders for the first time since December 1955. After successive home wins over Cardiff and Hull, a slump followed a 2-0 defeat at Charlton Athletic in late-October and by mid-February they were languishing in eighteenth place. A late rally lifted them clear of the relegation zone and City finished a creditable eighth despite the record £100,000 sale of England Under-23 star Chris Garland to Chelsea. The campaign saw Geoff Merrick establish himself and at Blackpool on January 22nd, 1972 he became the club's youngest captain at the age of twenty.

The find of the season had been Welsh amateur internationl mid-fielder John Emanuel. Signed from Ferndale after impressing on trial in the 1-1 draw with Bristol Rovers at Eastville in the Gloucestershire Senior Cup Final at the end of 1970/71, he quickly secured a regular place and his absence coincided with City's slump.

WATNEY CUP

City's improved form continued in 1972/73 after a worrying opening spell of five games without a win left them bottom of the table. A 2-0 victory at Orient in their next match signalled a sequence of nine games without defeat which saw they rise thirteen places, though City failed to win at home until defeating Sunderland 1-0 in late-November. Alan Dicks' side eventually finished fifth, scoring 63 goals to qualify for the Watney Cup.

By then just two years old, the Watney Cup was English football's first sponsored competition. Qualification for the pre-season tournament went to the two highest scoring teams not promoted in each division. Bristol Rovers had won the cup the previous year, and in seeking to emulate their local rivals, City gained a 2-1 victory at Peterborough in the opening round on August 11th, 1973 before going down 4-1 at Stoke City in the Semi-finals.

A 3-1 home win over Hull City on September 18th put City top of the Second Division table once more. The 10,711 fans at windswept Ashton Gate that night will long remember the game as they witnessed an extraordinary goal from City 'keeper Ray Cashley. The goalkeeper volleyed a clearance from a yard inside his own penalty area, the ball bounced just before the Hull penalty area and soared high into the net with Jeff Wealands stranded ten yards off his line.

Future Ashton Gate colleagues, Gerry Sweeney and Joe Jordan battle it out in the FA Cup Fifth Round tie at Ashton Gate on Saturday, February 16th, 1974.

CUP GIANT-KILLERS

Alan Dicks' team achieved national fame when they beat Leeds United in an FA Cup Fifth Round replay at Elland Road in February 1974, and a Donnie Gillies' goal after 73 minutes saw Bristol City elevated to the front page of *The Times* newspaper. It was a sensational defeat of the Cup favourites, unbeaten in the League and destined to clinch the championship. Rival manager Don Revie was statesmanlike in defeat, and City were to benefit from a good relationship built up in their two meetings when they signed Jimmy Mann and John Shaw from Leeds at the end of the season. City's reward for this shock win was a Sixth Round tie with Liverpool who were lucky to win 1-0 at Ashton Gate. Liverpool went on to beat Newcastle United 3-0 in the Wembley final.

THE CHAIRMAN STEPS DOWN

Harry Dolman stepped down as chairman on March 13th, 1974 when Robert Hobbs took over. Before Dolman left for his annual Barbados holiday, he is believed to have thought that Alan Dicks' assistant John Sillett would be a better choice as manager. He left instructions to the other board members that he was against offering Dicks more than a one-year extension of contract and also stresssed the need for further investment. He returned just in time to witness the epic win at Leeds, but was shocked when his fellow directors not only disagreed with his views on the managership, but told him that his ultimatum to resign had been accepted. Some commentators reckoned that the great cup run had saved Alan Dicks and seen Harry Dolman become the club's first president.

Harry Dolman remains City's longest-serving Chairman. He joined the board in 1939, and guided the club through the long war years. He became Chairman in 1949, serving as such for 25 years. Among his many contributions to the club's well-being, it was he who brought John Atyeo to Ashton Gate; in later years he fondly remembered walking along the railway line to the signal box where John's father worked to obtain the crucial signature.

An end-of-season fifth place was again City's fate in 1974/75 as Dicks' side failed to gain the promotion prize that seemed well within their grasp. City achieved their first-ever League success at Southampton, winning 1-0 on Good Friday to put themselves in the third promotion spot, but Norwich's 1-0 victory at Ashton Gate the following day ultimately brought them promotion at City's expense. Despite a notable 1-0 double over eventual champions, Manchester United, City were hampered by a low scoring attack which netted only 47 goals in the season.

FIRST-CLASS RETURN

Although City's scoring rate did not greatly improve, it was enough to regain First Division status in 1975/76. They finished runners-up after suffering two unexpected defeats by Blackpool and Notts County in the closing weeks. Promotion was clinched in the last-but-one game on April 20th, 1976, when a rare Clive Whitehead score brought a single-goal win over relegated Portsmouth in front of 27,394 fans at Ashton Gate.

A HOT START

Bristol City made a great start in the top flight after an absence of 65 years, with an impressive 1-0 win at Arsenal, and were undefeated in second place after four games. The loss of centre-forward Paul Cheesley, injured in the first home League match against Stoke City, was a key factor as the season declined into a relegation struggle, despite Alan Dicks' signing former internationals Norman Hunter and Peter Cormack from Leeds United and Liverpool respectively, then bringing Chris Garland back from Leicester City. With two games remaining, City looked doomed but a crucial 2-1 home success over champions Liverpool set the scene for a do-or-die battle with Coventry City at Highfield Road.

Geoff Merrick and Brian Drysdale sit up-front of the promotion-winning squad as they take an open-top bus ride through the streets of Bristol.

CHAPTER SIX

RISE AND FALL

With Spurs and Stoke already condemned to the drop, the third relegation place was between Coventry, Sunderland and Bristol City. All had the same points total, but with the Sky Blues having an inferior goal average, City need just the one point to be safe. Coventry needed a win, in case Sunderland won their final game at Everton. A tense atmosphere on May 19th, 1977 was heightened as the start was delayed five minutes to allow all 36,903 spectators into the ground.

Tommy Hutchinson's second goal gave Coventry a 2-0 lead seven minutes into the second half and appeared to finally dash Bristol City's survival hopes. Gerry Gow and, with just eleven minutes left, Donnie Gillies had other thoughts, and only four minutes remained when the electronic scoreboard flashed up the news that Sunderland had lost 2-0, to cheers from the crowd who appreciated that a draw was enough to enable both clubs to avoid the drop. The heart-pounding action came to a halt, with Bristol City players keeping possession of the ball in their own half until a bemused referee blew time.

Alan Dicks celebrates the controversial 1977/78 escape from relegation to the Second Division with an equally relieved Gordon Milne, the Coventry City manager.

ANTI-CLIMAX

To many supporters, it was this survival in the First Division that would, paradoxically, eventually bring about the formation of Bristol City FC (1982) plc. Chairman Robert Hobbs realised that investment was required if the club was to make any real impression at the highest level, and he announced that £25,000 would buy potential directors a seat on the board. It was a strategy not supported by the full board and led, on May 23rd, 1977 to his replacement by Stephen Kew, with the backing of Bill Garland, Graham Griffiths and Norman Jones. A costly legal battle ensued which – together with the decision to award excessively long contracts to many City players after centre-half Gary Collier had become the first British footballer to exercise his rights under freedom of contract in the 1979 close-season – brought the club close to extinction.

The club had finished seventeenth in 1977/78. The highlight of a modest season was the 4-1 home victory

Joe Royle puts pen to paper under the gaze of Alan Dicks.

over Middlesbrough on November 26th, when ex-England centre-forward Joe Royle, on loan from Manchester City, marked his debut by netting all four goals. He soon became a permanent signing, but the team's shortcomings were highlighted when they were unable to beat Third Division Wrexham in either cup competition – a weakness repeated the following season when City were defeated in both cup competitions by Second Division Crystal Palace.

The following season saw City finish mid-table after looking at one stage to be possible qualifiers for European competition, as they twice occupied fifth position in the table and were in seventh place as late as April 10th. City defended the Anglo-Scottish Cup won in 1977/78 when St Mirren were beaten 3-2 on aggregate, winning all three of their group matches, including a 6-1 success over Bristol Rovers. The Paisley side gained revenge in the quarter-finals, but City were destined to sign their star mid-fielder, Tony Fitzpatrick for a Club record fee of £250,000 in the summer of 1979. St. Mirren were to defeat City in the 1979/80 Final, winning both legs.

RELEGATION

Although as high as sixth early on, Bristol City lost First Division status in 1979/80 after finishing third from bottom. Although they suffered only four defeats in their opening fourteen league matches, the side struggled to overcome the departure of central defenders Norman Hunter and Gary Collier. City were in a relegation position from Boxing Day, when they lost 3-0 at West Bromwich Albion, through to the end of the season.

Back in the Second Division after four seasons in the First, Bristol City were quoted at 12-1 to make an immediate return, optimistic odds not entirely shared by fans or the local press. Joe Royle left for Norwich City just before the 1980/81 season got underway and after a poor start, Alan Dicks, the League's longest serving manager, was dismissed on September 8th. Assistant Tony Collins and coach Ken Wimshurst took over until Bob Houghton was appointed from the Greek side, Ethnikos three weeks later. Much was expected of Houghton, who had been in charge of Swedish club Malmo when they reached the European Cup Final in 1979, but with little cash at his disposal, he could do little to avoid relegation.

With City's Eastville rivals propping up the Second Division table, Bristol set an unenviable record by providing the first instance of two teams from the same provincial city being relegated from the same division together. Ironically, after the South Stand fire at Eastville, the two clubs had shared Ashton Gate early in the campaign. This season also brought a return of cricket to Ashton Gate for the first time since the Bedminster club had moved to the Clanage in 1912, when just under 8,000 watched a Rest of the World XI beat an England XI in September, 1980.

Further boardroom disagreements led to an attempted 'coup' by a group of rebel shareholders. Although they later withdrew their challenge, Stephen Kew, who had been Chairman since the departure of Robert Hobbs, was soon to step aside in favour of Archie Gooch, a long-standing City supporter who had been on the board for just under a year.

In the Third Division for the first time in sixteen years, Bristol City were now expected to stabilise their position and possibly make a bid for promotion. Optimism was fuelled by the summer signing of Mick Harford from Newcastle United, but nothing could stop the slide and further relegation at the end of 1981/82 meant that City were the first club – since emulated by Wolves – to fall from the First to the Fourth Division in successive seasons.

THE ASHTON GATE EIGHT

Behind the scenes, though, the directors were in crisis as the club's financial position worsened by the day. It was a question by the autumn of 1981, with creditors pressing in, of just how long the club could hold out. By the New Year their League future was on a match-by-match thread.

In the background a group of businessmen in Bristol were beavering away at a rescue plan. A financial expert, an accountant who specialised in collapsing companies, advised them their suggested package to take over control could only succeed by ending the long-term contracts of eight players.

This became the story of the Ashton Gate Eight: Geoff Merrick, Peter Aitken, Chris Garland, Jimmy Mann, Julian Marshall, David Rodgers, Gerry Sweeney and Trevor Tainton. Two others who had similar contracts, Kevin Mabbutt and Clive Whitehead, had already been transferred as the financial crisis gathered pace.

This then, is the next part of our history.

There has been no sadder episode in the story of Bristol City than that of the Ashton Gate Eight. Players who had given the club the glory days in the First Division were being sacrificed so the club – a new club – could rise like Phoenix from the ashes.

Two factors were involved: freedom of contract and the view that the football club could run on a permanent overdraft. An agreement between the League and the Professional Footballers Association had given players the right to change clubs when their contracts expired.

Bristol-born Gary Collier, who had played 216 League and Cup games for City, made history by becoming the first player in the country to do so. He joined Coventry City in an overnight deal which stunned manager Alan Dicks for he had been expecting the 24-year-old defender to re-sign as the 1979/80 season approached.

After the transfer went to arbitration City received a record fee of £350,000 but Dicks and the board had decided their best protection would be to sign the players they really wanted on long-term contracts.

Winger Clive Whitehead signed for 11 years – the longest contract ever given anywhere – although he had moved to West Brom, under pressure from the club, before the Ashton Gate crisis broke.

That came in the winter of 1981/82. On October 21st the board announced the club's debts exceeded £700,000 and falling gates after relegation from the First Division were not enough to pay the wages or the interest charges on the bank overdraft.

There was talk of rescue packages and a body called Friends of Bristol City was formed. Two local businessmen, Deryn Coller and Ken Sage, became the prime moves though with the dramatic suggestion of forming a new board, Bristol City (1982) to take over the running of the club.

The players were aghast when they were told they would have to tear up their contracts because the new company would not be able to honour them. The eight called in Gordon Taylor, secretary of their Association, as City travelled to Newport County on January 30th, 1982, with the real threat that this would be their last game.

As the crisis built up one director, unknown to his wife, re-mortgaged the family home to help out but the stark warning from the outside accountant was that the club would fold unless the eight went.

The deadline was set, midday February 2nd. The players were in turmoil, their careers and family security on the line.

Geoff Merrick (who began as a boy standing behind Tony Cook's goal at Ashton Gate and rose to captain City in the First Division) felt they were treated with contempt in being told to make themselves redundant.

But, with an hour to the deadline, the Ashton Gate Eight took the ultimate decision which sees League football being played at Ashton Gate today – they put club before self.

For most of them it was the end of their settled careers. All found other clubs, Jimmy Mann went to Barnsley, Julian Marshall to Blackburn Rovers, Trevor Tainton and David Rodgers joined Torquay United, Gerry Sweeney and Peter Aitken went to York City.

Merrick, the schoolboy international who played 400 times for City, and Chris Garland, flew off for a spell in Hong Kong. Garland came back briefly to play for City on a match basis the following season, Sweeney went on to become assistant manager at Walsall and later here at Ashton Gate but Merrick's League days were over.

A special match was played for the Eight at Ashton Gate between Ipswich Town and Southampton. A crowd of 6,020 helped towards the sum of £82,750 shared between them.

The most traumatic period City has ever known was at an end. The eight who had given so much felt neglected and forgotten as the club moved on to grapple with new problems in a fresh era. Time is a healer, they were to become very welcome guests and the Legends Bar is there in their honour.

The sacrifice they made should never be forgotten. Nor will it be.

CHAPTER SEVEN

NEW BEGINNINGS

The departure of the Ashton Gate Eight gave the new board a little breathing space – but not much. There were now effectively two boards, the old one charged with selling as many assets as they could for the benefit of creditors; the new one looking for the backing to build a sound financial platform for the future.

An uneasy situation was that the players still remaining at Ashton Gate had their registrations retained by the old club while the new one was paying their wages. With many being sold as soon as good offers were received, City fielded a number of untried youngsters – notably Wayne Bray, Rob Newman and Alan Nicholls – during the final three months of the season. Former assistant Roy Hodgson took over as caretaker-manager when Bob Houghton announced his resignation following the 3-1 home defeat by Wimbledon on January 2nd, 1982 and had the difficult task of operating within tight financial constraints.

Undaunted, he signed on loan and short-term transfers Aidan McCaffery from Bristol Rovers, Ray Gooding (Coventry City) and Les Carter (Crystal Palace), but when the Football League would not allow the monthly contracts to be renewed, McCaffery and Gooding departed. Meanwhile, Swedish international keeper Jan Moller followed Bob Houghton to Toronto Blizzards for £85,000 and Mick Harford, who later gained England honours, joined Birmingham City for £125,000.

The fate of the new organisation remained in the balance, with everything depending on the outcome of the share issue in April 1982. Public response was less than expected, and the issue succeeded only with the injection of capital by local businessmen – Bob Boyd, Bob Marshall, John Pontin and David Russe – which, together with further investment from the board members, eventually ensured the successful launch of Bristol City FC (1982) plc. The new company finally assumed full control on April 30th. Youth team manager Gerry Sharpe took over from Roy Hodgson for the rest of the season, with City losing only once in six games. The directors appointed former full-back Terry Cooper as player-manager on May 19th, just twelve days after purchasing Ashton Gate from the old club for £565,000.

TOUCHING BOTTOM, THEN TAKING OFF AGAIN

In the Fourth Division for the first time in 1982/83, City's early form did little to encourage the missing fans, except for the displays of striker Glyn Riley from Barnsley and winger Alan

Bobby Williams holds aloft the 1986 Freight Rover Trophy.

Crawford, a capture from Chesterfield. A 7-1 humiliation at Northampton Town was made worse when a 1-0 defeat at Rochdale on December 4th saw the club hit rock bottom. Another single-goal defeat at Chester a week later kept them there before a 2-2 draw at Bury lifted City and improvement during the rest of the campaign, with Forbes Phillipson-Masters from Plymouth Argyle adding steel to the defence, left them in mid-table.

Fans could look forward to better things in 1983/84, and seven wins from the opening eleven League matches confirmed their optimism. City finally claimed the fourth promotion place behind runaway champions York City, Doncaster Rovers and Reading.

Further promotion in 1984/85 looked a distinct possibility, with wingers Howard Pritchard and Alan Walsh, who was the supporters' 'Player of the Year', in great form, but a disappointing defeat at Bristol Rovers, following a 1-0 reverse at Plymouth in the previous away match, saw City finish in fifth place.

CITY AT WEMBLEY

Second favourites for promotion in the following season, Cooper's team started disappointingly with five successive defeats including one in the League (Milk) Cup, to find themselves bottom of the table. Recovery began when Wigan Athletic were beaten 1-0 at Ashton Gate and City eventually finished ninth. The season's highlight was City's first Wembley appearance – in the Freight Rover Trophy Final on May 24th, 1986. Facing Third Division rivals Bolton Wanderers, in front of 54,502 spectators, City withstood early pressure to win 3-0.

This success, along with the summer signings of John MacPhail from York City and Gordon Owen from Barnsley, saw City start as promotion favourites in 1986/87. Poor away form kept them out of the promotion frame, though, and it was only the introduction of the Play-Offs that kept the fans' interest alive. Despite an unexpected home defeat at the hands of Brentford, City began their last League match in fifth place, confident of beating Swindon Town at Ashton Gate. Cooper's team took an early lead, but the visitors drew level midway through the second half. A missed penalty meant City losing the opportunity to take part in the historic play-offs, as Gillingham's win over Bolton Wanderers pushed them down to sixth place.

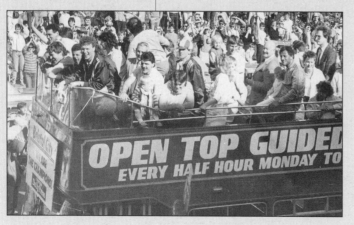

A team tour of the city passes through the City Centre in celebration of the victory over Bolton Wanderers in the 1986 Freight Rover Trophy Final.

Supporters took solace in the Freight Rover Trophy as City won through to Wembley for the second year running, with the Final being played on a Sunday for the first time. Facing Third Division Mansfield in front of a record 58,586 crowd, City struggled to get back in the game after falling behind, and it was a surprise when Glyn Riley netted a late equaliser to take the match into extra time. With no further goals, a Wembley Final went to a penalty shoot-out for the first time, which, perhaps justly, gave the match to the northern club.

Freight Rover Trophy 1986 – Glyn Riley nets City's third and his second to ensure the Trophy comes to Bristol . . . and then celebrates in style!

Roof extension on the Williams Stand affording shelter to supporters using the Enclosure below.

FAREWELL, TERRY COOPER

City had the chance of quick revenge over Mansfield, where they opened the 1987/88 season. The Stags proved their Wembley win was no fluke, though, as they won 2-0 and completed the double at Ashton Gate later in the season. Undeterred by this initial setback, City ended September on top of the table after a run of nine League games without defeat. Form then fluctuated, and City slipped out of contention, bringing Terry Cooper's reign to an end in mid-March. He had create football history when he became Britain's first player-director, and was popular with the fans who enjoyed his appearances for the side during his first three years in charge.

Cooper's assistant, Joe Jordan then took over on a temporary basis, and was soon confirmed as player-manager after he guided City into the Play-Offs with only two defeats in their final eleven League games. The Semi-Final stage brought City into two-legged confrontation with Second Division Sheffield United and a well earned 1-0 home victory on May 15th, 1988 set the scene for a difficult return three days later. A first-half goal from Carl Shutt gave City a battling 1-1 draw at Bramall Lane to take them through to the Final against Walsall. Walsall had an unexpected 3-1 first-leg success at Ashton Gate on May 25th, which left City with a mountain to climb.

After a superb 2-0 win at Fellows Park three days later, City had to concede ground advantage for a third meeting after losing another penalty shoot-out and returned to Walsall on May 30th. The players and supporters were in confident mood, but Eire international striker David Kelly scored a hat-trick in Walsall's 4-0 victory.

A poor League showing in 1988/89 and a disappointing mid-table position were offset by City's memorable exploits in the two main cup competitions. A marathon contest with Aldershot in the FA Cup Second Round went to three replays before City squeezed through 1-0 at Ashton Gate, only to lose by the same score at Hartlepool in the next round.

RECORD RUN

In the League (Littlewoods) Cup, City equalled their feat of 18 years earlier and progressed to the Semi-Finals, creating a new record in the competition by winning seven successive games in a season. A 1-1 draw at Brian Clough's Nottingham Forest in the first leg set up an interesting clash for the Ashton Gate return on February 26th, 1989. Although this second leg was shown live on television it attracted a record receipts crowd of 28,084 who witnessed a dour contest which Forest eventually won with six minutes of extra time remaining.

BRISTOL'S DOUBLE PROMOTION

After nine seasons in the lower echelons of the Football League, City put together many fine displays to clinch promotion in 1989/90. A magnificent haul of 91 points would normally have been enough to win the championship, but on this occasion City had to be content with the runners-up spot. Jordan's team, spearheaded by Bob Taylor, were thwarted by Bristol Rovers who, with minimal resources, deserved all credit for the way they remained in pursuit and then took

The Open End as it stood on November 12th, 1993, soon to be demolished to make way for the Atyeo Stand.

over at the top – the penultimate game taking City to Twerton Park where they lost 3-0. So the two clubs which went down together in 1980/81 created a new record by returning together.

City had a thrilling success against Chelsea in the FA Cup Fourth Round at Ashton Gate to earn an apparently easy home tie against Fourth Division Cambridge United. The East Anglians had other ideas and surprised the 20,676 crowd with the quality of their football in a goal-less draw on February 17th, 1990. The replay four days later ended in a 1-1 draw, but Jordan's side were heavily beaten 5-1 in the second replay at Abbey Stadium.

DEATH OF DEAN HORRIX

Ashton Gate was stunned by the tragic death, on March 11th, 1990, of Dean Horrix, a player signed from Millwall only a few weeks previously. After an evening out with friends to celebrate the move, he was killed instantly when the vehicle in which he was a passenger went out of control and crashed. A collection at Ashton Gate at the following home match raised £6,772 for his widow, and there was a benefit match at Milwall later in the season.

Back in the Second Division for 1990/91, City opened in fine form and were unbeaten until losing 2-1 at West Bromwich Albion on September 15th. Events were overshadowed by the resignation of Joe Jordan four days later to join Scottish club Hearts, only a month after signing a new three-year contract. His assistant, Jimmy Lumsden, was appointed as acting manager and the team responded with three straight wins, including a fine 1-0 first-leg victory in the League (Rumbelows) Cup. The day after Lumsden was confirmed as manager, though, Sunderland won 6-1 in the second-leg at Ashton Gate to inflict City's worst defeat in the competition.

After challenging strongly for a place in the play-offs, City had to settle for a commendable ninth place. The campaign was marred by the sudden death of 66-year old chairman Des Williams, who suffered a fatal heart attack while getting ready for City's home game with Oxford United on February 23rd, 1991. He was succeeded by Les Kew, another who had done much to save the club from disaster in 1982.

Jacki Dziekanowski shoots for goal in the 1992/93 Division One match against Southend United, City lost 0-1.

JACKI SIGNS

After a good start to the 1991/92 season, with only one defeat in the opening eight games, City's form declined to such an extent that relegation became a serious threat. A fine 2-1 win at Leicester, with new signing Polish international Jacki Dziekanowski having a great game, took City into the FA Cup Fifth Round, but a spell of eleven League games without a win put them next to bottom. Jimmy Lumsden and assistant Tony Taylor left the club on February 24th, 1992, and senior players Mark Aizlewood, Russell Osman and Gary Shelton were put in temporary charge while steps were taken to fill the vacancy. Denis Smith was appointed manager two weeks later and some astute dealings in the transfer market – securing the services of Leroy Rosenior from Fulham and Andy Cole initially on loan from Arsenal – made survival possible. A 2-0 home success over Wolves on March 17th started the recovery and eight games without defeat ensured survival.

Andy Cole was signed for a record £500,000 in the summer, but other acquisitions – such as Ray Atteveld for £250,000 from Everton, Brian Mitchell from Bradford City and David Thompson from Millwall in exchange for Andy May – were less successful.

THE NEW FIRST DIVISION

City started the 1992/93 season with a new defensive line-up, but were soon struggling in the newly designated First Division after the formation of the Premier League. Two days after a 2-0 FA Cup defeat at Luton in January 1993 – when City's full-back Martin Scott was sent off – Russell Osman took over from Denis Smith, initially on a temporary basis. He was rewarded with a three-year managerial contract after guiding City from relegation danger to a final position of fifteenth. Andy Cole was sold to Newcastle United for a record £1.75 million on March 13th, 1993 and even with the signings of Ian Baird from Hearts and Liam Robinson from Bury, there was something of a goal-scoring void after the departure of the England Under-21 striker who went on to gain full international honours.

BOARDROOM DIFFERENCES

After the resignation of Ivor Williams, who sold his five per cent holding of foundation shares to the Supporters Club for £35,000, boardroom differences became public property. In May, 1993 the FA announced an inquiry with regard to monies claimed by City from the

Football Trust for ground improvements. A 'Reform Group' now emerged and issued their blueprint for the future, 'The Way to Win!' There was an Extraordinary General Meeting at Whitchurch Sports Centre on November 12th, 1993, the day on which the FA found there had been a misuse of grants from the Football Trust. Punitive action included the club being fined £40,000 (£30,000 suspended for two years). Club chairman, Les Kew was banned from soccer for nine months, and along with three other directors – Oliver Newland, Peter Manning and Ken Sage – left the board following the EGM, to be replaced by 'Reform' rebels Peter Burchill, Deryn Coller, John Clapp, Mike Fricker and David Russe.

The new board met that afternoon. David Russe was elected chairman, with Mike Fricker his deputy. Supporters Club chairman Gary Williams was co-opted to the body, and a statement promised a new start: 'We must now start the task of rebuilding bridges which have been broken. We must start the task of uniting this great club, its staff and its supporters, so that we can now surge forward to one common goal.'

Ironically, while City were in eighth place when the new board took over, by the season's conclusion they had slipped to thirteenth. There was, however, a great win at Liverpool in the FA Cup Third Round to savour – a success almost on a par with the victory at Leeds twenty years earlier. It did not have a similar effect on City's fortunes, though, as Russell Osman had little money at his disposal and was obliged to look for budget signings. City had a three-match close season tour of Zimbabwe and were unbeaten in Africa, with a win and two draws.

FIVE-YEAR CYCLE

The 1994/95 season was City's fifth since promotion and, reflecting the five-year cycle so often evident in the club's history, relegation did not come as a complete shock to the faithful fans. Russell Osman was sacked on November 14th, 1994, following a 3-0 defeat at Sheffield United and the following day Joe Jordan was re-appointed City's manager. Jordan took over with City struggling in the relegation zone, starting with a thrilling 3-2 home win over Swindon before a sequence of six defeats. Signings like mid-fielders Gary Owers from Sunderland for Martin Scott in a £750,000 part-exchange and Martin Kuhl from Derby County for £300,000, together with central defender Richard Dryden for £200,000 from Birmingham City, did little to improve matters.

In the close season, the pitch needed relaying and City Reserves played many of their games at Clevedon Town's ground. With the pitch needing time to bed down, the Gloucestershire Cup Final was cancelled for the first time (other than during the war years) since its inception in 1887.

With City's return to the re-designated Second Division in 1995/96 and not playing well, pressure mounted on the board. David Russe resigned as chairman in September and his successor, vice-chairman Mike Fricker, faced a difficult task with the club losing money and support. Despite the goal-scoring ability of Australian striker David Seal, only one win from the opening ten League games saw City next to bottom, and a much needed 4-0 home success over Hull City was timely. A four-match unbeaten run starting in late-January lifted City and a great 4-2 win at Bristol Rovers – their first League success at Twerton Park – sparked a fine run to the end of the season. The £175,000 signing of Darren Barnard from

Chelsea and rapidly improving performances from Paul Agostino, who scored with a brilliant header against Rovers, helped City to a final placing of thirteenth.

THE CHANGING FACE OF FOOTBALL – AND A NEW CRISIS

In the years leading up to City's centenary, football throughout the world had been going through immense change, nowhere greater than in the English game. Gone were the days when many clubs were kept going by enthusiastic supporters who raised a few pounds with raffles and appeals or, as in City's case, where the first chairman had found £40 to put together the club's first professional football team. By the 1990s, football had become big business; and sponsorship, the successful marketing of everything from shirts to food, together with profits from the buying and selling of players, were all increasingly essential to supplement clubs' finances.

Legislation to provide better and safer facilities and to control the operation of football stadia required big investment, along with substantial running costs, and players' signing-on fees and salaries had reached levels undreamed of a playing generation earlier, yet alone back in the 1890s. But for Bristol City Football Club, as for other enlightened clubs, the most important element was still the supporter – loyal as ever, but now expecting vastly better standards of safety, comfort and hospitality as well as demanding entertaining and, of course, winning football.

The club had invested heavily in Ashton Gate, now widely recognised as the finest stadium west of London and south of the Midlands. Its players were thought to be on some of the best contracts outside the highest divisions, but with promotion from the Second Division still proving elusive, gates were not high enough to allow the club to break-even financially. Its off-the-field activities had not kept pace with the changing face of football, leading to the comment that City was 'a multi-million pound business being run as a village shop'. For some years, the club had run at a substantial loss and by 1995 was on the edge of bankruptcy. For the third time in its history, redundancies proved essential to survival. This time it was the support staff who were sacrificed, while the players were in the main retained in the hope that they could provide the success on the field to boost the club's fortunes.

These pressures produced another of City's periodic boardroom battles. A recently appointed director, Scott Davidson – in his thirties and with a successful track record as pop musician and magazine tycoon – stepped in to help the club. He had been a

Work begins on the addition of a Family Enclosure at the front of the Dolman Stand.

supporter from his youth, and was now in the habit of phoning from as far afield as Japan to get the match results; along with existing directors John Clapp and Bob Neale, he was joined by John Laycock – another highly successful local businessman – to head a new group willing to take control of the club's direction.

A NEW START

Proposals were put forward to revive the club's flagging fortunes in December 1995 and a deal was struck in the following March. The intense negotiations were concluded when Davidson and Laycock sealed their purchase of Bristol City by acquiring the 54 per cent shareholding of Mike Fricker, Deryn Coller, David Russe and Peter Manning.

The public response to new chairman, Scott Davidson's share issue during 1996 was better than hoped for, with shareholders paying £457,080 for 4,854 supporters shares, all of which was put into a fund to purchase new players. Supporters also responded by purchasing season tickets, joining the new membership scheme and clubs such as the Legends Bar, Boot Room and the Chairman's Club. The chairman's plans also included rescinding the five per cent voting rule, and at the club's AGM that year there was only one dissenting shareholder.

SHIP-SHAPE AND BRISTOL CITY FASHION

Ongoing problems with the pitch saw it relaid again, at a cost of £180,000, and it looked splendid on City's Open Day on July 21st, 1996. It was ready to stage the 99th Gloucestershire Cup Final two weeks later when £150,000 signing, Shaun Goater from Rotherham United, scored in City's 1-0 win over Rovers. Ashton Gate had a pitch to be proud of throughout the new season. Only Crewe Alexandra's Gresty Road being voted better in the Second Division.

The stadium's appearance was also much improved with the building of the new GWR Family Enclosure which hid the unsightly wall in front of the Dolman Stand and with the introduction of European-style goalposts, all looked set for a great Centenary season.

On the pitch, City looked out of contention for league honours when Joe Jordan was replaced in March, 1997 by ex-Bristol Rovers boss John Ward, who took over on a two-year contract, but the new manger immediately set his sights on a Play-Off place. His first game in charge saw ex-City defender Matt Bryant inspire Gillingham's 1-0 win at Ashton Gate, but after an encouraging draw at Luton Town, a run of five straight wins offered the opportunity for promotion via the play-offs and saw Ward named as Bells' Second Division Manager of the Month.

In the first leg of the Play-Off Semi-Finals, though, City came up against a well-motivated Brentford side that had lost their previous four games without scoring a goal, and it was no surprise to the disappointingly small crowd of 15,581 that they went down 2-1. No doubt many fans were put off by the monsoon conditions and the fact that the game was shown live on Sky Sports. For some, the star of the show was the referee, Uriah Rennie of Sheffield, who allowed the game to flow as in days gone by. City improved slightly in the return three days later, but Brentford won 2-1 to clinch their place in the Final at Wembley where they lost 1-0 to Crewe Alexandra.

The visit by Sky TV for the semi-final was their second to Ashton Gate that season.

Their previous coverage had been of the home 'derby' with Bristol Rovers on December 15th, 1996. After 100 years of keen local rivalry, passions can still run high whenever the two clubs meet. On this occasion, a small section of 'fans' over-reacted to the visitors' last-minute equaliser, which led to the FA Disciplinary Commission imposing a two-point deduction, suspended to the end of 1997. The Commission were doubtless mindful that this behaviour was completely at odds with the family atmosphere which the board had successfully encouraged at Ashton Gate, and that the Chairman was quick to emphasise that it would not be tolerated. The club identified fifteen hooligans through video recordings and banned them from the ground for life. Throughout the rest of the season City fans, as confidently expected, behaved impeccably in the best traditions of the club.

CENTENARY YEAR

Although there was disappointment that the club had not quite achieved promotion in its centenary year, an appearance in the play-offs was a measure of how far the club had come. On the field and off, there was an impressive programme of centenary celebrations, including visits by Everton and Liverpool, and the staging of a special celebration cricket match against Bedminster CC, who were marking their 150th anniversary. Nationally, City's 100 years was also commemorated by the generous presentation of a cut-glass trophy from the Football Association.

Supporters were now kept in touch by the setting up of a database, and the publication of an occasional 'Gatepost' newsletter. The fans of the future were cultivated in an imaginative schools project which brought up to 3,000 boys and girls to most home games during the year.

A centenary kit and a range of centenary mementoes were avidly taken up by supporters and brought in valuable revenue for the club. An award-winning video also proved highly popular, while a re-union dinner was much appreciated by past players, including several from before the war. Crucially, the board demonstrated their continuing commitment to improved performances on the field by acquiring five key new players.

All in all, the club now stood poised for even better things in the years running up to the year 2000 – as is outlined in this centenary history in the chapter 'Towards the Millennium'.

DAVID M. WOODS

Fans' Eye View

❝ Supporting Bristol City – a team whose only FA Cup Final appearance was so long ago you would have to be a centenarian to remember it – is all about being part of the crowd and having fun with the other fans.

Managers, players, terraces, chairmen – they all come and go. We fans are there every week. It makes no sense – but it's what football is all about.

Supporting City – it's irrational, it's insane, but it's been brilliant. What else would I have done with all those Saturday afternoons?

I had vowed never to attend a match at Wembley until my team ran out there. The fans stood and sang, the lads ran up the steps and lifted the cup and they ran round the track dancing, with us all going mad – how else can you describe crying and laughing and having a quasi-religious experience all at the same time?

A Bristol City season ticket holder since the age of ten, I have never once enjoyed a match. How can you, when your whole happiness depends on the outcome, an outcome that is totally out of your control no matter how many lucky shirts, jumpers, cigarettes you care to bring to the game?

With slightly superstitious tendencies and accepting the entire blame for City's disappointments, I sometimes wonder should I stop watching them?

An American friend accompanies me to Ashton Gate. He finds it difficult to understand why it is the Bristol City fans who seem to hurl most abuse at the home team.

The years of cheering on the players in red at Ashton Gate all merge into one tense, but glorious blur of colour, spectacle and passion.

My ultimate dream must be to watch Bristol City beat Manchester United in the Final of the FA Cup and so avenge that 1909 defeat.

Like thousands of others, I will always be a City fan. Perhaps we are suckers for punishment; or perhaps, as I have always secretly believed, we are all mad. ❞

Young Reds taking advantage of the 'Quid A Kid' initiative, first introduced in the nineties by Bristol City's first Community Officer, Shaun Parker.

Not Just For the Lads

JOE, NICKY AND ME

Most of my female – and indeed some of my male friends – find it difficult to understand exactly why football is so important to me.

There's probably some dark psychological reason why I prefer to spend Saturday afternoons at Ashton Gate (after watching 'Football Focus' of course) rather than shopping or doing something constructive.

Friends at University too, were bemused by the fact that I would spend much-needed funds on an overnight trip during midweek to watch an evening match and return in time for lectures the next day.

Unfortunately, the obsession is not only with Bristol City. I am constantly told off for letting my eyes drift towards the TV in the pub when they are screening football. I have even been to see Charlton Athletic (my local team at University) when I'm sure I should have been doing something else.

When BBC2 broadcast Goal TV, I not only sat through the whole thing but video'd it and watched it over and over again. And yes, when we beat Liverpool, I taped every 'Match of the Day' bit involving us, even the 'Nugget' bit.

I failed every attempt to explain to my friends in London why I am like this – although they came up with some insulting answers – and in a vain attempt to justify my obsession I invited one friend, Nicky, to visit the hallowed ground with me during a weekend visit to Bristol. Well, I did invite her, but friend or not, I was going and she could either come with me or spend the afternoon at home alone.

It was November 20th, Joe's first match back at The Gate, and it was a derby. A perfect introduction to the mighty Reds.

I bought a T-shirt, and explained each team member listed in the programme in excessive detail. As far as I can remember, her only reaction was disappointment that Keith Welch was injured (although he was listed in the programme).

Unfortunately for Nicky, this led to one of my over-preached sermons on how it is not becoming to lust after members of your own team. This tends to vary a little depending upon how much I have had to drink, as whether or not I confess to my own personal stud muffins.

Well, the game began, and soon she was chanting along like a true Red, JOE, JOE, SUPER-JOE . . . the first half came and went . . . and then they did something I hadn't seen them do so far this season.

They scored.

Not a particularly pretty goal, but little Junior had scored. Nicky knew that she had witnessed a miracle and didn't mind a bit as my brother and I went slightly insane.

Lo and behold, just as we had calmed down, Wayne gets another, just two minutes later. I couldn't believe it, we were all over them. Just as my brother and I were telling Nicky she had to come to every match as she was obviously a lucky omen, Swindon got one back. Ha! Ha! said the Swindon fans, that'll teach you . . . and then Wayne shut them up with our third. Beautiful. The sheer delight and noise was such that we didn't notice their second go in. And Nicky's reaction? When's the next one?

Nicky didn't actually get to another game, so it is all her fault that we were condemned to the Second Division (although hopefully just for one season, after which we can return to First Division obscurity). Despite this, she still claims to be a supporter and is now the proud owner of an original circa 1994 scarf.

At least after a game like that the journey back up the M4 was a happy, if not hung-over one. I knew I had succeeded when we passed the Swindon junction. After seeing where we were, a small voice next to me whispered . . . you're so shit it's unbelievable.

KATHRYN BRITTON

Emma Bishop and Anna Browning of Ashton, and Hazel Carr of Bedminster come up with a new idea to allow the goalkeeper to play a more attacking role.

Third Division (South) Champions 1954/55

Back row: Wilf Copping (Trainer), Arthur Milton, Ivor Guy, Bob Anderson, John Atyeo, Cyril Williams, Mike Thresher.
Front row: Ernie Peacock, Jimmy Rogers, Jack White, Tommy Burden, Jack Boxley.

Second Division Promotion Challengers 1965/66

Back row: Chuck Drury, Jack Connor, Tony Ford, Mike Gibson, Alec Briggs, Gordon Low.
Front row: Roger Peters, John Atyeo, Terry Bush, Brian Clarke, Peter Hooper.

FA Cup Fifth Round 1967/68

Back row: Alec Briggs, Trevor Jacobs, Gordon Parr, Mike Gibson, Gordon Low, Trevor Tainton, Terry Bush.
Front row: Jantzen Derrick, John Quigley, Hugh McIlmoyle, Chris Crowe, Roger Peters.

Second Division 1968/69

Back row: Jantzen Derrick, John Galley, Jack Connor, Mike Gibson, Gordon Parr, Alec Briggs, Terry Bush.
Front row: Trevor Jacobs, Chris Garland, Gerry Sharpe, Bobby Kellard, Ken Wimshurst.

FA Cup Giantkillers 1973/74

Back row: Gerry Sweeney, Joe Durrell, Malcolm Rogers, Pat Crowley, Clive Whitehead, Don Gillies.
Middle row: Alan Dicks (Manager), Gary Collier, Tom Ritchie, Ray Cashley, Len Bond, Bob Wardle, David Rodgers, Bobby Gould, John Sillett (Coach).
Front row: Edward Woods, Kevin Griffin, Trevor Tainton, John Emanuel, Geoff Merrick, Keith Fear, Gerry Gow, Brian Drysdale.
Inset: Ernie Hunt

Second Division Promotion Winners 1975/76

Back row: Don Gillies, Ray Cashley, John Shaw, Clive Whitehead.
Middle row: Alan Dicks (Manager), Paul Cheesley, David Rodgers, Tom Ritchie, Gary Collier, Ken Wimshurst (Chief Coach), Les Bardsley (Physio).
Front row: Mike Brolly, Jimmy Mann, Brian Drysdale, Geoff Merrick, Trevor Tainton, Gerry Sweeney, Gerry Gow.

Anglo-Scottish Cup Winners 1977/78

Back row: Kevin Mabbutt, Don Gillies, Ray Cashley, Norman Hunter, John Shaw, Clive Whitehead, Howard Pritchard. Middle row: Ken Wimshurst (Coach), Paul Cheesley, Tom Ritchie, David Rodgers, Gary Collier, Chris Garland, Brian McNeill, Les Bardsley (Physio). Front row: Alan Dicks (Manager), Jimmy Mann, John Bain, Trevor Tainton, Geoff Merrick, Gerry Sweeney, Gerry Gow, Keith Fear, Tony Collins (Assistant Manager).

Fourth Division 1982/83

Back row: Phil Thompson, Gary Williams, John Shaw, Russell Musker, Alan Crawford.
Middle row: Alex Lockhart (physio), Paul Stevens, Jon Economou, Gary Smith, Wayne Bray, Terry Cooper (Manager).
Front row: Ricky Chandler, Alan Nicholls, Terry Boyle, Tom Ritchie, Rob Newman, Glyn Riley.

Freight Rover Trophy Winners 1985/86

Back row: Clive Middlemass (Chief Coach), Gary Marshall, Rob Newman, Alan Walsh, Keith Waugh, David Moyes, Keith Curle, Howard Pritchard, Alex Lockhart (Physio).
Front row: Andy Llewellyn, Glyn Riley, Bobby Hutchinson, Steve Neville, David Harle, Brian Williams.

Freight Rover Trophy Runners-up 1986/87

Back row: Paul Fitzpatrick, Gary Marshall, Micky Tanner, Rob Newman, David Moyes, John MacPhail, Keith Curle, Alan Walsh.
Front row: Glyn Riley, Joe Jordan, Gordon Owen, Brian Williams, Steve Neville, Steve Galliers, Andy Llewellyn.
Keith Waugh was absent.

Littlewoods Cup Semi-Finalists 1988/89

Back row: Gary Stanley, Paul Mardon, Alan Walsh, Tony Sheppard, Nicky Dent, Scott McGarvey, Chris Honor.
Middle row: Buster Footman (Physio), Carl Shutt, Russel Bromage, John Pender, Keith Waugh, Andy Leaning, Rob Newman, John Bailey, Glenn Humphries, Alan Crawford (Youth Team Manager).
Front row: Steve Galliers, Mark Cooper, Nigel Hawkins, Jimmy Lumsden (Assistant Manager), Joe Jordan (Manager), Steve McClaren, Andy Llewellyn, Mark Gavin.

Third Division Promotion Winners 1989/90

Back row: Dave Smith, Matt Bryant, Paul Mardon, Robbie Turner, Cameron Toshack, Paul France, Ronnie McQuilter.
Middle row: John Pender, David Rennie, Ronnie Sinclair, Rob Newman, Russel Bromage, Andy Leaning, Bob Taylor, Glenn Humphries.
Front row: Gary Shelton, Mark Gavin, Jason Eaton, Alan Theobald, Micky Mellon, John Bailey, Andy Llewellyn.

'First Division' Founder Members 1992/93

Back row: Micky Mellon, Nicky Morgan, Gerry Harrison, James McIntyre, Ray Atteveld, Mark Gavin, Terry Connor.
Middle row: Buster Footman (Physio), Denis Smith (Manager), Wayne Allison, Dariusz Dziekanowski, Robert Edwards, Gary Campbell, Andy Leaning, Keith Welch, David Thompson, Matt Bryant, Brian Mitchell, Leroy Rosenior, Steve Benton, Mark Harrison, Alan Crawford.
Front row: Deion Vernon, Andy Paterson, Shaun Rouse, Andy Cole, Russell Osman, Gary Shelton, Mark Aizlewood, Andy Llewellyn, Martin Scott, Junior Bent, Andy Hogg.

Gloucestershire Cup Winners 1996/97

Back row: Junior Bent, Martin Kuhl, Dominic Barclay, Shaun Goater, Keith Welch, Rob Edwards, David Seal, Jim Brennan, Louis Carey.
Middle row: Buster Footman (Physio), Gerry Sweeney (Assistant Manager), Paul Agostino, Kevin Nugent, Mark Shail, Scott Alderman, Stuart Naylor, Mommainais Bokoto, Richard Perry, Kevin Langan, Dr S. Dasgupta (Club Doctor), Mike Gibson (Goalkeeper Coach).
Front row: Dave Bell (Youth Coach), Matt Hewlett, Brian Tinnion, Dwayne Plummer, Gareth Loyden, Joe Jordan (Manager), Alan McLeary, Gary Owers, Darren Barnard, Scott Partridge, Tony Fawthrop (Chief Scout).

TOWARDS THE MILLENNIUM

The publication of this official history brings to a close Bristol City's centenary celebrations. Throughout 1997 there have been a number of events to commemorate and celebrate our centenary year; players' reunion dinners, a centenary video release, a Golf Day and a Centenary Dinner and Dance (attended by over 500 people) – all culminating in two very prestigious pre-season friendlies against Premiership giants Liverpool and Everton.

Everyone concerned with the Club is now in a position to look towards the 21st century. What does the future hold?

Promotion to Division One is regarded a priority by the Board, staff and supporters of the club and, as this chapter is written, City are well-placed – riding high in Division Two under the management of John Ward – a string of good results earning him the Nationwide Division Two Manager of the Month award for October.

The summer of '97 saw a fluster of transfer activity with the manager being provided with over £1m of funds which enabled him to bring in five new players; Paul Tisdale, Adam Locke, Colin Cramb, Sean Dyche and Mickey Bell – an influx of talent largely afforded by the transfer fund created by the new share issue of 1996, but also an investment which bears testimony to the present Board's dedication to the Club's advancement.

The Club is also very much aware of the fundamental changes to our favourite game, and these changes will continue up to and beyond the year 2000. Football attendances are on the increase and more and more family groups attend matches than ever before. Indeed, it would be foolish for any football club to ignore the fact that its future lies firmly in the hands of its community.

Following the awful tragedies of Heysel, Bradford and Hillsborough and the radical changes recommended by the ensuing Taylor Report, we have seen the majority of football grounds convert their terracing into seating in a bid to establish all-seater stadia – our very own Ashton Gate being a fine example and which is now regarded as the premier sports arena in the south west.

Another initiative invoked by Lord Justice Taylor's Report was the introduction of the Football in the Community Programme. Funded by the PFA, the initiative has been taken up by nearly every League club, and Bristol City was amongst the forerunners when they appointed Shaun Parker as their first Community Officer back in 1990.

Over the following four years this new department generated a broad spectrum of community projects including women's and girl's football, fun days, soccer schools, 'Quid A Kid' and the founding of Senior Reds (a club for senior City supporters) – all of which have proved highly successful and gained the BCFC Community Department national recognition when they were voted the Jewson Family Football Club of the Year in 1994.

Parker's successor is former youth team coach Dave Bell who now runs the Bristol City Community Programme which continues to go from strength to strength and last year introduced a new incentive named 'Fans for the Future' under which schools are supplied free match tickets for the use of their pupils, the aim being to attract potential supporters.

The community is also regarded as a pivotal source of new players. How many instances can we think of where good local talent can be found playing in the Premiership after being 'lost' by their hometown teams? It is City's Centre of Excellence which has the job of developing local talent right the way through to genuine first-team contenders.

With spiralling fees and the changing structure of the transfer system post-Bosman ruling, a Club will always be better-placed having the facilities to receive and nurture local footballing talent. With a large investment by the Club followed by financial assistance from the Youth Foundation Scheme run by Chairman David Fear, the Centre of Excellence has now been running for 7 years. David Burnside was persuaded away from his post at the Football Association by present Vice-Chairman John Laycock to become Bristol City's Director of Youth. David is most ably assisted by Youth Development Officer and Director of the Centre of Excellence Peter Coleman, Youth team coach Peter Amos and their team of coaches. Already products of City's Youth Development have appeared in the first-team – Tommy Doherty being the most recent.

Communication between Club and supporter is crucial and something, perhaps, that has been lacking in the past. One of the first efforts by the present Board to address this shortcoming was the publication of a full-colour newsletter. 'Gatepost' is mailed, free of charge to 17,000 addresses which have been accumulated on the Club's database.

The installation of this database was City's first significant step towards embracing the new technologies – the ticket sales administration is now fully computerised and the Club's popular Clubcall telephone information service is soon to be supplemented by Bristol City's very own web site, allowing fans and other interested parties to access City info via the Internet. Indeed, by season 1998/99 it will be possible to order City SuperShop merchandise via your computer!

Developments are taking place around the ground too, with executive boxes due to be installed at the rear of the Dolman Stand during the close season of 1998, and there is also an option to add a second tier to the Wedlock Stand should the need arise.

These developments all require funding, and the stadium itself is seen as an ideal source of revenue. Ashton Gate has staged other events in the past such as the Rolling Stones concert in 1978. This year saw the FA choose the stadium as the venue for an under-21 international: England v Italy. The summer of '97 saw two religious festivals held at the ground and November '97 will see an England rugby international against the All Blacks take place. With an intended American Football match featuring the England Monarchs in April '98, Ashton Gate is fast becoming host to a whole gamut of entertainment.

Other developments in the pipeline are a Bristol City Museum which the Club is hoping will display artefacts and memorabilia from our 100-year history and utilising the new technologies already mentioned – the release of a City CD-ROM.

With the City Society lottery being replaced by 'City 2000 – Building The Dream', offering supporters prizes of up to £10,000 and the profits made from the scheme being funnelled back into the transfer fund and youth development, it is hard to remember a time when Bristol City FC was in possession of such a solid foundation for future advancement.

Of course, the last (but not least) piece in this jigsaw is the likes of you and me – the fan. Last season saw City gain the highest average attendance in Division Two and this season looks to emulate that as attendances are starting to exceed the 10,000 mark. With that amount of people encouraging the lads on the pitch we ought to be able to secure promotion by communal will-power alone!

The old chestnut 'A city the size of Bristol deserves a Premiership club' has been bandied around long enough – if the city deserves a Premiership club then a lot of hard work is called for – promotion never comes gift-wrapped. Perhaps that old chestnut should be adjusted slightly . . . City deserves to be a Premiership club?

STEVE HENDERSON
Programme Editor
November 3rd, 1997

THE BRISTOL CITY
A – Z

THE BRISTOL CITY FC

A TO Z

Paul Agostino

Young Australian international striker Paul Agostino was Bristol City's joint top goalscorer in 1995/96. He impressed as a 16-year-old with West Adelaide in the Australian Premier League and helped his country to reach the Youth World Cup semi-finals. Moving to Young Boys of Berne, he gained UEFA Cup experience during three years in Switzerland and had a ten day trial at Ashton Gate soon after Joe Jordan returned as City's manager in November 1994. He joined Bristol City for £50,000 in June 1995 and quickly formed an exciting striking partnership with fellow Aussie David Seal, making his full international debut as substitute against Chile in April 1996. He netted 19 goals in 84 Second Division games before moving to Munich 1860 shortly after helping City to reach the play-offs in 1996/97.

Peter Aitken

Versatile ex-Welsh U-23 defender Peter Aitken was one of Bristol City's 'Ashton Gate Eight' during the fateful 1981/82 campaign. A former Bristol Rovers apprentice, he signed professional in July 1972 and featured in the 1973/74 promotion success – appointed captain and making almost 250 appearances before Bob Houghton signed him on a free transfer in November 1980. His sole goal in 41 League outings came on his home debut the following month as City beat Bolton Wanderers 3-1. The finan-

cial crisis at Ashton Gate forced his release in February 1982 and he had spells with York City, Bulova (HK), AFC Bournemouth, Bath City, Trowbridge Town and Forest Green Rovers, then was assistant-manager at Bath City and Cheltenham Town. He still lives in Bristol and currently works for Rolls Royce.

Mark Aizlewood

Experienced Welsh international defender Mark Aizlewood was capped 21 times while at Ashton Gate. He initially joined his elder brother Steve at Newport County and made his League debut before signing professional from apprentice in October 1977. Sold to Luton Town for a record £50,000 in April 1978, he helped to win the Second Division title in 1981/82 and joined Charlton Athletic for £50,000 in November 1982. He scored the goal that clinched a First Division return in 1985/86, moving to Leeds United for £200,000 in February 1987, then Bradford City for a similar fee in August 1989. Joe Jordan paid £125,000 for him a year later and he starred in the 1991/92 FA Cup run, netting three goals in 101 League games prior to joining Cardiff City in November 1993. He became Merthyr Tydfil's player-coach in August 1995.

Paul Allen

Vastly experienced former England U-21 and B international midfielder Paul Allen made a significant contribution as Bristol City reached the Second Division play-offs in 1996/97. From a notable footballing family, he signed professional for West Ham in August 1979 and became the

youngest-ever FA Cup winner nine months later. Also featuring in their 1980/81 Second Division title campaign, he moved to Spurs for £400,000 in June 1985 and was an FA Cup finalist again in 1987 and a winner in 1991. He joined Southampton for £550,000 in September 1993, then had loan spells with Luton Town, Stoke City and Southend United prior to joining Swindon Town in October 1995. Starring in their 1995/96 Second Division title success, he followed Shaun Taylor to Ashton Gate on a free transfer in January 1997 and made 14 Second Division appearances before joining Millwall in June 1997.

Wayne Allison

Exciting striker Wayne Allison finished leading goalscorer three times at Bristol City and was voted 'Player of the Year' in 1993/94. He began as a Halifax Town trainee, making his League debut prior to signing professional in June 1987 and starring in a struggling team. Sold to Watford for a club record £250,000 in July 1989, he failed to secure a regular slot and Joe Jordan signed him for newly-promoted City in exchange for Mark Gavin in August 1990. An influential figure in the 1991/92 and 1993/94 FA Cup runs, he partnered the likes of Bob Taylor, Andy Cole and Leroy Rosenior while at Ashton Gate – netting 48 goals in 195 League outings before joining Swindon Town for £475,000 in July 1995. He was top scorer in their 1995/96 Second Division title success.

Anglo-Italian Cup

A table of Bristol City's record in this competition can be found at the end of this A to Z.

● Paul Agostino

● Wayne Allison

● **Bob Anderson**

Bob Anderson

Popular goalkeeper Bob Anderson deputised for injured Tony Cook during Bristol City's 1954/55 Third Division (South) title success. Following RAF service, he signed professional for Middlesbrough in November 1945 and moved to Crystal Palace via Blackhall Colliery in October 1951. 'Gentleman Bob' joined Bristol Rovers in March 1953 to replace injured Bert Hoyle during the 1952/53 Third Division (South) title campaign and Pat Beasley paid £500 for him in April 1954. He made 106 League appearances before a back injury ended his playing career in 1961, then coached St. Aldhelms and Bristol Federation of Boys Clubs while a district manager for Bollom dry cleaners. He retired in October 1986 after a stroke, remaining local until his death in November 1994.

Anglo-Scottish Cup

Bristol City won the Anglo-Scottish Cup at the third attempt in 1977/78, beating St. Mirren 3-2 on aggregate. After qualifying from Group B above Birmingham City, Plymouth Argyle and Bristol Rovers, City beat Partick Thistle 3-2 and Hibernian 6-4 to reach the final. Goals by Kevin Mabbutt and Peter Cormack gave the following team a 2-1 first-leg win at Love Street on 23rd November 1977: John Shaw, Gerry Sweeney, Don Gillies, Gerry Gow, Gary Collier, Geoff Merrick, Trevor Tainton, Tom Ritchie, Kevin Mabbutt, Peter Cormack, Jimmy Mann. Clive Whitehead replaced Cormack in the Ashton Gate second-leg two weeks later when Mabbutt's goal clinched a 1-1 draw. St. Mirren beat City 4-3 in the 1978/79 quarter-finals, then 5-1 in the 1979/80 final.

Archie Annan

Scottish right-back Archie Annan formed a notable defensive partnership with Joe Cottle as Bristol City won the Second Division title in 1905/06 and were FA Cup finalists in 1908/09. Initially with West Calder and St. Bernards, he joined Sunderland in July 1903 and Sheffield United five months later. He followed Harry Thickett to Ashton Gate for £200 in April 1905

● **John Atyeo**

and was ever-present in his first two seasons at Bristol City, making 143 League appearances prior to joining Burslem Port Vale in July 1911. Appointed manager of Mid-Rhondda a year later where he was assisted by Cottle and Bill Demmery, he subsequently returned to City as coach for five years in March 1921 and was later a police constable stationed at St. George.

Dick Armstrong

Long-serving, versatile inside-right Dick Armstrong was Bristol City's leading goalscorer in 1935/36. He impressed with Willington and Easington Colliery before joining Nottingham Forest in January 1930 and provided reliable cover for long-serving right-half Billy McKinlay, starring as Forest reserves finished Central Combination runners-up in 1934/35. Bob Hewison signed him in May 1935 and he partnered the likes of Bill Lane and Jack Haycox in attack before reverting to right-half, featuring prominently in City's 1937/38 promotion challenge. He scored 18 goals in 112 Third Division (South) games and remained on the books at Ashton Gate until March 1944, subsequently returning to Nottingham where he resided until his death in March 1969.

Ashton Gate Eight

On 21st October 1981, Bristol City directors announced that the club was over £700,000 in debt. By the end of January 1982 the financial situation was so bad that closure seemed imminent and a new company Bristol City (1982) Plc was formed to rescue the club. This takeover initially depended on the acceptance of redundancy by eight leading players – Peter Aitken, Chris Garland, Jimmy Mann, Julian Marshall, Geoff Merrick, David Rodgers, Gerry Sweeney and Trevor Tainton – who were on high wages and lengthy contracts. Dubbed the 'Ashton Gate Eight', they eventually accepted an improved redundancy offer an hour before the mid-day deadline on 2nd February 1982 and shared £82,500 including the proceeds of a special match between Ipswich Town and Southampton on 24th March 1982.

Associate Members Cup

A table of Bristol City's record in this competition can be found at the end of this A to Z.

Attendances

The record Football League attendance at Ashton Gate is 39,583 for the Second Division 'derby' against Bristol Rovers in October 1955, while the visit of Nottingham Forest in December 1993 produced record League gate receipts of £134,142. The 42,594 gate for the FA Cup fourth round tie against Blackpool in January 1959 compared with the record 43,335 FA Cup crowd against Preston NE in February 1935 and a record 30,002 saw the League Cup semi-final first-leg visit of Spurs in December 1970. The FA Cup fourth round visit of Everton in January 1995 produced record £174,231 receipts. In contrast, the 1,421 gate for the Football League Trophy tie against Torquay United in August 1982 is the lowest post-war attendance for a first-team game at Ashton Gate.

Ray Atteveld

Versatile Dutch midfielder Ray Atteveld was an early Denis Smith signing for Bristol City. Born in Amsterdam, he impressed in junior soccer with Slotervaart, Osdorp and DCG prior to joining Haarlem from school. Initially a sweeper, he gained 'B' international selection before moving to Everton for £250,000 in August 1989. Following the return of Howard Kendall as manager, he had a loan spell with West Ham and Smith paid £250,000 for him shortly before the transfer deadline in March 1992. He regularly featured as substitute, netting his sole goal in 14 League outings in the 2-1 defeat by Derby County in April 1992. Successive injuries and disciplinary problems marred his stay at Ashton Gate and he joined Belgian club Waregem on a free transfer in November 1993. Since returning to Holland, he has played for Roda and Vitesse.

John Atyeo

Widely regarded as Bristol City's finest post-war player, John Atyeo set the club appearance and goalscoring records during 15 years at Ashton Gate. Initially with Westbury United, he played in the

First Division as an amateur for Portsmouth prior to joining City as a part-timer in June 1951 – signing full-time only after qualifying as a surveyor. Ever-present and top scorer in the 1954/55 Third Division (South) title win, he was capped six times by England and remained at Ashton Gate despite big-money offers from clubs like Liverpool and Chelsea. Also a key figure in the 1964/65 promotion success despite reverting to part-time status to train as a teacher, he scored 314 goals in 596 League outings before retiring in 1966 to teach maths at a Warminster school. He died of a heart-attack in June 1993.

Phil Bach

Former England full-back Phil Bach was an influential figure as Bristol City were Southern League runners-up in 1900/01. Initially with Middlesbrough, he moved to Reading in July 1895 and was ever-present in 1895/96. Joining Sunderland in June 1897, he helped them to finish First Division runners-up in 1897/98 and gained international recognition before rejoining Middlesbrough in April 1899. He moved to Bristol City in June 1900 and made 29 Southern League appearances before reinstated as an amateur in 1904. Becoming a Middlesbrough director in February 1911 and chairman five months later, he held that post during two spells until 1935. He was also an FA Councillor and International Selector, serving on the Football League Management Committee until his death in December 1937.

Jack Bailey

Fast, genial left-back Jack Bailey formed a memorable partnership with Ivor Guy at Bristol City during the early post-war era. Born locally, Bob Hewison signed him from BAC in December 1944 and he made his first-team debut at Cardiff City in April 1945 – also playing in the

marathon War League Cup tie at Ninian Park twelve days later. Ever-present in 1947/48, he starred in the 1950/51 FA Cup run and overcame a broken arm in City's 1954/55 Third Division (South) title campaign, making 348 League appearances prior to joining Trowbridge Town in July 1958. He subsequently coached Welton Rovers, working in the dispatch department at DRG Robinson until retiring just six months before a fatal heart-attack on New Year's Eve 1986.

John Bailey

Former England 'B' left-back John Bailey was an influential figure as Bristol City became Littlewoods Cup semi-finalists in 1988/89 and won promotion in 1989/90. Initially an outside-left, he signed professional from apprentice for Blackburn Rovers in April 1975 and was reunited with Gordon Lee at Everton following a £300,000 move in July 1979. Ever-present in 1979/80, he helped to win the FA Cup in 1983/84 and League Championship in 1984/85 before joining Newcastle United for £80,000 in October 1985. Joe Jordan signed him on a free transfer in September 1988 and his sole goal in 80 League outings clinched a 1-0 win at Crewe Alexandra in October 1989. After a spell on City's coaching staff, he rejoined Everton as a coach in 1992 and has coached Sheffield United since March 1996.

David Bain

Experienced Scottish right-half David Bain was an influential figure as Bristol City managed to avoid relegation in successive years under Alex Raisbeck. Initially a centre-forward with Rutherglen Glencairn, he joined Manchester United in May 1922 and was soon followed by his younger brother Jimmy who subsequently played for and managed Brentford. He moved to Everton in July 1924 and featured in their 1927/28 League Championship triumph before Raisbeck paid £1,500 for him in November 1928. Scoring twice in 50 Second Division outings, he followed Raisbeck to Halifax Town in August 1930 and moved to Rochdale two years later.

Ian Baird

Former England Schoolboy striker Ian Baird was an experienced member of Joe Jordan's squad. An ex-Southampton apprentice, he signed professional in April 1982 and gained early First Division and UEFA Cup experience. After loan spells at Cardiff City and Newcastle United, he joined Leeds United for £100,000 in March 1985 and helped to reach the FA Cup semi-finals and play-offs in 1986/87. Sold to Portsmouth for £385,000 in August 1987, he returned to Elland Road nine months later and featured in the 1989/90 Second Division title success, then moved to Middlesbrough for £500,000 in January 1990 and Jordan's Hearts for £350,000 in July 1991. Russell Osman paid £295,000 for him in June 1993 and he scored 11 goals in 57 League outings before swapped for Plymouth Argyle's Kevin Nugent in September 1995. He joined Brighton for £35,000 in August 1996, starring in their 1996/97 'Great Escape'.

Albert Banfield

Inside-right Albert Banfield featured in Bristol City's 1934/35 FA Cup run alongside the likes of Teddy Harston and Jack Hodge. Born locally he impressed with St. Philip's Marsh Adult School and Joe Bradshaw signed him in October 1931. Given his League debut at Swindon Town in January 1934, he made a significant contribution as City pulled clear of re-election danger and lifted the Welsh Cup for the first time in 1933/34. He scored eight times in 38 Third Division (South) games prior to joining York City in May 1935, then Clapton Orient a year later. He subsequently returned to Bristol and resided locally until his death in August 1970.

Laurie Banfield

Small, tough-tackling left-back Laurie Banfield formed a notable defensive partnership with Charlie Treasure while at Bristol City. Initially with Old Mills, Sam Hollis signed him from Paulton Rovers in July 1911 and he made his League debut at home to Hull City in April 1912. Appointed captain at Ashton

● Jack Bailey

● John Bailey

● Ian Baird

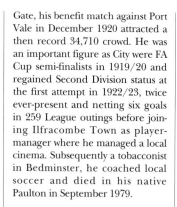

• Darren Barnard

Gate, his benefit match against Port Vale in December 1920 attracted a then record 34,710 crowd. He was an important figure as City were FA Cup semi-finalists in 1919/20 and regained Second Division status at the first attempt in 1922/23, twice ever-present and netting six goals in 259 League outings before joining Ilfracombe Town as player-manager where he managed a local cinema. Subsequently managed a tobacconist in Bedminster, he coached local soccer and died in his native Paulton in September 1979.

Bertie Banks

Stocky ex-England inside-left Bertie Banks was Bristol City's leading marksman in 1901/02, the club's first season in the Football League. He developed in Leamington junior soccer and joined Everton in April 1897 after representing the Army while on service in India. Moving to Millwall via Third Lanark in March 1899, he was top scorer in two consecutive seasons including 1899/00 when The Lions were FA Cup semi-finalists. Millwall's first international when capped against Ireland in March 1901, he joined Aston Villa a month later and Sam Hollis signed him in November 1901. He scored 17 goals in 43 Second Division games before returning to Southern League action with Watford in May 1903 and helping to win promotion. Subsequently employed by a Birmingham engineering firm, he died in Smethwick in 1947.

Stan Barber

Versatile half-back Stan Barber featured in successive relegation battles at Bristol City. Initially with Bishop Auckland and Wallsend he joined Newcastle United for £100 in September 1925 and gained top-flight experience before Alex Raisbeck paid £500 for him in June 1928. His sole goal in 23 Second Division outings came in the 6-0 trouncing of Oldham Athletic in November 1928. He joined Exeter City in June 1930 in exchange for Alec Sheffield, starring in their 1930/31 FA Cup run and 1932/33 promotion challenge. Moving to Brighton in May 1934, he subsequently returned to his native North-East as a carpenter and died in April 1984.

Les Bardsley

Popular trainer/physio Les Bardsley gave Bristol City excellent service during 21 years at Ashton Gate. A former Manchester City junior, he played for Derry City and Linfield during National Service before moving to Bury in April 1948 where he became captain and made 200 League appearances prior to joining Barrow in September 1955. Following a spell as Mossley player-manager, he joined City in July 1957 initially as assistant-trainer to Wilf Copping and was three times caretaker-manager at Ashton Gate after the departures of Pat Beasley (1958), Peter Doherty (1960) and Fred Ford (1967). He was the club's longest-serving full-time employee when he left in May 1978 to concentrate on his own physiotherapy practice and still lives locally.

Vic Barney

Fast-raiding inside-left Vic Barney was a big favourite during his brief spell at Ashton Gate. He represented the Army in Italy during war-time service, turning professional with Reading in September 1946. Bob Hewison signed him in October 1948 and he partnered Don Clark and Len Townsend in Bristol City's attack, netting four times in 28 Third Division (South) outings before joining Grimsby Town for £2,000 in June 1949. He subsequently captained Headington United, then played for Guildford City and Pressed Steel (P/M) where he worked on the production line until retiring in April 1986. Now residing in Witney, his son of the same name played for Bristol Rovers during the late 1960's.

Darren Barnard

Versatile attacking left-back Darren Barnard scored at Brentford in the 1996/97 Play-off semi-final second leg. A former England Schoolboy midfielder, he starred as Wokingham Town were Vauxhall League Premier Division runners-up in 1989/90 and gained Vauxhall League representative honours. He moved to Chelsea in July 1990 and gained top-flight experience under Glenn Hoddle, coming on as substitute in their 1994 FA Cup semi-final win over Luton Town. Following a loan spell at Reading,

Joe Jordan splashed out £175,000 for him in October 1995 and he quickly established an effective left-wing partnership with Brian Tinnion. He netted 15 goals in 78 Second Division outings for City prior to joining Premiership new-boys Barnsley for £750,000 in August 1997.

Danny Bartley

Ex-England Youth international Danny Bartley contested the left-wing slot with the likes of Lou Peters and Gerry Sharpe at Bristol City. Initially an apprentice, he signed professional in October 1964 and made his League debut as substitute in front of 36,184 at home to promotion rivals Wolves in December 1965. He netted seven goals in 101 Second Division games before moving to Swansea City in a joint £10,000 deal with Dave Bruton in August 1973 and starred as an attacking left-back in their rise under John Toshack. Released to join Hereford United in March 1980, he has since played for Trowbridge Town, Forest Green Rovers, Maesteg Park, Port Talbot (P/C) and now Bridgend Town (P/C). He still lives in Swansea and is a manager for a leading finance company.

Pat Beasley

Former England outside-left Pat Beasley managed Bristol City to the Third Division (South) title in 1954/55 with a record-equalling 70 points. Real name Albert, he joined Arsenal from Stourbridge in May 1931 and featured in successive League Championship campaigns prior to joining Huddersfield Town in October 1936, playing in the 1938 FA Cup final. He moved to Fulham in December 1945, switching to left-half and skippering the 1948/49 Second Division title win. Appointed City's player-manager in July 1950, he scored five goals in 66 League outings before concentrating on management. His contract was terminated by mutual agreement in January 1958 and he managed Birmingham City and Dover until retiring, living in Chard until his death in February 1986.

Walter Bennett

Skilful ex-England outside-right Walter Bennett was a key figure as Bristol City won the Second

• Danny Bartley

Division title in 1905/06. 'Cocky' impressed with Mexborough prior to joining Sheffield United and scored in their 1899 FA Cup final triumph, also helping to win the League Championship in 1897/98 and featuring in the 1901 and 1902 FA Cup finals. Capped against Wales and Scotland in 1901, he followed Harry Thickett to Ashton Gate in April 1905 and formed a prolific goalscoring partnership with Billy Maxwell and Sammy Gilligan. He netted 22 goals in 48 League outings before returning to South Yorkshire with Denaby United in May 1907, working at Denaby Main Colliery until tragically killed in a mining accident in April 1908.

Junior Bent

Fast, exciting right-winger Junior Bent helped Bristol City to reach the Second Division play-offs in 1996/97. A former Huddersfield Town trainee under ex-City favourite Gordon Low, he made his Second Division debut before signing professional in December 1987. Following a loan spell at Burnley, Jordan paid £30,000 for him on transfer deadline day in March 1990 and he helped to beat top-flight sides Wimbledon and Liverpool in the 1991/92 and 1993/94 FA Cup runs. Loaned to Stoke City and Shrewsbury Town, he created numerous goalscoring opportunities for the likes of Bob Taylor, Nicky Morgan, Andy Cole and Wayne Allison at Ashton Gate and has now managed 20 goals in 181 League outings for Bristol City before joining Blackpool in August 1997.

Roy Bentley

Centre-forward Roy Bentley gained 12 England caps including the 1950 World Cup after leaving Bristol City. Born locally, he was an amateur with Bristol Rovers prior to joining City in August 1939 and made his first-team debut at Bournemouth in the South Regional League in September 1940. Signed professional in August 1941, he netted 49 goals in 102 wartime games and joined Newcastle United for a record £8,500 in June 1946 – spearheading the 1947/48 promotion push before joining Chelsea for £12,500

in January 1948. He skippered the 1954/55 League Championship success, then switched to centre-half with Fulham (1958/59 promotion) and QPR before managing Reading and Swansea City. Subsequently a newsagent, then secretary at Reading and Aldershot, he is now retired and still lives in Reading.

Roy Bicknell

Centre-half Roy Bicknell provided reliable defensive cover while at Ashton Gate. A former Wolves junior, he signed professional under Major Buckley in September 1943 and moved to FA Cup winners Charlton Athletic in May 1947 where he gained First Division experience. He followed Bob Wright to Bristol City in June 1949 and made 21 Third Division (South) appearances prior to joining Cliff Edwards' Gravesend & Northfleet with George Brewster in June 1951, then moved to Colchester United in June 1952 and subsequently managed Clacton Town to the Southern League First Division title in 1959/60. He still lives in Colchester where he ran the Hythe Coffee House for 28 years, then worked at the County Court until retiring in May 1987.

Len Birks

Left-back Len Birks was an experienced figure as struggling Bristol City managed to avoid the re-election zone in 1933/34. Initially with Butt Lane Star, he joined Port Vale in May 1920 and was ever-present in 1923/24. Moving to Sheffield United in October 1924, he was a member of their 1925 FA Cup-winning squad and made almost 200 First Division appearances prior to joining newly-promoted Plymouth Argyle in February 1931. Bob Hewison paid £150 for him in September 1933, and he partnered Bill Roberts in defence, making 30 Third Division (South) appearances before joining Yeovil & Petters in August 1934. Featuring prominently as they reached the FA Cup third round in 1934/35, he later coached Bristol City and ran a shop in Bedminster, remaining local until his death in March 1975.

Cecil Blakemore

Much-travelled, experienced inside-left Cecil Blakemore was joint top

scorer with Percy Vials as Bristol City managed to avoid the re-election zone in 1928/29. He impressed in non-League soccer with Fairfield Villa, Stourbridge and Redditch prior to joining Crystal Palace in September 1922. Forming a notable forward partnership with big Percy Cherrett they starred in the 1925/26 FA Cup run and Alex Raisbeck paid £1,420 for the pair in May 1927. Blakemore netted 20 goals in 42 Third Division (South) games prior to joining Brentford with Jackie Foster in May 1929 and starred in successive promotion near-misses. Sold to Norwich City in August 1931, he was top scorer in 1931/32 and joined Swindon Town in June 1933 and Brierley Hill Alliance a year later. He was subsequently a publican in his native Stourbridge until his death in September 1963.

Jim Blessington

Former Scottish international inside-right Jim Blessington netted a hat-trick on his Bristol City home debut, later expunged from records when Southern League opponents Cowes disbanded. Initially with Leith Hibernians and Leith Athletic, he won Scottish League and Cup honours during six seasons with Celtic prior to joining Preston NE in February 1898 and Derby County in June 1899. He moved to City in November 1899 and scored seven times in 21 Southern League outings before joining Luton Town in August 1900. Leading marksman in 1900/01 he was ever-present in 1902/03 and moved to Leicester Fosse in May 1903. Appointed their first player-manager in January 1907, he subsequently coached Belfast Celtic and was a Newton Abbot licensee until his death in April 1939.

Len Bond

Young goalkeeper Len Bond understudied Mike Gibson and Ray Cashley at Bristol City during the early 1970's. Given his League debut at Blackburn Rovers in May 1971, four months before signing professional from apprentice, he was loaned to Exeter City, Torquay United, Scunthorpe United and Colchester United – making 30 League appearances prior to joining Brentford for £8,000 in August

● **Junior Bent**

● **Roy Bentley**

● **Jack Boxley**

1977. He starred in the 1977/78 promotion success, moving to Exeter City via St. Louis Stars (USA) for £10,000 in October 1980 and helping to reach the FA Cup sixth round in 1980/81. Followed Brian Godfrey to Weymouth in July 1984, then played for Bath City, Yeovil Town and Gloucester City (reunited with Godfrey) and is currently a newsagent in Exeter.

Lew Booth

Welsh inside-forward Lew Booth made a significant contribution as Bristol City narrowly missed promotion and were Third Division (South) Cup finalists in 1937/38. Unable to secure a regular first-team place with Swansea Town, he was a prolific goalscorer for Bangor City before Bob Hewison paid £350 for him in November 1936. He partnered the likes of Jack Haycox and Alfie Rowles in City's attack, scoring 22 goals in 63 Third Division (South) outings before the outbreak of World War Two. Also playing for City in war-time competition, he remained on the books at Ashton Gate until May 1946 and resided locally until his death in July 1984.

Tom Boucher

Skilful centre-forward Tom Boucher spearheaded two successive promotion challenges under Sam Hollis at Bristol City. He developed in non-League soccer with Redditch and Stourbridge prior to joining Notts County in July 1896 and was ever-present top scorer in their 1896/97 Second Division title triumph. Moving to Hollis' Bedminster with George Toone in July 1899 he joined local rivals Bristol Rovers a year later and was reunited with Hollis at Football League new-boys Bristol City in July 1901. He netted 14 goals in 51 Second Division outings before returning to Southern League action with New Brompton for two years in July 1903.

Clarrie Bourton

One of the club's finest servants, centre-forward Clarrie Bourton spearheaded Bristol City's 1937/38 promotion challenge. Born locally. Alec Raisbeck snapped him up from Paulton Rovers in January 1927 and he made his League debut at Stoke City in April 1928.

Moving to FA Cup winners Blackburn Rovers with Albert Keating for £4,000 in May 1928, he scored regularly in the top-flight and joined Coventry City in April 1931 where he scored a club record 171 League goals and starred in their 1935/36 Third Division (South) title success. He rejoined Bristol City via Plymouth Argyle in January 1938 and was player-manager during Bob Hewison's FA suspension, netting 15 goals in 61 League games overall before retiring in May 1944. He subsequently worked in City's Pools Office until shortly before his death in April 1981.

Ted Bowen

Centre-forward Ted Bowen was Bristol City's leading marksman in 1932/33. He impressed with Wath Wanderers prior to joining Arsenal for £500 in February 1926 and gained top-flight experience, also top scorer as their reserves won the London Combination title in consecutive years. Moving to Northampton Town in February 1928, he was their leading goalscorer in four successive seasons as they came close to achieving Second Division status for the first time. Bob Hewison paid £310 for him in August 1932 and he quickly became a favourite with three hat-tricks in his first season at Ashton Gate, scoring 33 goals in 55 Third Division (South) outings overall.

Archie Bown

Inside-forward Archie Bown was an experienced figure in Bristol City's 1920/21 promotion challenge as Joe Palmer's side went close to regaining First Division status. After impressing with Swindon Casuals and Whiteheads, he joined Swindon Town in July 1906 and was leading marksman four times in their greatest-ever forward-line including England star Harold Fleming. He gained Southern League representative honours prior to joining Bristol City in July 1919 and netted five goals in 35 League outings before moving to Weymouth in July 1922. Skippering their Southern League side under Billy Walker, he ran a sports shop in Weymouth and died in Southampton in August 1958.

Steve Bowyer

Diminutive inside-forward Steve Bowyer formed an exciting partnership with 'Ginger' Owers in Bristol City's attack. Initially with Lostock, he once scored four times in six minutes against Altrincham, then impressed with Earlestown before joining Liverpool in July 1907. He gained First Division experience, helping them to finish League Championship runners-up in 1909/10 and Sam Hollis signed him and Joe Brough in February 1912. Scoring 14 goals in 49 Second Division outings for City, he returned to Merseyside with South Liverpool in July 1913 and died in April 1967.

Jack Boxley

Fast, tricky outside-left Jack Boxley was a key figure in Bristol City's 1954/55 Third Division (South) title success. Initially with Stourbridge, Pat Beasley paid £2,000 for him in October 1950 and he created numerous goalscoring opportunities for the likes of Arnold Rodgers and John Atyeo prior to joining Coventry City with Jimmy Rogers in December 1956. He helped to win promotion in 1958/59, returning to Ashton Gate for a year in August 1960 and netting City's first-ever League Cup goal against Aldershot in October 1960. Scored 34 times in 207 League outings overall before playing for Chippenham Town, Welton Rovers and Bath City – settling in Bristol where he sold cars at Winterstoke Garage for 34 years until retiring in March 1995.

Danny Boxshall

Versatile forward Danny Boxshall partnered the likes of Don Clark, Len Townsend and Arnold Rodgers in Bristol City's early post-war attack. Initially a right-back, he developed in the Bradford Amateur League with Alston Works, Wilsden and Salem Athletic – representing the British Army of the Rhine prior to joining QPR in January 1946 and featuring in the 1947/48 Third Division (South) title success and FA Cup run. Bob Hewison signed him in May 1948 and he netted ten goals in 52 Third Division (South) games before moving to Bournemouth in July 1950, subsequently playing for Rochdale and Chelmsford City. An insurance agent for Prudential in Chelmsford for 25 years until retiring in April 1981, he now lives in Shipley, West Yorkshire.

Terry Boyle

Welsh international central defender Terry Boyle skippered Bristol City during a difficult period at Ashton Gate. A former Spurs apprentice, he joined Crystal Palace in January 1978 and gained First Division experience. Following a loan spell at Wimbledon, Bob Houghton signed him in a £200,000 exchange deal involving Kevin Mabbutt in October 1981 and he made 37 League appearances before released to join Newport County in November 1982. Sold to Cardiff City for £22,000 in August 1986, he was ever-present in the 1987/88 promotion success and switched to Swansea City for £11,000 in August 1989. Sub-sequently with Merthyr Tydfil, he helped Barry Town to win the Welsh League and Cup 'double' in 1993/94 and has since played for Merthyr again, Ebbw Vale (P/C), Inter Cardiff (P/C) and now Cinderford Town.

John Bradbury

Much-travelled outside-right John Bradbury created numerous goalscoring chances for Bertie Banks during Bristol City's 1901/02 Football League debut campaign. Initially with Stockport County, he had spells with Lincoln City, Blackburn Rovers and Ashton NE prior to joining Derby County in May 1899 where he contested a first-team slot with Dickie Wombwell. Moving to Barnsley a year later, Sam Hollis signed him in June 1901 and he scored four goals in 31 Second Division outings before moving to New Brompton in May 1902. He subsequently assisted Millwall, Carlisle United and Penrith.

Joe Bradshaw

Joe Bradshaw managed Bristol City during a difficult period at Ashton Gate. As an outside-right, he had played for Southampton, Woolwich Arsenal, Fulham (under his father Harry Bradshaw) and Chelsea before appointed Southend United's player-manager in

February 1911. He plotted their 1912/13 promotion triumph and took charge of Swansea Town in July 1919, guiding them to the Third Division (South) title in 1924/25 and FA Cup semi-finals in 1925/26 prior to rejoining Fulham as manager in May 1926. Succeeding Alex Raisbeck as City's manager in August 1929, he was sacked in February 1932 with the club facing relegation and in a desperate financial position. He later worked in insurance.

Joe Brain

Welsh inside-forward Joe Brain was an influential figure as Bristol City narrowly missed promotion and were Third Division (South) Cup finalists in 1937/38. Initially with Ebbw Vale, he joined Sunderland in March 1930 but failed to secure a First Division place at Roker Park and moved to Norwich City in May 1931. He joined Barrow in September 1932 and was top scorer in 1932/33, sold to Preston for £300 in April 1933. Returning to South Wales with Swansea Town in August 1934, he was leading marksman in two successive seasons before Bob Hewison signed him in June 1937. He netted nine goals in 32 Third Division (South) games before the outbreak of war and was a PE instructor in the Royal Artillery. Settling in Norwich, he ran a newsagent kiosk and died in March 1981.

Wayne Bray

Teenage midfielder Wayne Bray gained an early League chance with Bristol City following the 'Ashton Gate Eight' crisis in 1981/82. A member of the Bristol Boys side that won the English Schools Trophy in 1979, he signed professional from apprentice for City on his 17th birthday in November 1981 and made his League debut at home to Fulham three months later. He scored twice in 29 League outings prior to joining Weymouth in September 1983, then played for Bath City, Forest Green Rovers, Bristol Manor Farm, East Worle, Weston-Super-Mare and Dundry Athletic (where his brothers Gary and Andy also played) until receiving a five year ban in October 1991. Now living in Brislington, he is a fitter for Christie's Bedrooms.

Cyril Bridge

Long-serving left-back Cyril Bridge featured prominently in Bristol City's 1934/35 FA Cup run. Born locally, he starred for St. Philip's Marsh Adult School in the Bristol & District League before Joe Bradshaw snapped him up in August 1930. He made his League debut in the 3-3 draw at home to Crystal Palace in November 1932 and partnered the likes of Bill Roberts and Reg Brook in defence, also making a significant contribution to City's 1937/38 promotion near-miss and making 155 Third Division (South) appearances. He remained local until his death in January 1988 when his ashes were scattered on the pitch at Ashton Gate.

Alec Briggs

Long-serving full-back Alec Briggs featured prominently in Bristol City's 1964/65 promotion success. Pat Beasley signed him from Soundwell in April 1957 and he made his League debut at Cardiff City a year later, failing to secure a regular place until Fred Ford's appointment as manager. He subsequently formed a notable partnership with Mike Thresher, then Tony Ford and was three times ever-present – helping to reach the FA Cup fifth round in successive years and netting his sole goal in 351 League outings in the 3-1 defeat at Derby County in April 1968. Left City in May 1970 to concentrate on his clothing business, then was a partner of Bobrig Hotels Ltd providing holidays for handicapped people. He retired in June 1992 and still lives in Wrington.

Ernie Brinton

Stylish left-half Ernie Brinton made a significant contribution to Bristol City's 1934/35 FA Cup run. Born locally, he represented Bristol Boys and signed professional for City from Avonmouth in February 1930. Given his League debut at home to Blackpool a month later, he scored seven goals in 249 League outings and played alongside his younger brother Jack at Ashton Gate before joining Newport County in June 1937. He starred in their 1938/39 Third Division (South) title success and guested for City during the war while working at BAC. Joining Aldershot in August 1946, he subse-

● Terry Boyle

● Alec Briggs

● Russel Bromage

● Matt Bryant

● Tommy Burden

quently played for Street and Chippenham Town in the Western League and remained local until suffering a fatal heart-attack in September 1981.

Tommy Broad

Noted for his pace, much-travelled outside-right Tommy Broad was ever-present for Bristol City in 1913/14. He developed in junior soccer with Redgate Albion, Denton Wanderers and Openshaw Lads Club prior to joining West Brom in September 1905 after a trial with Manchester City. Moving to Chesterfield in February 1908, he was sold to Oldham Athletic for £250 in May 1909 and ever-present in their 1909/10 promotion success. Sam Hollis paid £5,000 for him in May 1912 and he created numerous goalscoring chances for the likes of Ginger Owers and Billy Brown, netting eight goals in 106 Second Division outings prior to joining Manchester City in March 1919. He helped to finish League Championship runners-up in 1920/21, then moved to Stoke City in May 1921 and starred in their 1921/22 promotion triumph, later playing for Southampton, Weymouth and Rhyl.

Mike Brolly

Ex-Scottish Schoolboy winger Mike Brolly featured in Bristol City's 1975/76 promotion campaign. Initially a Chelsea junior, he signed professional in October 1971 and gained First Division experience alongside Chris Garland before Alan Dicks signed him on a free transfer in June 1974. He scored twice in 30 Second Division outings prior to joining Tommy Casey's Grimsby Town for £6,000 in September 1976 and starred in their rise from Fourth Division to Second in successive years, moving to Derby County on a free transfer in August 1982 and newly-promoted Scunthorpe United a year later. Subsequently with Scarborough (1986/87 GM Vauxhall Conference title win) and Goole Town, he now teaches PE and history at St. Mary's RC School in Grimsby.

Russel Bromage

Experienced left-back Russel Bromage was an influential figure

as Bristol City reached the Third Division play-offs in 1987/88. A former Port Vale apprentice, he signed professional in November 1977 and starred in the 1985/86 promotion success – making almost 350 League appearances for Vale before Terry Cooper signed him in August 1987. He also featured in City's 1988/89 Littlewoods Cup run and 1989/90 promotion campaign as cover for John Bailey, netting his sole goal in 46 Third Division outings in the 1-1 draw against Preston NE in September 1988. Moved to Brighton in August 1990 and following a loan spell at Maidstone United, he became Southwick player-coach and was appointed Littlehampton Town player-manager in July 1995.

Reg Brook

Right-back Reg Brook featured prominently in Bristol City's 1937/38 promotion near-miss. Initially with Loughborough Corinthians, he joined Coventry City in July 1932 where he understudied Vic Brown and Charlie Bisby and helped to win the Third Division (South) Cup in 1935/36. Sold to Southend United in May 1936, Bob Hewison signed him in June 1937 and he formed a reliable defensive partnership with Cyril Bridge. His sole goal in 71 Third Division (South) outings came in the 8-2 win over Walsall in February 1938 and he guested for both Nottingham clubs during the war before retiring.

Billy Brown

Inside-right Billy Brown was Bristol City's leading marksman in the two seasons immediately prior to the Great War. He impressed with Kettering and briefly continued in the Southern League with QPR before joining Chelsea in July 1911. Despite featuring in their 1911/12 promotion success and netting goals regularly in their Combination side, he failed to establish a regular first-team place at Stamford Bridge and George Hedley signed him in November 1913. He scored 23 goals in 62 Second Division games prior to joining Swansea Town in September 1919, then had spells with Portsmouth and North-ampton Town prior to becoming a civil servant in London.

Dave Bruton

Young central defender Dave Bruton provided reliable cover for Dickie Rooks and David Rodgers while at Ashton Gate. He signed professional from apprentice for Bristol City in July 1971 and made his League debut at Sunderland four months later, amassing 17 Second Division appearances prior to joining Swansea City in a joint £10,000 deal with Danny Bartley in August 1973. Featured in successive promotion campaigns under John Toshack, moving to Newport County for a record £17,500 in October 1978 after an earlier loan spell and skippered the 1979/80 promotion triumph (alongside younger brother Mick). Subsequently with Gloucester City, Forest Green Rovers, Trowbridge Town, Pontllanfraith, Caerleon, Cwmbran Town (P/M) and Wotton Rovers (P/M), he now lives in Thornbury and is an Area Manager for Provident Finance Group

Matt Bryant

Tall central defender Matt Bryant was voted Bristol City's 'Player of the Year' in 1994/95. Born locally, he was initially a trainee at Ashton Gate and signed professional under Joe Jordan in July 1989. He moved to Kenny Hibbitt's Walsall on loan a year later where he made his League debut on the opening day of the 1990/91 campaign, returning to make his City debut at Plymouth Argyle in January 1991. Held his place alongside Welsh International Mark Aizlewood for the remainder of that season, helping City to consolidate Second Division status after promotion and featured in the 1991/92 and 1993/94 FA Cup runs. He netted seven goals in 204 League outings prior to joining Gillingham for £65,000 in August 1996.

Tommy Burden

Noted for his consistency, experienced wing-half Tommy Burden skippered Bristol City during the late 1950's. An ex-Wolves junior, he was wounded during wartime Army service and joined Chester in November 1945. Reunited with Major Buckley at Leeds United in July 1948, he became captain at

Elland Road with almost 250 Second Division appearances until the travelling from his job with Clarks Shoes in Street became too much. Pat Beasley was delighted to sign him for £3,000 in October 1954 and he helped City to clinch the Third Division (South) title in 1954/55, scoring 20 goals in 231 League outings prior to briefly joining Glastonbury in May 1961. Subsequently a senior executive in the shoe trade, he retired in 1987 and still lives in Glastonbury.

Andy Burton
Scottish inside-left Andy Burton was an influential figure during Harry Thickett's successful reign at Ashton Gate. He developed with Thompson's Rovers and Lochgelly Juniors prior to joining Motherwell and Thickett signed him in July 1905. Starring as City won the Second Division title in 1905/06, were League Championship runners-up in 1906/07 and FA Cup finalists in 1908/09, he netted 45 goals in 192 League games before moving to Everton in July 1911. Within a year, he had moved to Reading and later coached in Belgium. He was not related to Edwin Burton who was killed in action during the First World War after two seasons at Ashton Gate.

Terry Bush
Versatile forward Terry Bush netted several spectacular goals during Bristol City's 1964/65 promotion campaign. A former junior, he featured in the 1959/60 FA Youth Cup run and signed professional in February 1960 – scoring twice to earn a 2-2 draw against Torquay United on his League debut in March 1961. Groomed as John Atyeo's successor, he also featured at wing-half and netted 43 times in 162 League outings before a knee injury ended his career prematurely in 1970. He was subsequently City's Assistant Secretary, then Manager of the Dolman Stand Indoor Bowling Club and in July 1973 became Regional Officer for the Transport & General Workers' Union in Bristol. Since July 1993 he has been District Secretary of the Newport branch, still living in Easton-in-Gordano.

Sandy Caie
Versatile Scottish forward Sandy Caie was leading marksman as Bristol City were runners-up in their first Southern League campaign of 1897/98. Real name Alex, he developed with Victoria United in his native Aberdeen and spent a period with Woolwich Arsenal before following Sam Hollis to City in July 1897 as they turned professional and entered the Southern League. He helped City to repeat their Southern League runners-up placing in 1898/99, then moved to Millwall in February 1900 and later played for Newcastle Utd, Brentford and Motherwell. Subsequently emigrating to Canada, he played for Westmount and Sons of Scotland in Montreal before being murdered on the railway in Massachusetts in December 1914.

Percy Cainey
Outside-left Percy Cainey featured prominently in Bristol City's 1934/35 FA Cup run. Born locally, he developed with Kingsway and Wesley Rangers before Joe Bradshaw signed him in September 1930. He scored on his League debut as City defeated Swindon Town 5-1 in February 1933 and created numerous goalscoring opportunities for the likes of Ted Bowen, Joe Riley and Teddy Harston, netting 12 goals in 77 Third Division (South) games before joining Bradford PA in May 1936. Subsequently with Bath City, Bournemouth, Glastonbury and Coalpit Heath, he was publican at the 'Engineers Arms' then worked at Albion Dockyard and remained local until his death in March 1966.

Arthur Capes
Former England inside-left Arthur Capes partnered Sammy Gilligan and Albert Fisher in Bristol City's attack. Initially with Burton Wanderers, 'Sailor' joined Nottingham Forest with his brother Adrian in July 1896 and was ever-present and top scorer in 1896/97. He netted two goals in Forest's

1898 FA Cup final triumph and moved to Stoke in July 1902. Sam Hollis signed him in May 1904 and he was an experienced figure as City finished fourth in the Second Division for the third successive season, netting seven goals in 29 League outings. He briefly moved to Swindon Town in July 1905, then played for Langton Hall in the North Staffs Combination. He died in his native Burton in February 1945.

Louis Carey
Versatile young midfielder Louis Carey made a significant contribution as Bristol City reached the Second Division play-offs in 1996/97 and has impressed as an emerging member of John Ward's squad. Born locally, he attended Headley Park and Chew Valley schools and was spotted playing as a right-back for Bristol Boys. He graduated from City's school of excellence to sign professional under Joe Jordan and made a surprise League debut in the 1-0 win at York City in October 1995. He has now made 65 Second Division appearances for Bristol City.

Albert Carnelly
Much-travelled centre-forward Albert Carnelly impressed with his dribbling skills alongside Sandy Caie as Bristol City were Southern League runners-up in successive seasons. Initially with Notts Mapperley, he was a prolific goalscorer for Notts County, Loughborough, Nottingham Forest and Leicester Fosse before Sam Hollis recruited him for Southern League new-boys Bristol City in July 1897. Scoring 27 goals in 35 Southern League games, he left St. John's Lane for Southern League rivals Thames Ironworks in July 1899 and was leading marksman in 1899/00, then spent a season with East London neighbours Millwall.

Tommy Casey
Tough-tackling left-half Tommy Casey played under Peter Doherty for Northern Ireland and Bristol City. He developed with Belfast YMCA, East Belfast and Bangor prior to joining Leeds United in May 1949, then Bournemouth in August 1950. Sold to Newcastle United for £7,000 two years later, he played in the 1955 FA Cup final

● Terry Bush

● Louis Carey

● Tommy Casey

● Ray Cashley

triumph and the World Cup quarter-finals shortly before moving to Portsmouth for £8,500 in June 1958. Capped 12 times, Doherty signed him in March 1959 and he scored nine goals in 122 League outings, appointed Gloucester City player-manager in July 1963. Subsequently with Swansea Town (trainer), Ammanford Town and Distillery (P/M), he coached Everton and Coventry City, then managed Grimsby Town, KR (Reykjavik) and Harstaad. He was a mobile fishmonger based in Portbury for 17 years until retiring in February 1997 and now lives in Nailsea.

Ray Cashley
Goalkeeper Ray Cashley was twice ever-present for Bristol City, including the 1975/76 promotion success. Initially a left-back, he switched to goalkeeping during the 1969/70 FA Youth Cup run and signed professional in September 1970. He made his debut in the FA Cup third round tie at Southampton four months later and starred in the 1973/74 FA Cup run, scoring from a clearance in that season's 3-1 League win over Hull City. Displaced by John Shaw and Jan Moller in Division One, he made 227 League appearances and briefly retired after a loan spell at Hereford United. He revived his career with Bristol Rovers in August 1982 and subsequently played for Trowbridge Town, Chester City, East Worle, Bristol City (as cover in 1986/87) and Weston-super-Mare where he is now Lottery Manager.

Tommy Cavanagh
Experienced inside-right Tommy Cavanagh partnered John Atyeo and Jimmy Rogers while at Bristol City. He began with Preston NE, joining Stockport County in January 1950 and Huddersfield Town in May 1952 – helping to regain top-flight status at the first attempt in 1952/53. Moved to Doncaster Rovers in May 1956 and followed Peter Doherty to Ashton Gate in July 1959, scoring six goals in 24 Second Division outings. After relegation he joined Carlisle United in June 1960, then managed Cheltenham Town (P/M) and Brentford before becoming

● Paul Cheesley

trainer/coach at Nottingham Forest, Hull City and Manchester United (assisting ex-Preston teammate Tommy Docherty). He later assisted Arthur Cox at Newcastle United, then managed Rosenborg and Burnley prior to coaching Wigan Athletic and now lives in Humberside.

Chairmen
A table listing Bristol City's chairmen, with dates of office, can be found at the end of this A to Z.

Peter Chambers
Highly-rated, jovial left-half Peter Chambers played an important role in Bristol City's 1905/06 Second Division title success. After helping Black Diamonds to win the Cumberland League & Cup in his native Workington, he joined Blackburn Rovers in July 1897 and moved to Bedminster two years later. Following the merger in 1900 he starred as Bristol City were Southern League runners-up in 1900/01 and entered the Football League. He netted ten goals in 173 League games overall before joining Swindon Town with Freddie Fenton and Billy Jones in July 1907 and helped to finish runners-up in two consecutive seasons before they won the Southern League title in 1910/11. Subsequently landlord of the 'Red Lion' pub, he remained in Swindon until his death in 1952.

Ricky Chandler
Ex-England Schoolboy striker Ricky Chandler was a young member of Bristol City's squad that slipped from the First Division to Fourth in successive years. The son-in-law of Ken Wimshurst, he signed professional from apprentice in October 1978 and made his League debut as substitute at home to Watford in January 1981, scoring 13 goals in 61 League outings before joining Bath City in July 1983. Sold to Yeovil Town for £4,000 in July 1986, he featured in the 1987/88 Isthmian League and Cup 'double' campaign and moved via a spell back at Bath to Gloucester City in October 1988 – starring in the 1988/89 Midland Division title win and since playing for Weston-super-Mare, Clevedon Town, Mangotsfield United and Nailsea Town. Now living in Headley Park, he is UK Sales Manager for Hi-Tec Sports.

Paul Cheesley
Renowned for his heading ability, burly striker Paul Cheesley formed a notable partnership with Tom Ritchie in Bristol City's 1975/76 promotion campaign. Born locally, he signed professional from apprentice for Norwich City in October 1971 and gained First Division experience before moving to Ashton Gate for £30,000 in December 1973 – initially struggling to secure a regular place. He netted City's first goal back in the top flight to clinch a 1-0 win at Arsenal in August 1976 but a knee injury sustained against Stoke City three days later effectively ended his career after scoring 20 times in 64 League outings. Subsequently with Shepton Mallet, Frome Town, Odd Down and Yeovil Town, he now lives in Whitchurch and is a salesman for building materials and plastics, as well as a matchday host at Ashton Gate.

Percy Cherrett
Big, bustling centre-forward Percy Cherrett displaced Tot Walsh in Bristol City's attack alongside Albert Keating. Initially with Bournemouth Poppies, he joined Boscombe and impressed in their inaugural Southern League campaign. Moving to Portsmouth in February 1921, he was top scorer in 1921/22 and repeated this feat at Plymouth Argyle in 1923/24 as they finished Third Division (South) runners-up. He joined Crystal Palace in September 1925 and starred in their 1925/26 FA Cup run, leading marksman in two consecutive seasons before Alex Raisbeck signed him and striking partner Cecil Blakemore in May 1927. Netting 15 goals in 25 Second Division games, he rejoined Bournemouth in July 1928 and partnered record goalscorer Ron Eyre in attack before joining Cowes in May 1929. He was subsequently a publican in Southampton and Bournemouth.

Ken Chilcott
Welsh outside-right Ken Chilcott played for Bristol City either side of the Second World War and featured prominently in the 1946/47 promotion challenge. He developed with Eastville United before joining Bath City in August 1935 and scored regularly in the

Southern League. Moving to Ashton Gate in October 1937, he made his League debut at Gillingham on New Year's Day 1938. During the war he worked for Godwin, Warren & Co with Cliff Morgan, then at BAC (Filton) while guesting for their works team and Aberaman Athletic. He scored six goals in 46 Third Division (South) games prior to joining Bridgwater Town in July 1949 and subsequently worked as a window-cleaner in Bristol, emigrating to Australia in 1992.

Frank Clack

Experienced goalkeeper Frank Clack was ever-present for Bristol City in 1947/48. Initially with Witney Town, he joined Birmingham in May 1933 and gained First Division experience as understudy to England star Harry Hibbs. Moving to Brentford in July 1939, he guested for Mansfield Town and Notts County during the war and following relegation, Bob Hewison paid £1,500 for him in May 1947 to replace Alex Ferguson. He made 67 Third Division (South) appearances despite competition from George Marks prior to joining Guildford City in July 1949, then Dover for a brief spell. Settling in Witney, he worked as a welder and a sawyer, then spent 21 years in the finishing department at Early's blanket company until retiring in March 1977 and died in February 1996.

Brian Clark

Tall, stylish inside-forward Brian Clark was ever-present in three successive seasons and top scorer in Bristol City's 1964/65 promotion triumph. The son of Don Clark, he signed professional for City in March 1960 and made his League debut against Brentford in April 1961. Also leading marksman in 1962/63 alongside John Atyeo, he netted 83 goals in 195 League outings before joining Huddersfield Town in exchange for John Quigley in October 1966, then Cardiff City in February 1968. He formed a lethal striking partnership with John Toshack, then played for AFC Bourne-mouth, Millwall, Cardiff again and Newport County where he joined the coaching staff. Subsequently

manager/coach of Maesteg, AFC Cardiff and Bridgend Town, he still lives in Cardiff and is now a sales representative for safety equipment.

Don Clark

Dashing centre-forward Don Clark scored a club record 36 League goals in Bristol City's 1946/47 promotion challenge, including four in the record 9-0 League win over Aldershot. Born locally, Bob Hewison signed him as a wing-half from North Bristol Old Boys in May 1937 and he made his League debut against Mansfield Town in March 1939. Successfully switched to attack during war-time soccer, he partnered the likes of Roy Bentley, Cyril Williams and Len Townsend – netting 67 goals in 117 Third Division (South) outings until appointed City's Assistant Secretary for five years in 1951 after a serious knee injury. Subsequently bottling/transport manager for Harvey's wine merchants, he was then transport manager for BAC at Filton until retiring in August 1982 and now lives in Paignton.

Harry Clay

Long-serving goalkeeper Harry Clay was a key figure as Bristol City won the Second Division title in 1905/06 and were FA Cup finalists in 1908/09. Initially with Kimberley St. Johns, Sam Hollis signed him in November 1901 and he made his League debut in the 5-2 win at home to Chesterfield the following month. He was ever-present in three successive seasons and had a benefit match against Nottingham Forest in November 1907, making 311 League appearances despite competition from the likes of Bill Demmery and Talbot-Lewis before retiring in 1913. Serving in the Army during the Great War, he was head groundsman at the BAC Ground in Southmead Road then at Canford Park and remained local until his death in August 1964.

Billy Coggins

Goalkeeper Billy Coggins was ever-present in Bristol City's 1926/27 Third Division (South) title campaign. Born locally, he developed with Victoria Albion and represented the Bristol Suburban League

before joining Bristol St. George from where Alex Raisbeck signed him in September 1925. Displacing Frank Vallis in goal, he made his League debut at Southend United on Boxing Day 1925 and made 171 League appearances before being sold to Everton for £2,000 in March 1930. He made his Everton debut in the 2-4 defeat at home to Grimsby Town that condemned Everton to relegation and was ever-present in their 1930/31 Second Division title success before displaced by emerging Ted Sagar. Subsequently with QPR and Bath City, he became landlord of the 'Rising Sun' pub in Backwell where he died in July 1958.

Andy Cole

England U-21 striker Andy Cole was Bristol City's leading marksman in 1992/93 and remains the club's most expensive purchase and record sale. He graduated from the FA School of Excellence, signing professional for Arsenal in October 1989 and gaining limited opportunities behind Ian Wright & Co. Following a loan spell at Alan Dicks' Fulham, he moved to Ashton Gate on loan in March 1992 and Denis Smith paid £500,000 for him in July 1992. He netted 20 goals in 41 First Division outings before joining Newcastle United for £1,750,000 in March 1993, helping to clinch the First Division title. A big favourite on Tyneside as the Premiership's top scorer in 1993/94, he moved to Manchester United in a sensational £7,000,000 record deal in January 1995 and has since gained full England recognition, featuring in United's 1995/96 'double' triumph.

Gary Collier

Central defender Gary Collier made history as the first player to change clubs under freedom of contract. A former Bristol City apprentice, he signed professional in November 1972 and made his League debut at Luton Town in March 1973. He starred alongside Geoff Merrick in the 1973/74 FA Cup run, voted 'Player of the Year' in 1974/75 and a key figure in the 1975/76 promotion success. Ever-present in 1976/77, he netted three goals in 193 League outings before joining Coventry

● Brian Clark

● Don Clark

● Andy Cole

● **Gary Collier**

● **Tony Cook**

● **Terry Cooper**

City for a record £325,000 in July 1979 and his move precipitated the financial crisis at Ashton Gate as established players were given long contracts. Sold to Portland Timbers for £365,000 in March 1980, he later joined San Diego Sockers and has now settled in Florida – coaching teams like Fort Lauderdale.

Roger Collinson
England Youth right-back Roger Collinson partnered Mike Thresher while at Bristol City. A former schoolboy international and Doncaster Rovers amateur, he followed Peter Doherty to Ashton Gate in October 1958 and made his Second Division debut at Scunthorpe United in the opening game of the disastrous 1959/60 campaign in place of Gordon Hopkinson. He featured in the record 11-0 FA Cup victory over Chichester City in November 1960 and his sole goal in 50 League outings was a spectacular long-range effort at promotion-chasing Aston Villa in front of 38,556 in April 1960. Released to join Stockport County in July 1961, he later played for Alfreton Town and Skegness Town (with Johnny McCann). He tragically died of leukaemia in December 1989.

Terry Compton
Born locally, centre-half Terry Compton gave Bristol City loyal service during ten years at Ashton Gate. Initially with Phildown Rovers, Bob Hewison signed him in December 1948 and he made his League debut in the 2-1 win over Swindon Town in March 1952. He provided reliable defensive cover for the likes of Dennis Roberts, Jack White and Ernie Peacock, making 44 League appearances prior to joining Western League champions Salisbury for six years in July 1958. Four times ever-present, he starred in the 1959/60 FA Cup run and 1960/61 Western League title success, then assisted Arnold Rodgers at Welton Rovers. He settled in Hartcliffe, a long distance driver for British Road Services, then a local bus driver for 16 years until a fatal heart-attack in October 1991.

Jack Connor
Big centre-half Jack Connor was a popular figure in Bristol City's 1964/65 promotion success. A former Huddersfield Town junior, he signed professional in October 1952 and gained First Division experience before Fred Ford signed him in exchange for Johnny McCann in October 1960. He established a notable central defensive partnership with ex-Huddersfield team-mate Gordon Low and was three times ever-present, netting ten goals in 355 League outings prior to joining City's coaching staff in 1971. Subsequently coach at Everton, he then played for Formby (1973/74 FA Cup run), Fleet-wood Hesketh and Littlewoods (P/C). He still lives in Formby and after 18 years as Area Manager for Package Control Ltd, he ran the Littlewoods Sports & Social Club and is now groundsman at the Everton School of Excellence.

Tony Cook
Extrovert goalkeeper Tony Cook was renowned for his penalty saves during 15 years at Bristol City. Born locally, Bob Wright signed him from Clifton St. Vincents in December 1949 and he made his League debut against Swindon Town in November 1952. He missed the 1954/55 Third Division (South) title run-in with a broken arm and subsequently contested the goalkeeping slot with Bob Anderson. Ever-present in 1959/60, he amassed 320 League appearances before joining Worcester City on a free transfer in July 1964, then playing for Cinderford Town and in the Downs League for Manor Farm Boys Club (P/C) and Sneyd Park. After working in Bristol Docks, he was a Horfield Prison Officer for 27 years until retiring in October 1994 and sadly died in March 1996.

Terry Cooper
Ex-England left-back Terry Cooper managed Bristol City to promotion in 1983/84 and Freight Rover Trophy success in 1985/86. As a player, he starred in the glorious Don Revie era at Leeds United, capped 20 times before following Jack Charlton to Middlesbrough for £50,000 in

March 1975. Reunited with Norman Hunter at Ashton Gate after Alan Dicks paid £20,000 for him in July 1978, he joined Bristol Rovers in August 1979 and became player-manager for 18 months. Briefly at Billy Bremner's Doncaster Rovers, he returned to City as player-manager in May 1982 and later joined the board – scoring once in 71 League games overall. Sacked in March 1988, he managed Exeter City to the Fourth Division title 1989/90 and Birmingham City to promotion in 1991/92. Rejoining Exeter as manager in January 1994, ill-health forced his resignation and he joined Southampton's coaching staff in July 1996.

Fred Corbett
Versatile inside-forward Fred Corbett was Bristol City's joint leading goalscorer with Alf Dean in 1903/04. Initially with Old St. Lukes, he impressed with Thames Ironworks before joining Bristol Rovers in January 1902 and Sam Hollis signed him for City in July 1903. He made his League debut at Manchester United in the opening game of the 1903/04 campaign and netted 14 goals in 49 Second Division outings before rejoining Bristol Rovers in April 1905 after a brief spell at Brentford. He settled in his native London and died in April 1924.

Peter Cormack
Former Scottish international midfielder Peter Cormack was one of several experienced players recruited to boost Bristol City's First Division survival hopes during the 1976/77 campaign. Initially a striker with Hibernian, he was top scorer in successive years prior to joining Nottingham Forest for £80,000 in March 1970. Sold to Liverpool for £115,000 in July 1972, he featured in the 1972/73 UEFA Cup and 1973/74 FA Cup triumphs as well as two League Championship campaigns before Alan Dicks paid £50,000 for him in November 1976. He helped to win the Anglo-Scottish Cup in 1977/78, netting 15 goals in 67 First Division outings before rejoining Hibs on a free transfer in February 1980 and later managing Partick Thistle. Since July 1994 he has assisted Allan McGraw at Greenock Morton.

Joe Cottle

England left-back Joe Cottle formed a notable defensive partnership with Archie Annan as Bristol City won the Second Division title in 1905/06, were League Championship runners-up in 1906/07 and FA Cup finalists in 1908/09. Born locally, he developed with Dolphins and Harry Thickett signed him in June 1905. He made his League debut at Bradford City three months later and was ever-present in 1909/10, gaining his sole international cap alongside City team-mate Billy Wedlock against Ireland in February 1909. He made 204 League appearances before breaking a leg in January 1911 and subsequently played for Bristol Rovers before joining Archie Annan's Mid-Rhondda with Bill Demmery. Later a Bedminster publican, he remained local until his death in February 1958.

John Cowell

Centre-forward John Cowell was Bristol City's leading marksman in 1909/10. Initially with Castleford Town, he moved via Selby Mizpah to Rotherham Town and Harry Thickett signed him in April 1909. Given his League debut at home to Manchester City in the final game of the 1908/09 campaign, his 20 goals the following season included four at home to Nottingham Forest. He netted 20 times in 37 League games overall before moving to First Division rivals Sunderland in October 1910 and subsequently played for Belfast Celtic.

Alan Crawford

Experienced winger Alan Crawford featured prominently in Bristol City's 1983/84 promotion success. He signed professional from apprentice for Rotherham United in October 1971 and was ever-present in three successive campaigns, including the 1974/75 promotion triumph. Leading scorer in 1976/77, he joined Chesterfield for £30,000 in August 1979 and helped to win the Anglo-Scottish Cup in 1980/81. Terry Cooper signed him on a free transfer in August 1982 and he netted 26 goals in 92 League outings prior to joining Exeter City in July 1985, scoring the goal that beat City in the 1985/86 FA Cup.

Subsequently with Bath City, then Bristol Manor Farm before rejoining City as youth coach, he is currently a painter and decorator in Backwell.

Chris Crowe

Former England inside-forward Chris Crowe partnered the likes of John Quigley, Chris Garland and John Galley while at Bristol City. Initially a Leeds United junior, he signed professional in June 1956 and moved to Blackburn Rovers for £25,000 in March 1960, then Wolves for £28,000 in February 1962. He followed Alan Hinton to Nottingham Forest in August 1964 and Fred Ford signed him in January 1967 to boost City's relegation fight. Scored 13 goals in 67 Second Division outings and had a brief spell with Auburn in Australia prior to joining Walsall in September 1969, then managed Greenway Sports (P/M) and Fram in Norway. Still living in Whitchurch, he was a financial representative, then a newsagent, shoe shop owner, estate agent and taxi-driver until ill-health in 1994.

Keith Curle

An influential figure as Bristol City won the Freight Rover Trophy at Wembley in 1986, Keith Curle later became Britain's most expensive defender. Initially a midfielder, he signed professional from apprentice for Bristol Rovers in November 1981 and joined Bruce Rioch's Torquay United in November 1983. Reunited with Terry Cooper at Ashton Gate in March 1984, he helped to clinch promotion that season and featured in two successive Freight Rover Trophy finals – netting his sole goal in 121 League outings in the 3-1 win over Newport County in March 1986. He moved to Reading in October 1987, then Bobby Gould's Wimbledon for £500,000 a year later and Man-chester City for a record £2,500,000 in August 1991 where he gained full England honours and was captain until joining Wolves for £650,000 in July 1996.

Dermot Curtis

Eire international centre-forward Dermot Curtis was capped five times while at Bristol City. A prolific goalscorer for Shelbourne before Pat Beasley paid £5,000 for

him in November 1956 to replace Jimmy Rogers, he netted 16 goals in 26 Second Division outings alongside John Atyeo prior to joining Ipswich Town in September 1958 and featuring in the successes under Alf Ramsey. He moved to Exeter City in August 1963, forming a notable goalscoring partnership with Alan Banks and helping to win promotion in 1963/64 – rejoining Exeter in June 1967 after a season at Torquay United under ex-Eire team-mate Frank O'Farrell. Subsequently with Bideford and Elmore (P/M), he still lives in Exeter and after returning to his trade as a sheet-metal worker, is now a roofer for ABC Roofing.

● Peter Cormack

Bob Davies

Consistent left-back Bob Davies played in Bristol City's first-ever Football League game at Blackpool in September 1901. He developed with Tonge Lower End, Haugh Albion, Bolton Lads Club and Halliwell Rovers before joining Bolton Wanderers in July 1895. Moving to Bedminster in July 1899, he was one of several players retained after the amalgamation with Bristol City in 1900 and partnered Phil Bach in defence as City were Southern League runners-up in 1900/01. He played alongside Billy Tuft in City's 1901/02 Football League debut campaign and scored twice in 78 League games before rejoining Bolton in July 1903.

Frank Davies

Welsh centre-half Frank Davies joined Bristol City in their vain bid to avoid relegation in 1923/24. Initially with Swansea Town, he had a spell with Bath City before Alex Raisbeck signed him in July 1923. He made his League debut at Fulham three months later and contested a first-team slot with Fred Hawley, making 54 League appearances before joining Charlton Athletic in October 1926. Moving to First Division Portsmouth in July 1928, he joined

● Chris Crowe

● Keith Curle

● Harry Davy

● Jantzen Derrick

● Alan Dicks

Nantwich Town a year later and scored twice in the 1930 Cheshire Senior Cup final. He returned to League action with Northampton Town in July 1930 and gave them fine service over four seasons, residing in that area until his death on New Year's Day 1970.

Harry Davy
Right-back Harry Davy was an influential figure during Bristol City's Southern League era. Initially with Padiham, he had spells with Heywood Central and Blackpool prior to joining Leicester Fosse in July 1895 where he gained considerable Second Division experience. Sam Hollis recruited him as Bristol City turned professional in 1897 and he played in City's first-ever Southern League game at home to Wolverton in September 1897. He partnered Alex Milligan, then George Baker in defence and netted his sole goal in 53 Southern League games in the 2-1 win at New Brompton in October 1897.

Ted Dawson
Goalkeeper Ted Dawson made a significant contribution as Bristol City were Third Division (South) runners-up in 1937/38. He developed in his native North-East with Pouston Juniors, Annfield Plain and Blyth Spartans prior to joining Manchester City in December 1934 but failed to gain a first-team place at Maine Road behind Frank Swift. Bob Hewison signed him in May 1936 and he made his League debut at home to Swindon Town eleven months later. Displacing Jim Wilson in goal, he made 66 Third Division (South) appearances and played for City in war-time soccer prior to joining Gateshead in March 1944.

Alf Dean
Diminutive outside-right Alf Dean was Bristol City's joint leading goalscorer with Fred Corbett in 1903/04. He had spells with Walsall, West Brom, Nottingham Forest and Grimsby Town before Sam Hollis signed him in April 1902. Creating numerous goalscoring chances for the likes of Sammy Gilligan and Albert Fisher, he netted 35 goals in 84 Second Division outings before joining Swindon Town in July 1905 and continued in the Southern League with Millwall, also playing for Dundee and Wellington Town. He became a Walsall publican and died on New Year's Day 1959.

Defeats
Bristol City's record post-war defeat in the Football League is 7-1 at Northampton Town on 19th September 1982 (three months before City hit rock-bottom in Division Four) and 6-0 at Tranmere Rovers on 29th September 1989 – compared to the all-time record 9-0 League defeat at Coventry City in April 1934. City lost a record 26 games in 1959/60 when the 'split camp' team finished bottom of the Second Division, in contrast to just six defeats in the 1954/55 Third Division (South) title campaign and two in the 1905/06 Second Division title success. City's record FA Cup defeat is 6-1 in the fourth round at Sunderland in January 1964, while they lost 6-1 in the League Cup second round second leg at West Ham in October 1984 and at Sunderland in October 1990, then 5-0 against Newcastle United in September 1995.

Bill Demmery
Born locally, goalkeeper Bill Demmery featured prominently as Bristol City were First Division runners-up in 1906/07, the club's highest-ever final placing. Initially with Warmley, he starred as they won the Western League title and Gloucestershire Senior Cup in successive years and rejoined them after a spell with Staple Hill for their final season. Upon their demise, he played for newly-formed Bristol East and joined Bristol City in July 1902 as understudy to Harry Clay. He made 38 League appearances prior to joining Bristol Rovers in July 1908 and had a City benefit match against Middlesbrough in October 1908. Subsequently following Archie Annan to Mid-Rhondda, he then played for Bath City and remained local until his death in December 1955.

Jantzen Derrick
Enigmatic ex-England Schoolboy winger Jantzen Derrick was the youngest player to appear in a League game for Bristol City at 16 years 324 days at Lincoln City in November 1959. Born locally, he starred for Bristol Boys as they won the English Schools Trophy in 1958 and signed professional for City in January 1960. He helped to regain Second Division status in 1964/65, netting 32 goals in 260 League outings before released after a loan spell at Mansfield Town to join French side Paris St Germain in July 1971. Subsequently with Bath City, Keynsham Town and Redwood Lodge (P/M), he was a financial representative for Chartered Trust, then Associate Capital Corporation and since June 1991 has been sales manager for New Town Motors in Nailsea. His son Paul played for City reserves in the mid-1980's.

Jimmy Dickie
Scottish outside-left Jimmy Dickie created numerous goalscoring opportunities for the likes of Percy Vials and Bertie Williams as Bristol City narrowly managed to avoid relegation in successive seasons under Alex Raisbeck and Joe Bradshaw. Initially with Buckie Thistle, he had spells with Preston NE, Forres Mechanics and St. Johnstone prior to joining New Brighton in July 1927 where he was ever-present in 1927/28. Alex Raisbeck paid £1,550 for him in December 1928 and he contested the left-wing slot with Arthur Johnson at Ashton Gate, scoring four goals in 48 Second Division outings before moving to Chester for £700 in August 1930. He subsequently rejoined New Brighton but was unable to prevent them having to apply for re-election in 1932/33. He died in June 1960.

Alan Dicks
Alan Dicks guided Bristol City back to the First Division after 65 years' absence and became the Football League's longest-serving manager while at Ashton Gate. An amateur wing-half with Dulwich Hamlet, Rainham Town and Millwall, he signed professional for Chelsea in September 1951 and featured in the 1954/55 League Championship success. Sold to Southend United for £12,000 in November 1958, he joined Coventry City as Jimmy Hill's assistant in February 1962 and helped to plot the 'Sky Blue Revolution'. He resigned to succeed Fred Ford as City's manager in October 1967, plotting the

1970/71 League Cup and 1973/74 FA Cup runs as well as the 1975/76 promotion success. Dismissed in September 1980 after relegation, he returned to management with Jimmy Hill's Fulham for 18 months in June 1990 and now runs a soccer school in Florida.

Peter Doherty

Outstanding ex-Northern Ireland inside-forward Peter Doherty managed Bristol City for two controversial years. An FAI Cup winner with Glentoran in 1932/33, he joined Blackpool for £1,500 in November 1933, then Manchester City for £10,000 in June 1936 – top scorer in the 1936/37 League Championship win. Sold to Derby County for £6,000 in December 1945, he was an FA Cup winner in 1946 and moved via Huddersfield Town to Doncaster Rovers as player-manager in June 1949. He plotted the 1949/50 Third Division (North) title success and also managed Northern Ireland, taking charge of City in January 1958. With his 'split camp' side facing relegation, he was sacked in March 1960 and held scouting/coaching posts at Notts County, Aston Villa, Preston NE, Sunderland and Blackpool – living in Fleetwood until his death in April 1990.

Bill Dolman

Goalkeeper Bill Dolman was a key figure as Bristol City took Preston NE to an FA Cup fifth round replay in 1934/35. Initially with Willenhall, he joined Chesterfield for £200 in February 1929 and was ever-present in their 1930/31 Third Division (North) title triumph. Bob Hewison paid £150 for him in May 1934 and he made 62 Third Division (South) appearances before joining Luton Town for £250 in March 1936 and featured in their 1936/37 Third Division (South) title campaign.

Harry Dolman

Described as a benevolent dictator, Harry Dolman was chairman of Bristol City for 25 years and became the club's first president. He served with the Wiltshire Yeomanry during the First World War and joined the Bristol engineering firm of Brecknell, Munro & Rogers as a junior draughtsman in 1921, becoming a director of the compa-

ny seven years later and taking it over during a financial crisis when it became Brecknell, Dolman & Rogers. Joining the Bristol City board in 1939, he succeeded George Jenkins as chairman in March 1949 and held that post until stepping down in March 1974 – overseeing significant ground improvements including the 'Dolman Stand' opened for the start of the 1970/71 campaign. Harry was also instrumental in securing the signature of John Atyeo. With the intention of gaining the signature under the noses of other larger clubs, Harry took Atyeo's contract and walked along a railway line to a signal box where John Atyeo's father worked – he returned with the contract signed! Harry Dolman died aged 80 in November 1977.

Louie Donowa

Ex-England U-21 winger Louie Donowa created numerous goalscoring chances for Bob Taylor and Nicky Morgan while at Bristol City. Initially a Norwich City apprentice, he signed professional in September 1982 and helped to win the FA Youth Cup in 1982/83 and Milk Cup in 1984/85. Following a loan spell with Stoke City, he joined Spanish side La Coruna for £40,000 in February 1986 and returned to Ipswich Town in August 1989 after a trial with Willem II Tilburg. Joe Jordan paid £55,000 for him in August 1990 and he scored three goals in 24 Second Division outings prior to joining Birmingham City for £60,000 in August 1991. Loaned to Burnley, Crystal Palace and Shrewsbury Town in 1993/94, he helped Blues to win the Second Division title in 1994/95 and followed Barry Fry to Peterborough United in November 1996, then joined Walsall in August 1997.

Alex Downie

Young Scottish right-half Alex Downie was one of Bristol City's most notable graduates during the Southern League era. He played for Third Lanark before joining City in July 1899 and scored on his debut at home to Swindon Town in the opening game of the 1899/00 campaign. Making 23 Southern League appearances, he moved to Swindon in July 1900 and joined

Manchester United two years later. He featured prominently as United were promoted to the First Division with Bristol City in 1905/06 and won the League Championship in 1907/08. Sold to Oldham Athletic for £600 in October 1909, he starred in their 1909/10 promotion success and later played for Crewe Alexandra. He died in Manchester in December 1977.

Chuck Drury

Tough-tackling former England Youth wing-half Chuck Drury helped Bristol City to regain Second Division status in 1964/65. Real name Charles, he represented SE Staffs Boys and joined West Brom from FH Lloyds in September 1954. He made almost 150 First Division appearances before Fred Ford paid £7,500 for him in June 1964 and also featured prominently in the 1965/66 promotion challenge, netting twice in 51 League outings prior to joining struggling Bradford PA in March 1968. Subsequently with Tamworth, Bromsgrove Rovers and Warley, he was a market-trader, then a driver and for the past twelve years has been a departmental manager for a national haulage company, living in Acton Trussell.

Jackie Dryden

Speedy, skilful outside-left Jackie Dryden supplied the ammunition for prolific marksman Alfie Rowles as Bristol City were Third Division (South) runners-up in 1937/38. Initially with Ashington, he joined Newcastle United for £175 in September 1932 and gained top-flight experience before moving to Exeter City on a free transfer in May 1934. He scored 13 goals in 63 Third Division (South) outings prior to joining Burnley in June 1938 and guested for Aberdeen during the Second World War. He returned to his native North-East where he died in September 1975.

Richard Dryden

Versatile defender Richard Dryden was an influential member of Joe Jordan's squad. A former Bristol Rovers trainee, he made his League debut under Bobby Gould seven months before signing professional in July 1987 and joined Exeter City in March 1989 following an initial loan spell. He fea-

● **Harry Dolman**

● **Chuck Drury**

● Brian Drysdale

● Jackie Dziekanowski

● Jon Economou

tured prominently in the 1989/90 Fourth Division title success under Terry Cooper, moving to newly-promoted Notts County for £250,000 in August 1991 where he gained top-flight experience. Reunited with Cooper at Birmingham City for £165,000 in March 1993 after being loaned to Plymouth Argyle, he joined Bristol City for £200,000 in December 1994 and scored once in 37 League outings before linking up with Cooper again at Southampton for £150,000 in August 1996.

Brian Drysdale

Long-serving left-back Brian Drysdale was a key figure in Bristol City's 1975/76 promotion success. Initially a Lincoln City junior, he made his League debut prior to signing professional in September 1960 and joined Hartlepools United on a free transfer in July 1965 where he played under the Brian Clough/Peter Taylor partnership and starred in the 1967/68 promotion campaign. Alan Dicks paid £10,000 for him in May 1969 and he was three times ever-present, featuring in the 1970/71 League Cup and 1973/74 FA Cup runs. He scored three goals in 282 League outings before joining Oxford United in July 1977 after a loan spell at Reading, then played for Frome Town (P/M), Shepton Mallet (P/M), Clevedon Town, Clandown (P/M) and Hengrove (P/M). Now a self-employed carpenter living in Stockwood, his son Jason plays for Swindon Town.

Reg Dyer

Tall, versatile full-back Reg Dyer featured in Bristol City's 1922/23 Third Division (South) title success. Born locally, he developed with Ashton City before Joe Palmer signed him in October 1921 and he made his League debut as Dick Hughes' deputy at The Wednesday four months later. Also providing reliable defensive cover for Laurie Banfield, he featured in City's 1924/25 promotion challenge and made 49 League appearances prior to joining Fulham in May 1925 where he gave fine service over five seasons. Subsequently with Tunbridge Wells Rangers and Bath City, he returned to Ashton Gate to assist his former Fulham manager Joe Bradshaw. He died in Harlow in January 1990.

Jackie Dziekanowski

Capped 62 times, Polish international striker Jackie Dziekanowski was idolised by Bristol City fans. Real name Dariusz, he played for F50 Cars, Widzew Lodz and Legia Warsaw prior to joining Celtic for £650,000 in July 1989. Leading scorer in 1989/90 when he netted four goals against Partizan Belgrade in the ECWC and was a Scottish Cup finalist, he also played in the 1990/91 Scottish League Cup final. Jimmy Lumsden paid £250,000 for him in January 1992 and he scored on his debut the next day in a 2-2 home draw with Southend United, then again to beat Leicester City 2-1 in the FA Cup fourth round. Netting seven goals in 43 League outings before rejoining Legia Warsaw in September 1993, he now runs an electrical business in his native Warsaw.

Jon Economou

Midfielder Jon Economou was one of several teenage players to appear in the League for Bristol City in the wake of the 1981/82 'Ashton Gate Eight' crisis. He represented Islington Schools, joining City as an apprentice and signing professional under Alan Dicks in October 1979. Given his League debut at home to Fulham in February 1982, he featured in the 1983/84 promotion campaign and netted three goals in 65 League outings before released by Terry Cooper in May 1984. He subsequently had spells with Cardiff City (on trial), Devizes Town, Gloucester City, Yeovil Town (under Gerry Gow), Forest Green Rovers, Minehead (under Chris Garland) and Weston-Super-Mare. Since October 1986 he has worked for ICL and is now a Southern Regional manager, living in Clevedon.

Cliff Edwards

Versatile half-back Cliff Edwards joined Bristol City in an exchange deal involving Cyril Williams. Initially with Cannock Town, he joined West Brom as an amateur in October 1938 and turned professional the following May. He guested for Bath City, Blackpool and Carlisle United during World War Two, moving to Ashton Gate in June 1948 and displacing Cliff Morgan alongside skipper Dennis Roberts. Scoring three times in 33 Third Division (South) outings, he became Gravesend & Northfleet's first player-manager in August 1950 and later signed Roy Bicknell and George Brewster. He rejoined West Brom as a director in 1971, remaining on the board until retiring in 1986 and died three years later.

Rob Edwards

Welsh U-21 skipper Rob Edwards remains a versatile member of John Ward's squad. Initially a Carlisle United trainee, Clive Middlemass gave him his League debut in the same promotion-chasing side as Paul Fitzpatrick and Tony Shepherd a month before he signed professional in April 1990. His impressive displays tempted Jimmy Lumsden to pay £135,000 for him in March 1991 and he featured as a midfielder in the 1991/92 and 1993/94 FA Cup runs, helping to beat top-flight sides Wimbledon and Liverpool. Switched to a left-back role in 1995/96, he has now netted three goals in 156 League outings for Bristol City and helped to reach the Second Division play-offs in 1996/97.

Alec Eisentrager

Popular, skilful winger Alec Eisentrager thrilled Bristol City fans with his powerful shooting during the 1950's. Real name Alous, he was born in Hamburg and came to Britain as a prisoner-of-war in February 1945. A prolific goalscorer for Trowbridge Town, Bob Wright signed him in August 1949 and he made his League debut at home to Northampton Town that month. He netted four goals against Newport County two weeks later, scoring 47 times in 229 League games overall before joining Merthyr Tydfil in July 1958, then playing for Chelmsford City and Westbury Park while running his own printing business in Bristol. Now living in Clevedon where he was a machine operator for Cam-Gear for 20 years until retiring in February 1989, his sons Andy and Ian play for Backwell United and Yate Town respectively.

Sid Elliott

Centre-forward Sid Elliott was Bristol City's leading marksman in 1930/31. A prolific goalscorer for Arcade Mission in his native Sunderland, he was snapped up by Durham City in June 1926 and quickly impressed as a 16-year-old. Moving to Joe Bradshaw's Fulham in May 1927, he was ever-present and top scorer alongside Teddy Craig in 1927/28 and joined Chelsea for £3,000 in May 1928. He helped to regain top-flight status in 1929/30 and was reunited with Bradshaw at Ashton Gate for £1,000 in July 1930, netting 24 goals in 50 Second Division games before joining Notts County in March 1932. He subsequently played for Bradford City, Rochdale and FB Minter Sports.

John Emanuel

Skilful Welsh international midfielder John Emanuel was capped twice while at Ashton Gate and voted 'Player of the Year' in 1972/73. A relatively late starter in League soccer, he was an amateur with Blaenrhondda, Swansea Town and Ferndale before Alan Dicks signed him in May 1971. 'Ivor' made his League debut at home to Millwall three months later and netted ten goals in 128 Second Division outings before joining Newport County on a free transfer in June 1976 after loan spells with Swindon Town and Gillingham. Subsequently with Barry Town and Ton Pentre where he is now manager after a period in charge of Maesteg Park, he was an office worker for the NCB in Treforest and is currently a fork-lift driver for Porth Decorative Products in Treorchy.

Bobby Etheridge

Footballing-cricketer Bobby Etheridge was ever-present at right-half for Bristol City in 1961/62. He initially starred for Gloucester City, leading scorer in 1954/55 and a key figure in the 1955/56 Southern League Cup success. Pat Beasley signed him in September 1956 and he made his League debut in the 5-1 win over Lincoln City three months later, impressing at inside-right alongside John Atyeo. Also Gloucestershire's wicket-keeper for ten years, he netted 42 goals in 259 League games prior to joining Cheltenham Town as player-manager in July 1965 and returned to Gloucester as manager in November 1973, remaining local until his death in April 1988. His brother Dick has served Gloucester City as a player, secretary, coach, manager (for three spells), director and now president.

FA Cup

A table of Bristol City's record in this competition can be found at the end of this A to Z.

FA Cup Final

Having beaten Southampton, Bury, Norwich City, Glossop and Derby County after a semi-final replay, Bristol City faced First Division rivals Manchester United in the FA Cup final at the Crystal Palace on 24th April, 1909. Watched by 71,401, Sandy Turnbull's first-half goal gave United a 1-0 win over the following City team: Harry Clay, Archie Annan, Joe Cottle, Pat Hanlin, Billy Wedlock, Arthur Spear, Fred Staniforth, Bob Hardy, Sammy Gilligan, Andy Burton and Frank Hilton. It remains Bristol City's sole FA Cup final appearance, although they were unlucky to lose 2-1 to Second Division rivals Huddersfield Town in the semi-final at Stamford Bridge on March 27th, 1920.

FA Cup Giantkillers

Alan Dicks masterminded one of the biggest FA Cup shocks of the decade in 1973/74. After beating Hull and Hereford United, Bristol City faced Cup favourites Leeds United at Ashton Gate in the fifth round and forced a replay when

Keith Fear equalised Billy Bremner's first half goal in front of 37,141 on 16th February 1974. Three days later, City earned national headlines when Donnie Gillies' second-half strike clinched a sensational 1-0 win at Elland Road and narrowly lost 1-0 at home to eventual Cup winners Liverpool in the sixth round. City have reached the fifth round on nine other occasions since the war – beating top-flight sides Chelsea (1989/90), Wimbledon (1991/92) and Liverpool (1993/94) in recent seasons.

Albert Fairclough

Centre-forward Albert Fairclough was Bristol City's leading goalscorer in three successive seasons including the 1922/23 Third Division (South) title triumph. 'Fairy' developed with Windle Villa, St. Helen's Town, St. Helen's Recreational and Eccles Borough prior to joining Manchester City with his brother Peter in April 1913 where he gained top-flight experience. Moving to Southend United in May 1920, he was top scorer in their 1920/21 Football League debut campaign and Joe Palmer paid £2,300 for him in March 1921 to boost City's promotion challenge. He netted 44 goals in 91 League outings while at Ashton Gate prior to joining Derby County in July 1924 and was their top scorer in 1924/25. Featuring in their 1925/26 promotion campaign, he moved to Gillingham in February 1927 and died in Stockport in November 1958.

Keith Fear

Ex-England Schoolboy striker Keith Fear was leading scorer in 1973/74 as Bristol City reached the FA Cup sixth round. Born locally, he signed professional under Alan Dicks in June 1969 and made his League debut at Middlesbrough in October 1970. His equaliser against Leeds United earned an FA Cup fifth round replay in 1973/74 and he featured in the 1975/76 promotion success, netting 32 goals in 151 League outings prior to joining Plymouth Argyle in February 1978 after loan spells at John Sillett's Hereford United and Blackburn Rovers. Subsequently with Brentford (on loan), Chester, Bangor City and Scarborough, he

● Alec Eisentrager

● John Emanuel

● Bobby Etheridge

● Keith Fear

● Tony Fitzpatrick

● Fred Ford

still lives in Bristol and works in the fruit and veg market at Temple Meads. His younger brother Viv was a City apprentice in the early 1970's.

Freddie Fenton

Diminutive outside-left Freddie Fenton featured in Bristol City's 1905/06 Second Division title success. He impressed with Preston NE prior to joining West Brom in July 1903 where he gained top-flight experience. Sam Hollis signed him in July 1904 and he created numerous goalscoring opportunities for the likes of Sammy Gilligan, Albert Fisher and Billy Maxwell. Displaced by Frank Hilton, his sole goal in 36 League outings came in the 2-0 win at Doncaster Rovers in March 1905. He moved to Swindon Town with Peter Chambers and Billy Jones in July 1907.

Pat Finnerhan

Skilful ex-Irish international inside-right Pat Finnerhan was an influential figure as Bristol City were Southern League runners-up for the second successive season in 1898/99. Initially with Northwich Victoria, he joined Manchester City in June 1894 after being spotted by their director Lawrence Furness while refereeing a match. He was ever-present in their 1895/96 promotion challenge, playing for the Football League against the Irish League in November 1895 and for the North versus the South in March 1896. Moving to Liverpool in May 1897, he gained top-flight experience before Sam Hollis signed him in July 1898. He combined well with the likes of Billy Langham, Albert Carnelly and Sandy Caie while at City, scoring eight times in 22 Southern League outings.

Albert Fisher

Speedy Scottish inside-forward Albert Fisher partnered the likes of Fred Corbett and Sammy Gilligan in Bristol City's attack. He impressed with Asbury Richmond, East Stirling, St. Bernards and Soho Caledonian before joining Aston Villa in July 1902 and was top scorer in their reserves, gaining top flight experience. Sam Hollis signed him in July 1904 and he netted 21 goals in 50 Second Division outings before moving to Brighton

in August 1905, then played for Manchester City, Bradford PA and Coventry City. He became Merthyr Town's manager in June 1912 and took charge of Notts County a year later, plotting their 1913/14 and 1922/23 Second Division title triumphs and 1921/22 FA Cup run. Resigning in May 1927, he was a Nottingham businessman until his death in December 1937.

Paul Fitzpatrick

Lanky midfielder Paul Fitzpatrick came on as substitute for Bristol City in the 1986/87 Freight Rover Trophy final at Wembley. A former Tranmere Rovers junior, he joined Bolton Wanderers in March 1985 and Terry Cooper signed him in August 1986. He helped to reach the promotion play-offs in 1987/88, scoring seven goals in 44 Third Division outings prior to joining Clive Middlemass' Carlisle United in October 1988 and featured prominently in the 1989/90 promotion challenge after a loan spell at Preston NE. Sold to Leicester City for £40,000 in July 1991, he has since played for Birmingham City (under Cooper), Bury (on loan), Hamilton Academical, Northampton Town, Leicester United, RC Warwick, Forest Green Rovers and Corby Town (P/M).

Tony Fitzpatrick

Fiery Scottish U-21 midfielder Tony Fitzpatrick cost Bristol City a then club record £225,000 in August 1979. He skippered St. Mirren while still a teenager and starred in the 1976/77 Scottish First Division title success, impressing Alan Dicks in the Anglo-Scottish Cup ties. Moving to Ashton Gate after protracted transfer negotiations, he faced his former club in the 1979/80 Anglo-Scottish Cup final and his sole goal in 75 League outings clinched a 1-1 draw against Oldham Athletic in November 1980. Following two successive relegation campaigns, he rejoined St. Mirren for £150,000 in June 1981 and helped to win the Scottish Cup in 1987, making a club record 351 appearances overall. He was manager for three years until resigning in March 1991, then was St. Mirren's Community Develop-ment Officer before being re-appointed as manager in September 1996.

Robert Fleck

Scottish international striker Robert Fleck attracted considerable interest during his two month loan spell at Bristol City in 1994/95. Initially with Possil YM, he joined Glasgow Rangers in May 1983 and starred in the 1986/87 Scottish League and Cup 'double' success. He moved to Norwich City for a record £580,000 in December 1987 and was leading marksman in four successive seasons, voted 'Player of the Year' in 1991/92. Following his disastrous £2,100,000 move to Chelsea in August 1992, he was loaned to Bolton Wanderers and Joe Jordan signed him on loan in January 1995. His sole goal in 10 First Division outings came in the 3-0 win over Swindon Town in February and he rejoined Norwich from Chelsea for a cut-price £650,000 in August 1995.

Floodlights

The first floodlit game at Ashton Gate was a friendly against Wolves on 27th January 1953. Primitive by today's standards, the £3,500 system consisted of 14 poles 40 ft high with a cluster of three lights on top of each. Sold to Burton Albion in July 1965, a new system costing £27,000 was officially switched on for the Second Division game against Wolves on 28th December 1965. Consisting of four 160 ft high pylons with 48 lamps on each angled head, they gave Ashton Gate much of its character until removed in June 1992 and are now at Wigan Athletic's Springfield Park. City's current set of lights were erected on the roofs of the Des Williams Stand and Dolman Stand and used for the first time on 5th November 1991 for the Second Division game against Plymouth Argyle.

Football League

A table of Bristol City's record in this competition, analysed by season and opposition, can be found at the end of this A to Z.

Fred Ford

Popular manager Fred Ford plotted Bristol City's 1964/65 promotion success. He was a centre-half with Erith & Belvedere, Arsenal, Charlton Athletic, Millwall and

Carlisle United where he became trainer-coach when a knee injury ended his playing career in 1949. Appointed Bristol Rovers coach in 1955, he also coached the England U-23 and 'B' teams prior to succeeding Peter Doherty as Bristol City's manager in July 1960 and his discoveries included Chris Garland, Geoff Merrick and Trevor Tainton. Dismissed in September 1967, he coached Swindon Town before rejoining Bristol Rovers as manager in April 1968, then Swindon as manager in October 1969. He later coached Torquay United, then was Oxford United chief scout/Youth Development Officer for seven years until his death in October 1981.

Tony Ford
Tall, ex-England Youth right-back Tony Ford was ever-present in Bristol City's 1964/65 promotion campaign. He signed professional from apprentice in November 1961 and made his League debut in the 4-0 win at Swindon Town in March 1962, netting ten goals in 171 League outings before switching to Bristol Rovers in December 1969 where he was appointed captain. A ruptured spleen ended his playing career eight months later and he became reserve coach at Plymouth Argyle, then assisted John Sillett at Hereford United and Bobby Moncur at Hearts. Now living back in Thornbury, he spent ten years as a sales rep for Marley Roof Tiles and since January 1993 has been a sales executive for Colas. His son Mike is currently Oxford United's captain.

Jackie Foster
Much-travelled outside-right Jackie Foster created numerous goalscoring chances for the likes of Percy Cherrett and Albert Keating while at Ashton Gate. Initially with Murton CW, he joined Sunderland in July 1920 and gained top-flight experience before moving to Ashington in July 1921 and helping to consolidate Football League status. He was ever-present in 1922/23 and moved to Halifax Town in September 1923, joining Grimsby Town in May 1925 and featuring

in their 1925/26 Third Division (North) title campaign. Alex Raisbeck signed him in June 1926 and he featured in the 1926/27 Third Division (South) title campaign as Cyril Gilhespy's understudy, netting four goals in 47 League outings prior to joining Brentford with Cecil Blakemore in May 1929 and starred in their 1932/33 Third Division (South) title success. He moved to Barrow in July 1933 and was ever-present in 1933/34 when they scored a club record 116 League goals.

Freight Rover Trophy
Goals by Glyn Riley (2) and Howard Pritchard gave the following Bristol City side a 3-0 win over Bolton Wanderers in the Freight Rover Trophy final at Wembley on 24th May 1986: Keith Waugh, Rob Newman, Brian Williams, Keith Curle, David Moyes, Glyn Riley, Howard Pritchard, Bobby Hutchinson, David Harle, Alan Walsh, Steve Neville. City were Wembley finalists again under Terry Cooper a year later when Glyn Riley's goal earned the following team a 1-1 draw against Mansfield Town on 24th May 1987: Keith Waugh, Rob Newman, Brian Williams, David Moyes, John MacPhail, Andy Llewellyn (Paul Fitzpatrick), Gordon Owen, Alan Walsh (Keith Curle), Glyn Riley, Gary Marshall, Joe Jordan. City lost 5-4 in a penalty shoot-out after extra-time.

Billy Fulton
Fast, clever Scottish inside-left Billy Fulton partnered Jim Stevenson in Bristol City's attack. Initially with Alva Albion Rangers, he had a trial with Preston NE prior to joining Sunderland in May 1898. He gained First Division experience and moved to Bristol City in June 1900 and netted eight goals in 25 Southern League outings before returning to the top-flight with Derby County in May 1901. Scoring on his debut, he was soon displaced by emerging England star Ben Warren and injuries hampered him at the Baseball Ground. He moved back to Scotland with Alloa in June 1902 where he became a publican.

John Galley
Centre-forward John Galley was Bristol City's leading goalscorer four times. Initially a Wolves junior, he signed professional in May 1961 and moved to Rotherham United in December 1964. Alan Dicks paid £25,000 for him in December 1967 to replace Hughie McIlmoyle and he scored a hat-trick on his debut as City won 3-0 at Huddersfield Town. A key figure in the 1967/68 relegation escape, he netted 84 goals in 172 Second Division outings before joining Nottingham Forest for £30,000 in December 1972. Following a loan spell with Peterborough United, he joined John Sillett's Hereford United in December 1974 and starred at centre-half in the 1975/76 Third Division title success. Subsequently with Telford United and Atherstone Town, he is now a sales rep for William Guppy Paper Group and runs a hostel for Nottingham Forest apprentices.

Steve Galliers
Diminutive midfield dynamo Steve Galliers skippered Bristol City to the Littlewoods Cup semi-finals in 1988/89. Initially with Chorley, he joined new-boys Wimbledon for £1,500 in June 1977 and was twice voted 'Player of the Year' – returning from a ten month period at Crystal Palace to feature prominently in the Crazy Gang's meteoric rise from the Fourth Division to First. Terry Cooper signed him in September 1987 after a loan spell at Ashton Gate the previous season and he was an experienced figure as City reached the promotion play-offs in 1987/88. He netted six goals in 77 Third Division games overall before joining new-boys Maidstone United for £20,000 in July 1989 where he became youth coach, then moved to Kingstonian and is now manager of a telephone marketing company.

Chris Garland
England U-23 striker Chris Garland was a key figure as Bristol City reached the League Cup semi-

● Tony Ford

● John Galley

● Chris Garland

● Mike Gibson

● Don Gillies

● Shaun Goater

finals in 1970/71. He signed professional from apprentice in May 1966 and partnered John Galley in attack prior to joining Chelsea for a record £100,000 in September 1971. A League Cup finalist in 1972, he moved to Leicester City for £100,000 in February 1975 and Alan Dicks re-signed him for £110,000 in December 1976 – helping to retain top-flight status until a knee injury restricted his appearances. One of the 'Ashton Gate Eight' in February 1982, he played on a match-by-match basis the following season and scored 42 goals in 207 League games overall before spells at Yeovil Town (P/C) and Minehead (P/M). Still living in Nailsea, he now suffers from Parkinson's Disease and had a benefit game against Manchester United in May 1993.

Mark Gavin

Skilful Scottish midfielder Mark Gavin featured prominently as Bristol City reached the Littlewoods Cup semi-finals in 1988/89 and won promotion in 1989/90. A former Leeds United apprentice, 'Gavs' signed professional in December 1981 and moved to Carlisle United in July 1985 after a loan spell at Hartlepool United. He joined Bolton Wanderers in March 1986 and faced City in the Freight Rover Trophy final two months later, then had spells with Rochdale and Hearts before Joe Jordan signed him for £35,000 in October 1988. Swapped for Watford's Wayne Allison in August 1990, Jimmy Lumsden paid £60,000 to bring him back to Ashton Gate in December 1991 and he netted eight goals in 110 League games overall prior to joining Terry Cooper's Exeter City in February 1994.

Mike Gibson

Ex-England Youth goalkeeper Mike Gibson was ever-present in three successive seasons for Bristol City, including the 1964/65 promotion campaign. His early career owed much to former England star Sammy Crooks who signed him for Gresley Rovers and then recommended him to his ex-Derby teammate Angus Morrison at Nuneaton Borough. He moved to Shrewsbury Town in March 1960, helping to reach the League Cup semi-finals

in 1960/61 and Fred Ford paid £6,000 for him in April 1963. A League Cup semi-finalist again in 1970/71, he made 332 League appearances prior to joining Gillingham in July 1972 and starred in the 1973/74 promotion success. When a shoulder injury ended his playing career soon after, he returned to Bristol as a postman and still assists at Ashton Gate on a part-time basis.

Cyril Gilhespy

Outside-right Cyril Gilhespy featured prominently in Bristol City's 1926/27 Third Division (South) title success. Initially with Chester-le-Street, he joined Sunderland in July 1920 and gained top-flight experience prior to joining Liverpool a year later. He featured in the 1921/22 and 1922/23 League Championship successes and Alex Raisbeck paid £350 for him in May 1925, creating numerous goalscoring chances for the likes of Tot Walsh, Albert Keating and Percy Cherrett. Netting 25 goals in 117 League outings, he returned to First Division action with Blackburn Rovers in June 1929, then had a season each at Reading, Mansfield Town and Crewe Alexandra.

Donnie Gillies

Scottish U-23 star Donnie Gillies made headlines with his goal that knocked Leeds United out of the FA Cup in 1973/74. Initially with Inverness Clachnacuddin, he joined Morton in October 1971 and was twice top scorer before Alan Dicks paid £30,000 for him in March 1973 as Steve Ritchie moved in the opposite direction. Bristol City's leading marksman in 1974/75, he featured at right-back in the 1975/76 promotion campaign and 1977/78 Anglo-Scottish Cup win, netting 26 goals in 220 League outings before moving from Terry Cooper to Bristol Rovers for £50,000 in June 1980. Subsequently with Paulton Rovers, Gloucester City, Bath City, Anorthosis (Cyprus) and Yeovil Town, he was a sales rep until his wife's tragic death in July 1990 and currently lives in Temple Cloud.

Sammy Gilligan

Popular centre-forward Sammy Gilligan was three times leading

goalscorer for Bristol City, including 1908/09 when Harry Thickett's side were FA Cup finalists. After three years with Belmont Athletic, he joined Dundee and helped to finish Scottish League runners-up and was a Scottish Cup winner with Celtic before Sam Hollis signed him in July 1904. He starred as City won the Second Division title in 1904/05 and were League Championship runners-up in 1905/06, netting 78 goals in 188 League outings prior to joining Liverpool in May 1910. Subsequently Gillingham's player-manager, he played for Dundee Hibernian during the Great War and then Forfar Athletic. He emigrated to Vancouver in 1969.

Ernie Glenn

Versatile left-back Ernie Glenn was an influential figure in Bristol City's 1926/27 Third Division (South) title success. He impressed with Willenhall before Alex Raisbeck signed him in May 1923 and made his League debut at home to Blackpool six months later. Partnering the likes of Dick Hughes and Jack Walsh in City's defence, he made 276 League appearances before deciding to retire in May 1931 after failing to accept new terms offered and being placed on the transfer-list. He intended to take over his late father's pub in Birmingham and subsequently worked in a Coventry factory. He died in Coventry in February 1965.

Gloucestershire Cup

A table of Bristol City's record in this competition can be found at the end of this A to Z.

Shaun Goater

Big Bermudan international striker Shaun Goater was leading marksman as Bristol City reached the Second Division play-offs in 1996/97. Spotted by Manchester United during a mid-season break in Bermuda, he signed professional at Old Trafford in May 1988 but failed to secure a first-team place behind the likes of Mark Hughes and Brian McClair and moved to Rotherham United in October 1989. Featuring in their 1991/92 promotion success, he was briefly loaned to Notts County before finishing top scorer in two successive seasons including 1995/96 when he helped to win the Auto Windscreens Shield at Wembley. He was Rotherham's most capped player when Joe Jordan paid £175,000 for him in July 1996 and has now scored 23 goals in 42 Second Division outings for City.

Greg Goodridge

Skilful Barbados international winger Greg Goodridge remains a popular member of John Ward's squad. He impressed as a teenager in his native country for Lambada and was recommended to Torquay United by Devonian Kevin Millard who coached Barbados. Signing professional at Plainmoor in March 1994, he helped Torquay to reach the Third Division play-offs in 1993/94 and moved to QPR for an initial £100,000 after starring against them during their 1995 summer tour. Despite captaining his country, 'Lalu' failed to secure a regular Premiership place at Loftus Road and was so frustrated by the lack of first-team opportunity that he returned to Barbados. Joe Jordan paid £25,000 for him in August 1996 after organising a work permit and he has now scored six goals in 28 Second Division games for Bristol City.

Bobby Gould

Much-travelled striker Bobby Gould replaced John Galley in Bristol City's attack. A former Coventry City apprentice (where Alan Dicks was coach), he signed professional in June 1964 and was top scorer in the 1966/67 Second Division title success. Following spells with Arsenal, Wolves and West Brom, Dicks paid £69,000 for him in December 1972 and he netted 15 goals in 35 Second Division outings prior to joining West Ham for £70,000 in November 1973. He later played for Wolves again, Bristol Rovers and Hereford United, then assisted Geoff Hurst at Chelsea before managing Bristol Rovers (twice), Coventry City (twice), Wimbledon (1988 FA Cup final win) and West Brom. He was appointed manager of Wales in September 1995 and his son Jonathan is a goalkeeper with Celtic.

Gerry Gow

Tough-tackling Scottish U-23 midfielder Gerry Gow was ever-present in Bristol City's 1975-76 promotion success. A former junior, he signed professional in June 1969 and made his League debut at Charlton Athletic in April 1970. Ever-present and top scorer in 1972/73, he was a key figure in the 1973/74 FA Cup run and netted 48 goals in 374 League outings before joining Manchester City for £175,000 in October 1980. An FA Cup finalist in 1981, he moved to Rotherham United for £80,000 in January 1982 and was reunited with John Bond at Burnley in August 1983. Appointed Yeovil Town player-manager in May 1984, he resigned in January 1987 and ran the 'White Horse' pub in Bedminster then became Wey-mouth manager for a year in February 1989. Now living in nearby Portland, he helps out at the 'Punchbowl Inn'.

Malcolm Graham

Scheming inside-left Malcolm Graham joined Bristol City with Johnny McCann in exchange for Bert Tindill plus £14,500 in May 1959. Initially with Hall Green, he was snapped up by Barnsley in April 1953 and featured in the 1954/55 Third Division (North) title campaign. Peter Doherty brought him to Ashton Gate amid high expectation but a knee injury restricted him to eight goals in 14 Second Division games before he moved to Leyton Orient for £5,250 in June 1960. An influential figure as they reached the First Division in 1961/62, he joined QPR with Derek Gibbs for £8,000 in July 1963 and returned to Barnsley a year later, then played for Alfreton Town and coached Wolves' U-16 team. Still living in Barnsley, he spent 23 years as a sales representative for East Midlands Gas Board until ill-health forced retirement in December 1991.

Grounds

Bristol City initially played home matches at the St. John's Lane ground, leased from the Trustees of the Ashton Court Estate. Following amalgamation with Bedminster, City played several matches on their Ashton Gate ground during 1900/01 season and, after failing to improve the lease on St. John's Lane, have played home games at Ashton Gate since 1904. The original Number One Grandstand was destroyed during an air-raid in 1941 and the replacement Des Williams Stand dates from 1953. The original Number Two Grandstand became unsafe and was demolished in 1966, replaced four years later by the Dolman Stand. The original Covered End had seats installed in 1991 and is now known as the Billy Wedlock Stand, while the open Park End was replaced by the John Atyeo Stand in 1994.

Ivor Guy

Noted for his consistency, right back Ivor Guy formed a notable partnership with Jack Bailey at Bristol City during the early post-war era. Born locally, Bob Hewison signed him from Hambrook Villa in August 1944 and he made his first team debut at Swansea Town two months later, scoring an incredible 70 yard goal at Cardiff City in October 1945. Twice ever-present, including the 1950/51 FA Cup run, he missed just one game in City's 1954/55 Third Division (South) title campaign and scored twice in 404 League outings before reunited with Hewison at Bath City in August 1957. He subsequently ran his own grocery business in Fishponds until his death after a short illness in September 1986.

Bruce Halliday

Central defender Bruce Halliday featured prominently in Bristol City's 1983/84 promotion success. A former Newcastle United apprentice, he signed professional in January 1979 and gained an early Second Division chance in the same side as Peter Johnson and Mick Harford. Following a loan spell at Darlington, he joined Bury on a free transfer in November 1982 and Terry Cooper signed him in August 1983. He formed an effective defensive pairing with Forbes Phillipson-Masters until Keith Curle switched to defence,

● Gregory Goodridge

● Bobby Gould

● Gerry Gow

● Ivor Guy

● Vegard Hansen

● Gerry Harrison

making 53 League appearances before moving to Hereford United in June 1985, then Bath City two years later. Since playing for Apia (Australia) and Gateshead, he is currently with Dunston Federation Brewery.

Jack Hamilton

Experienced Scottish wing-half Jack Hamilton skippered Bristol City in the Southern League. Initially with Ayr United, he had spells with Wolves, Derby County, Ilkeston Town and Loughborough before Sam Hollis signed him as City turned professional and entered the Southern League in 1897. His fine distribution helped City to finish runners-up in two consecutive seasons and he scored twice in 71 Southern League outings before joining Brentford in July 1900, featuring in their 1900/01 promotion campaign. He had a spell with Leeds City, returning to Brentford in July 1907 where he was an influential figure for five seasons. Moving back to Ashton Gate in charge of the reserves, he was City's war-time manager in place of George Hedley and became a newsagent, remaining local until his death in October 1931.

Pat Hanlin

Former Scottish junior international half-back Pat Hanlin helped Bristol City to clinch the Second Division title in 1905/06 and played against Manchester United in the 1909 FA Cup Final. Initially with Burnbank Athletic, he had a spell with Everton but failed to establish a first-team slot at Goodison Park and Harry Thickett signed him in July 1905. He made his League debut in the 2-1 win at Bradford City in September 1905 and featured prominently alongside Billy Wedlock and Reuben Marr as City were League Championship runners-up in 1906/07, netting three goals in 162 League outings.

Vegard Hansen

Versatile Norwegian defender Vegard Hansen was a popular member of Joe Jordan's squad. Born in Drammen, he developed with Vikersund prior to joining Stromsgodset in November 1988 and featured in their 1989 promo-

tion and 1991 Norwegian Cup final successes and then skippered their 1993 promotion and Cup final campaign. Following trials with Bristol City and Barnsley, Jordan signed him on loan and he made his League debut in the 3-2 televised home win over Swindon Town in November 1994. Displacing Marvin Harriott at right-back, he was signed on a permanent basis for £105,000 in January 1995 and partnered Stuart Munro throughout the latter half of City's 1994/95 relegation battle. He made 37 League appearances for Bristol City before returning to Norway in June 1996.

Bob Hardy

Noted for his pace, former England Amateur international outside-right Bob Hardy scored Bristol City's winner in the 1909 FA Cup semi-final replay against Derby County. A notable schoolboy footballer, he impressed with South Bank Celtic and South Bank Amateurs, capped against Wales. Harry Thickett signed him in May 1908 and he made his League debut at home to Woolwich Arsenal in September 1908, netting 13 goals in 74 First Division outings.

Mick Harford

Leading marksman in Bristol City's fateful 1981/82 campaign, centre-forward Mick Harford has twice played for England since leaving Ashton Gate. Initially with Lambton Street BC, he joined Lincoln City in July 1977 and was top scorer in three successive seasons. Sold to Newcastle United for £180,000 in December 1980, Bob Houghton signed him for £160,000 in August 1981 and he netted 11 goals in 30 Third Division outings before joining Birmingham City in March 1982 with the £100,000 fee going directly to Newcastle. He moved to Luton Town for a record £250,000 in December 1984 and featured in the 1988 Littlewoods Cup final success, then had big-money moves to Derby County, Luton again, Chelsea, Sunderland and Coventry City prior to joining Wimbledon for £75,000 in August 1994.

David Harle

Ex-England Youth midfielder David Harle featured in Bristol

City's Freight Rover Trophy final success at Wembley in 1986. A former Doncaster Rovers apprentice, he made his League debut before signing professional in November 1980 and featured in the 1980/81 promotion campaign. Released to join Exeter City in July 1982, he rejoined Doncaster in September 1983 and starred in the 1983/84 promotion triumph, then followed Billy Bremner to Leeds United in December 1985. Reunited with Terry Cooper at Ashton Gate in March 1986, he scored twice in 23 Third Division outings prior to joining Scunthorpe United in November 1986 and returned to Doncaster via Peterborough United in March 1990. Subsequently with Stafford Rangers (on loan), Hatfield Main (P/M), Goole Town, Mossley and Brodsworth, he is now a factory supervisor for Limpack Ltd in Scunthorpe.

Joe Harris

Scottish outside-left Joe Harris made a significant contribution as Bristol City were FA Cup semi-finalists in 1919/20, scoring both goals in the 2-0 quarter-final win at home to Bradford City. The brother of Newcastle United leader Neil Harris, he developed with Vale of Clyde and Glasgow Ashfield prior to joining Burnley in July 1910 where he starred in their 1911/12 promotion challenge. Sam Hollis signed him in May 1912 and he created numerous goalscoring opportunities for the likes of Ginger Owers, Billy Brown, Tommy Howarth and Billy Pocock. Ever-present in 1920/21, he netted 26 goals in 205 League outings before joining Leeds United in May 1922 and starred in their 1923/24 Second Division title success. He moved to Fulham in July 1925 for two seasons, residing in Leeds until his death in 1966.

Gerry Harrison

Versatile midfielder Gerry Harrison secured a regular first team place during Denis Smith's reign at Bristol City. A former Watford trainee, he signed professional in December 1989 and Colin Lee gave him his Second Division debut four months later. He played alongside Wayne Allison and Mark Gavin while at Vicarage Road and Jimmy Lumsden signed him on a free transfer in June 1991. Often featuring as substitute, his sole goal in 38 League outings clinched a 2-1 win over Charlton Athletic in October 1992. Following loan spells at Cardiff City, Hereford United and Bath City, he briefly joined Huddersfield Town in March 1994 and is currently playing for Burnley.

Teddy Harston

Prolific goalscoring centre-forward Teddy Harston was leading marksman as Bristol City took Preston NE to an FA Cup fifth round replay in 1934/35. Initially with Cudworth and Barnsley Co-op, he joined Sheffield Wednesday in July 1928 but failed to secure a first-team place at Hillsborough. Moving to Barnsley in May l930, he joined Reading a year later and Bob Hewison signed him in May 1934. He scored 17 times in 28 Third Division (South) outings prior to joining Mansfield Town for £250 in October 1935 and replaced record goalscorer Harry Johnson at Field Mill. Netting an all-time record 55 Third Division (North) goals in 1936/37, he moved to Liverpool for a record £3,000 in June 1937. Following a broken leg, he was appointed player-manager of Ramsgate in June 1939, then worked for Shorts in Rochester.

Fred Hawley

Much-travelled centre-half Fred Hawley was an experienced figure as Bristol City narrowly failed to regain Second Division status at the first attempt in 1924/25. Initially with Derby Midland and Ripley Athletic, he joined Sheffield United in July 1912 and gained top-flight experience, helping to reach the FA Cup Final in 1915. Following the Great War, he played for Coventry City and Birmingham before joining Swindon Town in July 1920 and helped to consolidate Football League status. Alex Raisbeck paid £1,500 for him in March 1923 and he helped to clinch the Third Division (South) title the following month, netting his sole goal in 75 League games in the 1-1 draw at Coventry City in September 1923. Moving to Brighton in August 1925, he joined

QPR a year later, then played for Loughborough Corinthians. He died in May 1954.

Alan Hay

Scottish left-back Alan Hay was a member of Bristol City's side that plummeted from the First Division to Fourth in successive years. Initially with Dundee and Bolton Wanderers, Alan Dicks signed him in July 1978 and he came on as substitute for his League debut at Everton in September 1979. He featured in the 1980 Anglo-Scottish Cup final, netting his sole goal in 74 League games in the 3-1 win over Orient in April 1981. Moving to Denis Smith's York City in August 1982, he starred alongside John MacPhail in the 1983/84 Fourth Division title triumph and consecutive FA Cup runs, then had spells with Tranmere Rovers, Hill of Beath, York again, Sunderland under Smith and Torquay United where he became youth development officer. Subsequently assisting MacPhail at Hartlepool United and South Tyneside United, he now runs 'Hat-tricks Vans' in Stockton-on-Tees.

Jack Haycox

Clever centre-forward Jack Haycox was Bristol City's leading goalscorer in 1936/37. Initially with Cheltenham Town, he signed professional for Newport County in June 1934 and was a prolific marksman in their reserves. Bob Hewison signed him in May 1936 and he featured in City's 1937/38 promotion challenge, netting 25 goals in 43 Third Division (South) outings prior to joining Torquay United in February 1938. He was swapped for Northampton Town's Ralph Allen in November 1938 and subsequently played for Peterborough United.

Jimmy Heale

Young inside-forward Jimmy Heale showed great promise alongside Ted Bowen in Bristol City's attack. Born locally, he represented South Bristol Central School and Bristol Boys before Joe Bradshaw signed him initially as an amateur in June 1931. He made his League debut at Stoke City six months later and scored eight goals in 26 League outings prior to joining Manchester City for £3,750 in January 1934 after helping to take Derby County

to an FA Cup third round replay. He featured in Manchester City's 1936/37 League Championship success but was unable to prevent their shock relegation the following season and subsequently became a policeman in Man-chester where he resided until his death from cancer in May 1997.

George Hedley

Former England centre-forward George Hedley managed Bristol City for the two seasons immediately prior to World War One. Initially with South Bank, he signed professional from amateur for Sheffield United in May 1898 and featured in three FA Cup finals – a winner in 1899 and 1902. He joined Southampton in May 1903 and starred alongside Fred Harrison in the 1903/04 Southern League title success. Moving to Wolves in May l906, he scored in their 1908 FA Cup final triumph and succeeded Sam Hollis in charge at Ashton Gate in April 1913 until called up in January 1917. He was a Bristol licensee throughout the inter-war period, then briefly ran a boarding house in Wolverhampton until his death in August 1942.

Bob Hewison

Bob Hewison managed Bristol City for 17 years and was awarded a Football League long-service medal in 1946. A right-half with Newcastle United and Leeds City, he was Northampton Town player-manager for five seasons prior to taking charge of QPR in July 1925 and succeeded Joe Bradshaw as Bristol City manager in April 1932. Plotting the 1934/35 FA Cup run and 1937/38 promotion challenge, he was suspended for eight months soon after for illegal payments to players and resigned in March 1949. He subsequently managed Guildford City, then scouted for Bristol Rovers until appointed as Bath City's manager for four years in May 1957 – guiding them to the Southern League title in 1959/60 and remaining local until his death in April 1964.

Matt Hewlett

Hard-working, young midfielder Matt Hewlett made a significant contribution as Bristol City reached the Second Division play-offs in 1996/97 and remains an

● Alan Hay

● Matt Hewlett

● **Wally Hinshelwood**

● **Martin Hirst**

● **Sam Hollis**

important member of John Ward's squad. Born locally, he was rated amongst City's best prospects in years when making his League debut at Wolves on the opening day of the 1993/94 season. He ended that campaign as a regular first-teamer but suffered a loss of form as City were relegated in 1994/95 and rebuilt his career alongside Dwayne Plummer in the reserve team. His first-team recall came at Wycombe Wanderers in December 1995 and he has since partnered the likes of Martin Kuhl, Louis Carey and Brian Tinnion in midfield, netting four goals in 76 League games to date.

Sandy Higgins
Centre-half Sandy Higgins was Bristol City's first captain. He developed in non-League soccer with Woodfield, Albion Swifts and Birmingham St. Georges prior to joining Grimsby Town in July 1892 and featured in successive promotion challenges. Sam Hollis recruited him for City as they turned professional in 1897 and he played in the club's first-ever Southern League game at home to Wolverton in September 1897. He scored six goals in 21 Southern League outings as City were runners-up in 1897/98, then moved to Newcastle United in May 1898 where he was also captain and his debut coincided with their first-ever Division One game. He joined Middlesbrough in May 1900, then played for Newton Heath.

Frank Hilton
Outside-left Frank Hilton represented the Football League whilst at Bristol City. He impressed with Doncaster St. James before Harry Thickett signed him in July 1905 and made his League debut at Lincoln City in October 1905. Creating numerous goalscoring chances for Sammy Gilligan and Billy Maxwell as City won the Second Division title in 1905/06, were First Division runners-up in 1906/07 and FA Cup finalists in 1908/09, he scored 21 goals in 116 League outings before leaving Ashton Gate in May 1910.

Wally Hinshelwood
Popular outside-right Wally Hinshelwood created numerous goalscoring chances for John Atyeo

while at Ashton Gate. An ex-Fulham junior, he signed professional in October 1946 and was swapped for Chelsea's Jimmy Bowie in January 1951. Rejoining Fulham just four months later, he moved to Reading in exchange for Gordon Brice in December 1952 and was reunited with Pat Beasley at Bristol City for £15,000 in February 1956, scoring 16 times in 148 Second Division outings before joining Millwall for £1,100 in June 1960. Subsequently with Toronto Italia (Canada), Newport County, Dartford, Canterbury City, Sittingbourne and Deal Town, he was a caretaker in New Addington for 26 years until retiring in February 1993 and now lives in Selsey. His sons Martin and Paul both played for Crystal Palace and his grandson Danny Hinshelwood is currently with Portsmouth.

Martyn Hirst
Ex-England Schoolboy midfielder Martyn Hirst made a significant contribution to Bristol City's 1983/84 promotion success while studying at Bristol University. He impressed in the Alliance Premier League with Bath City before Terry Cooper signed him in October 1983 and gave him his League debut at home to Chesterfield a month later. He scored in City's FA Cup second round victory at Bristol Rovers and his sole goal in 41 League outings came in the 2-1 home win over Crewe Alexandra in April 1984. Following a loan spell at Torquay United, he joined Weymouth on a free transfer in January 1986 and has since played for St. Albans City, Wealdstone, Tooting & Mitcham, Harrow Borough and Chesham United while working for a major travel firm.

Jack Hodge
Versatile outside-right Jack Hodge featured prominently in Bristol City's 1934/35 FA Cup run, helping to take Preston NE to a fifth round replay. Initially with St. Austell, he joined Plymouth Argyle in July 1932 but failed to secure a first-team place at Home Park and Bob Hewison paid £100 for him in July 1934. He scored on his League debut in the 3-1 home in over Watford a month later and created numerous goalscoring opportuni-

ties for Teddy Harston, netting eight goals in 62 Third Division (South) outings prior to joining Luton Town for £800 in March 1936 to boost their promotion push. Supplying the ammunition for Joe 'Ten Goal' Payne during their 1936/37 Third Division (South) title campaign, he moved to newly-formed Colchester United for £500 in July 1937 and starred in their Southern League successes before joining Hereford United.

Roy Hodgson
Now widely regarded as one of Europe's leading coaches, Roy Hodgson managed Bristol City during the fateful 1981/82 season. A former defender with Crystal Palace, Tonbridge, Gravesend & Northfleet, Maidstone United (under Bob Houghton), Ashford Town, Berea Park (SA) and Carshalton Athletic, he managed Halmstad BK to the Swedish League Championship in 1976 and 1979 before reuniting with Houghton at Ashton Gate as assistant-manager in October 1980. He succeeded him as manager in January 1982 and his brief reign coincided with the 'Ashton Gate Eight' crisis. Dismissed in April 1982, he joined Malmo and plotted two successive Swedish League & Cup 'double' triumphs prior to managing Neuchatel Xamax. He took charge of the Swiss national team in December 1991 and became Inter-Milan's coach in October 1995, guiding them to the 1996/97 UEFA Cup final before leaving to manage Blackburn Rovers.

Sam Hollis
Sam Hollis was Bristol City's first manager and a very influential figure during the club's formative years. Born in Nottingham, he worked in a Probate Office and the Post Office before managing Woolwich Arsenal for three years. He was appointed manager of City in April 1897 and bought eight players for just £40 as he prepared the club for Southern League football. Resigning in March 1899 after interference from directors, he managed local rivals Bedminster until they amalgamated with City. He returned as City's manager in June 1901 after the shock departure of Bob Campbell and

remained in charge until March 1905. He ran the Southville Hotel until January 1911 when he returned for a third spell as manager until April 1913, then managed Newport County for four years. Sub-sequently chairman of Bristol City's shareholders association, he was a local publican until his death in April 1942.

Syd Homer

Diminutive outside-right Syd Homer was an influential figure as Bristol City won the Welsh Cup in 1933/34. He developed with Bloxwich White Star and Bloxwich Strollers, helping the latter to win the 1924/25 Birmingham Combination title prior to joining Wolves in May 1925. Moving to Bristol Rovers in June 1927, he scored on his debut at Eastville and Joe Bradshaw paid £350 for him in November 1929. He netted 13 goals in 179 League outings for City before joining Worcester City in August 1934 and died in Walsall in January 1983.

Chris Honor

Versatile defender Chris Honor featured in Bristol City's 1989/90 promotion campaign. An ex-apprentice, he made his League debut at Darlington in May 1986 and signed professional under Terry Cooper two months later. Also helping to reach the promotion play-offs in 1987/88 and Littlewoods Cup Semi-final in 1988/89, his sole goal in 60 Third Division games came in the 5-0 win at Swansea City in March 1990. Following loan spells at Torquay United, Hereford United and Swansea City, he joined Airdrie for £20,000 in August 1991 and played alongside Gus Caesar in the 1992 Scottish Cup final, gaining ECWC experience. During a protracted dispute, he joined Cardiff City in August 1994 and has since played for Bath City and Slough Town.

Peter Hooper

Noted for his powerful shot, outside-left Peter Hooper was an experienced figure in Bristol City's 1964/65 promotion success. Initially with Dawlish Town, he joined Bristol Rovers in May 1953 and became a great favourite at Eastville alongside Geoff Bradford. An expert penalty-taker, he was twice ever-present including 1960/61 when he was top scorer. Sold to Cardiff City for £10,000 in July 1962, he was reunited with Fred Ford at Ashton Gate for £11,000 in July 1963 and netted 14 goals in 54 league outings prior to joining Worcester City in July 1966. Subsequently with Barnstaple Town, he ran the 'Three Pigeons' pub in Bishop's Tawton for ten years and has worked in the probation service since June 1979. He is now Community Service Projects Manager in Barnstaple.

Dai Hopkins

Former Welsh international outside-right Dai Hopkins continued his partnership with Len Townsend at Ashton Gate. Real name Idris, he began with Merthyr Town and had spells with Sheffield Wednesday, Dartford and Crystal Palace prior to joining Brentford in November 1932. Ever-present in three successive seasons, he was a key figure in their rise from the Third Division (South) to First and Bob Hewison signed him as well as Townsend and Maurice Roberts in May 1947. Making 24 Third Division (South) appearances before leaving a year later to manage Swiss side Sleipner and Portadown, he subsequently ran a general stores in Cheam, a similar shop in Harefield, then was a courier for Parker Knoll in High Wycombe. He died of a heart attack in October 1994.

Gordon Hopkinson

Right-back Gordon Hopkinson was one of several players who followed Peter Doherty from Doncaster Rovers to Ashton Gate. He impressed with Beighton MW before joining Rovers in June 1957 but was unable to prevent relegation in 1957/58 and reunited with Doherty at Bristol City in July 1958. Breaking into the side after an injury to Ernie Peacock, he kept his place alongside Mike Thresher for the remainder of the 1958/59 campaign and helped to beat his former club in the FA Cup third round. He was displaced by another ex-Doncaster player Roger Collinson during the following season when City were relegated, netting his sole goal in 67 League games in the 2-0 win at Lincoln City in December 1958. Surprisingly released in May 1961, he subse-quently played in the Southern League for Cheltenham Town and Margate.

Bob Houghton

Bob Houghton succeeded long-serving Alan Dicks as manager of Bristol City. Formerly a defender with Stevenage Town, Fulham, Brighton, Tonbridge, Crawley Town and Hastings United, he became Maidstone United player-manager for a year in May 1971. After a spell as Ipswich Town's youth coach, he was appointed manager of Malmo and guided them to three Swedish League and Cup 'doubles' and the 1979 European Cup final. Briefly in charge of Ethnikos, he began his traumatic reign at Ashton Gate in October 1980 and was dismissed in January 1982 with City facing a third successive relegation and bankruptcy. Subsequently managing Toronto Blizzard and Orgryte IS, he returned as Southend United's assistant-manager in July 1992, then coached FC Zurich and Colorado Rapids and scouted for Roy Hodgson at Inter Milan before being appointed Nottingham Forest's assistant-manager in May 1997.

Tommy Howarth

Centre-forward Tommy Howarth was leading marksman as Bristol City reached the FA Cup semi-finals in 1919/20. Initially with Bury, he impressed in Army soccer and joined City in January 1919. He scored on his League debut at home to his former club in August 1919 and netted 15 goals in 46 Second Division outings prior to joining Leeds United for £460 in March 1921. Returning to Bristol with Rovers for £500 in November 1922, he joined Lovells Athletic for £750 in May 1923 and became their player-manager three months later – guiding the Toffeemen to the Western League title in 1923/24, three successive Welsh Amateur Cup triumphs and into the Southern League in 1928/29. He died in Newport in November 1946.

Ted Howling

Former England Amateur international Ted Howling was Bristol City's first-choice goalkeeper immediately prior to the Great

● Chris Honor

● Bob Houghton

● Glenn Humphries

● Ernie Hunt

● Norman Hunter

War. He impressed with South Bank and gained First Division experience with Middlesbrough as understudy to England star Tim Williamson who set the club appearance record at Ayresome Park. George Hedley signed him in May 1913 and despite competition from Tommy Ware, he made 55 Second Division appearances and briefly returned to First Division action with Bradford PA after the First World War.

Dick Hughes
An ex-England Schoolboy captain, right-back Dick Hughes featured prominently in Bristol City's 1922/23 and 1926/27 Third Division (South) title successes. Initially with Castletown, he joined Sunderland as an amateur in July 1919 and Joe Palmer signed him in September 1920. Making his League debut in the 2-0 win at home to Coventry City seven months later, he partnered the likes of Laurie Banfield, Reg Dyer and Ernie Glenn in City's defence. He made 268 League appearances despite competition from Jack Walsh and had a benefit match before moving to Exeter City in August 1932, helping them to finish as Third Division (South) runners-up in 1932/33. Subsequently landlord of the 'Old Inn' at Hutton near Weston-super-Mare, he died in Highbridge in April 1984.

Mark Hughes
Former Welsh Youth central defender Mark Hughes featured prominently in Bristol City's 1984/85 promotion challenge. An ex-Bristol Rovers apprentice, he signed professional in February 1980 and Terry Cooper gave him his League debut three months later. Loaned to Bruce Rioch's Torquay United, he joined Swansea City in July 1984 and was reunited with Cooper at Ashton Gate in February 1985. He made 22 Third Division appearances prior to joining Tranmere Rovers for £3,000 in September 1985 and like Jimmy Harvey was a key figure in their rise from the Fourth Division to the brink of the Premiership. A Leyland DAF Cup winner at Wembley in 1990, he also featured in the 1993/94 Coca-Cola Cup run and has been with Shrewsbury Town since July 1994.

Glenn Humphries
Ex-England Youth central defender Glenn Humphries made a significant contribution to Bristol City's 1989/90 promotion success. Initially a Doncaster Rovers apprentice with his elder brother Steve, he gained a regular League place before signing professional in August 1982 and starred in the 1983/84 promotion campaign alongside David Harle. Following a loan spell at Lincoln City, he was reunited with Terry Cooper at Ashton Gate for £20,000 in October 1987 and featured in the 1987/88 promotion play-offs and 1988/89 Littlewoods Cup run – making 85 League appearances prior to joining Scunthorpe United for £50,000 in March 1991. He has since played for Frickley Athletic, Goulding (HK), Gainsborough Trinity and Hull City.

Ted Humpish
Right-half Ted Humpish formed an effective half-back line with Allan Sliman and Ernie Brinton while at Ashton Gate. Initially with Walker Celtic, he joined Bury in July 1923 and Wigan Borough two years later where he became a key figure. Ever-present in 1928/29, he moved to Arsenal in January 1930 and gained top-flight experience before Joe Bradshaw paid £450 for him in December 1930. His sole goal in 36 Second Division outings came in the 1-3 defeat at Nottingham Forest in October 1931 and he joined Stockport County in August 1932. He moved to Rochdale two years later where he subsequently became trainer.

Ernie Hunt
Former England U-23 striker Ernie Hunt helped Bristol City to beat Leeds United in the 1973/74 FA Cup fifth round replay. Real name Roger, he began with Swindon Town and was leading marksman in their 1962/63 promotion triumph. He repeated this feat in 1966/67 after joining Wolves for £40,000 in September 1965, then moved to Everton for £80,000 in September 1967 and Coventry City for £65,000 in March 1968. Top scorer three times, he is well remembered with Willie Carr for the 'donkey-kick' goal against Everton in October

1970. Alan Dicks signed him for £8,000 in December 1973 after a loan spell at Doncaster Rovers and he scored twice in 12 Second Division outings before joining Atherstone Town in November 1974. Subsequently with Ledbury Town (where he ran the 'Full Pitcher' pub), he is currently an unemployed window-cleaner in Gloucester.

Norman Hunter
Tough-tackling ex-England central defender Norman 'Bites Yer Legs' Hunter was a key figure in Bristol City's 1976/77 First Division survival. He starred alongside Terry Cooper in the glorious Don Revie era at Leeds United, capped 28 times before Alan Dicks paid £40,000 for him in October 1976. Twice voted 'Player of the Year', he netted four goals in 108 First Division outings prior to joining Allan Clarke's Barnsley as player-coach in June 1979 and succeeding him as player-manager in October 1980. Plotting promotion in 1980/81, he became Rotherham United's manager in June 1985 and later coached West Brom, Leeds United and Bradford City. Still living near Leeds, he now combines media work with after-dinner speaking and helps run a property business with wife Suzanne.

Bobby Hutchinson
Experienced Scottish midfielder Bobby Hutchinson was voted 'Player of the Year' as Bristol City won the Freight Rover Trophy at Wembley in 1986. Initially a striker with Montrose, he joined Scottish League Cup winners Dundee in July 1974 and was swapped for Hibernian's Eric Schaedler in November 1977, featuring in the 1979 Scottish Cup final. He moved to Wigan Athletic in July 1980 and had spells with Tranmere Rovers and Mansfield Town prior to rejoining Tranmere in January 1984. Terry Cooper signed him on a free transfer six months later and he became captain, scoring 10 times in 92 Third Division outings. Sold to Walsall for £10,000 in February 1987, he was loaned to Blackpool and Carlisle United before returning to Scotland.

Trevor Jacobs

Popular right-back Trevor Jacobs partnered Alec Briggs and Brian Drysdale while at Ashton Gate. Signing professional from apprentice under Fred Ford in July 1965, he had the misfortune to score an own goal on his League debut at Rotherham United in November 1966 and displaced Tony Ford – featuring in the 1970/71 League Cup semi-final and netting three goals in 131 Second Division outings. Following a loan spell at Plymouth Argyle, he moved across Bristol to Rovers on a free transfer in May 1973 and was ever-present in the 1973/74 promotion success. Subsequently with Bideford, Paulton Rovers and Clevedon Town, he was a publican at the 'Horseshoe Inn' in Shepton Mallet, then the 'Baccy Jar' in Whitchurch. Since May 1986 he has been a local postman based at the delivery office in Kent Street.

Walter Jennings

Versatile right-half Walter Jennings displaced Ted Humpish in Bristol City's half-back line alongside Allan Sliman and Ernie Brinton. Born locally, he represented Bristol Boys and played for South Bristol Central OB before Alex Raisbeck signed him in May 1928 after trials with Bristol Rovers and Blackburn Rovers. He made his League debut at home to Hull City in September 1929 and his sole goal in 122 League outings came in the 4-1 win at Swindon Town in September 1932. Moving to struggling Cardiff City in June 1933, he later played for Bath City, Cheltenham Town and Bristol St. George. He was subsequently chief scout for Everton, Bristol Rovers and Bath City, remaining local until his death in November 1993.

Arthur Johnson

Outside-left Arthur Johnson made a significant contribution as Bristol City narrowly managed to avoid relegation in two successive seasons. He began with Thurston Town and

joined Huddersfield Town in November 1924, failing to secure a first-team slot as Herbert Chapman's side won three consecutive League Championships. Moving to Barnsley in October 1925, he joined Birmingham in May 1927 and gained top-flight experience before Alex Raisbeck signed him in May 1928. He created numerous goalscoring chances for the likes of Cecil Blakemore and Bertie Williams, contesting the left-wing slot with Jim Dickie at Ashton Gate and scoring seven goals in 60 Second Division outings before joining Coventry City in June 1931.

Joe Johnson

Diminutive outside-left Joe Johnson gained five England caps after leaving Ashton Gate. Initially with Cleethorpes Royal Saints, he impressed in the Midland League with Scunthorpe United before Joe Bradshaw signed him in May 1931. Given his League debut in the 4-0 win at home to Barnsley five months later, he made six further Second Division appearances before a financial crisis and relegation led to his £250 sale to Stoke City in April 1932. A key figure in their 1932/33 Second Division title success, he starred alongside fellow England internationals Stanley Matthews and Freddie Steele prior to joining West Brom for £6,000 in November 1937. He subsequently played for Northwich Victoria and Hereford United, then ran a cafe in Dartmouth Park and resided in West Bromwich until his death in August 1983.

Billy Jones

Dashing England right-half Billy Jones was the first player to gain international recognition while at Bristol City. Initially with Long Eaton Rangers and Wellington Athletic, he was top scorer for Loughborough Town in 1896/97 and Sam Hollis' first signing for City in May 1897. Capped against Ireland in March 1901, he was ever-present in City's 1901/02 Football League debut campaign and featured in the 1905/06 Second Division title success. He netted 44 goals in 290 League games before moving to Spurs in July 1906 and joined Swindon Town a year later with Freddie Fenton and Peter

Chambers. Subsequently landlord of the 'Barley Mow' pub in Bedminster, he resided locally until his death in September 1959.

Edwin Jones

Left-back Ted Jones gave Bristol City loyal service over eleven seasons. He had spells with Penrith, Chorley, Bolton Wanderers and Atherton prior to joining Exeter City in July 1909. Harry Thickett signed him in February 1910 and he understudied England star Joe Cottle before making his First Division debut at home to Liverpool in February 1911. Partnering the likes of Bob Young and John Kearns in City's defence, he was displaced by Laurie Banfield but remained at Ashton Gate long enough to earn two benefit matches. He scored four goals in 101 League outings before moving to Weymouth in July 1923, then was trainer at Bristol Rovers and Torquay United. He died in Birmingham in November 1953.

Ernie Jones

Born locally, left-half Ernie Jones featured prominently for Bristol City immediately after the Second World War. He represented Bristol Schools and was an England schoolboy triallist, impressing in local soccer with Caxtonians and Victoria Athletic before Bob Hewison signed him in February 1938. Serving with the 6th Airborne Division during the war, he was captured by the Germans at Arnheim. Making his League debut in City's first post-war Third Division (South) match at Aldershot in August 1946, his sole goal in 27 League outings came in City's record 9-0 victory at home to the same opposition four months later. He joined Wells City as player-manager in July 1948 and plotted the 1949/50 Western League title success, later coaching local soccer while working as a warehouseman.

Ernie Jones

Former Welsh international outside-right Ernie Jones created numerous goalscoring chances for John Atyeo and Arnold Rodgers while at Ashton Gate. During ten years with Swansea Town, he also played as an amateur for Bolton Wanderers and war-time guest for Bury and Chester. He joined Spurs

● Bobby Hutchinson

● Trevor Jacobs

● Billy Jones

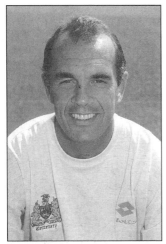

● Joe Jordan

● Bobby Kellard

● Martin Kuhl

in May 1947, then Southampton two years later in an exchange deal involving Alf Ramsey. Pat Beasley signed him as player-coach in November 1951 and he netted seven goals in 50 Third Division (South) outings prior to joining Rhyl as player-manager in April 1954, then returning to Southampton as youth coach. Subsequently settling in Bolton where he was an engineer for Hawker Siddeley until retiring in 1980, he became a member of the National Association of Inventors and Innovators and now designs water leisure products.

Joe Jordan

Ex-Scottish international centre-forward Joe Jordan had two spells as Bristol City's manager, plotting the 1988/89 Littlewoods Cup run and 1989/90 promotion success. He moved from Morton to Leeds United for £15,000 in October 1970 and featured in the 1973/74 League Champion-ship triumph as well as two European finals before joining Manchester United for a record £350,000 in January 1978 and playing in the 1979 FA Cup final. Sold to AC Milan for £325,000 in July 1981, he returned via Verona to Southampton for £150,000 in August 1984 and was reunited with Terry Cooper at Ashton Gate on a free transfer in February 1987. Succeeding him as player-boss in March 1988, he scored eight times in 57 Third Division games before appointed Hearts manager in September 1990, then assisted Liam Brady at Celtic and managed Stoke City prior to rejoining City in November 1994. He left by mutual consent in March 1997.

Syd Kearney

Experienced left-half Syd Kearney was a popular figure at Ashton Gate during the early post war era. He developed in Liverpool junior football, moving from Crowndale to Leicester City and turning professional in August 1936. Joining

Tranmere Rovers in May 1937, he featured in the 1937/38 Third Division (North) title success and moved to struggling Accrington Stanley for £125 in November 1938. Stationed in Nairobi during the war, he scored Accrington's first post-war League goal and success-fully switched from inside-forward to wing-half. Bob Hewison signed him in January 1947 and he dis-placed Ernie Jones, netting five goals in 65 Third Division (South) outings before joining Street in August 1950. Continuing in the Western League with Stonehouse, he died in London in October 1982.

John Kearns

Noted for his positional sense, right-back John Kearns formed a reliable defensive partnership with Laurie Banfield at Bristol City immediately prior to the Great War. He developed with Brownhills Albion, Hartshill United and Coventry City before gaining considerable top-flight experience with Birmingham, then joined rivals Aston Villa in July 1908 where he featured in their 1909/10 League Champion-ship success. Villa narrowly failed to retain the title the following season and Sam Hollis signed him in July 1912, netting his sole goal in 93 Second Division outings in the 2-0 home win over promotion chasing Bradford PA in January 1914.

Albert Keating

Inside-left Albert Keating formed a prolific goalscoring partnership with Tot Walsh as Bristol City won the Third Division (South) title in 1926/27. Starting with Prudhoe Castle, he joined Newcastle United for £130 in January 1922 and gained top-flight experience before Alex Raisbeck paid £650 for him in November 1925. Leading marks-man in 1927/28, he netted 39 goals in 79 League outings for City before being sold to FA Cup win-ners Blackburn Rovers for £4,000 with Clarrie Bourton in May 1928. He moved to Cardiff City in February 1931, then rejoined Bristol City in November 1932 and scored a further six goals in 21 League games prior to joining North Shields in July 1933. Subsequently with Throckley

Welfare, he became a referee on Tyneside and died in Newcastle in October 1984.

Bobby Kellard

Former England Youth midfielder Bobby Kellard skippered Bristol City during the late 1960's. Southend United's then youngest League debutant at 16 years 208 days, he was ever-present in 1961/62 and joined promotion-chasing Crystal Palace for £9,000 in September 1963. Moving via Ipswich Town and Portsmouth, he was reunited with Alan Dicks at Ashton Gate for £30,000 in July 1968 and scored six goals in 77 Second Division outings prior to joining Leicester City for £50,000 in August 1970. Subsequently returning to Palace and Portsmouth, he also played for Hereford United (on loan), Torquay United, Chelmsford City and Grays Athletic. After running a taxi business in Southend for several years, he is now an antiques dealer and was joint manager of Harlow Town with Len Glover until February 1995.

Bob Kirk

Scottish outside-left Bob Kirk cre-ated numerous goalscoring opportunities for Tot Walsh while at Bristol City and featured in the 1926/27 Third Division (South) title campaign. Initially with Clydebank, he impressed with Albion Rovers before Alex Raisbeck signed him in July 1924. He made his League debut at home to Exeter City two months later and faced competition for the left-wing slot from the likes of Billy Pocock and Arthur Rankin, netting five goals in 54 Third Division (South) outings before moving to Exeter City in July 1927.

Martin Kuhl

Experienced midfielder Martin Kuhl was Bristol City's ever-pre-sent 'Player of the Year' in 1995/96. A former Birmingham City apprentice, he made his League debut two months after signing professional in January 1983. He featured prominently in the 1984/85 promotion cam-paign, helping to regain top-flight status at the first attempt and joined Sheffield United in March

1987, then Watford in exchange for Tony Agana and Peter Hetherston in February 1988. Moving to Portsmouth for £125,000 in September 1988, he starred as they reached the FA Cup semi-finals in 1991/92 and joined Derby County for £650,000 in September 1992. Following a loan spell at Notts County, Jordan paid £330,000 for him in December 1994 and he scored seven goals in 94 League games for Bristol City before being released in May 1997 after helping to reach the Second Division play-offs.

Jack Landells
Scheming inside-forward Jack Landells starred in Bristol City's 1934/35 FA Cup run. Born in Gateshead, his family moved to Essex and he developed with Thames Board Mills, Jurgens and Grays Athletic prior to joining Millwall in March 1925 and scored on his League debut five months later. Leading marksman in 1927/28 alongside Jack Cock, he represented the FA and moved to West Ham in July 1933. Bob Hewison signed him in October 1934 and he scored twice in 21 Third Division (South) outings before joining Carlisle United in June 1935. Subsequently with Walsall, Clapton Orient and Chelmsford City where he starred in their 1938/39 FA Cup run under Allan Sliman, he returned to his native North-East and died in 1960.

Billy Lane
Experienced centre-forward Billy Lane netted several vital goals for Bristol City during the mid-1930's. Initially with Gnome Athletic, he joined Spurs in July 1921 and was subsequently a major source of goals at Leicester City, Reading, Brentford and Watford before Bob Hewison paid £310 for him in July 1935. He scored 11 times in 30 Third Division (South) outings prior to joining Clapton Orient in July 1937, then became a PE

Instructor during the war. Later assisting Harry Curtis at Brentford, he was appointed Guildford City's manager in June 1947, then took charge of Brighton in March 1951 and plotted their 1957/58 Third Division (South) title success. He later guided Gravesend & Northfleet to the FA Cup fourth round in 1962/63, then scouted for Arsenal. He died in Chelmsford in November 1985.

Billy Langham
Outside-right Billy Langham was leading marksman as Bristol City were Southern League runners-up in 1898/99. He developed with Stapleford and Hucknell Portland prior to joining Blackpool South Shore, then helped Notts County to win the Second Division title in 1896/97. Sam Hollis signed him in July 1898 and he scored 20 goals in 53 Southern League outings before joining Leicester Fosse in November 1900. He moved to Doncaster Rovers in July 1901 and helped consolidate Football League status, then joined Gainsborough Trinity for two seasons. Following another spell with Doncaster, he moved to Lincoln City in March 1907 and became their trainer/groundsman after the Great War, then was a licensee in Gainsborough.

League Cup
A table of Bristol City's record in this competition can be found at the end of this A to Z.

League Cup Semi-Finalists
Bristol City have twice been League Cup semi-finalists, narrowly beaten both times by the eventual Cup winners. In 1970/71, Alan Dicks' Second Division side beat Rotherham United. Blackpool, Leicester City and Fulham en route to a semi-final clash with Spurs. Alan Skirton' goal earned a 1-1 first-leg draw in front of 30,022 at Ashton Gate on 16th December 1970 but City lost the second-leg 0-2 after extra-time. In 1988/89, Joe Jordan's Third Division side beat Exeter City, Oxford United, Crystal Palace, Tranmere Rovers and Bradford City en route a semi-final clash with Nottingham Forest in the sponsored Littlewoods Cup. Paul Mardon's goal gave City a 1-1

first leg draw in front of 30,016 at the City Ground and 28,084 watched the second-leg on 26th February 1989, won 1-0 by Forest in extra-time.

Andy Leaning
Goalkeeper Andy Leaning made a significant contribution to Bristol City's 1989/90 promotion campaign and FA Cup run, He joined Denis Smith's York City from Rowntree Mackintosh in June 1985, playing in the same team as John MacPhail and Alan Hay and helping to take Liverpool to an FA Cup fifth round replay in 1985/86. Moving to Sheffield United in May 1987, Joe Jordan paid £10,000 for him in September 1988 after an initial loan spell as cover for injured Keith Waugh. Also contesting City's goalkeeping slot with Ronnie Sinclair and Keith Welch, he made 75 League appearances prior to joining Lincoln City on a free transfer in March 1994 and was their 'Player of the Year' in 1994/95. He joined Chesterfield in September 1996 and was a member of their 1996/97 FA Cup run squad.

George Lewis
Experienced left-back George Lewis partnered Billy Tuft in Bristol City's defence during the club's early days in the Football League. Initially with Chasetown Rovers, he also played for Walsall Town Swifts and Wellingborough prior to joining Notts County in February 1897. Helping to clinch the Second Division title four months later, he featured prominently in their 1900/01 League Championship challenge and Sam Hollis signed him in July l902. His sole goal in 30 Second Division outings was a penalty that clinched a 1-1 draw at home to Glossop in January 1903. He moved to Stourbridge in July 1903, briefly returning to League action with Leicester Fosse three months later.

Andy Llewellyn
Long-serving former England Youth right-back Andy Llewellyn was ever-present in Bristol City's 1989/90 promotion success. Born locally, he attended The Chase School, Mangotsfield and Terry Cooper gave him his League debut at Rochdale in December 1982 just five months after joining City as an

● Andy Leaning

● Andy Llewellyn

● **Gordon Low**

● **Kevin Mabbutt**

apprentice. Partnering the likes of Rob Newman, Brian Williams, John Bailey and Martin Scott, he played in the 1987 Freight Rover Trophy final at Wembley and the 1987/88 promotion play-offs, also featuring in the FA Cup wins over Chelsea in 1989/90 and Liverpool in 1993/94. Voted 'Player of the Year' in 1990/91, he scored three times in 313 League outings prior to joining Cooper's Exeter City on loan in March 1994 and has since played for Yeovil Town, Bishop Sutton and now Weston-Super-Mare.

Jimmy Loftus

Versatile, scheming inside-left Jimmy Loftus partnered the likes of Ted Bowen, Joe Riley and Teddy Harston in Bristol City's attack. Initially with Willington, he joined South Shields in July 1926 and moved to Nottingham Forest three years later. Bob Hewison paid £100 for him in June 1932 and he scored on his home debut against Torquay United, featuring in the 1934/35 FA Cup run and netting 29 goals in 93 Third Division (South) games. He moved to Gillingham in August 1935, then had a brief spell with Burton Town prior to joining Barrow in June 1936.

Gordon Low

Scottish wing-half Gordon Low skippered Bristol City's 1964/65 promotion triumph. A former Huddersfield Town junior, he signed professional in July 1957 and followed Jack Connor to Ashton Gate in March 1961. He established a notable central defensive partnership with his ex-Huddersfield team-mate and was ever-present in two successive seasons, netting 12 goals in 200 League outings before moving to Stockport County in July 1968. Subsequently with Crewe Alexandra and Selby Town, he still lives in Huddersfield and was a sales rep for Lilywhites, then ran the Cavalry Arms pub. He has been an agent for several toy firms since January 1989 and during 14 years as Huddersfield Town's part-time youth coach, graduates included Junior Bent and Robbie Turner.

George Lowrie

Ex-Welsh international inside-forward George Lowrie partnered Arnold Rodgers while at Ashton Gate. Initially a Swansea Town amateur, he signed professional in January 1937 and joined Preston NE in December 1937. He moved to Coventry City for £1,750 in June 1939 to replace Clarrie Bourton, guesting for Bristol City, Nottingham Forest and Northampton Town during the war. Twice leading goalscorer, he joined Newcastle United for a record £18,500 in March 1948 and Bob Wright paid £10,000 for him in September 1949. He netted 21 goals in 48 Third Division (South) games before rejoining Coventry for £2,750 in February 1952, then skippering Lovells Athletic to the Southern League Cup final in 1953/54. Settling in Bristol and working for Messrs Douglas in Kingswood, he died in May 1989.

Jimmy Lumsden

Jimmy Lumsden succeeded Joe Jordan as manager of Bristol City in September 1990. As an inside-forward, he signed professional from apprentice for Leeds United in November 1966 and gained top-flight experience prior to joining Southend United in September 1970. Subsequently with Morton twice, St. Mirren and Cork Hibernian, he moved to Clydebank in July 1975 and starred in their rise from Scottish Second Division to Premier in successive seasons. He became Celtic's youth team manager until July 1982, then assisted Eddie Gray at Leeds United and Rochdale before his appointment as assistant manager at Ashton Gate in July 1988. Taking charge when Jordan left to manage Hearts, he plotted Second Division survival until dismissed in February 1992 after just one win in 14 games.

Kevin Mabbutt

Exciting young striker Kevin Mabbutt was Bristol City's top scorer and 'Player of the Year' in 1980/81. From a notable local footballing family, his father Ray and younger brother Gary (now Spurs) both starred for Bristol Rovers. An England Youth international, he signed professional from apprentice in January 1976 and made his League debut at Nottingham Forest in August 1977. He scored twice in the 1977/78 Anglo-Scottish Cup final triumph and netted 29 goals in 129 League outings prior to joining Crystal Palace in a £200,000 exchange deal involving Terry Boyle in October 1981. Leading marksman in successive seasons, he briefly played in Canada, Belgium and Cyprus after injury and now lives in California, running his own family restaurant called 'Delicias'.

Peter McCall

Young right-half Peter McCall featured prominently during Peter Doherty's controversial reign at Ashton Gate. Discovered playing with King's Lynn, he signed professional for Bristol City in April 1955 and made his League debut at Cardiff City in April 1958, netting his sole goal in 78 league games in the 3-0 home win over Brighton five months later. He moved to Oldham Athletic in May 1962 and was ever-present in the 1962/63 promotion success, then joined Hereford United in July 1965 and starred in the 1965/66 FA Cup run. Still living locally, he was an accountant for Jack Tully's bookmakers and UBM building supplies, then an estimator for Bristol City Parks Deparment until early retirement in May 1992. A champion bowls player, he represented England 12 times in the mid-1980's and is now assistant-chairman of Bristol Indoors Bowls Club (Mens Section).

Johnny McCann

Ex-Scottish 'B' outside-left Johnny McCann joined Bristol City with Malcolm Graham in exchange for Bert Tindill plus £14,500 in May 1959. Initially with Bridgeton Waverley, he joined Barnsley in December 1955 and quickly impressed in the Second Division. Peter Doherty brought him to Ashton Gate and he overcame a broken leg on Boxing Day 1959 to make 30 League appearances before he was swapped for Huddersfield Town's Jack Connor in October 1960. Reunited with Tim Ward at Derby County for £6,000 in September 1962, he subsequently played for Darlington, Chesterfield, Skegness Town and

Lockheed Leamington. Still living in Barnsley, he was Senior Inspector (Quality Control) at Shaw Carpets for 25 years until December 1994 and is currently unemployed .

Steve McClaren
All-action midfielder Steve McClaren was a key figure as Bristol City reached the Littlewoods Cup semi-finals in 1988/89. He signed professional from apprentice for Hull City in April 1979 and starred in their rise from the Fourth Division to Second, then joined Derby County for £75,000 in August 1985 and featured in their rise from the Third Division to First. Following loan spell at Lincoln City, Terry Cooper signed him for £50,000 in February 1988 and he helped to reach the promotion play-offs in 1987/88, scoring twice in 61 Third Division games before moving to Oxford United in exchange for Gary Shelton in August 1989. When injury ended his playing career, he became youth and reserve coach under Denis Smith and rejoined Derby as first-team coach in June 1995.

Scott McGarvey
Former Scottish U-21 striker Scott McGarvey featured alongside Alan Walsh in Bristol City's attack. An ex-Manchester United apprentice, he signed professional in April 1980 and gained top-flight experience. Following a loan spell at Wolves, he joined Portsmouth for £50,000 in July 1984, then Carlisle United in July 1986 after another loan period. He moved to Grimsby Town in March 1987 and was reunited with Joe Jordan at Ashton Gate in exchange for Tony Caldwell in September 1988. Ineligible to play as City reached the Littlewoods Cup semi-finals in 1988/89 he netted nine goals in 26 Third Division outings prior to joining Joe Royle's Oldham Athletic in May 1989. Subsequently loaned to Wigan Athletic, he moved to Japanese club Mazda in May 1990 and now runs 'Moneystone' sand suppliers at Levenseat Quarry, Glasgow.

Hugh McIlmoyle
Classy, much-travelled centre-forward Hugh McIlmoyle cost Bristol City a then record £27,000 when Fred Ford signed him in March 1967. Initially with Port Glasgow, he joined Leicester City in August 1959 and played in the 1961 FA Cup Final. He moved via Rotherham United to Carlisle in March 1963 and was leading marksman in the 1963/64 promotion success and FA Cup run, joining Wolves for £30,000 in October 1964. Netting a brilliant goal on his City debut, he scored four times in 20 Second Division outings overall prior to rejoining Carlisle for a cut-price £22,000 in September 1967 and was ever-present and top scorer in 1968/69. Subsequently with Middlesbrough, Preston NE, Morton (twice) and Carlisle again, he now lives in Oadby and since June 1977 has been a warehouseman for Walkers Crisps.

Jack McLean
Tireless ex-Scottish junior international centre-half Jack McLean was ever-present in Bristol City's 1901/02 Football League debut campaign. Starting with Greenock Volunteers, he joined Liverpool in July 1894 and helped to win the Second Division title in 1895/96. He moved to Grimsby Town in June 1897 and Sam Hollis paid £40 for him in May 1898, starring as City were Southern League runners-up in 1898/99 and 1900/01. Scoring ten goals in 158 appearances prior to joining local rivals Bristol Rovers in July 1902, he subsequently continued in the Southern League with Millwall and QPR where he starred in the 1907/08 Southern League title triumph
.

Alan McLeary
Experienced former England U-21 and B international central defender Alan McLeary partnered Matt Bryant in the heart of Bristol City's defence. An ex-Millwall apprentice, he signed professional as a midfielder in October 1981 and scored in their 1982/83 Football League Trophy final triumph. He was twice ever-present, starring in their rise from the Third Division to top of the First and had loan spells at Sheffield United and Wimbledon before joining Charlton Athletic on a free transfer in May 1993. Featuring in their 1993/94 FA Cup run, Joe Jordan signed him in July 1995 and he made 34 Second Division appearances prior to rejoining Millwall in January 1997.

John MacPhail
Central defender John MacPhail played for Bristol City in the 1987 Freight Rover Trophy final at Wembley. He began with Dundee, joining Sheffield United for £30,000 in January 1979 and starred in the 1981/82 Fourth Division title campaign. Moving to Denis Smith's York City on a free transfer in February 1983, he repeated this feat in 1983/84 and was a key figure in consecutive FA Cup runs before Terry Cooper paid £15,000 for him in July 1986. His sole goal in 25 Third Division outings clinched a 2-1 home win over Walsall in December 1986 and he was reunited with Smith at Sunderland in July 1987, featuring prominently in the rise from Third Division to First. He joined Hartlepool United in September 1990, becoming player-manager for ten months until sacked in September 1994 and now manages South Tyneside United.

● John MacPhail

Managers
A table listing Bristol City's managers, with dates of office, can be found at the end of this A to Z.

George Mann
Scottish right-half George Mann was ever-present as Bristol City were runners-up in their 1897/98 Southern League debut campaign. Initially with East Stirling, he moved to Blackburn Rovers in July 1892 and gained First Division experience prior to joining Manchester City in July 1894. He featured in their 1895/96 promotion challenge alongside Pat Finnerhan and Sam Hollis recruited him as Bristol City turned professional in 1897. Forming a reliable half-back line with Sandy Higgins and Jack Hamilton, he scored nine goals in 25 Southern League games before an injury sustained in the match at Chatham in January 1899 forced him to retire.

● Hugh McIlmoyle

Jimmy Mann
Noted for his lethal free-kicks, long-serving midfielder Jimmy Mann made a significant contribu-

● Jimmy Mann

● Paul Mardon

tion to Bristol City's 1975/76 promotion campaign. A former Leeds United apprentice, he signed professional in December 1969 but had limited first-team opportunities before moving to Ashton Gate on a free transfer with John Shaw in May 1974. Also helping to win the Anglo-Scottish Cup in 1977/78, he netted 31 goals in 231 League outings prior to the 'Ashton Gate Eight' crisis in February 1982 when he joined Norman Hunter's Barnsley, then played for Scunthorpe United, Doncaster Rovers, Goole Town and Bentley Victoria. Now living back in Goole he was a mobile security officer for Securicor, then a Co-op Milkman and since May 1994 has been a marine operator at Goole docks.

Paul Mardon

Young central defender Paul Mardon's first senior goal gave Bristol City the lead in the 1988/89 Littlewoods Cup semi-final first-leg at Nottingham Forest. Born locally, he signed professional from trainee under Terry Cooper in January 1988 and was given his league debut at Preston NE the same month. Also featuring in the 1989/90 promotion campaign, he regularly featured as substitute and made 42 League appearances prior to joining Cooper's Birmingham City for £65,000 in August 1991 after a loan spell at Doncaster Rovers. An influential figure in the 1991/92 promotion success alongside David Rennie and Louie Donowa, he moved to West Brom for £50,000 in November 1993. Now captain at The Hawthorns, he was 'Player of the Year' in 1994/95 and has gained full Welsh International recognition.

Gary Marshall

Midfielder Gary Marshall played for Bristol City in the 1987 Freight Rover Trophy final at Wembley. Born locally, Terry Cooper signed him from Shepton Mallet in July 1983 and gave him his League debut as substitute at home to Chesterfield four months later. He regularly featured as substitute after a loan spell at Torquay United and helped to reach the promotion play-offs in 1987/88, netting seven goals in 68 League

● Gary Marshall

outings before following Clive Middlemass to Carlisle United in July 1988. Briefly partnering Paul Fitzpatrick at Brunton Park, he moved to Scunthorpe United in July 1989 and was reunited with Cooper at Exeter City for £22,000 in October 1990. Since injury ended his League career prematurely, he has played for Shortwood and Forest Green Rovers.

Julian Marshall

Tall Welsh central defender Julian Marshall was one of Bristol City's 'Ashton Gate Eight' during the fateful 1981/82 campaign. Initially with Merthyr Tydfil, he joined John Sillett's Hereford United in August 1975 and played alongside John Galley and Peter Spiring in the Second Division. Following successive relegations, Alan Dicks signed him on a free transfer in August 1980 and he provided reliable defensive cover for injured Geoff Merrick in the heart of defence alongside David Rodgers. Experiencing further relegation as City dropped into the Third Division, he made 29 League appearances before the financial crisis at Ashton Gate forced his release in February 1982 and subsequently played for Blackburn Rovers, Walsall, Worcester City and Stourbridge.

Reuben Marr

Long-serving right-half Reuben Marr shared with Billy Wedlock the distinction of featuring in Bristol City's 1908/09 and 1919/20 FA Cup runs. He developed in Doncaster junior soccer and Harry Thickett snapped him up from Mexborough in July 1906. Making his League debut at Birmingham in September 1906, he quickly impressed alongside Wedlock and Pat Hanlin as City were League Championship runners-up in 1906/07. Given a benefit match against Burnley in February 1913, he scored 11 goals in 178 League outings before retiring in May 1920 and remained local until his death in March 1961.

David Martin

Versatile ex-England Youth midfielder David Martin featured prominently in Bristol City's

1993/94 FA Cup run. A former Millwall apprentice, he helped to win the FA Youth Cup in 1979 and made his League debut two months before signing professional in May 1980. Scoring twice in the 1982/83 Football League Trophy final triumph, he joined Wimbledon for £35,000 in September 1984 and was a member of the 'Crazy Gang' that reached the First Division. Sold to Southend United for £15,000 in August 1986, he starred in the rise from Fourth Division to Second in successive years. Russell Osman signed him in July 1993 and his sole goal in 38 First Division outings clinched a 1-1 draw at Watford in November 1993. Following a loan spell at Northampton Town, he moved to Gillingham on a free transfer in July 1995 and starred in the 1995/96 promotion success.

Jimmy Martin

Much-travelled inside-right Jimmy Martin displaced Johnny Paul in Bristol City's attack during the 1926/27 Third Division (South) title campaign. Initially with Stoke St. Peters and Basford, he joined Stoke in July 1919 and moved to Aberdare Athletic two years later. He helped Wolves to win the Third Division (North) title in 1923/24, then played for Reading before rejoining Aberdare in July 1925 where he was top scorer in 1925/26. Alex Raisbeck paid £100 for him in May 1926 and he netted 16 goals in 40 League outings prior to joining Blackpool in February 1928. He was subsequently with Southend United, Halifax Town and Congleton Town, residing in his native Stoke until his death in June 1969.

Billy Matthews

Tall, cultured Welsh international centre-half Billy Matthews featured prominently in Bristol City's 1922/23 Third Division (South) title success. Initially a centre-forward with Colwyn Bay, he joined Liverpool in July 1916 and followed Alex Raisbeck to Ashton Gate for £750 in March 1922. Capped against England in March 1923, his sole goal in 42 League outings for City clinched a 1-1 draw at Luton Town in December 1922. He moved to Wrexham for £350 in

November 1923, then played for Northwich Victoria and Barrow prior to joining Bradford PA in January 1926 and starred in their 1927/28 Third Division (North) title success. Subsequently with Stockport County, New Brighton, Chester, Oswestry Town, Witton Albion, Sandbach Ramblers, Colwyn Bay and Rossendale United, he resided in Wrexham until his death in December 1987.

Billy Maxwell

Experienced Scottish inside-right Billy Maxwell was leading marksman as Bristol City won the Second Division title in 1905/06 and were League Championship runners-up the following season. Initially with Hearts Strollers, he played for Arbroath, Hearts and Third Lanark prior to joining Sunderland in July 1902 where he featured in their 1902/03 League Championship challenge. Moving via Millwall, Harry Thickett signed him in July 1905 and he netted 58 goals in 120 League games before joining Belgian club Leopold as coach in July 1909. He later coached Brussels and the Belgian national team in the 1912 Olympic Games and died in Bristol in July 1940.

Andy May

Former England U-21 midfielder Andy May was an influential figure in Bristol City's 1991/92 FA Cup run. An ex-Manchester City apprentice, he made his League debut nine months before signing professional in January 1982. Everpresent in 1983/84, he starred in the 1984/85 promotion campaign and played in the 1986 Full Members Cup Final at Wembley. Moving to Huddersfield Town in July 1987, he followed Junior Bent to Ashton Gate for £90,000 in August 1990 after a loan spell at Bolton Wanderers and helped newly-promoted City consolidate higher status. He netted four goals in 90 Second Division outings prior to joining Millwall in exchange for David Thompson in June 1992 and moved to Bromley on a free transfer in July 1995.

Geert Meijer

Dutch international winger Geert Meijer made a significant contribution as Bristol City consolidated top-flight status in 1978/79. A qual-

ified schoolmaster, he represented the Dutch Army and played for DWS Amsterdam, FC Amsterdam and Ajax where he featured in two Dutch League title successes. Alan Dicks paid £80,000 for him in March 1979 at the same time as Finnish international Perti Jantunen arrived at Ashton Gate for £50,000. He made an immediate impact, scoring on his City debut in the 2-1 home win over Birmingham City and enabling Clive Whitehead to switch to a fullback role. Netting twice in 15 First Division games before losing his place after injury and a change of policy, he returned to Holland with Sparta Rotterdam for £50,000 in February 1980 and is now coaching Feyenoord.

Micky Mellon

Young Scottish midfielder Micky Mellon featured in Bristol City's 1989/90 promotion campaign. Initially with Bishopbriggs Boys Club, he moved to Ashton Gate as a trainee from Hearts in April 1989 and made rapid progress. Joe Jordan gave him his League debut as substitute at home to Wigan Athletic two months before he signed professional in December 1989, contesting a first-team slot with the likes of Mark Gavin, Gary Shelton and Junior Bent. Netting his sole goal in 35 League outings in the 3-0 win at Luton Town in August 1992, he joined West Brom for £75,000 in February 1993 and helped to clinch promotion via the play-offs three months later. He moved to Blackpool for £50,000 in November 1994 and was 'Player of the Year' in their 1995/96 promotion near-miss.

Arthur Mercer

Much-travelled inside-right Arthur Mercer partnered the likes of Sid Elliott and Percy Vials in Bristol City's attack. Starting with Parr St. Peters, he helped Wigan Borough to consolidate Football League status before moving to Bury in July 1925. He continued in the First Division with Sheffield United the following season, then helped Leeds United to win promotion in 1927/28. After spells with Rhyl and Connah's Quay, Joe Bradshaw paid £425 to sign him and right-wing partner Cuthbert Robson for City in May 1930 and he netted eight

goals in 31 Second Division outings before joining Chester with Robson in October 1931. He featured in successive promotion challenges, then had spells with Halifax Town and Dartford prior to rejoining Rhyl.

Geoff Merrick

Twice 'Player of the Year', loyal defender Geoff Merrick skippered Bristol City's 1975/76 promotion success. An ex-England Schoolboys captain, he signed professional from apprentice in August 1968, three months after making his League debut at Aston Villa. Three times ever-present, he starred in the 1973/74 FA Cup run and switched from central defence to left-back after the arrival of Norman Hunter. He had a testimonial in May 1980 and netted ten goals in 367 League outings before the 'Ashton Gate Eight' crisis forced his release in February 1982. Subsequently with Yeovil Town, Carolina Hills (HK), Bath City, Gloucester City, Bridgwater Town, Minehead, Bristol Rovers reserves, Port of Bristol, Shirehampton, Hengrove Athletic and Nailsea Town. He still lives in Nailsea and is now a self-employed builder.

Andy Micklewright

Inside-forward Andy Mickle-wright partnered John Atyeo in Bristol City's attack during the mid 1950's. Initially a West Brom amateur, he represented the Combined Services and moved from Smethwick Highfield to Bristol Rovers in January 1952. He featured in the 1952/53 Third Division (South) title success and repeated this feat with City in 1954/55 after Pat Beasley signed him in May 1953, netting 17 goals in 39 outings before moving to struggling Swindon Town in September 1955. He joined Exeter City in July 1959 and later played for Nuneaton Borough, Hinckley Athletic, Brierley Hill Alliance and Redditch United prior to rejoining Smethwick as player-manager. During 27 years with Smethwick/Sandwell Borough Council, he became Chief Estimator for the Works Department until retiring in October 1988 and now lives in Brixham.

● Geert Meijer

● Micky Mellon

● Geoff Merrick

● Jan Moller

● Hugh Monteith

● Trevor Morgan

Ralph Milne

Former Scottish U-21 midfielder Ralph Milne was an experienced figure as Bristol City reached the promotion play-offs in 1987/88. He starred in Dundee United's successes under Jim McLean, helping to win the Scottish League title in 1982/83 and reach the European Cup semi-finals in 1983/84. Sold to Charlton Athletic for £130,000 in January 1987, he played in the Full Members Cup final at Wembley two months later and Terry Cooper paid £60,000 for him in January 1988. He scored on his City debut in the 3-2 home win over Bury, featuring in the 1988/89 Littlewoods Cup run and netting six goals in 30 Third Division outings prior to joining Manchester United for £170,000 in November 1988. Released after making controversial press revelations, he had spells with West Ham (on loan), Bury and in Hong Kong. He is currently unemployed, living in Backwell.

Arthur Milton

England's last dual international at cricket and football, outside-right Arthur Milton made a significant contribution as Bristol City clinched the Third Division (South) title in 1954/55. Born locally, he attended Cotham School and signed professional for Arsenal in July 1946. He was capped against Austria at Wembley in November 1951, featuring in the 1952/53 League Championship success and Pat Beasley paid £4,000 for him in February 1955. After scoring three times in 14 League games, Arsenal repaid half the fee when he chose to retire in May 1955 to concentrate on his cricket for Gloucestershire and he played 585 matches over 26 years until 1974. Still living in Henleaze, he was a postman for ten years and since March 1988 has kept fit by delivering morning newspapers.

Jan Moller

Tall, Swedish international goalkeeper Jan Moller followed manager Bob Houghton from Malmo to Bristol City in December 1980. Working as a sports organiser for a Malmo bank, he was a Swedish League and Cup 'double' winner with Malmo in 1977 and played in the 1978 European Cup Final against Nottingham Forest.

Displacing Ray Cashley and John Shaw in goal after his £120,000 move, he made his League debut in the Boxing Day clash at home to Cardiff City and helped to reach the FA Cup fifth round but was unable to prevent relegation for the second successive year. He made 48 League appearances prior to following Houghton to Toronto Blizzard for a cut-price £85,000 in March 1982 after the financial crisis at Ashton Gate and played in the 1983 Soccer Bowl Final before returning to Sweden.

Hugh Monteith

Noted for his consistency, popular Scottish goalkeeper Hugh Monteith was ever-present as Bristol City were Southern League runners-up in 1897/98. Previously with Parkhead Juniors, Celtic and Loughborough Town, he followed Billy Jones to City in July 1897 as they entered the Southern League and made 70 Southern League appearances prior to joining West Ham in July 1900. He moved to Bury in July 1902 and starred in their 1902/03 FA Cup run when they did not concede a goal and trounced Derby County by a record 6-0 margin in the final.

Cliff Morgan

Popular right-half Cliff Morgan still holds the record as Bristol City's longest-serving player and gave outstanding service in various capacities over 45 years at Ashton Gate. Born locally, he played for Bristol Boys Brigade and joined City as an amateur inside-forward in September 1930. Joe Bradshaw gave him his League debut at Spurs in March 1931 and after switching to half-back, he featured prominently in the 1934/35 FA Cup run and 1937/38 promotion near-miss. A dead-ball specialist, he was appointed captain and netted eight goals in 235 League games (plus 15 in 203 war-time games prior to becoming player-coach in April 1948). Subsequent-ly City's chief scout, he died of cancer at Frenchay Hospital in July 1975 just two months after his third benefit match.

Nicky Morgan

Experienced, skilful striker Nicky Morgan helped Bristol City to clinch promotion in 1989/90. A former West Ham apprentice, he

signed professional in November 1977 and featured in the 1980/81 Second Division title success. Following a loan spell with Den Haag, he joined Portsmouth for £50,000 in March 1983 and helped to win the Third Division title two months later. Top scorer as Pompey narrowly missed promotion for the second consecutive year in 1985/86, he joined Stoke City for £30,000 in November 1986. Joe Jordan paid a similar fee for him in March 1990 and he was leading marksman in 1990/91, netting 23 goals in 80 League games. He moved to Terry Cooper's Exeter City in February 1994 after being loaned to AFC Bournemouth and has since played for Dorchester Town and Salisbury.

Syd Morgan

Goalkeeper Syd Morgan gave Bristol City loyal service over ten years at Ashton Gate. Born locally, this former Royal Marine was discovered playing on the Downs for works team AG Farmer & Sons and signed by Bob Hewison in December 1947. Given his League debut at Torquay United in March 1949, he provided reliable cover for the likes of Frank Clack, Frank Coombs, Con Sullivan, Tony Cook and Bob Anderson. He made 71 Third Division (South) appearances before following assistant-manager Jimmy Seed to Millwall in March 1958 and later played for Salisbury in the Western League, then assisted Arnold Rodgers at Welton Rovers and Bath City. Still living in Stapleton, he was an electrician for Hector Tanner & Co until retiring in August 1991.

Trevor Morgan

Much-travelled striker Trevor Morgan was a popular figure during two spells at Ashton Gate. He impressed with Tonbridge, Dartford and Leytonstone & Ilford before joining AFC Bournemouth for £3,000 in September 1980. Featuring in the 1981/82 promotion campaign after a brief spell at Mansfield Town, Terry Cooper paid £10,000 for him in March 1984 and he netted the goals that clinched promotion two months later. Moving to Exeter City in November 1984, Cooper re-signed him from Bristol Rovers in January 1987 and he scored 15 times in 51 league outings overall prior to joining Bolton Wanderers in June 1987. He starred in the 1987/88 promotion success and 1988/89 Sherpa Van Trophy final triumph, then played for Colchester United and Happy Valley (HK) before assisting Cooper at Exeter City (twice) and Birmingham City.

Jack Morris

Small, versatile inside-forward Jack Morris played alongside Fred Corbett in attack as Bristol City finished fourth in Division Two for the second successive season in 1903/04. He developed with Sterling Youth Club and Rock Ferry before a spell at Liverpool, then had a good goalscoring record in limited Second Division outings for Blackpool. Scoring regularly in the top-flight after moving to Notts County in July 1901, Sam Hollis signed him in July 1903 and he netted 11 goals in 29 Second Division outings prior to joining New Brompton in July 1904.

Arthur Moss

Versatile half-back Arthur Moss played alongside Billy Wedlock at Bristol City immediately prior to the Great War. Initially with Crewe Central, he had spells with Willeston White Star, Crewe Alexandra and Whitchurch prior to joining Aston Villa for £250 in September 1908. He understudied Chris Buckley as Villa won the League Championship in 1909/10 and Sam Hollis signed him in July 1912. Making 85 Second Division appearances, he served with distinction in the Army during the First World War and subsequently played for Runcorn before rejoining Crewe Alexandra and helping them to re-establish Football League status.

David Moyes

Popular ex-Scottish Youth central defender David Moyes featured prominently as Bristol City contested two successive Freight Rover Trophy Finals and was a Wembley winner in 1986. He developed with Celtic under youth team boss Jimmy Lumsden, featuring in the 1981/82 Scottish League title success and gaining European Cup experience.

Moving to Cambridge United in October 1983, Terry Cooper paid £10,000 for him two years later and he became captain, netting six goals in 83 Third Division outings before following Brian Williams to Shrewsbury Town for £25,000 in October 1987. Ever-present in 1989/90, he moved to Dunfermline Athletic in July 1990 and was top scorer in 1991/92. Briefly with Hamilton Academicals, he joined Preston NE in September 1993 and starred in their 1995/96 Third Division title success.

Stuart Munro

Versatile ex-Scottish 'B' left back Stuart Munro was an experienced figure in Bristol City's 1993/94 FA Cup run including the third round replay defeat of Liverpool. Initially with Bo'ness United, he moved via St. Mirren to Alloa in July 1982. Ever-present in 1982/83, he joined Glasgow Rangers in January 1984 and featured prominently in the successes under Graeme Souness including three Scottish League Cup 'double' triumphs. sold to Don Mackay's Blackburn Rovers for £350,000 in August 1991, he languished in the reserves after Kenny Dalglish took charge and revived his career at Ashton Gate after Russell Osman signed him in February 1993. Helping to preserve First Division status that season, he made 94 League appearances prior to joining Falkirk on a free transfer in November 1995.

Russell Musker

Young midfielder Russell Musker was at Ashton Gate while Bristol City plummeted from the First Division to Fourth in successive years. Representing Devon and SW England Schoolboys, he signed professional from apprentice in August 1979 and Bob Houghton gave his League debut at home to Chelsea in April 1981. His sole goal in 46 League outings came in the 2-1 home win over Hull City in August 1982 and following a loan spell at Exeter City, he joined Gillingham for £7,500 in November 1983. Moving to Torquay United in August 1986, he has since played for Gloucester City, Weymouth and Taunton Town where he is now manager.

Stuart Naylor

Former England B goalkeeper Stuart Naylor made a significant contribution as Bristol City qualified for the Second Division play-offs in 1996/97. An ex-Youth international, his father and uncle both played for Oldham Athletic and he joined Lincoln City from Yorkshire Amateurs in June 1980. Following loan periods with Peterborough United and Crewe Alexandra, he succeeded David Felgate in goal and was Ron Saunders' first signing for West Brom at £110,000 in February 1986. Ever-present 'Player of the Year' in 1986/87, he lost his place to Tony Lange during Albion's 1992/93 promotion campaign after successive injuries and was their longest-serving player when Joe Jordan signed him on a free transfer in August 1996. He has now made 35 Second Division appearances for City, contesting the goalkeeping slot with Keith Welch.

Bert Neesam

Long-serving, versatile right-half Bert Neesam was an experienced figure in Bristol City's 1922/23 and 1926/27 Third Division (South) title successes. As an inside-right, he was leading marksman for Brampton in the Northallerton League and moved via Grange-town Athletic to Ashton Gate in September 1913. George Hedley gave him his League debut at Glossop six months later and he played throughout the Great War, appointed captain and scoring 18 goals in 282 League outings before joining Bath City in July 1928. Reinstated as an amateur in January 1932, he played locally for George's Brewery and was a keen cricketer. He died in Northallerton in July 1969.

Billy Nesbitt

Experienced outside-right Billy Nesbitt contested Bristol City's right-wing slot with Charlie Worlock during the 1923/24 cam-

● David Moyes

● Stuart Munro

● Stuart Naylor

● **Steve Neville**

● **Rob Newman**

● **Alan Nicholls**

paign. He developed with Portsmouth Rovers and Hebden Bridge prior to joining Burnley in September 1911, featuring prominently alongside England star Bob Kelly as they won the FA Cup in 1913/14 and League Championship in 1920/21. Displaced at Turf Moor by the arrival of Peter Benine, Alex Raisbeck signed him in May 1923 but persistent injury problems restricted him to 26 Second Division appearances while at Ashton Gate. He briefly joined Clapton Orient in July 1924, then became a tobacconist in Paddington.

Steve Neville

Skilful striker Steve Neville was leading goalscorer as Bristol City won the Freight Rover Trophy at Wembley in 1986. An ex-Southampton apprentice, he signed professional in September 1975 and featured in the 1977/78 promotion campaign. He was sold to Exeter City for £20,000 in September 1978, moving to Sheffield United for £80,000 in October 1980 and starring in the 1981/82 Fourth Division title success. Rejoining Exeter in October 1982, Terry Cooper swapped Trevor Morgan for him in November 1984 and he scored 40 goals in 134 Third Division games before following Cooper back to Exeter for £10,000 fixed by tribunal in July 1988. A key figure in the 1989/90 Fourth Division title win, he has since played for South China (HK), Dorchester Town, Torrington (P/C) and now Clyst Rovers (P/M).

George Newlands

Scottish goalkeeper George Newlands was ever-present for Bristol City in 1931/32. Initially with Shotts Battlefield, Alex Raisbeck signed him in July 1927 and he understudied Billy Coggins at Ashton Gate. Making his League debut at Swansea Town in November 1927, he established himself as City's first-choice keeper after Coggins' departure to Everton in March 1930 and made 90 League appearances prior to joining Belfast Distillery in November 1932. He gave them four years' service before resigning from that club and died in February 1969.

Rob Newman

Versatile central defender Ron Newman skippered Bristol City's 1989/90 promotion success. Signing professional from apprentice in October 1981, 'Biff' made his League debut at home to Fulham four months later immediately after the 'Ashton Gate Eight' crisis. He was an influential figure as City won promotion in 1983/84, reached two consecutive Freight Rover Trophy finals at Wembley, the promotion play-offs in 1987/88 and were Littlewoods Cup semi-finalists in 1988/89. Three times ever-present, he was 'Player of the Year' in 1986/87 and scored 52 goals in 394 League outings before moving to Norwich City for £600,000 in July 1991, a year after his benefit match against Aston Villa. He helped to reach the FA Cup semi-finals in 1991/92, then gained UEFA Cup experience in 1993/94.

Alan Nicholls

Tall, young central defender Alan Nicholls was at Ashton Gate while Bristol City plummeted from the First Division to Fourth in successive years. An England Youth trialist, he signed professional from apprentice on his 17th birthday in February 1980 and Bob Houghton gave him his League debut at home to Sheffield Wednesday a year later. Also featuring in the 1980/81 FA Cup fifth round tie at Nottingham Forest when he marked England star Trevor Francis. He succeeded Julian Marshall in the heart of City's defence and scored five goals in 70 League outings before he suffered a very badly broken right leg during a reserve game at Backwell in August 1983. He failed to recover full fitness and announced his retirement from League football 18 months later.

Ron Nicholls

Footballing-cricketer Ron Nicholls contested the goalkeeping slot with long-serving Tony Cook whilst at Bristol City. An ex-Fulham amateur, he signed professional for Bristol Rovers in November 1954 and shared goalkeeping duties with Howard Radford – helping to beat Manchester United's 'Busby's Babes' 4-0 in the 1955/56 FA Cup

third round tie at Eastville. Moving to Cardiff City for £10,000 in August 1958, he helped to regain top-flight status in 1959/60 and was reunited with Fred Ford at Ashton Gate in July 1961. He made 39 Third Division appearances before briefly following Bobby Etheridge to Cheltenham Town in July 1965. An opening batsman for Gloucestershire, he played 534 matches during his 24 year county career. He died in July 1994.

Jock Nicholson

Long-serving Scottish left-half Jock Nicholson succeeded Billy Wedlock as Bristol City's captain and featured prominently in the 1919/20 FA Cup run and 1920/21 promotion challenge. He impressed with Glasgow Ashfield before Sam Hollis signed him in July 1911 and he made his League debut at home to Fulham in the opening game of City's 1911/12 campaign. Awarded two benefit matches while at Ashton Gate, he scored four goals in 197 Second Division outings prior to joining Glasgow Rangers in July 1921. He moved to St. Johnstone a year later, then coached Swiss club Etoile-Carouse for two seasons prior to rejoining City as trainer for six years in 1925. Subsequently holding a similar post at Manchester United, he then coached in Sweden and settled locally. He died in Weston-super-Mare in June 1970.

Kevin Nugent

Tall ex-Eire Youth international striker Kevin Nugent featured in Bristol City's 1996/97 promotion challenge. A former Leyton Orient trainee, he signed professional under Frank Clark in July 1987 and played on loan for Cork City in the 1989 FAI Cup final. Leading marksman in 1991/92, he moved to Peter Shilton's Plymouth Argyle for a record £200,000 in March 1992 and starred as they reached the Second Division play-offs in 1993/94. Unable to prevent relegation the following season, Joe Jordan signed him in exchange for Ian Baird plus £75,000 in September 1995 and he scored 14 goals in 70 Second Division outings for Bristol City prior to joining Cardiff City for £65,000 in July 1997.

Paddy O'Brien

Tricky little inside-left Paddy O'Brien scored both goals as Bristol City defeated Blackpool 2-0 in their first Football League game in September 1901. He developed in Glasgow junior soccer with Elm Park and Glasgow Northern before joining Woolwich Arsenal in July 1893 and quickly impressed alongside Jock Russell with his consistent displays. One of four players who followed Sam Hollis to Bristol City in July 1897, he scored 44 goals in 106 League outings before moving to Swindon Town in July 1902. He subsequently ran a newsagents in Bedminster, then was landlord of the 'Avon Packet' pub and remained local until his death in October 1950.

Russell Osman

As Bristol City's player-manager, stylish former England central defender Russell Osman plotted the FA Cup third round replay defeat of Liverpool in 1993/94. The son of an ex-Derby County player, he signed professional from apprentice for Ipswich Town in March 1976 and was twice ever-present including the 1980/81 UEFA Cup success. Capped 11 times by Bobby Robson, he joined Leicester City for £240,000 in July 1985, then moved to Southampton in June 1988. Jimmy Lumsden paid £60,000 for him in October 1991 and he helped to beat Wimbledon in the FA Cup third round replay three months later. He succeeded Denis Smith in charge in March 1993 and scored three times in 70 League games before his dismissal in November 1994. After spells at Plymouth Argyle, Sudbury Town and Brighton he is now Cardiff City's player-manager.

Gordon Owen

Much-travelled right-winger Gordon Owen played for Bristol City in the 1987 Freight Rover Trophy Final at Wembley. A former Sheffield Wednesday junior, he signed professional in November 1976 and featured in the 1979/80 promotion success under Jack Charlton. Following loan spells at Rotherham United, Doncaster Rovers and Chesterfield, he moved to Cardiff City on a free transfer in August 1983 and joined Barnsley for £27,000 a year later. Terry Cooper paid £30,000 for him in August 1986 and he netted 11 goals in 52 Third Division outings before moving to Freight Rover Trophy holders Mansfield Town for £35,000 in January 1988 after a loan period at Hull City. Sold to Blackpool for £15,000 in July 1989, he was loaned to Carlisle United and Cooper's Exeter City before joining Frickley Athletic and now lives in Cudworth.

Gary Owers

Versatile midfielder Gary Owers was ever-present as Bristol City reached the Second Division play-offs in 1996/97. An ex-Sunderland apprentice, he signed professional in October 1986 and starred in Sunderland's 1987/88 Third Division title success under Denis Smith. He helped to beat rivals Newcastle United in the 1990 Second Division play-offs and appeared at Wembley when Sunderland were promoted after Swindon Town were punished for financial irregularities. Ever-present in the top-flight in 1990/91, he returned to Wembley as right-back in the 1992 FA Cup Final and Joe Jordan signed him as part of the £450,000 exchange deal that took Martin Scott to Roker Park in December 1994. Married to former British ice-skating champion Joanne Conway, he has now scored eight goals in 104 League outings for Bristol City.

Ginger Owers

Once selected as a reserve for England, centre-forward Ginger Owers was leading marksman in both spells with Bristol City. Real name Ebenezer, he played for Leyton and Blackpool prior to joining West Brom in November 1907. Moving to Chesterfield in January 1909, he had a season with Darlington before Harry Thickett signed him in July 1910 and was top scorer in 1910/11. He rejoined Darlington in July 1911, then returned to Ashton Gate a year later and topped City's goal charts again in 1912/13 with 32 goals in 62 League games overall before joining Clyde in March 1913. He had a period with Celtic prior to serving in the Sportsmans Battalion and a war wound ended his playing career.

Joe Palmer

Noted for his strict discipline, Joe Palmer managed Bristol City to the FA Cup semi-final in 1919/20. A former Army sergeant-major, he had been City's trainer before the Great War and took charge at Ashton Gate in August 1919. He also plotted City's 1920/21 promotion challenge but fortunes dipped the following season and he resigned after disagreements with the directors as City faced relegation. After three years as Bradford PA's trainer he was appointed Bristol Rovers' manager in May 1926 but had little success during three years in charge at Eastville.

Jack Parker

Centre-half Jack Parker replaced Allan Sliman in the heart of Bristol City's defence following relegation in 1932. He impressed with Morton before joining Manchester United in July 1930 where he gained top-flight experience. Bob Hewison paid £150 for him in May 1932 and his sole goal in 54 Third Division (South) games came in the 2-4 defeat at Gillingham in November 1932. Moving to struggling Carlisle United in July 1934, he joined Stalybridge Celtic a year later and settled in Manchester until his death in November 1964.

Gordon Parr

Uncompromising defender Gordon Parr gave Bristol City marvellous service over 15 years at Ashton Gate. Born locally, he captained Bristol Boys and was an England Schools trialist. He signed professional for City in February 1957 and Pat Beasley gave him his League debut at home to Middlesbrough ten months later but he did not secure a regular first team slot

● Kevin Nugent

● Russell Osman

● Gary Owers

● Gordon Parr

● Ernie Peacock

● John Pender

until 1962/63. Featuring in City's 1964/65 promotion campaign, he helped to reach the FA Cup fifth round in two consecutive seasons and the League Cup semi-finals in 1970/71. He was ever-present in 1968/69, scoring four goals in 287 League games before joining Irish League Champions Waterford on a free transfer in July 1972 and playing in the European Cup. Subsequently with Minehead, he still lives in Abbots Leigh and is a self-employed electrician.

Johnny Paul
Long-serving Scottish inside-right Johnny Paul featured in Bristol City's 1922/23 and 1926/27 Third Division (South) title campaigns. Initially with Torpedo Athletic, he had four seasons with Port Glasgow before Alex Raisbeck signed him in August 1922. He made his League debut in the 3-0 win at Southend United two months later and partnered the likes of Albert Fairclough, Tot Walsh and Albert Keating in City's attack, scoring 49 goals in 206 League outings prior to joining Taunton Town in November 1930. A serious knee injury ended his playing career soon after and he became a leading bowls player. Subsequently landlord of the 'Coopers Arms' pub in Ashton Gate, then the 'Angel Inn' in Taunton, he died in January 1979.

Ernie Peacock
Long-serving, fiery, red-haired right-half Ernie Peacock was a popular member of Bristol City's 1954/55 Third Division (South) championship side. Born locally, 'Ginger' represented Barleyfields School and played for Syston, Notts County and as a guest for Bath City before Bob Hewison signed him in October 1946. Ever-present in 1952/53, he switched to centre-half for a period after Dennis Roberts' retirement and his tireless displays were a key factor as City reached the FA Cup fifth round in two consecutive years. He scored seven goals in 343 League outings before joining Weymouth in June 1959, then became Taunton Town player-manager. Subsequently a car salesman, heart trouble led to his premature death at Bristol General Hospital in February 1973.

Jim Pearce
Former Welsh Amateur international centre-half Jim Pearce was a key figure as Bristol City narrowly missed promotion in 1937/38. He impressed with Chirk and represented the Royal Tank Corps before Bob Hewison signed him in August 1934. Making his League debut at home to Reading a month later, he featured prominently as City took Preston NE to an FA Cup fifth round replay in 1934/35. He scored twice in 148 Third Division (South) games before joining Rochdale in May 1939 and represented the British Army during wartime service in Greece and the Middle East.

John Pender
Former Eire U-21 central defender John Pender was a key figure as Bristol City were Littlewoods Cup semi-finalists in 1988/89. An ex-Wolves apprentice, he signed professional in November 1981 and helped to regain top-flight status at the first attempt in 1982/83. He joined Charlton Athletic in July 1985, featuring prominently in the 1985/86 promotion triumph and Terry Cooper paid £55,000 for him in October 1987 to replace David Moyes. Sent off on his City debut, he helped to reach the promotion play-offs in 1987/88 and clinch a Second Division return in 1989/90 – netting three goals in 83 Third Division outings before moving to Burnley for £70,000 in September 1990. Starring in the 1991/92 and 1993/94 promotion successes, he joined Wigan Athletic for £30,000 in August 1995 and helped to win the Third Division title in 1996/97 before moving to Rochdale for £11,500 in July 1997.

Glenn Pennyfather
Experienced, versatile midfielder Glenn Pennyfather featured in Bristol City's 1993/94 FA Cup run. A former Southend United apprentice, he made his first-team debut before signing professional in February 1981 and was a key figure in the 1986/87 promotion success. Sold to Crystal Palace for a record £150,000 in November 1987, he helped to win promotion via the play-offs in 1988/89 and moved to Ipswich Town in October 1989. Featuring in the 1991/92 Second Division title campaign, Russell

Osman paid £80,000 for him in March 1993 after a loan spell and his sole goal in 26 First Division outings clinched a 2-1 home win over Watford that month. Released in May 1994, he has since played for Colchester United, Stevenage Borough and Canvey Island.

Frank Peters
Outside-right Frank Peters created numerous goalscoring chances for the likes of Jack Haycox and Alfie Rowles while at Bristol City. Initially with Wellington St. George, he was briefly with Coventry City but failed to secure a first-team slot at Highfield Road and moved to Charlton Athletic in July 1930. Following a spell with Fulham, he joined Swindon Town in July 1933 and was a regular goalscorer before Bob Hewison signed him in May 1936. He scored 22 goals in 113 Third Division (South) outings prior to the outbreak of World War Two.

Lou Peters
Speedy ex-England Youth winger Lou Peters was an influential member of Bristol City's 1964/65 promotion-winning side. Real name Roger, he signed professional from apprentice in March 1961 and Fred Ford gave him his League debut at home to Brentford a month later. Creating numerous goalscoring opportunities for the likes of John Atyeo, Brian Clark and Terry Bush, he also starred in City's 1965/66 promotion challenge and successive FA Cup runs. He was leading scorer in 1966/67, netting 25 goals in 158 League games before joining Bournemouth for £5,000 in June 1968 and subsequently playing for Bath City under Arnold Rodgers. Currently living in Weston-in-Gordano, he has spent over 25 years with Sun Life of Canada and is now a Senior Consultant back in Bristol after a spell in Plymouth.

Player of the Year
A table listing Bristol City's 'Player of the Year' since the award was instigated in 1970/71 can be found at the end of this A to Z.

Forbes Phillipson-Masters
Whole-hearted central defender Forbes Phillipson-Masters made a significant contribution to Bristol

City's 1983/84 promotion success. Starting as a Southampton apprentice goalkeeper, he switched to central defence and signed professional in June 1974. He featured in the 1977/78 promotion campaign with Steve Neville and after loan spells at Exeter City, AFC Bournemouth and Luton Town, he joined Plymouth Argyle for £50,000 in August 1979. Terry Cooper signed him, initially on loan, in November 1982 and he partnered Alan Nicholls, then Bruce Halliday in the heart of defence. Scoring four goals in 94 League outings, he had another loan spell at Exeter before moving to Gerry Gow's Yeovil Town in August 1985 and later Weston-Super-Mare (Player/Coach) and Poole Town. Now living in Verwood, he is a self-employed builder and decorator.

Jon Picken
Scottish inside-left Jon Picken featured prominently in Bristol City's attack immediately prior to the Great War. Initially with Kilmarnock Shawbank, he joined Bolton Wanderers with Willie Brown in July 1899 and featured in their 1899/1900 promotion campaign. Ever-present in 1900/01, he was reunited with Bob Jack at Plymouth Argyle as they entered the Southern League in 1903 and was top scorer in two consecutive seasons. He moved to Manchester United in June 1905 and was top scorer as they won promotion with Bristol City in 1905/06. Also helping United to win the League Championship in 1907/08 and 1910/11, he moved to Burnley in December 1911 and Sam Hollis signed him in October 1913 as a replacement for Steve Bowyer. He netted 13 goals in 51 Second Division outings for City before retiring and died in Plymouth in July 1952.

Billy Pocock
Fast, skilful outside-left Billy Pocock was an important figure as Bristol City reached the FA Cup semi-finals in 1919/20 and regained Second Division status at the first attempt in 1922/23. Born locally, he impressed with Bedminster St. Francis and in Army soccer before Joe Palmer signed him in August 1919. He made his League debut in City's opening game of the

1919/20 campaign at home to Bury and created numerous goalscoring chances for the likes of Jonah Wilcox, Albert Fairclough and Tot Walsh, scoring 46 times in 236 League outings prior to joining St. Johnstone in July 1926. Subsequently head groundsman at Bedminster Down Sports Ground, he remained local until his death in February 1959.

Howard Pritchard
Welsh international winger Howard Pritchard was ever-present in Bristol City's 1983/84 promotion campaign. Capped at Youth level, he signed professional from apprentice under Alan Dicks in August 1976 and made his League debut at home to Aston Villa two years later. Allowed to join Swindon Town on a free transfer in August 1981, Terry Cooper re-signed him in August 1983 and he scored in the 1986 Freight Rover Trophy Final success at Wembley – netting 24 goals in 57 League games overall, prior to joining Gillingham for £22,500 in August 1986. Ever-present in 1986/87, he moved to Walsall for £20,000 in July 1988, then played for Maidstone United, Yeovil Town, Yate Town and Nailsea Town. He is now a driver for Frenchay Health Authority and runs his own driving school in Backwell.

Promotion Winners
Photography of the eight promotion-winning teams can be found in the colour section of this book.

John Quigley
Skilful, tenacious Scottish inside-left John Quigley was a popular figure as Bristol City reached the FA Cup fifth round in two successive years during the mid-1960's. Initially with Celtic, he joined Nottingham Forest from Ashfield Juniors in July 1957 and helped to win the FA Cup in 1959 after scoring the semi-final winner against Aston Villa. Moving to Huddersfield Town in February 1965, Fred

Ford swapped Brian Clark for him in October 1966 and he became captain at Ashton Gate. Netting seven goals in 66 Second Division games before surprisingly sold to Mansfield Town for £3,000 in July 1968, he skippered the 1968/69 FA Cup run side and became assistant-manager for a year in November 1970. Subsequently coaching at Doncaster Rovers and in the Middle East, he is now living back in Nottingham.

Alex Raisbeck
Former Scottish international centre-half Alex Raisbeck managed Bristol City to the Third Division (South) title in 1922/23 and 1926/27. One of seven brothers, he impressed with Larkhall Thistle, Royal Albert and Hibernian prior to joining Stoke in March 1898. Moving to Liverpool for £350 in May l898, he starred in the League Championship triumphs of 1900/01 and 1905/06 and returned to Scotland with Partick Thistle for £500 in July 1909. Appointed Hamilton Academical's secretary-manager in April 1914, he became a director before taking charge of struggling Bristol City in December 1921. Resigning in July 1929, he later managed Halifax Town (1932/33 FA Cup run), Chester and Bath City, then scouted for Liverpool until his death in March 1949.

Arthur Rankin
Scottish outside-left Arthur Rankin made a significant contribution as Bristol City won the Third Division (South) title in 1926/27. He impressed with Dykehead before Alex Raisbeck signed him in August 1926 and made his League debut at Gillingham in the opening game of City's promotion campaign. Creating numerous goalscoring chances for the prolific forward partnership of Tot Walsh and Albert Keating, he netted 12 goals in 70 League outings before joining Charlton Athletic in July 1928

● Lou Peters

● Howard Pritchard

● Alex Raisbeck

● David Rennie

● Glyn Riley

● Tom Ritchie

and starred in their 1928/29 Third Division (South) title campaign. Following a brief spell with Exeter City, he joined Yeovil & Petters in July 1930 and was later landlord of the 'Heart of Oak' and 'Albion Inn' pubs in Yeovil. He resided in Yeovil until his death in November 1962.

Dickie Reader

Outside-right Dickie Reader was a prominent figure as Bristol City reached the FA Cup semi-finals in 1919/20. Initially with Ripley Athletic, he sampled First Division soccer with Derby County before George Hedley signed him in June 1914. He featured in wartime competition for City and supplied the ammunition for leading marksman Tommy Howarth, netting four goals in 52 Second Division outings prior to joining Luton Town on a free transfer in June 1922. He subsequently emigrated to the United States where he worked as an insurance salesman in Methuen, Massachusetts.

Doug Regan

Experienced outside-left Doug Regan created numerous goalscoring chances for the likes of Arnold Rodgers, John Atyeo and Jimmy Rogers while at Ashton Gate. He represented the Fleet Air Arm before joining Exeter City in March 1945 and was twice top scorer, helping to reach the FA Cup fourth round in two successive years. Pat Beasley signed him in December 1952 and he contested the left-wing slot with Jack Boxley as City swept to the Third Division (South) title in 1954/55, netting 11 goals in 36 League outings before reunited with Arthur Coles at Weymouth in July 1956. He helped to beat Shrewsbury Town in the 1956/57 FA Cup run, then joined Bridgwater Town and worked for Westland in his native Yeovil until retiring in November 1985.

Jimmy Regan

Dependable right-half Jimmy Regan featured prominently in Bristol City's 1954/55 Third Division (South) title campaign. Initially with Moorthorpe Colliery, he moved to Rotherham United in August 1949 and gained Second Division experience under ex-Bristol City star Andy Smailes

before Pat Beasley signed him in June 1953. Partnering Ernie Peacock and Jack White at Ashton Gate, he made 51 League appearances prior to joining Coventry City in March 1956. Followed to Highfield Road by Jack Boxley and Jimmy Rogers nine months later, he joined Yeovil Town in July 1957, he then played for Burton Albion. He subsequently settled back in South Elmsall and was a miner at Moorthorpe Colliery until his sudden death from a cerebral haemorrhage in April 1976.

David Rennie

Versatile ex-Scottish Youth midfielder David Rennie was a key figure in Bristol City's 1989/90 promotion triumph and FA Cup run. A former Leicester City apprentice, he signed professional as a central defender in May 1982 and joined Leeds United in January 1986. Scoring in the 1987 FA Cup semifinal. Joe Jordan paid £175,000 for him in July 1989 and he helped to beat Wimbledon in the 1991/92 FA Cup replay. He netted eight goals in 104 League outings before following Louie Donowa and Paul Mardon to Terry Cooper's Birmingham City for £120,000 in February 1992 and made a significant contribution as they clinched promotion that season. Swapped for Coventry City's David Smith in March 1993, he gained Premiership experience prior to joining Northampton Town in July 1996 and starred in their 1996/97 promotion success.

Glyn Riley

Popular striker Glyn Riley was twice top scorer at Bristol City including the 1983/84 promotion campaign. He signed professional from apprentice for Barnsley in July 1976 and starred in the rise from Fourth Division to Second as well as successive Cup runs under Norman Hunter. Following a loan spell at Doncaster Rovers, Terry Cooper signed him on a free transfer in August 1982 and he was 'Player of the Year' in 1982/83. Forming a prolific goal scoring partnership with Alan Walsh, he scored twice at Wembley in City's 1986 Freight Rover Trophy Final triumph and grabbed the equaliser in the 1987 final. He netted 61 goals in 199

League outings before joining Aldershot for £15,000 in October 1987 after being loaned to Torquay United, then helped Bath City to regain Conference status in 1989/90.

Joe Riley

Centre-forward Joe Riley was leading marksman in 1933/34 as Bristol City won the Welsh Cup for the first time, scoring twice in the final replay triumph over Tranmere Rovers. Initially with Denaby United, he moved via Goldthorpe United to Bristol Rovers in May 1931 and was their first player to score a hat-trick on his debut. Overshadowed by England internationals Tommy Cook and Viv Gibbins at Eastville, he was signed by Bob Hewison in May 1933 and scored all five goals in City's 5-0 win over Brighton in February 1934. Netting 21 goals in 59 Third Division (South) games overall, he moved to Bournemouth in May 1935 and was top scorer in two successive years then joined Notts County in exchange for Harry Mardon in December 1937. Subsequently a Bristol City scout, he recommended Dennis Roberts to the club.

Willis Rippon

Centre-forward Willis Rippon made a significant contribution as Bristol City were FA Cup finalists in 1908/09 with two vital penalties against Derby County in the semifinal, but he missed the final at the Crystal Palace against Manchester United with a knee injury. He developed with Heckenthorpe, Rawmarsh Albion, Sandhill Rovers and Kilnhurst Town before Harry Thickett signed him in July 1907. Given his League debut at home to Manchester City three months later, he netted 13 goals in 36 First Division games prior to joining Arsenal in July 1910. Moving to Brentford in October 1911, he joined Grimsby Town via Hamilton Academicals in October 1913 (where his younger brother Tom also played) and later Rotherham Town. He died in 1956.

Tom Ritchie

Versatile, lanky Scottish striker Tom Ritchie was Bristol City's leading goalscorer in five successive years including the 1975/76 promotion campaign when he was ever-present. Snapped up from Bridgend Thistle in July 1969, Alan Dicks gave him his League debut at home to Millwall in August 1972 and his younger brother Steve briefly followed him into City's first team. Featuring prominently in the 1973/74 FA Cup run and 1977/78 Anglo-Scottish Cup win, he joined Sunderland for £180,000 in January 1981. Loaned to promotion-winning Carlisle United during 1981/82, Terry Cooper re-signed him on a free transfer in June 1982 and he skippered the 1983/84 promotion success – netting 102 goals in 414 League games overall before moving to Gerry Gow's Yeovil Town in December 1984. He is now a postman living in Clevedon.

Bill Roberts
Tough-tackling Welsh right-back Bill Roberts was an influential figure as Bristol City won the Welsh Cup in 1933/34. After impressing in Army football, he had a spell with Spurs before Bob Hewison signed him in September 1933 and made his League debut at home to Aldershot that month. He starred alongside Cyril Bridge as City took Preston NE to an FA Cup fifth round replay in 1934/35, netting seven goals in 136 League outings before following Ernie Brinton to Newport County in July 1938. An important figure in their 1938/39 Third Division (South) title success, he was captured by the Germans in France during the war. He subsequently ran the 'Elm Tree' pub in Bishopsworth then worked for the Customs & Excise and remained local until his death in February 1976.

Dennis Roberts
Commanding centre-half Dennis Roberts gave Bristol City outstanding service during 16 years at Ashton Gate. Initially a Huddersfield Town amateur, he joined Notts County in August 1937 and Bob Hewison signed him on a free transfer a year later. Given his League debut at Clapton Orient in September 1938, he succeeded Joe Pearce in central defence and became captain. Twice ever-present, he starred in the 1950/51 FA Cup run and scored two goals in 303 Third Division (South) games (with a further 205 war-time appearances) before leaving in May 1954. He was subsequently mine host at the 'Avon Packet' and the 'Ship Inn' at Cathay, then a forklift driver at GKN Bedminster until retirement in February 1983. On the death of his wife, he moved back to Emley.

Liam Robinson
Striker Liam Robinson made a significant contribution as Bristol City beat Liverpool in the 1993/94 FA Cup third round replay. A former Nottingham Forest apprentice, he joined Huddersfield Town in January 1984 and was top scorer for their reserves. After a loan spell at Tranmere Rovers, he moved to Bury for a tribunal fee in July 1986 and finished leading marksman in three successive seasons including 1989/90 when they reached the Third Division promotion play-offs. Russell Osman paid £130,000 for him in July 1993 and he scored four times in 41 First Division outings alongside Wayne Allison prior to joining newly-promoted Burnley for a record £250,000 in July 1994, moving to Scarborough on a free transfer in July 1997.

Arnold Rodgers
Prolific goalscoring centre-forward Arnold Rodgers was Bristol City's leading marksman in four consecutive seasons and featured prominently in the 1954/55 Third Division (South) title campaign. Initially a left-half with Wickersley, he moved to Huddersfield Town in March 1942 and gained top-flight experience before Bob Wright paid £4,450 for him in October 1949. Starring in the 1950/51 FA Cup run and successive promotion challenges, he partnered the likes of John Atyeo, Jimmy Rogers and Alec Eisentrager in City's attack and netted 106 goals in 195 League outings prior to briefly joining Shrewsbury Town in June 1956. He later had managerial success at Welton Rovers and Bath City while running his own florists business in North View for 37 years until a fatal heart attack in October 1993.

David Rodgers
Ex-England Schoolboy central defender David Rodgers gave Bristol City loyal service over 13 years at Ashton Gate. Born locally, the son of Arnold Rodgers, he signed professional under Alan Dicks in July 1969 and scored on his first-team debut in the League Cup replay win over Leicester City in November 1970. Partnering Geoff Merrick in central defence, he featured in the 1973/74 FA Cup run and regained his place from Gary Collier in the First Division. He netted 15 goals in 192 League outings before the 'Ashton Gate Eight' crisis forced his release in February 1982, then played for Torquay United, Lincoln City and Forest Green Rovers. Briefly groundsman at Bristol Grammar School, since January 1985 he has worked at Clifton College and is now General Manager (Services).

Jimmy Rogers
Brave, flying winger Jimmy Rogers was a popular figure as Bristol City won the Third Division (South) title in 1954/55. Joining Wolves from Rubery Owen FC in May 1948, he represented the combined services and Bob Wright signed him on a free transfer in May 1950. Forming a thrilling partnership with John Atyeo, he moved to Coventry City with Jack Boxley in December 1956 and featured in the 1958/59 promotion campaign before Peter Doherty re-signed him for £3,000 in December 1958. He scored 102 goals in 270 League games overall prior to his appointment as Cinderford Town player-manager in July 1962, then ran his own company First Bristol Finance. After a heart-attack in 1976, he set up KGC Panels and was chairman of the trustees of Westbury Wildlife Park until his death in December 1996.

Lee Rogers
Young central defender Lee Rogers was an emerging member of Bristol City's squad during the mid-1980's. Born locally, he was an Associate Schoolboy with Manchester United before signing professional from apprentice under Terry Cooper in December 1984. Given his League debut at

● Dennis Roberts

● David Rodgers

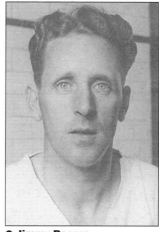
● Jimmy Rogers

● Dickie Rooks

● Leroy Rosenior

● Jock Russell

home to Wigan Athletic in August 1984, a broken leg in January 1986 was a severe set-back to his progress and he struggled to recapture his form. He made 30 Third Division appearances prior to loan spells at Hereford United and York City, then followed Cooper to Exeter City on a free transfer in June 1988. Featuring in the 1989/90 Fourth Division title success, he joined Gloucester City in July 1991 and Weston-Super-Mare a year later where he now partners Andy Llewellyn in defence.

Dickie Rooks

Centre-half Dickie Rooks was an experienced figure as Bristol City reached the League Cup semi-finals in 1970/71. A former Sunderland junior, he signed professional in June 1957 and sampled top-flight soccer as Charlie Hurley's understudy before moving to Middlesbrough for £20,000 in August 1965 and helping to regain Second Division status at the first attempt in 1966/67. Alan Dicks paid £17,000 for him in June 1969 and he scored four times in 96 Second Division outings prior to joining Willington as player-coach in July 1972. Subsequently managing Scunthorpe United for 14 months until sacked in January 1976, he then coached Zanzibar and was an FA Coach for Tyne and Wear linked with Sunderland's School of Excellence. He is now a self-employed builder in his native Sunderland.

Leroy Rosenior

Ex-England Youth striker Leroy Rosenior helped Bristol City to beat Liverpool in the 1993/94 FA Cup third round replay. Born in Clapton, of parents from Sierra Leone, his full name is Leroy De Graft Rosenior. He signed professional for Fulham in August 1982 and moved to QPR for £100,000 in September 1985, appearing as substitute in the 1986 Milk Cup Final. Returning to Fulham in June 1987 in an exchange deal involving Paul Parker and Dean Coney, he joined West Ham in March 1988 to replace Frank McAvennie. Denis Smith signed him in March 1992 after loan spells with Fulham and Charlton Athletic. Partnering the likes of Andy Cole and Wayne

Allison in attack, he became player-coach and scored 12 times in 51 league games until released in May 1995. After a spell at Fleet Town, he has been Gloucester City's player-manager since March 1996 with a benefit match in May 1997.

Alfie Rowles

Free-scoring centre-forward Alfie Rowles was leading marksman as Bristol City were Third Division (South) runners-up in 1937/38. Born locally, he impressed with St. Pancras and Weston-super-Mare before City's scout Sam Poople brought him to Ashton Gate for a trial. Netting a hat-trick on his League debut against Exeter City in January 1938, he set a Football League record by scoring in each of his first six games but a knee injury sustained against Notts County in September 1938 effectively ended his playing career and he retired after scoring 20 goals in 24 League outings. He returned to his trade as a fitter with Harry Dolman's firm, also acting as trainer to City's junior team for six seasons. Still living locally, he attended Bristol City's Centenary Reunion Dinner in March 1997.

Joe Royle

Former England striker Joe Royle starred as Bristol City consolidated top-flight status under Alan Dicks. He became Everton's youngest debutant seven months before signing professional in August 1966 and was an FA Cup finalist in 1968. Ever-present and top scorer in the 1969/70 League Championship success, he joined Man-chester City for £200,000 in December 1974 and was a League Cup winner in 1976. Dicks paid £90,000 for him in November 1977 and he netted four goals on his debut at home to Middlesbrough, scoring 18 times in 101 First Division games prior to joining Norwich City for £60,000 in August 1980. Appointed manager of Oldham Athletic July 1982, he plotted promotion and Cup success before rejoining Everton as manager in November 1994 and guiding them to FA Cup final glory in 1995. He resigned in March 1997.

Tommy Rudkin

Experienced outside-left Tommy Rudkin, created numerous goalscoring chances for the likes of

Arnold Rodgers and Alec Eisentrager while at Ashton Gate. A former Wolves amateur, he joined Lincoln City in May 1938 and guested for Darlington, Hartlepool United, Middles-brough and Southampton during the war. Following a spell with Peterborough United, he joined Arsenal in January 1947 and sampled top-flight soccer prior to joining Southampton with George Curtis as part of the Don Roper exchange deal in August 1947. Bob Wright signed him in May 1949 and he netted four goals in 34 Third Division (South) games before moving to Southern League strugglers Hastings United in June 1951. He was subsequently player-manager of Weston-super-Mare, then settled in his native Peterborough.

Jock Russell

Diminutive Scottish outside-left Jock Russell was an important figure during Bristol City's Southern League era. Real name John, he developed with Glasgow Thistle and Leith Athletic and had two seasons with St. Mirren prior to joining Woolwich Arsenal in June 1896 where he partnered Paddy O'Brien. The pair followed Sam Hollis to Bristol City as they turned professional and entered the Southern League in 1897, with Russell ever-present in 1897/98 as City were Southern League runners-up and won the Western League title. He netted 30 goals in 92 League outings prior to joining Blackburn Rovers in July 1900 and tragically died in Glasgow in August 1905.

Charlie Sargeant

Speedy outside-left Charlie Sargeant was leading marksman during Bristol City's 1931/32 relegation campaign. He impressed with Cornsay Park Albion, Esh Winning Juniors, Washington Colliery, Bishop Auckland and White-le-Head Rangers before joining Norwich City in March 1930. Joe Bradshaw paid £100 for him in

June 1931 and he netted ten goals in 27 Second Division outings before the club's poor financial position forced his sale to Hull City in May 1932. A key figure in their 1932/33 Third Division (North) title success, he moved to Chester in March 1934 and was twice a Welsh Cup finalist, then played for Stockport County, Plymouth Argyle, Blackhall CW and Cornsay Park Albion again. He resided in his native North-East until his death in September 1988.

Ray Savino

Diminutive outside-right Ray Savino featured prominently in Bristol City's 1964/65 promotion success. Initially with Thorpe Village, he signed professional for Norwich City in February 1957 after national service and featured in the 1959/60 promotion success, also helping to reach the League Cup Final in 1961/62. Fred Ford brought him and Derrick Lythgoe to Ashton Gate in July 1962 and he set up numerous goalscoring opportunities for the likes of John Atyeo and Brian Clark, netting twice in 75 League outings before joining King's Lynn in March 1968. Reunited with Lythgoe at Lowestoft Town in July 1970, he helped to retain the Eastern Counties League title in 1970/71, then played for Wisbech Town, Great Yarmouth and St. Andrews OB (P/M). He still lives in his native Norwich and is now a bricklayer.

Ken Scattergood

Goalkeeper Ken Scattergood made an important contribution as Bristol City won the Welsh Cup in 1933/34. The son of ex-England keeper Ernie Scattergood, he joined Wolves from Cresswell in November 1931 but failed to make an impact at Molineux or at Sheffield Wednesday from where Bob Hewison signed him in August 1933. He made his League debut at Norwich City in September 1933 and made 39 Third Division (South) appearances before being sold to Stoke City for £500 in May 1934. Gaining First Division experience before joining Derby County in July 1935, he had the traumatic experience of conceding seven goals on his Christmas Day debut at Everton.

Martin Scott

Versatile left-back Martin Scott was ever-present and 'Player of the Year' as Bristol City reached the FA Cup fifth round in 1991/92. He made his League debut for Rotherham United eight months before signing professional from apprentice in January 1986 and helped to clinch the Fourth Division title in 1988/89, becoming Rotherham's most expensive sale when Jimmy Lumsden paid £200,000 for him in December 1990. Also featuring prominently as City beat Liverpool in the 1993/94 FA Cup third round replay, he netted 14 goals in 171 League outings prior to joining Sunderland in a £450,000 exchange deal involving Gary Owers in December 1994. He starred in their 1995/96 First Division title success under Peter Reid.

Tommy Scott

Much-travelled inside-right Tommy Scott helped Bristol City to narrowly avoid relegation in two successive seasons. He developed with Pandon Temperance in his native North-East before joining Sunderland in December 1922 where he featured in their 1923/24 League Championship challenge. Moving to Darlington in June 1924, he was a member of their Third Division (North) championship squad in 1924/25 and joined Liverpool in December 1925. Alex Raisbeck signed him in October 1928 and he scored six goals in 35 Second Division outings before moving to Preston NE in June 1930, then Norwich City two years later where he starred in their 1933/34 Third Division (South) title triumph. He subsequently played for Exeter City, Hartlepool United and Bangor City, then was a Liverpool publican and died on Christmas Eve, 1979.

Aubrey Scriven

Experienced outside-left Aubrey Scriven scored in Bristol City's Welsh Cup final replay triumph over Tranmere Rovers in 1933/34. He developed in non-League soccer with Highley, Denaby United and Darnley United prior to joining Birmingham in December 1923

where he scored regularly in the First Division. Sold to Bradford City for £400 in May 1927 he starred in their 1928/29 Third Division (North) title success and Bob Hewison paid £250 for him in May 1932. Also scoring the goal that took Derby County to an FA Cup third round replay in 1933/34, he netted 12 goals in 54 Third Division (South) games prior to joining Worcester City in July 1934. He subsequently played for Brierley Hill Alliance and became a Birmingham publican.

David Seal

Australian international striker David Seal was Bristol City's joint top goalscorer with fellow Aussie Paul Agostino in 1995/96. He developed with Sydney Olympic, Sydney Croatia and Marconi in Australia, also representing his country at youth level as they reached the Youth World Cup semi-finals in 1991 and in the Olympic Games. Moving to Belgian side Aalst, he attracted the attention of several English clubs with his prolific goalscoring and had a trial with West Ham. He made a dramatic impact on trial at Bristol City, netting six goals in his first two reserve team appearances and Russell Osman paid £80,000 for him in October 1994. Making his League debut at home to Millwall that month, he scored 10 goals in 51 League outings for City before joining Northampton Town in June 1997.

Mark Shail

Central defender Mark Shail skippered Bristol City to victory over Liverpool in the 1993/94 FA Cup third round replay. Born in Sweden of English parents, he moved to England at the age of four and joined Worcester City from school. Continuing his studies, he gained a degree in Psychology and Sociology at Surrey University after moving to Yeovil Town for £5,000 in March 1989. Ever-present as Yeovil won the Bob Lord Trophy in 1989/90, their last season at The Huish, he was also a key figure as they beat Torquay United and Hereford United en route to an FA Cup third round clash with Arsenal in 1992/93. Russell Osman paid £45,000 for him in March 1993

● Martin Scott

● David Seal

● Mark Shail

● Gerry Sharpe

● Gary Shelton

● Carl Shutt

and he has now scored four times in 101 League games recovering from a cruciate ligament injury to feature in City's 1996/97 promotion challenge.

Arthur Sharp

Much-travelled inside-right Arthur Sharp partnered Ted Bowen in Bristol City's attack. Born in Nottingham, he was a prolific goalscorer in local soccer and had spells with Notts County and Loughborough Corinthians prior to joining Midland League champions Mansfield Town in February 1926 and helped to win the Notts Senior Cup in successive years. Moving to Blackpool in July 1927, he joined Reading in May 1928 and was briefly with West Ham and Newark Town before moving to Carlisle United in May 1930. Bob Hewison signed him in June 1932 and he scored nine goals in 28 Third Division (South) outings before joining Aldershot in May 1933. He subsequently played for Oldham Athletic, Shrewsbury Town (twice) and Darlington.

Gerry Sharpe

Young forward Gerry Sharpe netted several vital goals as Bristol City reached the League Cup semi-finals in 1970/71. A former apprentice, he signed professional in March 1964 and Fred Ford gave him his League debut at home to Carlisle United seven months later. Featuring in City's 1964/65 promotion campaign and 1967/68 FA Cup run, he was switched from inside-forward to left winger by Alan Dicks and was leading marksman alongside John Galley in 1969/70. He scored 48 goals in 153 League outings before a double compound leg fracture at home to Middlesbrough in January 1971 ended his playing career at the age of 25 after a vain comeback bid. Awarded a testimonial against Derby County in December 1973, he became City's youth coach and had a brief spell as acting manager in May 1982. Now coaching in Canada, he attended City's Centenary Reunion Dinner in March 1997.

John Shaw

Scottish goalkeeper John Shaw was three times ever-present for Bristol City, including the 1983/84 promotion campaign. An ex-Leeds United apprentice, he signed professional in February 1971 and gained UEFA Cup experience before following Jimmy Mann to Ashton Gate on a free transfer in May 1974. Initially understudying Ray Cashley and Len Bond, he made his First Division debut at home to Birmingham City in October 1976 and helped to win the Anglo-Scottish Cup in 1977/78 when he was tipped for international honours. Reclaiming his first-team place from Cashley and Jan Moller, he overcame the embarrassing loss of his hair due to a nervous complaint to make 295 League appearances prior to joining Exeter City in July 1985 and moved to Gloucester City three years later.

Ben Shearman

Noted for his accurate crosses, outside-left Ben Shearman created numerous goalscoring opportunities for the likes of John Cowell and Ginger Owers while at Bristol City. He impressed in the Midland League with Worksop Town and Rotherham Town before Harry Thickett signed him in April 1909, and made his League debut at Bradford City in the opening game of the 1909/10 season. Scoring four goals in 60 First Division outings, he remained in the top-flight after joining Second Division Champions West Brom in June 1911 where he twice represented the Football League and played in the 1912 FA Cup final. He moved to Nottingham Forest in August 1919 after the emergence of Howard Gregory and later played for Gainsborough Trinity and Norton Woodseats.

Gary Shelton

Tough-tackling ex-England U–21 midfielder Gary Shelton was an inspirational figure in Bristol City's 1989/90 promotion success. A former Walsall apprentice, he signed professional in March 1976 and moved to Aston Villa for £60,000 in January 1978. Following a loan spell at Notts County, he joined Sheffield Wednesday for £50,000 in March 1982 and starred in the 1983/84 promotion campaign as well as successive Cup runs. Sold to Oxford United for £150,000 in July 1987, Joe Jordan swapped Steve McClaren for him in August 1989 and he added much-needed steel and determination to the side. Scoring 24 times in 150 League outings, he was loaned to Rochdale before joining Chester City in July 1994 and has starred in successive promotion challenges.

George Showell

Versatile full-back George Showell provided experienced defensive cover during Bristol City's 1965/66 promotion challenge and was the club's first playing substitute on his debut. An ex-Wolves junior, he signed professional in August 1951 and made 200 First Division appearances over 14 years at Molineux. Featuring in the 1957/58 and 1958/59 League Championship successes as well as the 1960 FA Cup Final triumph, Fred Ford signed him for newly-promoted City in May 1965 and he made 11 Second Division appearances prior to joining Wrexham in November 1966. Subsequently trainer/physio and assistant manager, he gave them excellent service until forced to quit in 1990 due to new qualification requirements. Still living in Wrexham, he is now physio for Wrexham RUFC and at Maelor Hospital.

Carl Shutt

Striker Carl Shutt netted several vital goals as Bristol City reached the Littlewoods Cup semi-finals in 1988/89. He impressed with Spalding United before moving to Sheffield Wednesday in May 1985 and played alongside Gary Shelton in the top-flight. Terry Cooper paid £55,000 for him in October 1987 and he scored twice on his debut at Blackpool, helping to reach the promotion play-off final in 1987/88. He netted ten goals in 46 Third Division outings prior to joining Leeds United in exchange for Bob Taylor in March 1989 and made a notable contribution as they won the Second Division title in 1989/90 and First Division title in 1991/92. Briefly reunited with Cooper at Birmingham City for £50,000 in August 1993, he was loaned to Manchester City before joining Bradford City for £75,000 in September 1994. Voted 'Player of the Year' in their 1995/96 promotion success, he was swapped for Darlington's Robbie Blake in March 1997.

Ronnie Sinclair

Ex-Scottish Youth goalkeeper Ronnie Sinclair featured prominently in Bristol City's 1989/90 promotion success and FA Cup run. Initially a Nottingham Forest apprentice, he signed professional in October 1982 and had a loan spell at Wrexham prior to joining Leeds United in June 1986. Twice loaned to Halifax Town, Joe Jordan signed him on a free transfer in August 1989 and he took over City's goalkeeping slot from injured Andy Leaning while at Ashton Gate. Making 44 League appearances, he had another loan period at Walsall before moving to Stoke City in November 1991 where he helped to win the Second Division title in 1992/93 and was briefly reunited with Jordan. He joined Chester City in August 1996 and starred in their 1996/97 promotion challenge.

Alan Skirton

Experienced winger Alan Skirton gave Bristol City the lead in the 1970/71 League Cup semi-final first-leg at home to Spurs. Initially with West Twerton YC, he was an amateur with City and helped to reach the FA Youth Cup semi-finals in 1955/56 before impressing with Bath City. Sold to Arsenal for £5,000 in January 1959, he continued in the top-flight after moving to Blackpool for £30,000 in September 1966 and Alan Dicks paid £15,000 for him in November 1968. He scored 14 times in 78 Second Division outings prior to joining Torquay United on a free transfer in July 1971. Subsequently with Durban City (South Africa), he helped Weymouth to win the Southern League Cup in 1972/73, then rejoined Bath City in July 1974 where he was also commercial manager. He has been Yeovil Town's commercial manager since October 1981.

Allan Sliman

Scottish centre-half Allan Sliman was an influential figure as Bristol City narrowly managed to avoid relegation in successive seasons during the late 1920's. He impressed with

Arthurlie Juniors before Alex Raisbeck paid £280 for him in September 1928 and made his League debut at home to Southampton the following month. His sole goal in 136 Second Division outings came in the 5-3 win at home to Reading in September 1929 and he moved to Chesterfield for £2,000 in March 1932. He was a key figure in their 1933/34 promotion challenge and 1935/36 Third Division (North) title success, then became Chelmsford City's player-manager in October 1938 and starred in their 1938/39 FA Cup run. He died in an RAF plane crash in 1945.

Andy Smailes

Versatile half-back Andy Smailes was a key figure in Bristol City's 1926/27 Third Division (South) title success. Initially an inside-forward with Blyth Spartans he joined Newcastle United for £300 in October 1919 and scored regularly in the top-flight prior to joining Sheffield Wednesday for £1,500 in October 1922. Alex Raisbeck signed him for struggling City a year later in an exchange deal involving Billy Walker and he was ever-present in 1924/25. He netted 14 goals in 162 League games before moving to Rotherham United in August 1929 where he spent 18 years as trainer prior to succeeding Reg Freeman as manager in August 1952. Plotting their 1952/53 FA Cup run, he resigned in October 1958 and managed Scarborough for two years. He died in 1978.

Dave Smith

Fast, exciting left-winger Dave Smith was another important member of Bristol City's 1989/90 promotion side. A Charlton Athletic schoolboy, he had spells with Orpington Eagles, Welling United and Dartford prior to rejoining Welling in December 1984 and starring in the 1985/86 Southern League title success. Sold to Gillingham for £3,000 in August 1986, he helped to reach the Third Division promotion play-offs in 1986/87 and Joe Jordan paid £75,000 fixed by tribunal for him in August 1989. 'Smudger' scored ten goals in 97 League outings before moving to Plymouth Argyle for £200,000 in December 1991, then Notts County for £150,000 in July

1992. A serious knee injury ended his playing career two years later and he now lives in Norway with his Norwegian wife.

Denis Smith

Manager Denis Smith guided Bristol City to Second Division safety in 1991/92. As a tough-tackling central defender, he made over 400 League appearances over 16 years with Stoke City and was a key figure in their 1971/72 League Cup Final triumph and 1978/79 promotion success. Appointed York City player/manager in May 1982, he plotted the 1983/84 Fourth Division title success and consecutive FA Cup runs, then took charge of Sunderland in June 1987 and led them from the Third Division to First in three years. He replaced Jimmy Lumsden as City's manager in March 1992 and his ten month reign at Ashton Gate included the club record signings of Ray Atteveld and Andy Cole. Sacked after a disappointing start to the 1992/93 campaign, he has been manager of Oxford United since September 1993 and masterminded the 1995/96 promotion success.

George Sommerville

Scottish goalkeeper George Sommerville succeeded George Newlands in goal for Bristol City. Starting with Strathclyde Juniors, he joined Hamilton Academicals in July 1922 and helped to take Dundee to a Scottish Cup semi-final replay in 1924/25. Moving to Burnley in July 1926, 'Jock' displaced record appearance holder Jerry Dawson at Turf Moor and gained considerable top-flight experience before Bob Hewison signed him for £150 in August 1932. He made 34 Third Division (South) appearances prior to joining Burton Town in July 1934, then moved to Yeovil & Petters United a year later and subsequently worked at BAC in Filton.

Southern League

A table of Bristol City's record in this competition can be found at the end of this A to Z.

Arthur Spear

Versatile half-back Arthur Spear featured prominently in Bristol City's successes under Harry Thickett. Born locally, he joined

● Alan Skirton

● Dave Smith

● Denis Smith

● Paul Stevens

City from local soccer in July 1904 and made his League debut at Glossop in December 1904. He provided reliable cover for the likes of Billy Jones, Peter Chambers and Reuben Marr, helping City to win the Second Division title in 1905/06 and finish League Championship runners-up in 1906/07. Establishing a regular slot at Ashton Gate, he was an important figure as City were FA Cup finalists in 1908/09 and had a joint benefit match with Archie Annan against Everton in April 1911. His sole goal in 136 League games came in the 2-0 home win over Leeds City in April 1906. He later became landlord of the 'Golden Fleece Hotel' in Bath where he died in December 1946.

Peter Spiring

Ex-England Youth midfielder Peter Spiring was an emerging figure at Ashton Gate in the early 1970's. The son of a former City player, he signed professional under Alan Dicks in June 1968 and made his League debut at home to Birmingham City in October 1969. He featured in the 1970/71 League Cup semi-final second-leg at Spurs and netted 16 goals in 63 Second Division games before a surprise £60,000 move to Liverpool in March 1973. Remaining in the top-flight after joining Luton Town for £70,000 in November 1974, he was reunited with John Sillett at Hereford United for £8,000 in February 1976 and helped to clinch the Third Division title in 1975/76 during seven years at Edgar Street. Still living in Hereford, he has been an electrical contractor since October 1983 and his son Reuben is a Worcestershire County cricketer.

Fred Staniforth

Clever outside-right Fred Staniforth played for Bristol City in the 1909 FA Cup final against Manchester United. He developed with Kilnhurst Town, Rotherham Main and Mexborough Town before Harry Thickett signed him for Second Division champions City in July 1906. Given his League debut at Everton three months later, he created numerous goalscoring chances for the likes of Billy Maxwell and Sammy Gilligan and

netted 14 goals in 134 First Division outings prior to joining Grimsby Town after relegation in July 1911. Moving to Liverpool two years later, he subsequently settled in Bristol until his death in May 1955.

Paul Stevens

Young right-back Paul Stevens was twice ever-present for Bristol City, including the 1983/84 promotion campaign. Born locally, he attended Hartcliffe School and represented Bristol Boys before signing professional from apprentice under Alan Dicks in April 1978. Given his League debut four days later at Middlesbrough, he scored in the 1979/80 Anglo-Scottish Cup final second-leg and netted three goals in 147 League outings prior to joining Bath City on a free transfer in July 1985. He helped Bath to take Bristol City to an FA Cup second round replay in 1986/87 and regain Conference status in 1989/90 before a knee injury halted his playing career. Still living in Ashton, he is currently a sales rep for Remploy and playing again for Paul Derrick's Broad Plain.

Jim Stevenson

Skilful Scottish inside-forward Jim Stevenson was an influential figure as Bristol City finished Southern League runners-up in 1900/01. Starting with Ashfield Juniors, he joined Clyde in January 1895 and moved to Derby County in January 1896. He helped them to finish First Division runners-up in 1895/96 and was an FA Cup finalist in 1897/98, joining Newcastle United for £225 in October 1898. Moving to City in July 1900, he netted seven goals in 24 Southern League outings before returning to top-flight action with Grimsby Town in September 1901. He joined Leicester Fosse in January 1902 but was suspended within two months as an internal disciplinary action and rejoined Clyde in October 1902. He was tragically killed during the Great War.

Billy Stewart

Left-half Billy Stewart was noted for his long throw-ins involving a running and jumping technique that was eventually outlawed. Initially with Black Watch, he was

an Army Cup winner and helped Belfast Distillery to lift the Irish Cup while stationed in Ireland with the Royal Scots Greys. Preston NE bought him out of the services and he moved to Everton in July 1893, forming a notable half-back line with Johnny Holt and Richard Boyle and playing in the 1897 FA Cup final against Aston Villa. Sam Hollis signed him in July 1898 and he became captain, making 51 Southern League appearances.

Fred Stone

Full-back Fred Stone provided reliable cover for Ivor Guy and Jack Bailey in Bristol City's defence during the early post-war era. Born locally, he developed with Oldland Common and Warmley before Bob Hewison signed him in February 1947. Given his League debut in the 2-2 draw at home to Swindon Town in April 1948, he featured in the 1952/53 promotion challenge and netted three goals in 64 Third Division (South) outings prior to joining Chippenham Town in July 1953. Together with other one-time City players like Ron Tovey and Jimmy Terris, he helped them to finish as Western League runners-up in 1954/55, then continued in the Western League with Salisbury and settled in Kingswood.

Kenny Stroud

Experienced midfielder Kenny Stroud made a significant contribution to Bristol City's 1983/84 promotion success. He signed professional from apprentice for Swindon Town in March 1971 and made over 300 League appearances for Swindon, an influential figure as they reached the League Cup semi-finals in 1979/80. Released following relegation to join Newport County in August 1982, he starred in the 1982/83 promotion near-miss and Terry Cooper signed him on another free transfer in October 1983. He netted four goals in 69 League outings before retiring in June 1985 and has since run Kingsbridge House Hotel in Swindon, briefly reviving his playing career in the Southern League with Bath City and Newport AFC.

● Kenny Stroud

Con Sullivan

Young goalkeeper Con Sullivan was ever-present for Bristol City in 1951/52. Born locally, he played for Trowbridge Town and Horfield Old Boys before Bob Wright signed him in May 1949. Given his League debut at home to Bournemouth in December 1950, he contested the goalkeeping slot with Syd Morgan and Tony Cook whilst at Ashton Gate and made 73 Third Division (South) appearances prior to joining Arsenal in February 1954. He gained top-flight experience as Jack Kelsey's understudy before a dislocated shoulder ended his League career in 1960. Still living in Knowle West, he spent 20 years as a warehouseman for Robertson's in Brislington until the site closed in 1981, then worked for Courages in a similar capacity until retiring in June 1992.

Charlie Sutherland

Versatile Scottish inside-left Charlie Sutherland featured prominently as Bristol City won the Third Division (South) title in 1922/23. He impressed in Scottish football with St. Mirren, Clydebank and Third Lanark prior to joining Millwall in July 1920 and played in their first-ever Third Division game, helping to consolidate Football League status. Alex Raisbeck signed him in August 1922 and he partnered the likes of Albert Fairclough and Tot Walsh in City's attack, netting 23 goals in 103 League outings before moving to Merthyr Town with Frank Vallis in May 1926.

Gerry Sweeney

Versatile Scottish right-back Gerry Sweeney was an influential figure in Bristol City's 1975/76 promotion campaign. Initially with Celtic, he represented the Scottish League during five years at Morton before Alan Dicks paid £22,000 for him in August 1971 and displaced Trevor Jacobs in defence. Also helping City to reach the FA Cup sixth round in 1973/74 and win the Anglo-Scottish Cup in 1977/78, he was four times ever-present and netted 22 goals in 406 League games before the 'Ashton Gate Eight' crisis forced his release in

February 1982. Subsequently with Trowbridge Town, York City, Forest Green Rovers, Gloucester City, Paulton Rovers, Clevedon Town (P/M), Backwell United (P/C) and Walsall (A-M), he became a postman based at Portishead and part-time coach at Ashton Gate then City's assistant-manager during the 1996/97 campaign.

Trevor Tainton

Long-serving ex-England Schoolboy midfielder Trevor Tainton was three times ever-present for Bristol City, including the 1975/76 promotion success. Born locally, he signed professional from apprentice in September 1965 and Fred Ford gave him his League debut at home to Carlisle United two years later. He featured prominently as City reached the League Cup semi-finals in 1970/71, the FA Cup sixth round in 1973/74 and won the Anglo-Scottish Cup in 1977/78. Awarded a testimonial in October 1976, he netted 24 goals in 486 League games before the 'Ashton Gate Eight' crisis also forced his release in February 1982. Subsequently with Torquay United, Trowbridge Town, Odd Down, Imperial, Olveston (P/C) and Almondsbury Picksons (P/C), he has been a security officer at Oldbury Power Station since December 1985.

Alex Tait

Red-haired ex-England Youth centre-forward Alex Tait was a popular figure at Ashton Gate during the early 1960's. Signing as a part-time professional for Newcastle United in September 1952 while qualifying as a maths and PE teacher, he understudied Jackie Milburn and netted a memorable hat-trick at Sunderland on Boxing Day 1955. Fred Ford's first signing for City, he cost £5,000 in June 1960 and partnered the likes of John Atyeo, Bobby Williams and Brian Clark in attack. He scored 38 goals in 117 Third Division outings before joining

Doncaster Rovers in June 1964, then Burton Albion a year later where he succeeded Peter Taylor as player-manager and plotted the 1965/66 promotion and Merit Cup success. Still living in Tutbury, he became deputy head-master during 19 years at Allestree Woodlands Comprehensive until retiring in July 1991.

Micky Tanner

Aggressive young midfielder Micky Tanner helped Bristol City to reach the Freight Rover Trophy Final in 1986/87 and Third Division promotion play-offs in 1987/88. Born locally, he was a schoolboy with City but failed to secure an apprenticeship and impressed with Brian Drysdale's Shepton Mallet and Lawrence Weston Hallen before Terry Cooper signed him in July 1985. Given his League debut at Wigan Athletic seven months later, his only goal in 19 Third Division games clinched a 1-1 draw at York City in March 1987. He joined Bath City in July 1988 and has since played for Cheltenham Town, Weymouth (under Gerry Gow), Bath (again), Bristol Manor Farm (twice), Mangotsfield United (twice), Clevedon Town and now Shirehampton. A qualified fitter, he works for Seeking Toyota at Portbury.

Archie Taylor

Young winger Archie Taylor was one of several Doncaster Rovers players who followed manager Peter Doherty to Ashton Gate. An amateur with Doncaster, he joined Bristol City in May 1958 and scored on his Second Division debut at Charlton Athletic in September 1959. He understudied Jimmy Rogers and netted twice in 12 League games prior to joining Barnsley in July 1961, then had spells with Goole Town and Hull City. Moving to Halifax Town in July 1963, he was ever-present in 1964/65 and followed Willie Watson to Bradford City in December 1967, then joined York City in October 1968 and starred in the 1970/71 promotion campaign. Subsequently with Gainsborough Trinity, Frickley Athletic and Hatfield Main, he still lives in Doncaster and is now a sales agent for Revlon and Vidal Sassoon hair products.

● Gerry Sweeney

● Trevor Tainton

● Alex Tait

● Bob Taylor

● Shaun Taylor

● Mike Thresher

Bob Taylor

Goalscoring favourite Bob Taylor was leading marksman and 'Player of the Year' in Bristol City's 1989/90 promotion campaign, when he topped the Third Division charts with 27 goals. He joined Leeds United from Horden Colliery in January 1986 and secured a regular first-team place in 1987/88 until displaced by Ian Baird. Joe Jordan signed him in a £225,000 exchange deal involving Carl Shutt in March 1989 and he netted 50 goals in 106 League outings before Ashton Gate fans were upset by his £300,000 sale to Bobby Gould's West Brom in January 1992, where he replaced Don Goodman in attack. Three times top scorer at The Hawthorns including 1992/93 when Albion won promotion via the Wembley play-offs, he is now rated in the £2,000,000 class.

Jock Taylor

Scottish left-half Jock Taylor gave Bristol City reliable service over seven seasons. He developed in Scottish football with St. Johnstone, Cowdenbeath and Raith Rovers before Bob Hewison signed him in October 1927 and made his League debut at Stoke City in April 1928. Initially displacing Andy Smailes at left-half, he switched to left-back after the arrival of Ernie Brinton and made 148 League appearances prior to joining Halifax Town in May 1934. Featuring prominently in their 1934/35 promotion challenge he moved to Clapton Orient in July 1935 and briefly returned to Ashton Gate two years later but failed to make any further League appearances. He then coached Cork in Ireland and H.B.S. in Holland before settling in Bristol where he coached Horfield Sports and ran a sports shop in Totterdown. He died in March 1964.

Shaun Taylor

Experienced, fearless central defender Shaun Taylor was 'Player of the Year' as Bristol City reached the Second Division play-offs in 1996/97. He impressed with Bideford, scoring in their 1984/85 Western League Cup final triumph before joining Exeter City in December 1986. Ever-present in 1988/89, he starred in the 1989/90 Fourth Division title success under Terry Cooper and moved to Swindon Town for £200,000 in July 1991. Voted 'Player of the Year' three times at the County Ground, he featured prominently in Swindon's 1992/93 and 1995/96 promotion successes. Joe Jordan paid an initial £50,000 for him in September 1996 and he displaced Alan McLeary in City's defence, scoring once in 29 Second Division outings to date. His younger brother Craig plays for Swindon Town.

Harry Thickett

Former England right-back Harry Thickett managed Bristol City to the Second Division title in 1905/06, League Championship runners-up in 1906/07 and FA Cup final in 1908/09. Initially with Hexthorpe, he joined Sheffield United in July 1890 and moved to Rotherham Town two years later. He rejoined Sheffield United in December 1893 and starred in their 1897/98 League Championship triumph as well as two FA Cup final successes. Moving to Bristol City in May 1904, he made 14 Second Division appearances prior to succeeding Sam Hollis as manager in March 1905. Surprisingly sacked in October 1910, he was subsequently a licensee in Trowbridge until his death in November 1920.

Third Division (South) Cup

A table of Bristol City's record in this competition can be found at the end of this A-Z section.

Bill Thomas

Inside-forward Bill Thomas was a popular figure at Bristol City during the early post-war era. Initially with Derby Corinthians and Matlock Town, he switched from Rolls Royce in Derby to BAC during the war and represented both works teams before Bob Hewison signed him as a part-time professional in March 1944. He netted 18 goals in 77 Third Division (South) games before joining Stonehouse as player-coach in July 1950, then played for Cheltenham Town, Stonehouse (P/M), Forest Green Rovers (P/C), Cinderford Town (P/M) and managed

Retford Town. He took charge of City's juniors under Fred Ford and scouted for the club until 1982. He was a draughtsman for Harry Dolman's firm, then spent 20 years as a packaging systems engineer/consultant for Ashton Containers until retiring in May 1989 and still lives locally.

David Thompson

Tall, central defender David Thompson joined Bristol City in an exchange deal involving Andy May. An ex-Millwall trainee, he signed professional in November 1986 and featured in the 1987/88 Second Division title campaign. He gained a regular place in the top-flight alongside Alan McLeary, then helped to reach the Second Division promotion play-offs in 1990/91. Brought to Ashton Gate by Denis Smith in June 1992, he partnered the likes of Matt Bryant, Russell Osman and Mark Aizlewood in the heart of City's defence and made 17 First Division appearances prior to joining Brentford on a free transfer in February 1994. Moving to Blackpool seven months later, he has been with Cambridge United since March 1995.

Mike Thresher

Fast, tough-tackling left-back Mike Thresher shared with John Atyeo the distinction of featuring in both of Bristol City's 1954/55 and 1964/65 promotion campaigns. One of six footballing brothers to play for Chard Town, he represented the RAF and Pat Beasley signed him in January 1954. Given his League debut at Reading on Boxing Day 1954, he displaced Jack Bailey in defence and partnered the likes of Ivor Guy, Gordon Hopkinson, Roger Collinson and Alec Briggs while at Ashton Gate. His only goal in 379 League games clinched a 1-1 draw at Southend United in November 1963 and he moved to Bath City on a free transfer in July 1965, then rejoined Chard. A carpenter by trade, he worked for the family building firm until his wife's death in February 1995 and still lives in Langport.

Bert Tindill

Experienced, popular insid- right Bert Tindill was ever-present for Bristol City in 1958/59. Starting with South Hiendley, he joined Doncaster Rovers in April 1944 and featured in the 1946/47 and 1949/50 Third Division (North) title successes. Leading marksman in 1955/56, he made over 400 League appearances before following Peter Doherty to Ashton Gate for £8,000 in February 1958. His goalscoring partnership with John Atyeo was a key factor in City's relegation escape that season and he scored 29 goals in 56 Second Division games prior to joining Barnsley in a record £14,500 exchange deal involving Mal Graham and Johnny McCann in July 1959. Starring in the 1960/61 FA Cup run, he moved to Frickley Colliery in July 1962 and ran a hotel until a fatal heart attack in July 1973.

Brian Tinnion

Versatile midfielder Brian Tinnion scored Bristol City's winner against Liverpool in the 1993/94 FA Cup third round replay triumph at Anfield and remains an important member of John Ward's squad. A former Newcastle United apprentice, he signed professional in February 1986 and sampled top-flight soccer prior to joining Bradford City for £150,000 in March 1989. Russell Osman paid £180,000 for him in March 1993 and his first goal for City was the penalty that clinched a vital 2-1 home win over Bristol Rovers the following month. Overcoming a loss of form as City struggled towards relegation, he has now scored 13 times in 149 League outings for Bristol City and helped to reach the Second Division play-offs in 1996/97.

David Tong

Midfielder David Tong made a significant contribution to Bristol City's 1985/86 campaign that ended in Freight Rover Trophy Final success at Wembley. An ex-Blackpool apprentice, he signed professional in September 1973 and moved to Shrewsbury Town for £25,000 in September 1978. Starring in the 1978/79 Third Division title and Welsh Cup 'double' triumph, he moved to Cardiff City in August 1982 and helped to regain Second Division status at the first attempt in 1982/83. Terry Cooper signed him in October

1985 after a loan spell at Rochdale and he made 19 Third Division appearances prior to joining Gillingham on loan, then Cambridge United in August 1986. Subsequently with Merthyr Tydfil where he featured in the successes under Lyn Jones, he had a spell as Fleetwood's player-manager and is now coaching minor soccer in the Blackpool area.

George Toone

Ex-England goalkeeper George Toone was ever-present as Bristol City were Southern League runners-up in 1900/01. He developed with several teams in his native Nottingham before joining Notts County where he starred in the 1894 FA Cup final triumph and 1896/97 Second Division title success. Moving to Bedminster in 1899, he continued with Bristol City after the amalgamation in 1900 and made 30 Southern League appearances prior to rejoining Notts County in July 1901. He retired two years later to become a publican in Nottingham where he resided until his death in September 1943.

Sandy Torrance

Scottish left-half Sandy Torrance featured in Bristol City's 1922/23 and 1926/27 Third Division (South) title successes. Real name Alex, he impressed with Renfrew Juniors before Joe Palmer signed him in June 1921 and made his League debut at West Ham four months later. Appointed captain at Ashton Gate, he played alongside the likes of Bert Neesam, Frank Davies and Fred Hawley and had a benefit match against Gillingham in January 1927. Displaced by Andy Smailes, he netted ten goals in 167 League outings before joining Bath City in July 1928 and remained local until his tragic death during an air raid on Bedminster in April 1941.

Bill Tovey

Local-born left-half Bill Tovey featured prominently in Bristol City's 1952/53 promotion challenge. Signing professional as an outside-left under Bob Hewison in December 1948, he made his League debut at Leyton Orient two months later and scored twice in 57 Third Division (South) outings before a serious knee injury at

Colchester United in April 1953 ended his playing career. He became a semi-skilled fitter for Harry Dolman's firm and City's part-time junior/reserve team trainer, then full-time assistant trainer/kit manager from July 1971 until the financial crisis of February 1982. Now living in Henleaze, he worked for CRS Dairy and since October 1993 has been a member of the Corps of Commissionaires with matchday duties at Bristol Rovers.

Len Townsend

Experienced inside-right Len Townsend was Bristol City's leading marksman in two consecutive early post-war seasons. Initially with Hayes, he joined First Division Brentford in May 1937 and was top scorer in 1946/47. A war-time guest for Belfast Celtic, he followed Dai Hopkins to Ashton Gate in June 1947 and formed a notable goalscoring partnership with Don Clark. Netting 45 goals in 74 Third Division (South) outings, he moved to Millwall in July 1949 and was reunited with Bob Hewison at Guildford City a year later where he helped to reach two successive Southern League Cup finals. Subsequently player-coach at Hayes, Slough Town and Maidenhead United, he was a London-based sales rep for Carborundum and Tex Abrasives until retiring in May 1982 and now lives in Seaford.

Transfers

Andy Cole remains Bristol City's most expensive purchase and record sale. Costing £500,000 from Arsenal in July 1992, he joined Newcastle United for £1,750,000 in March 1993 and moved to Manchester United for a British record £7,000,000 in January 1995. The club's previous record buy was Ray Atteveld for £250,000 from Everton four months earlier and City's first six-figure purchase was Chris Garland from Leicester City for £110,000 in December 1976. Garland had been the club's first six-figure sale when he moved to Chelsea for £100,000 in September 1971. Gary Collier made history as the first player to change clubs under freedom of contract, joining Coventry City for a record £325,000 in July 1979 and his move precipi-

● Bert Tindill

● Brian Tinnion

● **Robbie Turner**

tated the financial crisis at Ashton Gate as established players were given long contracts.

Charlie Treasure

Right-back Charlie Treasure partnered Laurie Banfield in defence as Bristol City reached the FA Cup semi-finals in 1919/20. Born in Farrington Gurney, he developed with Old Mills and Paulton Rovers before joining City in July 1919. He made his League debut at Fulham in October 1919 and featured prominently in the 1920/21 promotion challenge. Injured during an FA tour of South Africa, he made 63 Second Division appearances prior to joining Halifax Town in June 1922. He subsequently played for Taunton United where he set up a timber business and remained there until his death in June 1985.

Billy Tuft

Tireless full-back Billy Tuft was ever-present in Bristol City's 1901/02 Football League debut campaign. Initially with Coseley United, he joined Wolves in July 1896 and gained top-flight experience before moving to neighbours Walsall in July 1900. Sam Hollis signed him in July 1901 as Bristol City entered the Football League and he operated on both flanks alongside the likes of Richard Davies, George Lewis and Alf Gilson as City mounted successive promotion challenges. He helped to launch the 1905/06 Second Division title campaign until displaced by Joe Cottle and had a benefit match against Southamp-ton in February 1907, making 138 Second Division appearances before retiring that summer and later settled in Bilston.

Robbie Turner

Much-travelled, gangling striker Robbie Turner formed a notable partnership with Bob Taylor in Bristol City's 1989/90 promotion success and FA Cup run. An ex-Huddersfield Town apprentice, he signed professional in September 1984 and joined Cardiff City in July 1985. After a loan spell at Hartlepool United, he moved to Bristol Rovers in December 1986 and followed Bobby Gould to Wimbledon a year later. Joe Jordan paid £45,000 for him in January

1989 and he scored 12 times in 52 Third Division outings prior to joining Plymouth Argyle for £150,000 in July 1990. Leading marksman in 1990/91, he joined Notts County for £90,000 in November 1992 and was loaned to Shrewsbury Town before joining Terry Cooper's Exeter City on a free transfer in February 1994. Subsequently with Cambridge United, he is now with Taunton Town.

Frank Vallis

Goalkeeper Frank Vallis was a key figure as Bristol City were FA Cup semi-finalists in 1919/20 and Third Division (South) champions in 1922/23. Born locally, he impressed with Trowbridge Town and Horfield United before joining City in April 1919 and made his League debut at home to Bury four months later. Ever-present in City's first two seasons after the Great War, he was later joined at Ashton Gate by his brothers Jack and Arthur. Given a benefit match against Merthyr Town in December 1924, he made 219 League appearances prior to joining Merthyr with Charlie Sutherland in May 1926 after being displaced by Billy Coggins. He subsequently played for Yeovil & Petters, then coached football and cricket at Monkton Combe School in Bath and remained local until his death in September 1957, serving as Chairman of the Parish Council.

Percy Vials

Noted for his pace, young centre-forward Percy Vials was Bristol City's joint leading goalscorer with Cecil Blakemore in 1928/29. Initially with Market Harborough Town and Little Rowden Albion, he helped Kettering Town to win the Southern League title in 1927/28 before Alex Raisbeck paid £125 for him in October 1928 after a trial with Leicester City. 'Tiny' scored twice on his League debut in the 6-0 home win over Oldham Athletic the following month and

was an influential figure as City narrowly managed to avoid relegation in successive seasons. Netting 36 goals in 73 Second Division outings, he joined First Division Middlesbrough in May 1932 but illness prevented him making an impact at Ayresome Park and he was top scorer for Hinckley United in 1933/34, then played for Atherstone Town.

Derek Virgin

Winger Derek Virgin provided reliable forward cover at Bristol City during the 1950's. Initially with Ilminster Town, Pat Beasley signed him as an amateur in August 1953 and he made his League debut in the 6-0 thrashing of Plymouth Argyle in December 1955. He skippered St. Lukes College while qualifying as a PE Geography teacher and taught at Ashton Park Comprehensive School while a part-time professional with City. Netting four goals in 21 League outings prior to joining Bath City in June 1961. After studying at Moorlands Bible College in Dawlish, he taught PE and Religious Studies at Homefield School in Christchurch and for 20 years at Wadham Community School in Crewkerne until retiring in July 1994. He is now an elder at Crewkerne Christian Fellowship.

Walter Wadsworth

Experienced centre-half Walter Wadsworth skippered Bristol City to the Third Division (South) title in 1926/27. Initially with Lingdale and Ormskirk, 'Waddy' joined Liverpool in July 1914 and was ever-present in 1920/21, starring in their 1921/22 and 1922/23 League Championship successes. He followed Alex Raisbeck to Ashton Gate for £400 in May 1926 and his sole goal in 67 League outings came in the 3-0 win at home to Fulham in October 1927. Moving back to Merseyside with New Brighton in August 1928, he later played for Flint Town (P/M) and Oswestry Town. Subsequently returning to Bristol, he became a publican and restaurateur and remained local until his death in October 1951.

Billy Walker

Skilful Scottish inside-right Billy Walker made a significant contribution as Bristol City won the Third Division (South) title in 1922/23. Initially with Lugar Boswell, he moved to Bradford City in August 1911 and had a spell with Birmingham prior to joining Coventry City in November 1919. He moved to Merthyr Town with Albert Lindon, Charlie Copeland and Joe Godfrey in May 1920 after they were not retained by a technical oversight and Alex Raisbeck paid £1,000 for him in October 1922. Combining well with Albert Fairclough in attack, he netted seven goals in 37 League outings for City before joining The Wednesday in exchange for Andy Smailes in October 1923. He was appointed Weymouth's player-manager in July 1924, joining Leamington Town a year later where he was a prolific goalscorer.

Alan Walsh

Skilful striker Alan Walsh was leading goalscorer and 'Player of the Year' for the second time as Bristol City reached the promotion play-offs in 1987/88. He joined Middlesbrough from Horden Colliery in December 1976 and gained top-flight experience before moving to Darlington in October 1978 where he scored a club record 90 League goals. Terry Cooper paid just £18,000 for him in August 1984 and he starred as City reached two successive Freight Rover Trophy finals, netting 77 times in 218 Third Division games prior to joining Besiktas in July 1989. Later with Walsall, Glenavon, Huddersfield Town, Shrewsbury Town, Cardiff City, Michalotti (HK), Clevedon Town, Taunton Town (1994 FA Vase Final), Hartlepool United (Player/Coach) and Bath City, he is now Bristol Rovers' Community Development Officer.

Jack Walsh

Jack Walsh succeeded long-serving Dick Hughes as Bristol City's right-back. Initially with Darwen,

he gained Lancashire County honours and had a spell with Blackburn Rovers prior to joining Aberdare Athletic in July 1925. Alex Raisbeck signed him in December 1926 and he helped City to clinch the Third Division (South) title in 1926/27, forming a notable defensive partnership with Ernie Glenn. His sole goal in 164 League games came in the 1-3 defeat at Charlton Athletic in September 1929 and he moved to Millwall in March 1932. Ever-present in 1932/33, he subsequently ran a pub in Thornbury and settled in Bristol until his sudden death in June 1965.

Tot Walsh

Diminutive centre-forward Tot Walsh was Bristol City's leading marksman in three consecutive seasons including the 1926/27 Third Division (South) title success netting six goals in the amazing 9-4 home win over Gillingham. Real name Tommy, he sampled top-flight soccer with Bolton Wanderers after scoring regularly in their reserves and Alex Raisbeck paid £1,550 for him in January 1924 in a vain bid to boost City's relegation fight. He netted 88 goals in 142 League outings prior to joining Crystal Palace in May 1928 and featured in their 1928/29 promotion challenge when Charlton pipped them to the Third Division (South) title on goal average. He subsequently returned to his native Lancashire with Hurst and died in November 1950.

John Ward

Current manager John Ward guided Bristol City to the Second Division play-offs in 1996/97. As a centre-forward, he signed professional for Lincoln City in March 1971 and was top scorer in three successive seasons including their 1975/76 Fourth Division title triumph. He followed Graham Taylor to Watford for £15,000 in July 1979 and had spells with Grimsby Town and Lincoln again before rejoining Watford as coach in May 1982. Subsequently assistant manager, he also assisted Taylor for Aston Villa and England until appointed York City manager in November 1991. He took charge of Bristol Rovers in

March 1993 and guided them to the 1994/95 Second Division play-off final at Wembley, assisting Adrian Heath at Burnley for eight months before succeeding Joe Jordan as City's manager in March 1997.

Tommy Ware

Local goalkeeper Tommy Ware impressed at Bristol City while deputising for the injured Harry Clay. He was home on leave from the Army at Christmas 1911 when he was called upon to make his League debut in a 3-0 defeat at Hull City, playing a further four games that season prior to leaving the forces. In November 1912 he was again drafted into the City goal after Clay sustained a leg injury and retained his place for the remainder of that campaign as Sam Hollis' side struggled to avoid the Second Division re-election zone. He made 51 Second Division appearances overall before war was declared in August 1914 and was one of the first to be called up because of his previous military service, tragically killed in action in June 1915.

Watney Cup

A table of Bristol City's record in this competition can be found at the end of this A-Z section.

Johnny Watkins

Ex-England Youth outside-left Johnny Watkins thrilled fans with his powerful shooting while at Ashton Gate. Born locally, he impressed with Clifton St. Vincents before signing professional for Bristol City under Pat Beasley in June 1951 and made his League debut at home to Norwich City in September 1953. He scored 19 times in 95 League outings prior to joining Cardiff City for £2,500 in June 1959 and helped to regain top-flight status in 1959/60. Swapped for Bristol Rovers' Dai Ward in February 1961, he joined Cyril Williams' Chippenham Town in July 1962, then played under Arnold Rodgers at Welton Rovers and Bath City before managing Shirehampton. Still living locally, he was a clerk for Harry Dolman's firm, then at Rolls Royce for 20 years until 1991 and now with Strachan Henshaw engineers.

● Alan Walsh

● John Ward

● Johnny Watkins

● **Keith Waugh**

● **Keith Welch**

● **Jack White**

Keith Waugh

Experienced goalkeeper Keith Waugh was 'Player of the Year' as Bristol City reached the Littlewoods Cup semi-finals in 1988/89. A former Sunderland apprentice, he signed professional in July 1974 and moved to Peterborough United on a free transfer in July 1976 where he was twice ever-present. Sold to Sheffield United for £90,000 in August 1981, he starred in their rise from the Fourth Division to Second before Terry Cooper signed him in July 1985 after a loan spell. Virtually ever-present as City reached two successive Freight Rover Trophy finals and the promotion play-offs in 1987/88, he made 171 Third Division appearances overall prior to joining John Sillett's Coventry City for £40,000 in August 1989, then Watford in February 1991. He is now a police constable stationed at Luton.

Billy Wedlock

Outstanding centre-half Billy Wedlock was capped a club record 26 times by England while at Bristol City. Born locally, 'Fatty' helped Arlington Rovers to win the Bristol & District League title before joining City in June 1900. His first-team chances were restricted and he was allowed to join Aberdare a year later where he featured in Welsh Cup and South Wales Cup successes. Harry Thickett re-signed him in June 1905 and he was ever-present in City's 1905/06 Second Division title campaign, also starring as City were League Championship runners-up in 1906/07 and FA Cup finalists in 1908/09. He netted 17 goals in 364 League games prior to retiring in May 1921 when he became licensee of the 'Star Inn' opposite the main entrance to Ashton Gate until a year before his death in January 1965.

Keith Welch

Voted 'Player of the Year' in 1992/93, goalkeeper Keith Welch remains an important member of John Ward's squad. Initially a Bolton Wanderers trainee, he joined Rochdale in March 1987 and was ever-present in three consecutive seasons including the 1989/90 FA Cup run when 'Dale reached the fifth round for the first time in their history. He followed Jimmy Lumsden to Ashton Gate in a record £200,000 deal in August 1991 and was an influential figure as City qualified for the new First Division in 1991/92 and beat Liverpool in the 1993/94 FA Cup third round replay at Anfield. Despite facing competition for the goalkeeping slot from the likes of Andy Leaning, Phil Kite, Sieb Dykstra and Stuart Naylor, he has now made 206 League appearances for Bristol City and helped to reach the Second Division promotion play-offs in 1996/97.

Welsh Cup

A table of Bristol City's record in this competition can be found at the end of this A to Z.

Welsh Cup Winners

Bristol City defeated Cardiff City, New Brighton and Port Vale en route to the Welsh Cup final in 1933/34. Bill Molloy scored to give the following City team a 1-1 draw against Tranmere Rovers in the first all-English final watched by 4,922 at Wrexham on 25th April 1934: Ken Scattergood, Bill Roberts, Jock Taylor, Cliff Morgan, Jack Parker, Ernie Brinton, Albert Banfield, Bill Molloy, Joe Riley, Jimmy Loftus, Aubrey Scriven. Eight days later, goals by Joe Riley (2) and Aubrey Scriven gave the following side a 3-0 win in the replay at Chester: Ken Scattergood, Bill Roberts, Len Birks, Cliff Morgan, Jack Parker, Ernie Brinton, Syd Homer, Bill Molloy, Joe Riley, Jimmy Loftus, Aubrey Scriven.

Arnie White

Popular inside-right Arnie White partnered the likes of Don Clark, Len Townsend and Arnold Rodgers in Bristol City's early post-war attack. Born locally, Bob Hewison signed him from Soundwell in March 1947 and he made his League debut in front of 51,621 at runaway leaders Cardiff City a month later. He scored 12 goals in 82 Third Division (South) games before moving to Millwall in August 1951, where he featured in successive promotion challenges, then joined Hereford United in July 1953. Subsequently with Chippenham Town, he then helped Trowbridge Town to win the Western League title in 1955/56 and consolidate Southern League status. Now living in Charfield, he was a property developer/builder in the Yate area until retiring in September 1987.

Jack White

Constructive centre-half Jack White skippered Bristol City to the Third Division (South) title in 1954/55 when he was ever-present. A former miner, he played for Broadworth Main and Frickley Colliery before turning professional with Aldershot in July 1944. Pat Beasley paid a record £5,300 for him in October 1952 and he displaced long-serving Dennis Roberts in the heart of City's defence alongside Ernie Peacock. He scored 11 goals in 216 League outings prior to joining Cambridge City as player-manager for three years in April 1958, then managed Wellington Town. Subsequently a service engineer for Harry Dolman's firm based in Tonbridge, then for Tonbridge Printers, he returned to Doncaster in 1978 and was a labourer at Thorpe Marsh Power Station until retiring in March 1989. Now living in Tonbridge, his younger brother Len was a goalscoring hero for Newcastle United.

Willie White

Much-travelled Scottish inside-forward Willie White netted several vital goals for Bristol City during the mid-1930's. Initially with Musselburgh Bruntonians, he joined Reading in June 1927 and Bristol Rovers a year later. Moving via Southport to Charlton Athletic in July 1930, 'Wattie' left the Valley five months later as they cut their wage bill and joined Gillingham where he was top scorer in 1931/32. After spells with Aldershot, Carlisle United and Newport County, Bob Hewison signed him in May 1935 and he netted 15 goals in 50 Third Division (South) outings prior to joining Lincoln City in December 1936. He subsequently played for Hull City and was a talented banjo player, being a member of a family group that toured Fife.

Clive Whitehead

Noted for his versatility, ex-England Youth winger Clive Whitehead netted the goal that beat Portsmouth 1-0 in April 1976 to clinch Bristol City's promotion to the First

Division. Alan Dicks signed him from Northfield Juniors in August 1973 and he scored on his league debut before City's worsening financial position forced his £100,000 sale to West Brom in November 1981 where he became captain. Moving to Portsmouth in June 1987 after a loan spell at Wolves, he joined Terry Cooper's Exeter City in July 1989 and starred in the 1989/90 Fourth Division title success, then had six months as Yeovil Town player-manager prior to rejoining Bristol City as coach. He followed Leroy Rosenior to Fleet Town in September 1995.

Jonah Wilcox

Centre-forward Jonah Wilcox was Bristol City's joint leading goalscorer with Billy Pocock in the 1920/21 promotion challenge. He developed with Coleford Athletic, Frome Town, Welton Rovers and Abertillery before Joe Palmer signed him in August 1919 after he had guested for City during the Great War. He scored on his League debut in the 2-1 win at Nottingham Forest in September 1919 and netted 20 times in 59 Second Division outings prior to joining Bradford PA for £600 in September 1922. Featuring in their 1922/23 promotion challenge, he joined New Brighton in July 1924 and broke their goalscoring record in 1924/25. Moving to Bristol Rovers in August 1925, he was their top scorer in 1925/26 and repeated this feat with Gillingham in 1927/28 after a season at QPR. He subsequently played for Kidderminster Harriers, then was a Bristol publican until his death in August 1956.

Alan Williams

Fair-haired centre-half Alan Williams was one of Bristol City's most notable discoveries of the 1950's. Born locally, he signed professional under Pat Beasley in September 1955 and made his League debut at Blackburn Rovers in February 1957. Unlucky not to gain England U-23 honours, he scored twice in 135 League outings before moving to Oldham Athletic for £1,000 in June 1961 and was ever-present skipper in the 1962/63 promotion campaign. He joined Watford in July 1965, then moved via Newport County to Swansea Town for £1,500 in October 1968 –

starring in the 1969/70 promotion success prior to joining Gloucester City in June 1972. Later manager of Keynsham Town and Almondsbury Greenway, he became mine host at the 'White Horse' in Bedminster and is now at the 'Horse & Groom'.

Bertie Williams

Skilful, diminutive Welsh international inside-forward Bertie Williams was Bristol City's leading marksman in 1929/30. Starting with Cyfartha Stars, Alex Raisbeck signed him from Merthyr Town in August 1926 and he made his League debut at South Shields on Christmas Eve 1927. Capped against Northern Ireland in February 1930 after scoring against Derby County in the FA Cup third round, he netted 26 goals in 103 League outings before moving to Sheffield United for £1,400 in January 1932. Controversially preferred to Don Bird in the 1936 FA Cup final, he left Bramall Lane in a dispute over terms during the summer of 1937 and took employment with a tool company.

Bobby Williams

Slight, skilful inside-left Bobby 'Shadow' Williams formed a notable goalscoring partnership with John Atyeo in Bristol City's attack. Born locally, he signed professional from amateur under Peter Doherty in May 1958 and made his League debut at home to Leyton Orient eleven months later. He scored 76 goals in 187 League outings and helped to launch City's 1964/65 promotion campaign before moving to Rotherham United for £10,000 in February 1965. Joining Bristol Rovers in March 1967, he moved to Reading in August 1969, then played for ASO Ostend, Cheltenham Town (under Bobby Etheridge) and Weymouth before he was almost killed in a car crash in September 1972. After a vain comeback attempt with Keynsham Town, he rejoined Reading as youth team manager.

Brian Williams

Left-back Brian Williams was an experienced figure as Bristol City reached two successive Freight Rover Trophy finals, including the 1985/86 Wembley triumph. A former Bury apprentice, he signed

professional in April 1973 and starred in the 1973/74 promotion campaign. He sampled top-flight soccer after joining QPR for £70,000 in July 1977, then moved to Swindon Town for £50,000 in June 1978 and starred in the 1979/80 League Cup run. Terry Cooper signed him for Bristol Rovers in exchange for Gary Emmanuel in July 1981, then brought him to Ashton Gate in July 1985 where he became captain and netted three goals in 77 Third Division outings before joining Shrewsbury Town in July 1987. Subsequently with Alvechurch and Oldswinford, he is now Hereford United's Community Develop-ment Officer.

Cyril Williams

Versatile inside-left Cyril Williams was an influential member of Bristol City's 1954/55 Third Division (South) Championship side. Born locally, he signed professional under Bob Hewison in May 1939 and guested for Reading and Spurs during the war. Moving to West Brom in exchange for Cliff Edwards plus £500 in June 1948, he featured prominently in the 1948/49 promotion campaign and returned to Ashton Gate for £4,500 in August 1951. Netting 69 goals in 296 League outings for City overall, he was appointed Chippenham Town player-manager in July 1958 and took charge of Gloucester City for a season in August 1966. He subsequently ran Greylands Hotel in Weston-super-Mare until 1975 and remained local until his tragic death in a car crash in January 1980.

Gary Williams

Ex-England Schoolboy left-back Gary Williams made a significant contribution to Bristol City's 1983/84 promotion triumph. Born locally, the son of ex-City centre-half Alan Williams, he signed professional in August 1980 and Bob Houghton gave him his League debut at Oldham Athletic in May 1981. Following the 'Ashton Gate Eight' crisis, he formed a young full-back partnership with Paul Stevens and his only goal in 100 League outings clinched a 2-1 win at home to Gillingham in May 1982. He had spells with Portsmouth, Swansea City and

● **Alan Williams**

● **Bobby Williams**

● **Brian Williams**

● Cyril Williams

Bristol Rovers before joining Oldham Athletic in August 1985 and featured in their successes under Joe Royle, then played for Hearts, Kitchee (HK) and Bath City. After running 'The Pineapple' and the 'Three Tuns' pubs, he is now with his father at the 'Horse & Groom'.

Sid Williams

Winger Sid Williams created numerous goalscoring chances for the likes of Don Clark, Len Townsend and Arnold Rodgers during the early post-war era. Born locally, he began with Eastville United and Bob Hewison signed him as an amateur in July 1937. He represented Northern Command and guested for Darlington during the war, turning professional with Bristol City in July 1945. Given his League debut in the local derby at home to Bristol Rovers seven months later, he contested the outside-left slot with Jackie Hargreaves and Tommy Rudkin and helped to reach the FA Cup fifth round in 1950/51. He scored 11 times in 100 Third Division (South) outings before joining Bill Thomas' Stonehouse in June 1952. Subsequently a self-employed decorator until retiring in December 1984, he still lives in Patchway.

George Willshaw

Outside-left George Willshaw created numerous goalscoring opportunities for Clarrie Bourton and Lew Booth at Bristol City immediately prior to the Second World War. He helped Walthamstow Avenue to win the Athenian League title in 1932/33 and 1933/34, then starred for Southall as they reached the FA Cup third round for the first time in 1935/36. Moving to Southend United in February 1936, Bob Hewison signed him in June 1938 and he scored nine times in 34 Third Division (South) outings before joining Leyton Orient in September 1942. He featured in their first post-war campaign and subsequently resided in Portsmouth until his death in September 1993.

Hugh Wilson

Former Scottish international Hugh Wilson was ever-present as Bristol City finished Southern League runners-up in 1900/01.

Initially with Newmilns, he joined Sunderland in July 1890 and helped to win the League Championship in 1891/92, 1892/93 and 1894/95 prior to joining Bedminster in July 1899. He skippered their Southern League side and was one of several players retained after the amalgamation with Bristol City in 1900, scoring nine goals in 31 Southern League games before returning to Scotland with Third Lanark in July 1901. He died in April 1940.

Les Wilson

Versatile right-back Les Wilson featured prominently in Bristol City's 1970/71 relegation escape. An ex-Wolves junior, he signed professional in September 1964 and gained First Division and UEFA Cup experience at Molineux. With City battling to avoid the drop, Alan Dicks signed him on a loan in March 1971 together with Coventry City's Brian Hill and he moved to Ashton Gate on a permanent basis for £15,000 in November 1971. His only goal in 43 Second Division outings earned a 1-1 draw at Sunderland that month and after a brief top-flight return with Norwich City in September 1973, he moved to Vancouver Whitecaps in May 1974 where he became coach. Now based in British Columbia, he is the National Teams' Administrator of the Canadian Football Association.

Ken Wimshurst

Experienced right-half Ken Wimshurst was an influential figure as Bristol City reached the League Cup semi-finals in 1970/71. Initially with South Shields, he was snapped up by Newcastle United in July 1957 and moved to Gateshead in November 1958. Following a spell with Wolves, he joined Southampton for £1,500 in July 1961 and starred as they reached the FA Cup semi-finals in 1962/63 and the First Division in 1965/66. Alan Dicks paid £15,000 for him in October 1967 and he scored nine times in 149 Second Division outings prior to becoming assistant-coach in July 1972, then succeeding John Sillett as chief coach two years later. After leaving Ashton Gate in June 1981, he briefly assisted Don Mackay at Dundee and now runs Southampton's School of Excellence in Bath. His son-in-law

Ricky Chandler played for City in the early 1980's.

Wins

Bristol City's record Football League win is 9-0 at home to Aldershot on 28th December 1946: John Eddolls, Cliff Morgan, Ray Fox, Ernie Peacock, Dennis Roberts, Ernie Jones, Ken Chilcott, Bill Thomas, Don Clark, Cyril Williams, Jackie Hargreaves. City's record FA Cup win is 11-0 at home to Chichester City in the first round on 5th November 1960: Tony Cook, Roger Collinson, Mike Thresher, Jack Connor, Alan Williams, Bobby Etheridge, Alex Tait, Bobby Williams, John Atyeo, Adrian Williams, Jantzen Derrick. Cardiff City were beaten 5-1 in the (Coca-Cola) League Cup first round second-leg at Ashton Gate on 25th August 1992: Keith Welch, Brian Mitchell, Martin Scott, David Thompson, Matt Bryant, Mark Aizlewood, Micky Mellon, Jackie Dziekanowski, Andy Cole, Leroy Rosenior (Wayne Allison), Gary Shelton (Gerry Harrison).

Dickie Wombwell

Ever-present in two consecutive seasons for Bristol City, versatile outside-left Dickie Wombwell was leading marksman in 1902/03. He developed with Bulwell and Ilkeston Town prior to joining Derby County in May 1899 where he gained considerable top-flight experience. Sam Hollis signed him in July 1902 and he partnered the likes of Fred Corbett, Albert Fisher and Sammy Gilligan in attack, netting 19 goals in 92 Second Division outings before being sold to Manchester United for £175 in March 1905. He helped United to win promotion with Bristol City in 1905/06, then moved to Hearts in January 1907 and played in that year's Scottish Cup final. After a spell in the Southern League with Brighton, he returned to First Division action with Blackburn Rovers in February 1908, then played for Ilkeston United.

Charlie Worlock

Outside-right Charlie Worlock made a significant contribution as Bristol City won the Third Division (South) title in 1922/23. Born

● Ken Wimshurst

locally, he developed with St. Philip's Marsh Adult School and Alex Raisbeck signed him in August 1922. He made his League debut in the first-ever Bristol 'derby' match in the Football League, at home to Rovers a month later, and created numerous goalscoring chances for the likes of Albert Fairclough and Tot Walsh while at Ashton Gate. Scoring nine goals in 73 League outings, he joined Bradford PA in May 1925. He died in Bristol in February 1973.

Jack Wren

Versatile half-back Jack Wren was an influential figure as Bristol City were Cup semi-finalists in 1919/20 and succeeded ex-England star Billy Wedlock in the heart of City's defence. He impressed in local soccer with Greenback and had a spell with Bristol Rovers before moving to Ashton Gate in July 1917. Making his League debut at home to Bury as League football resumed in August 1919, his sole goal in 104 Second Division games clinched a 1-0 win at home to Coventry City in November 1919. He joined Notts County for £1,500 in August 1922 and helped to win the Second Division title in 1922/23, then had spells with Huddersfield Town, Bradford City, Portsmouth and Norwich City. He subsequently ran the 'Ashley Hill Station Hotel' and remained in Bristol until his death in July 1948.

Tom Wyllie

Former Scottish international outside-right Tom Wyllie was an experienced figure as Bristol City finished runners-up in their 1897/98 Southern League debut campaign. Initially with Maybole, he spent three seasons with Glasgow Rangers, then had spells with Merseyside rivals Everton and Liverpool prior to joining Bury in July 1894. He featured prominently in their 1894/95 Second Division title success and gained top-flight experience before Sam Hollis signed him as City turned professional in 1897. He scored three times in 16 Southern League outings before retiring in May 1898 to become a Football League referee and subsequently ran a newsagents in Bedminster.

Bob Young

Ex-Scottish junior international right-back succeeded Archie Annan in Bristol City's defence. He developed with Vale of Eden and Dundee Violet before Harry Thickett beat stiff competition to sign him in July 1907 and made his League debut at home to Newcastle United in September 1907. Partnering England star Joe Cottle in City's defence, he switched to right-half after the arrival of John Kearns and made 168 League appearances prior to retiring in May 1920. He subsequently became a referee in the Bristol Suburban League and remained local until his death.

Zenith Data Systems Cup

A table of Bristol City's record in this competition can be found at the end of this A-Z section.

● **Tom Wyllie**

One Hundred Years of Bristol City FC Chairmen

May 1897	– July 1898	Albert E. Denby
July 1898	– July 1900	William Panes Kingston
July 1900	– June 1901	A.W. Francis*
June 1901	– June 1911	William Panes Kingston
June 1911	– March 1921	Ernest Murdock
March 1921	– June 1923	E. Gwynne Vevers
June 1923	– May 1925	Harry Drewett
May 1925	– March 1949	George Jenkins
March 1949	– March 1974	Harry J. Dolman
March 1974	– May 1977	Robert Hobbs
May 1977	– December 1980	Stephen Kew
December 1980	– April 1982	Archie Gooch
April 1982	– June 1982	Leslie Kew**
June 1982	– February 1991	Des Williams
February 1991	– November 1994	Leslie Kew
November 1994	– September 1995	David Russe
September 1995	– March 1996	Mike Fricker
March 1996	–	Scott Davidson

* Information regarding this ex-Bedminster director taking over as the initial Chairman of the amalgamated Club is not at all conclusive. Only one reference has been discovered in the local press in regard to him being the Chairman and it is therefore unfortunate that a report of City's AGM in 1900 has not been found.

** Interim Chairman of the reborn Bristol City.

$\mathcal{S}$TATISTICS
1897–1997

Season	Div.	Home						Away						Pts.	Pos.	Top Scorer	League Goals	Ever-present Players
		P	W	D	L	F	A	P	W	D	L	F	A					
SOUTHERN LEAGUE																		
1897/98	1	11	9	2	0	44	14	11	4	5	2	23	18	33	2	Caie	18	Mann/Montieth/Russell
1898/99	1	12	11	0	1	39	16	12	4	3	5	16	17	33	2	Langham	12	Hamilton/Langham/Russell
1899/00	1	14	9	0	5	33	23	14	0	7	7	10	24	25	9	Jones	14	
1900/01	1	14	12	2	0	40	6	14	5	3	6	14	21	39	2	Michael	14	Toone/Wilson
FOOTBALL LEAGUE																		
1901/02	2	17	13	1	3	39	12	17	4	5	8	13	23	40	6	Connor	10	Jones/McLean/Tuft
1902/03	2	17	12	3	2	43	18	17	5	5	7	16	20	42	4	Wombwell	11	Clay/Wombwell
1903/04	2	17	14	2	1	53	12	17	4	4	9	20	29	42	4	Dean/Morris	13	Clay/Wombwell
1904/05	2	17	12	3	2	40	12	17	7	1	9	26	33	42	4	Fisher	13	Clay
1905/06	2	19	17	1	1	43	8	19	13	5	1	40	20	66	1	Maxwell	25	Annan/Maxwell/Wedlock
1906/07	1	19	12	3	4	37	18	19	8	5	6	29	29	48	2	Maxwell	17	Annan
1907/08	1	19	8	7	4	29	21	19	4	5	10	29	40	36	10	Gilligan	16	
1908/09	1	19	7	7	5	24	25	19	6	5	8	21	33	38	8	Gilligan	10	
1909/10	1	19	9	5	5	28	18	19	3	3	13	17	42	32	16	Cowell	20	Cottle
1910/11	1	19	8	4	7	23	21	19	3	1	15	20	45	27	19	Owers	16	
1911/12	2	19	11	4	4	27	17	19	3	2	14	14	43	34	13	Bowyer/Copestake/Forbes	5	
1912/13	2	19	7	9	3	32	25	19	2	6	11	14	47	33	16	Owers	13	
1913/14	2	19	12	5	2	32	10	19	4	4	11	20	40	41	8	Brown	10	Broad
1914/15	2	19	11	2	6	38	19	19	4	5	10	24	37	37	13	Brown	13	Banfield/Brown
								Competition suspended due to war										
1919/20	2	21	9	9	3	30	18	21	4	8	9	16	25	43	8	Howarth	14	F. Vallis
1920/21	2	21	14	3	4	35	12	21	5	10	6	14	17	51	3	Pocock/Wilcox	14	Harris/F. Vallis
1921/22	2	21	10	3	8	25	18	21	2	6	13	12	40	33	22	Fairclough	12	Banfield
1922/23	3S	21	16	4	1	43	13	21	8	7	6	23	27	59	1	Fairclough	19	
1923/24	2	21	5	8	8	19	26	21	2	7	12	13	39	29	22	Fairclough	8	
1924/25	3S	21	14	5	2	40	10	21	8	4	9	21	31	53	3	Walsh	20	Smailes
1925/26	3S	21	14	3	4	42	15	21	7	6	8	30	36	51	4	Walsh	25	
1926/27	3S	21	19	1	1	71	24	21	8	7	6	33	30	62	1	Walsh	32	Coggins
1927/28	2	21	11	5	5	42	18	21	4	4	13	34	61	39	12	Keating	16	
1928/29	2	21	11	6	4	37	25	21	2	4	15	21	47	36	20	Blakemore/Vials	15	
1929/30	2	21	11	4	6	36	30	21	2	5	14	25	53	35	20	Williams	16	
1930/31	2	21	11	5	5	29	23	21	4	3	14	25	59	38	16	Elliott	15	
1931/32	2	21	4	7	10	22	37	21	2	4	15	17	41	23	22	Sargeant	10	Newlands
1932/33	3S	21	11	5	5	59	37	21	1	8	12	24	53	37	15	Bowen	28	Homer
1933/34	3S	21	7	8	6	33	22	21	3	5	13	25	63	33	19	Riley	13	
1934/35	3S	21	14	3	4	37	18	21	1	6	14	15	50	39	15	Harston	15	
1935/36	3S	21	11	5	5	32	21	21	4	5	12	16	38	40	13	Armstrong	11	
1936/37	3S	21	13	3	5	42	20	21	2	3	16	16	50	36	16	Haycox	17	
1937/38	3S	21	14	6	1	37	13	21	7	7	7	31	27	55	2	Rowles	18	
1938/39	3S	21	14	5	2	42	19	21	2	7	12	19	44	44	8	Booth	15	
								Competition suspended due to war										
1946/47	3S	21	13	4	4	56	20	21	7	7	7	38	36	51	3	Clark	36	Roberts
1947/48	3S	21	11	4	6	47	26	21	7	3	11	30	39	43	7	Townsend	31	Bailey/Clack
1948/49	3S	21	8	9	4	28	24	21	3	5	13	16	38	36	16	Townsend	14	
1949/50	3S	21	12	4	5	38	19	21	3	6	12	22	42	40	15	Rodgers	18	
1950/51	3S	23	15	4	4	41	25	23	5	7	11	23	34	51	10	Rodgers	20	Guy

Season	Div.	Home						Away						Pts.	Pos.	Top Scorer	League Goals	Ever-present Players
		P	W	D	L	F	A	P	W	D	L	F	A					
1951/52	3S	23	13	6	6	49	35	23	2	6	15	14	43	42	15	Atyeo/Rodgers	12	Roberts/Sullivan
1952/53	3S	23	13	8	2	62	28	23	9	7	7	33	33	59	5	Rodgers	26	Peacock
1953/54	3S	23	18	3	2	59	18	23	7	3	13	29	48	56	3	Atyeo	22	Guy
1954/55	3S	23	17	4	2	62	22	23	13	6	4	39	25	70	1	Atyeo	28	Atyeo/White
1955/56	2	21	14	4	3	49	20	21	5	3	13	31	44	45	11	Atyeo	30	
1956/57	2	21	13	2	6	49	32	21	3	7	11	25	47	41	13	Atyeo	23	
1957/58	2	21	9	5	7	35	31	21	4	4	13	28	57	35	17	Atyeo	23	Atyeo
1958/59	2	21	11	3	7	43	27	21	6	4	11	31	43	41	10	Atyeo	26	Tindill
1959/60	2	21	8	3	10	27	31	21	3	2	16	33	66	27	22	Atyeo/Rogers	16	Atyeo/Cook
1960/61	3	23	15	4	4	50	19	23	2	6	15	20	49	44	14	Atyeo	19	
1961/62	3	23	15	3	5	56	27	23	8	5	10	38	45	54	6	Atyeo	26	Briggs/Connor/Etheridge
1962/63	3	23	10	9	4	54	38	23	6	4	13	46	54	45	14	Clark	23	Briggs
1963/64	3	23	13	7	3	52	24	23	7	8	8	32	40	55	5	Atyeo	21	Atyeo/Clark
1964/65	3	23	14	6	3	53	18	23	10	5	8	39	37	59	2	Clark	24	Clark/Atyeo/Gibson/Low
1965/66	2	21	9	10	2	27	15	21	8	7	6	36	33	51	5	Atyeo	19	Clark/Gibson/Low
1966/67	2	21	10	8	3	38	22	21	2	6	13	18	40	38	15	Peters	9	Briggs/Connor/Gibson
1967/68	2	21	7	7	7	26	25	21	6	3	12	22	37	36	19	Galley	16	
1968/69	2	21	9	9	3	30	15	21	2	7	12	16	38	38	16	Galley	19	Connor/Kellard/Parr
1969/70	2	21	11	7	3	37	13	21	2	6	13	17	37	39	14	Sharpe	10	Drysdale
1970/71	2	21	9	6	6	30	28	21	1	5	15	16	36	31	19	Galley	12	Drysdale
1971/72	2	21	14	3	4	43	22	21	4	7	10	18	27	46	8	Galley	22	Drysdale/Merrick
1972/73	2	21	10	7	4	34	18	21	7	5	9	29	33	46	5	Gow	12	Gow
1973/74	2	21	9	5	7	25	20	21	5	5	11	22	34	38	16	Fear	8	Sweeney/Tainton
1974/75	2	21	14	5	2	31	10	21	7	3	11	16	23	50	5	Gillies	9	Cashley/Merrick/Sweeney
1975/76	2	21	11	7	3	34	14	21	8	8	5	25	21	53	2	Ritchie	18	Cashley/Gow/Merrick/Ritchie/Tainton
1976/77	1	21	8	7	6	25	19	21	3	6	12	13	29	35	18	Garland/Ritchie	7	Collier/Sweeney
1977/78	1	21	9	6	6	37	26	21	2	7	12	12	27	35	17	Royle	8	Shaw
1978/79	1	21	11	6	4	34	19	21	4	4	13	13	32	40	13	Mabbutt/Ritchie	9	Sweeney
1979/80	1	21	6	6	9	22	30	21	3	7	11	15	36	31	20	Ritchie	13	
1980/81	2	21	6	10	5	19	15	21	1	6	14	10	36	30	21	Mabbutt	9	
1981/82	3	23	7	6	10	24	29	23	4	7	12	16	36	46	23	Harford	11	Stevens
1982/83	4	23	10	8	5	32	25	23	3	9	11	27	45	56	14	Riley	16	Shaw
1983/84	4	23	18	3	2	51	17	23	6	7	10	19	27	82	4	Riley	16	Pritchard/Shaw
1984/85	3	23	17	2	4	46	19	23	7	7	9	28	28	81	5	Walsh	20	
1985/86	3	23	14	5	4	43	19	23	4	9	10	26	41	68	9	Neville	19	Neville
1986/87	3	23	14	6	3	42	15	23	7	8	8	21	21	77	6	Walsh	16	Waugh
1987/88	3	23	14	6	3	51	30	23	7	6	10	26	32	75	5	Walsh	12	
1988/89	3	23	10	3	10	32	25	23	8	6	9	21	30	63	11	Walsh	11	Newman/Walsh
1989/90	3	23	15	5	3	40	19	23	12	5	6	36	24	91	2	Taylor	27	Llewellyn/Newman
1990/91	2	23	14	5	4	44	28	23	6	2	15	24	43	67	9	Morgan	13	Newman
1991/92	2	23	10	8	5	30	24	23	3	7	13	25	47	54	17	Allison	10	Scott
1992/93	1*	23	10	7	6	29	25	23	4	7	12	20	42	56	15	Cole	12	
1993/94	1	23	11	7	5	27	18	23	5	9	9	20	32	64	13	Allison	15	
1994/95	1	23	8	8	7	26	28	23	3	4	16	16	35	45	23	Allison	13	
1995/96	2	23	10	6	7	28	22	23	5	9	9	27	38	60	13	Agostino/Seal	10	Kuhl
1996/97	2	23	14	4	5	43	18	23	7	6	10	26	33	69	5	Goater	23	Owers

With the introduction of the Premiership, Division 2 became Division 1

Season	Rnd	Venue	Opponents	Result
1897/98	1Q	H	Clifton Association	W 9-1
	2Q	A	Trowbridge Town	W 5-2
	3Q	A	Southampton	L 0-2
1898/99	3Q	A	Cowes	W 5-0
	4Q	A	Bristol St George	W 1-0
	5Q	H	Reading	W 3-2
	1	H	Sunderland	L 2-4
1899/1900	1	H	Stalybridge Rovers	W 2-1
	2	A	Aston Villa	L 1-5
1900/01	1	A	Reading	D 1-1
	1r	H	Reading*	D 0-0
	(Fading light ended play after 110 minutes)			
	1r²	N	Reading	L 1-2
	(Played on the 'County Ground', Swindon)			
1901/02	3Q	H	Bristol East	W 5-1
	4Q	A	Bristol Rovers	– 0-2
	(Abandoned due to fog after 80 minutes)			
	4Q	A	Bristol Rovers*	D 1-1
	(Fading light ended play after 116 minutes)			
	4Qr	H	Bristol Rovers	L 2-3
1902/03	1NT	H	Middlesbrough	W 3-1
	1	A	Bolton Wanderers	W 5-0
	2	A	Tottenham Hotspur	L 0-1
1903/04	1NT	A	New Brompton	D 1-1
	1NTr	H	New Brompton	W 5-2
	1	H	Sheffield United	L 1-3
1904/05	1NT	H	Blackpool	W 2-1
	(Blackpool drawn at home but agreed to switch to Ashton Gate for £200)			
	1	A	Woolwich Arsenal	D 0-0
	1r	H	Woolwich Arsenal	H 1-0
	2	H	Preston North End	D 0-0
	2r	A	Preston North End	L 0-1
1905/06	1	A	Brentford	L 1-2
1906/07	1	H	Leeds City	W 4-1
	2	A	Woolwich Arsenal	L 1-2
1907/08	1	H	Grimsby Town	D 0-0
	1r	A	Grimsby Town	L 1-2
1908/09	1	H	Southampton	D 1-1
	1r	A	Southampton	W 2-0
	2	H	Bury	D 2-2
	2r	A	Bury	W 1-0
	3	H	Norwich City	W 2-0
	4	A	Glossop	D 0-0
	4r	H	Glossop	W 1-0
	S/F	N	Derby County	D 1-1
	(Semi-final at 'Stamford Bridge')			
	S/Fr	N	Derby County	W 2-1
	(Semi-final replay at 'St Andrews', Birmingham)			
	F	N	Manchester United	L 0-1
	(Final at 'The Crystal Palace')			
1909/10	1	H	Liverpool	W 2-0

Season	Rnd	Venue	Opponents	Result
1909/10	2	H	West Bromwich Albion	D 1-1
	2r	A	West Bromwich Albion	L 2-4
1910/11	1	H	Crewe Alexandra	L 0-3
1911/12	1	A	Northampton Town	L 0-1
1912/13	1	A	Liverpool	L 0-3
1913/14	1	A	Queens Park Rangers	D 2-2
	1r	H	Queens Park Rangers*	L 0-2
1914/15	1	H	Cardiff City	W 2-0
	2	A	Everton	L 0-4
1919/20	1	A	Grimsby Town	W 2-1
	2	H	The Arsenal	W 1-0
	3	H	Cardiff City	W 2-1
	4	H	Bradford City	W 2-0
	S/F	N	Huddersfield Town	L 1-2
	(Semi-final at 'Stamford Bridge')			
1920/21	1	A	Aston Villa	L 0-2
1921/22	1	H	Nottingham Forest	D 0-0
	1r	A	Nottingham Forest	L 1-3
1922/23	1	H	Wrexham	W 5-1
	2	H	Derby County	L 0-3
1923/24	1	A	Norwich City	W 1-0
	2	A	The Wednesday	D 1-1
	2r	H	The Wednesday	W 2-0
	3	A	Cardiff City	L 0-3
1924/25	1	A	Bristol Rovers	W 1-0
	2	H	Liverpool	L 0-1
1925/26	1	A	West Bromwich Albion	L 1-4
1926/27	1	A	Merthyr Town	W 2-0
	2	H	Bournemouth & B.A.	D 1-1
	2r	A	Bournemouth & B.A.	L 0-2
1927/28	3	H	Tottenham Hotspur	L 1-2
1928/29	3	H	Liverpool	L 0-2
1929/30	3	A	Derby County	L 1-5
1930/31	3	A	Barnsley	L 1-4
1931/32	3	A	Notts County	D 2-2
	3r	H	Notts County	W 3-2
	4	A	Watford	L 1-2
1932/33	1	H	Romford	W 4-0
	2	H	Tranmere Rovers	D 2-2
	2r	A	Tranmere Rovers	L 2-3
1933/34	1	A	Kingstonian	W 7-1
	2	H	Barrow	W 2-1
	3	H	Derby County	D 1-1
	3r	A	Derby County	L 0-1
1934/35	1	H	Gillingham	W 2-0
	2	A	Rotherham United	W 2-1
	3	H	Bury	D 1-1
	3r	A	Bury*	D 2-2

● Alan Williams, 1956/57 – 1960/61

● Ernie Peacock, 1946/47 – 1958/59

● Mike Thresher, 1954/55 – 1964/65

● Bert Tindill, 1957/58 – 1958/59

● Bob Anderson, 1954/55 – 1958/59

● John Atyeo,
1951/52 – 1965/66

● John Galley, 1967/68 – 1972/73

● Chris Garland, 1966/67 – 1971/72
and 1976/77 – 1982/83

● Mike Gibson, 1962/63 – 1971/72

● Alec Briggs, 1957/58 – 1969/70

● Jack Connor, 1960/61 – 1970/71

● Brian Clark, 1960/61 – 1966/67

● Jantzen Derrick, 1959/60 – 1970/71

Clockwise from top left:
- Geoff Merrick, 1967/68 – 1981/82
- Gerry Gow, 1969/70 – 1980/81
- Gerry Sweeney, 1971/72 – 1981/82
- Don Gillies, 1972/73 – 1979/80
- Joe Royle, 1977/78 – 1979/80
- Trevor Tainton, 1967/68 – 1981/82
- Norman Hunter, 1976/77 – 1978/79

● **Paul Cheesley, 1973/74 – 1976/77**

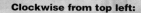

Clockwise from top left:

● Alan Walsh, 1984/85 – 1988/89

● Andy Llewellyn, 1982/83 – 1993/94

● Tom Ritchie, 1972/73 – 1980/81
and 1982/83 – 1984/85

● Rob Newman, 1981/82 – 1990/91

● Joe Jordan, 1986/87 – 1989/90

● David Moyes, 1985/86 – 1987/88

● Glyn Riley, 1982/83 – 1986/87

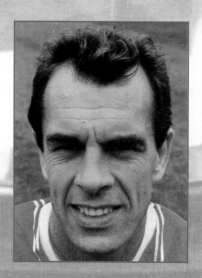

Clockwise from top left:

● Paul Agostino, 1995/96 – 1996/97

● Martin Scott, 1990/91 – 1994/95

● Dariusz Dziekanowski, 1991/92 – 1992/93

● Mark Aizlewood, 1990/91 – 1993/94

● Bob Taylor, 1988/89 – 1991/92

● Andy Cole, 1991/92 – 1992/93

● David Seal, 1994/95 – 1996/97

● Wayne Allison, 1990/91 – 1994/95

● **Shaun Goater, 1996/97 –**

Season	Rnd	Venue	Opponents	Result
1934/35	3r²	N	Bury	W 2-1
	(Played at 'Villa Park')			
	4	A	Portsmouth	D 0-0
	4r	H	Portsmouth	W 2-0
	5	H	Preston North End	D 0-0
	5r	A	Preston North End	L 0-5
1935/36	1	H	Crystal Palace	L 0-1
1936/37	1	A	Newport County	L 0-3
1937/38	1	H	Enfield	W 3-0
	2	A	Cardiff City	D 1-1
	2r	H	Cardiff City	L 0-2
1938/39	1	A	Bournemouth & B.A.	L 1-2
1945/46	1/1	A	Yeovil & Petters United	D 2-2
	1/2	H	Yeovil & Petters United	W 3-0
	2/1	H	Bristol Rovers	W 4-2
	2/2	A	Bristol Rovers	W 2-0
	3/1	H	Swansea Town	W 5-1
	3/2	A	Swansea Town	D 2-2
	4/1	H	Brentford	W 2-1
	4/2	A	Brentford	L 0-5
	(The 1945/46 FA Cup ties were played over two legs)			
1946/47	1	H	Hayes	W 9-3
	2	H	Gillingham	L 1-2
1947/48	1	A	Dartford*	D 0-0
	1r	H	Dartford	W 9-2
	2	H	Crystal Palace*	L 0-1
1948/49	1	A	Crystal Palace*	W 1-0
	2	H	Swansea Town	W 3-1
	3	H	Chelsea	L 1-3
1949/50	1	A	Nottingham Forest	L 0-1
1950/51	1	H	Gloucester City	W 4-0
	2	H	Wrexham	W 2-1
	3	H	Blackburn Rovers	W 2-1
	4	H	Brighton & Hove Albion	W 1-0
	5	A	Birmingham City	L 0-2
1951/52	1	A	Brighton & Hove Albion	W 2-1
	2	A	Colchester United	L 1-2
1952/53	1	A	Coventry City	L 0-2
1953/54	1	A	Torquay United	W 3-1
	2	A	Rhyl	W 3-0
	3	H	Rotherham United	L 1-3
1954/55	1	H	Southend United	L 1-2
1955/56	1	A	Everton	L 1-3
1956/57	3	H	Rotherham United	W 4-1
	4	H	Rhyl	W 3-0
	5	A	Aston Villa	L 1-2
1957/58	3	A	Accrington Stanley	D 2-2
	3r	H	Accrington Stanley	W 3-1
	4	A	Notts County	W 2-1

Season	Rnd	Venue	Opponents	Result
1957/58	5	H	Bristol Rovers	L 3-4
1958/59	3	A	Doncaster Rovers	W 2-0
	4	H	Blackpool	D 1-1
	4r	A	Blackpool	L 0-1
1959/60	3	H	Charlton Athletic	L 2-3
1960/61	1	H	Chichester City	W 11-0
	(Chichester drawn at home but requested			
	switch to Ashton Gate)			
	2	A	Kings Lynn	D 2-2
	2r	H	Kings Lynn	W 3-0
	3	A	Plymouth Argyle	W 1-0
	4	A	Leicester City	– 0-0
	(Abandoned at half-time due to waterlogged pitch)			
	4	A	Leicester City	L 1-5
1961/62	1	H	Hereford United	D 1-1
	1r	A	Hereford United	W 5-2
	2	H	Dartford	W 8-2
	3	H	Walsall	D 0-0
	3r	A	Walsall	L 1-4
1962/63	1	H	Wellington Town	W 4-2
	2	H	Wimbledon	W 2-1
	3	H	Aston Villa	D 1-1
	3r	A	Aston Villa	L 2-3
1963/64	1	A	Corby Town	W 3-1
	2	A	Exeter City	W 2-0
	3	A	Doncaster Rovers	D 2-2
	3r	H	Doncaster Rovers	W 2-0
	4	A	Sunderland	L 1-6
1964/65	1	H	Brighton & Hove Albion	W 1-0
	2	A	Bournemouth & B.A.	W 3-0
	3	H	Sheffield United	D 1-1
	3r	A	Sheffield United	L 0-3
1965/66	3	A	Birmingham City	L 2-3
1966/67	3	A	Halifax Town	D 1-1
	3r	H	Halifax Town	W 4-1
	4	H	Southampton	W 1-0
	5	A	Tottenham Hotspur	L 0-2
1967/68	3	H	Bristol Rovers	D 0-0
	3r	A	Bristol Rovers	W 2-1
	4	A	Middlesbrough	D 1-1
	4r	H	Middlesbrough	W 2-1
	5	A	Leeds United	L 0-2
1968/69	3	A	West Ham United	L 2-3
1969/70	3	A	Chester	L 1-2
1970/71	3	A	Southampton	L 0-3
1971/72	3	A	Preston North End	L 2-4
1972/73	3	A	Portsmouth	D 1-1
	3r	H	Portsmouth	W 4-1
	4	A	Wolverhampton Wndrs	L 0-1
1973/74	3	H	Hull City	D 1-1

Season	Rnd	Venue	Opponents	Result
1973/74	3r	A	Hull City	W 1-0
	4	A	Hereford United	W 1-0
	5	H	Leeds United	D 1-1
	5r	A	Leeds United	W 1-0
	6	H	Liverpool	L 0-1
1974/75	3	A	Sheffield United	L 0-2
1975/76	3	A	Coventry City	L 1-2
1976/77	3	A	Ipswich Town	L 1-4
1977/78	3	H	Wrexham	D 4-4
	3r	A	Wrexham	L 0-3
1978/79	3	H	Bolton Wanderers	W 3-1
	4	A	Crystal Palace	L 0-3
1979/80	3	H	Derby County	W 6-2
	4	H	Ipswich Town	L 1-2
1980/81	3	A	Derby County	D 0-0
	3r	H	Derby County	W 2-0
	4	A	Carlisle United	D 1-1
	4r	H	Carlisle United	W 5-0
	5	A	Nottingham Forest	L 1-2
1981/82	1	H	Torquay United	D 0-0
	1r	A	Torquay United	W 2-1
	2	H	Northampton Town	W 3-0
	3	A	Peterborough United	W 1-0
	4	H	Aston Villa	L 0-1
1982/83	1	A	Orient	L 1-4
1983/84	1	A	Corinthian Casuals	D 0-0

(Played at 'Champion Hill, the home of Dulwich Hamlet)

Season	Rnd	Venue	Opponents	Result
	1r	H	Corinthian Casuals	W 4-0
	2	A	Bristol Rovers	W 2-1
	3	A	Notts County	D 2-2
	3r	H	Notts County	L 0-2
1984/85	1	A	Fisher Athletic	W 1-0
	2	H	Bristol Rovers	L 1-3
1985/86	1	A	Swindon Town	D 0-0
	1r	H	Swindon Town	W 4-2
	2	H	Exeter City	L 1-2
1986/87	1	H	VS Rugby	W 3-1
	2	H	Bath City	D 1-1

(Bath drawn at home but requested switch to 'Ashton Gate')

Season	Rnd	Venue	Opponents	Result
	2r	H	Bath City	W 3-0
	3	H	Plymouth Argyle	D 1-1
	3r	A	Plymouth Argyle*	L 1-3
1987/88	1	H	Aylesbury United	W 1-0
1987/88	2	H	Torquay United	L 0-1
1988/89	1	H	Southend United	W 3-1
	2	A	Aldershot	D 1-1
	2r	H	Aldershot*	D 0-0
	2r²	A	Aldershot*	D 2-2

Season	Rnd	Venue	Opponents	Result
1988/89	2r³	H	Aldershot	W 1-0
	3	A	Hartlepool	L 0-1
1989/90	1	H	Barnet	W 2-0
	2	H	Fulham	W 2-1
	3	H	Swindon Town	W 2-1
	4	H	Chelsea	W 3-1
	5	H	Cambridge United	D 0-0
	5r	A	Cambridge United*	D 1-1
	5r²	A	Cambridge United	L 1-5
1990/91	3	A	Norwich City	L 1-2
1991/92	3	H	Wimbledon	D 1-1
	3r	A	Wimbledon	W 1-0
	4	A	Leicester City	W 2-1
	5	A	Nottingham Forest	L 1-4
1992/93	3	A	Luton Town	L 0-2
1993/94	3	H	Liverpool	– 1-1

(Abandoned after 65 mins due to floodlight failure)

Season	Rnd	Venue	Opponents	Result
	3	H	Liverpool	D 1-1
	3r	A	Liverpool	W 1-0
	4	A	Stockport County	W 4-0
	5	H	Charlton Athletic	D 1-1
	5r	A	Charlton Athletic	L 0-2

Sponsorship taken up by Littlewoods Pools

Season	Rnd	Venue	Opponents	Result
1994/95	3	H	Stoke City	D 0-0
	3r	A	Stoke City*	W 3-1
	4	H	Everton	L 0-1
1995/96	1	A	AFC Bournemouth	D 0-0
	1r	H	AFC Bournemouth	L 0-1
1996/97	1	A	Swansea City	D 1-1
	1r	H	Swansea City	W 1-0
	2	H	St Albans City	W 9-2
	3	A	Chesterfield	L 0-2

* denotes extra-time played

Season	Rnd	Venue	Opponents	Result
1960/61	2	A	Aldershot	D 1-1
	2r	H	Aldershot	W 3-0
	3	A	Nottingham Forest	L 1-2
1961/62	1	A	York City	L 0-3
1962/63	2	H	Rotherham United	L 1-2
1963/64	1	A	Gillingham	L 2-4
1964/65	2	A	Carlisle United	L 1-4
1965/66	2	A	Shrewsbury Town	L 0-1
1966/67	2	H	Swansea Town	D 1-1
	2r	A	Swansea Town*	L 1-2
1967/68	2	H	Everton	L 0-5
1968/69	1	H	Newport County	W 2-0
	2	H	Middlesbrough	W 1-0
	3	A	Leeds United	L 1-2
1969/70	1	A	Exeter City	D 1-1
	1r	H	Exeter City	W 3-2
	2	H	Leicester City	D 0-0
	2r	A	Leicester City*	D 0-0
	2r²	A	Leicester City	L 1-3
1970/71	2	A	Rotherham United	D 0-0
	2r	H	Rotherham United	W 4-0
	3	A	Blackpool	W 1-0
	4	A	Leicester City	D 2-2
	4r	H	Leicester Clty*	W 2-1
	5	A	Fulham	D 0-0
	5r	H	Fulham	W 1-0
	S/F-1	H	Tottenham Hotspur	D 1-1
	S/F-2	A	Tottenham Hotspur*	L 0-2
1971/72	1	A	Plymouth Argyle	L 0-1
1972/73	2	A	West Ham United	L 1-2
1973/74	2	A	Scunthorpe United	D 0-0
	2r	H	Scunthorpe United	W 2-1
	3	H	Coventry City	D 2-2
	3r	A	Coventry City	L 1-2
1974/75	1	H	Cardiff City	W 2-1
	2	A	Crystal Palace	W 4-1
	3	H	Liverpool	D 0-0
	3r	A	Liverpool	L 0-4
1975/76	2	A	West Ham United	D 0-0
	2r	H	West Ham United	L 1-3
1976/77	2	H	Coventry City	L 0-1
1977/78	2	H	Stoke City	W 1-0
	3	A	Wrexham	L 0-1
1978/79	2	H	Crystal Palace	L 1-2
1979/80	2/1	H	Rotherham United	W 1-0
	2/2	A	Rotherham United	D 1-1
	3	A	Peterborough United	D 1-1
	3r	H	Peterborough United	W 4-0
	4	H	Nottingham Forest	D 1-1
	4r	A	Nottingham Forest	L 0-3
1980/81	2/1	A	Birmingham City	L 1-2
	2/2	H	Birmingham City	D 0-0
1981/82	1/1	H	Walsall	W 2-0
	1/2	A	Walsall	L 0-1
	2/1	A	Carlisle United	D 0-0
	2/2	H	Carlisle United	W 2-1
	3	A	Queens Park Rangers	L 0-3

Season	Rnd	Venue	Opponents	Result
Milk Cup				
1982/83	1/1	A	Swindon Town	L 1-2
	1/2	H	Swindon Town	W 2-0
	2/1	H	Sheffield Wednesday	L 1-2
	2/2	A	Sheffield Wednesday*	D 1-1
1983/84	1/1	A	Oxford United	D 1-1
	1/2	H	Oxford United	L 0-1
1984/85	1/1	H	Newport County	W 2-1
	1/2	A	Newport County	W 3-0
	2/1	H	West Ham United	D 2-2
	2/2	A	West Ham United	L 1-6
1985/86	1/1	A	Hereford United	L 1-5
	1/2	H	Hereford United	W 2-0
Littlewoods Cup				
1986/87	1/1	A	AFC Bournemouth	W 1-0
	1/2	H	AFC Bournemouth*	D 1-1
	2/1	H	Sheffield United	D 2-2
	2/2	A	Sheffield United	L 0-3
1987/88	1/1	A	Swindon Town	L 0-3
	1/2	H	Swindon Town	W 3-2
1988/89	1/1	H	Exeter City	W 1-0
	1/2	A	Exeter City	W 1-0
	2/1	A	Oxford United	W 4-2
	2/2	H	Oxford United	W 2-0
	3	H	Crystal Palace	W 4-1
	4	H	Tranmere Rovers	W 1-0
	5	A	Bradford City	W 1-0
	S/F-1	A	Nottingham Forest	D 1-1
	S/F-2	H	Nottingham Forest*	L 0-1
1989/90	1/1	H	Reading	L 2-3
	1/2	A	Reading	D 2-2
Rumbelows Cup				
1990/91	1/1	A	West Bromwich Albion	D 2-2
	1/2	H	West Bromwich Albion	W 1-0
	2/1	A	Sunderland	W 1-0
	2/2	H	Sunderland	L 1-6
1991/92	2/1	A	Bristol Rovers	W 3-1
	2/2	H	Bristol Rovers*	L 2-4
(Rovers went through on away goals rule)				
Coca-Cola Cup				
1992/93	1/1	A	Cardiff City	L 0-1
	1/2	H	Cardiff City	W 5-1
	2/1	H	Sheffield United	W 2-1
	2/2	A	Sheffield United	L 1-4
1993/94	1/1	A	Swansea City	W 1-0
	1/2	H	Swansea City	L 0-2
1994/95	1/1	H	Notts County	L 0-1
	1/2	A	Notts County	L 0-3
1995/96	1/1	A	Colchester United	L 1-2
	1/2	H	Colchester United*	W 2-1
(City won penalty shoot-out 5-3)				
	2/1	H	Newcastle United	L 0-5
	2/2	A	Newcastle United	L 1-3
1996/97	1/1	A	Torquay United	D 3-3
	1/2	H	Torquay United	W 1-0
	2/1	H	Bolton Wanderers	D 0-0
	2/2	A	Bolton Wanderers*	L 1-3

* denotes extra-time played

Season	Rnd	Venue	Opponents	Result
Welsh Cup				
1932/33	7	H	Newport County	L 3-4
1933/34	6	A	Cardiff City	D 2-2
	6r	H	Cardiff City	W 1-0
	7	A	New Brighton	D 2-2
	7r	H	New Brighton	W 2-1
	S/F	N	Port Vale	W 1-0
(Played at 'Sealand Road', Chester)				
	F	N	Tranmere Rovers	D 1-1
(Played at 'The Racecourse Ground', Wrexham)				
	Fr	N	Tranmere Rovers	W 3-0
(Final replayed at 'Sealand Road', Chester)				
1935/36	6	A	Cardiff City	L 1-2
1936/37	6	H	Swansea Town	L 1-2
1937/38	6	A	Newport County	L 2-6
1961/62	5	H	Merthyr Tydfil	W 4-2
	6	H	Cardiff City	L 0-2

ASSOCIATE MEMBERS CUP COMPETITIONS
Third Division (South) Cup

Season	Rnd	Venue	Opponents	Result
1933/34	1	A	Bournemouth & B.A.	L 1-7
1934/35	2	A	Watford	L 1-4
1935/36	1	A	Bristol Rovers	W 4-2
	2	A	Bournemouth & B.A.	L 0-1
1936/37	1	H	Gillingham	L 0-2
1937/38	1	H	Torquay United	W 3-0
	2	H	Cardiff City	W 2-0
	3	A	Walsall	W 2-1
	S/F	H	Millwall	W 2-0
1938/39	F-1	A	Reading	L 1-6
(1937/38 Final, 1st leg played Sep 28)				
	F-2	H	Reading	W 1-0
(1937/38 Final, 2nd leg played Oct 12)				
	2	H	Cardiff City	W 6-0
	3	H	Torquay United	L 0-1

Football League Trophy

Season	Rnd	Venue	Opponents	Result
1982-83	GM	A	Exeter City	L 1-2
	GM	H	Torquay United	W 1-0
	GM	H	Newport County	L 1-4

Associate Members Cup

Season	Rnd	Venue	Opponents	Result
1983/84	1	A	Exeter City	L 1-3

Freight Rover Trophy

Season	Rnd	Venue	Opponents	Result
1984/85	1/1	A	Hereford United	D 1-1
	1/2	H	Hereford United	W 1-0
	2	H	Port Vale	W 2-1
	SQ/F	H	Newport County	L 1-2

Season	Rnd	Venue	Opponents	Result
1985/86	GM	H	Plymouth Argyle	D 0-0
	GM	A	Walsall	W 2-1
	SQ/F	H	Northampton Town	W 3-2
	SS/F	H	Gillingham	W 3-0
	SF-1	A	Hereford United	L 0-2
(Southern area Final, 1st leg)				
	SF-2	H	Hereford United*	W 3-0
(Southern area Final, 2nd leg)				
	F	N	Bolton Wanderers	W 3-0
(Final at 'Wembley Stadium')				
1986/87	GM	A	Exeter City	D 1-1
	GM	H	Bristol Rovers	W 3-0
	1	H	Southend United	W 1-0
	SQ/F	H	Brentford	W 3-0
	SS/F	H	Gillingham	W 2-0
	SF-1	A	Aldershot	W 2-1
(Southern area Final, 1st leg)				
	SF-2	H	Aldershot	W 2-0
(Southern area Final, 2nd leg)				
	F	N	Mansfield Town*	D 1-1
(Final at 'Wembley Stadium'. Mansfield won 5-4 on penalties)				

Sherpa Van Trophy

Season	Rnd	Venue	Opponents	Result
1987/88	GM	H	Swansea City	W 2-0
	GM	A	Wolverhampton Wndrs	L 1-3
	1	A	Aldershot*	L 0-1
1988/89	GM	A	Bristol Rovers	L 0-1
	GM	H	Exeter City	W 2-0
	1	A	Wolverhampton Wndrs	L 0-3

Leyland DAF Cup

Season	Rnd	Venue	Opponents	Result
1989/90	GM	H	Swansea City	W 2-1
	GM	A	Reading	D 1-1
	1	H	Notts County	L 0-1

Auto Windscreens Shield

Season	Rnd	Venue	Opponents	Result
1995/96	GM	A	Oxford United	L 0-3
	GM	H	Barnet	W 2-0
	1	A	Shrewsbury Town*	D 0-0
(Shrewsbury won 7-6 on penalties)				
1996/97	2	A	Swansea City	W 1-0
	SQ/F	A	Watford	L 1-2

FULL MEMBERS CUP COMPETITIONS
Zenith Data Systems Cup

Season	Rnd	Venue	Opponents	Result
1990/91	1	A	Oxford United*	D 2-2
(Oxford won 3-2 on penalties)				
1991/92	2	H	Southampton	L 1-2

* denotes extra-time played

WATNEY CUP

Season	Rnd	Venue	Opponents	Result
1973/74	1	A	Peterborough United	W 2-1
	S/F	A	Stoke City	L 1-4

ANGLO-SCOTTISH CUP

Season	Rnd	Venue	Opponents	Result
1975/76	GM	A	Chelsea	L 0-1
	GM	A	Fulham	D 2-2
	GM	H	Norwich City	W 4-1
1976/77	GM	H	West Bromwich Albion	W 1-0
	GM	H	Notts County	W 2-0
	GM	A	Nottingham Forest	L 2-4
1977/78	GM	H	Bristol Rovers	W 3-1
	GM	A	Plymouth Argyle	W 2-0
	GM	A	Birmingham City	L 0-1
	QF-1	A	Partick Thistle	L 0-2
	QF-2	H	Partick Thistle	W 3-0
	S/F-1	A	Hibernian	D 1-1
	S/F-2	H	Hibernian	W 5-3
	F-1	A	St Mirren	W 2-1
	F-2	H	St Mirren	D 1-1
1978/79	GM	H	Bristol Rovers	W 6-1
	GM	H	Cardiff City	W 1-0
	GM	A	Fulham	W 3-0
	QF-1	H	St Mirren	L 1-2
	QF-2	A	St Mirren	D 2-2
1979/80	GM	A	Birmingham City	W 4-0
	GM	A	Plymouth Argyle	D 0-0
	GM	H	Fulham	W 1-0
	QF-1	A	Partick Thistle	D 1-1
	QF-2	H	Partick Thistle	W 2-0
	S/F-1	H	Morton	D 2-2
	S/F-2	A	Morton	W 1-0
	F-1	H	St Mirren	L 0-2
	F-2	A	St Mirren	L 1-3
1980/81	GM	H	Fulham	W 2-0
	GM	H	Notts County	D 1-1
	GM	A	Orient	L 0-1

ANGLO-ITALIAN CUP

Season	Rnd	Venue	Opponents	Result
1992/93	PG	H	Watford	W 1-0
	PG	A	Luton Town	D 1-1
	GM	H	Cosenza	L 0-2
	GM	A	Pisa	L 3-4
	GM	H	Reggiana	L 1-2
	GM	A	Cremonese	D 2-2
1993/94	PG	A	Portsmouth	L 1-3
	PG	H	Oxford United	W 2-1

GLOUCESTERSHIRE CUP

Season	Rnd	Venue	Opponents	Result
1897/98	2	H	Eastville Rovers	W 2-0
	S/F	N	Bristol St George	D 1-1
	(Semi-final at 'The Chequers')			
	S/Fr	N	Bristol St George	W 2-0
	(Semi-final replay at 'Ashton Gate')			
	F	N	Warmley	W 2-1
	(Final at 'Eastville')			
1898/99	1	H	Bristol Amateurs	W 7-3
	S/F	H	Fishponds	W 8-1
	F	N	Bristol Rovers	W 2-1
	(Final at 'St George')			
1899/1900	S/F	A	Bristol Rovers	D 1-1
	S/Fr	H	Bristol Rovers	W 2-1
	F	N	Bedminster	L 1-3
	(Final at 'Eastville')			
1900/01	F	H	Bristol Rovers	W 4-0
1901/02	S/F	H	Bristol East	W 2-1
	F	A	Bristol Rovers	D 0-0
	Fr	H	Bristol Rovers	D 0-0
1902/03	F	A	Bristol Rovers	D 0-0
	Fr	H	Bristol Rovers	D 1-1
	Fr^2	H	Bristol Rovers	L 2-4
1903/04	S/F	A	Bristol East	W 4-0
	(Semi-final at 'Eastville')			
	F	H	Bristol Rovers	W 2-1
1904/05	S/F	H	Bristol East	W 5-1
	F	A	Bristol Rovers	D 2-2
	Fr	H	Bristol Rovers	L 1-3
1905/06	F	H	Bristol Rovers	W 4-0
1906/07	F	A	Bristol Rovers	W 2-0
1907/08	F	H	Bristol Rovers	W 2-0
1908/09	F	A	Bristol Rovers	D 1-1
	Fr	H	Bristol Rovers	D 1-1
	Fr^2	A	Bristol Rovers	W 2-1
	(Played 1909/10 season)			
1909/10	F	H	Bristol Rovers	W 2-0
1910/11	F	A	Bristol Rovers	W 1-0
1911/12	F	H	Bristol Rovers	W 1-0
1912/13	F	A	Bristol Rovers	L 0-1
1913/14	F	H	Bristol Rovers	W 2-0
Competition not held 1914/15 to 1918/19 inclusive.				
1919/20	F	A	Bristol Rovers	W 4-0
1920/21	F	H	Bristol Rovers	W 1-0
1921/22	F	A	Bristol Rovers	W 2-0
1922/23	F	H	Bristol Rovers	− 3-1
	(Abandoned after 80 minutes due to fading light)			
	F	H	Bristol Rovers*	W 1-0

Season	Rnd	Venue	Opponents	Result
1923/24	F	A	Bristol Rovers	D 1-1
	Fr	H	Bristol Rovers	W 2-0
1924/25	F	H	Bristol Rovers	D 1-1
	Fr	A	Bristol Rovers	L 0-2
1925/26	F	A	Bristol Rovers	W 4-1
1926/27	F	H	Bristol Rovers	W 4-0
1927/28	F	A	Bristol Rovers	L 0-1
1928/29	F	H	Bristol Rovers	W 2-0
1929/30	F	A	Bristol Rovers	D 0-0
	Fr	H	Bristol Rovers	W 4-1
1930/31	F	H	Bristol Rovers	W 3-1
1931/32	F	A	Bristol Rovers	W 1-0
1932/33	F	H	Bristol Rovers	D 3-3
	Fr	A	Bristol Rovers	W 4-3
1933/34	F	A	Bristol Rovers	D 0-0
	F	H	Bristol Rovers	W 2-1
1934/35	F	H	Bristol Rovers	L 1-2
1935/36	F	A	Bristol Rovers	L 1-3
1936/37	F	H	Bristol Rovers	W 1-0
1937/38	F	A	Bristol Rovers	L 1-2
1938/39	F	H	Bristol Rovers	W 3-0

Competition not held 1939/40 to 1943/44 inclusive.

Season	Rnd	Venue	Opponents	Result
1944/45	F	A	Bristol Rovers	W 5-0
1945/46	F	H	Bristol Rovers	W 3-1
1946/47	F	A	Bristol Rovers	D 2-2
	Fr	H	Bristol Rovers	W 2-0
1947/48	F	H	Bristol Rovers	L 1-2
1948/49	F	A	Bristol Rovers	L 0-2
1949/50	F	H	Bristol Rovers	W 2-0
1950/51	F	A	Bristol Rovers	D 1-1
1951/52	F	H	Bristol Rovers	W 2-1
1952/53	F	A	Bristol Rovers	W 2-0
1953/54	F	H	Bristol Rovers	D 2-2
1954/55	F	A	Bristol Rovers	L 1-2
1955/56	F	H	Bristol Rovers	L 0-1
1956/57	F	A	Bristol Rovers	W 2-1
1957/58	F	H	Bristol Rovers	W 4-1
1958/59	F	A	Bristol Rovers	D 1-1
1959/60	F	H	Bristol Rovers	W 3-2
1960/61	F	A	Bristol Rovers	W 3-1
1961/62	F	H	Bristol Rovers	W 3-1
1962/63	F	A	Bristol Rovers	L 1-2
1963/64	F	H	Bristol Rovers	D 2-2
1964/65	F	A	Bristol Rovers	L 2-3
1965/66	F	H	Bristol Rovers	L 0-1

Season	Rnd	Venue	Opponents	Result
1966/67	F	A	Bristol Rovers	W 3-0
1967/68	F	H	Bristol Rovers	D 1-1
1968/69	F	A	Bristol Rovers	W 5-0
1969/70	F	H	Bristol Rovers	W 2-1
1970/71	F	A	Bristol Rovers	D 1-1
1971/72	F	H	Bristol Rovers*	D 1-1

(Rovers secured the Cup by winning the new penalty shoot-out 4-2)

Season	Rnd	Venue	Opponents	Result
1972/73	F	A	Bristol Rovers*	D 2-2

(City won 5-3 on penalties)

Season	Rnd	Venue	Opponents	Result
1973/74	F	H	Bristol Rovers	L 0-2
1974/75	F	A	Bristol Rovers*	L 1-2
1975/76	F	H	Bristol Rovers*	L 3-2
1976/77	F	A	Bristol Rovers	W 1-0
1977/78	F	H	Bristol Rovers	W 3-0
1978/79	F	A	Bristol Rovers	W 2-0
1979/80	F	H	Bristol Rovers	W 1-0
1980/81	F	A	Bristol Rovers*	W 1-0
1981/82	F	H	Bristol Rovers	L 0-1
1982/83	F	A	Bristol Rovers	L 1-2
1983/84	F	H	Bristol Rovers*	L 2-3
1984/85	F	A	Bristol Rovers*	L 1-3
1985/86	F	H	Bristol Rovers	W 1-0
1986/87	F	A	Bristol Rovers	W 2-1

(Played 1987/88 season)

Season	Rnd	Venue	Opponents	Result
1987/88	F	H	Bristol Rovers	W 3-1
1988/89	F	A	Bristol Rovers	L 0-3
1989/90	F	H	Bristol Rovers	L 1-2
1990/91	F	A	Bristol Rovers	W 4-1
1991/92	F	H	Bristol Rovers	W 3-2
1992/93	F	A	Bristol Rovers	L 1-2
1993/94	F	H	Bristol Rovers*	D 1-1

(Rovers won 5-3 on penalties)

Season	Rnd	Venue	Opponents	Result
1994/95	F	A	Bristol Rovers	D 0-0

(Rovers won 11-10 on penalties)

Season	Rnd	Venue	Opponents	Result
1995/96				

Competition not held as City's new pitch not ready for pre-season game and no time later to play the Final

Season	Rnd	Venue	Opponents	Result
1996/97	F	H	Bristol Rovers	W 1-0

* Denotes extra-time played

(NOTE: The Competiton only became restricted to a City v Rovers contest from the 1907/08 season)

One Hundred Years of Bristol City FC Managers

April 1897	– April 1899	Sam Hollis
May 1899	– June 1901	Bob Campbell
June 1901	– April 1905	Sam Hollis
May 1905	– October 1910	Harry Thickett
October 1910	– January 1911	Frank Bacon
January 1911	– April 1913	Sam Hollis
April 1913	– January 1917	George Hedley
January 1917	– May 1919	Jack Hamilton
May 1919	– October 1921	Joe Palmer
December 1921	– July 1929	Alex Raisbeck
August 1929	– February 1932	Joe Bradshaw
April 1932	– March 1949	Bob Hewison
October 1938	– May 1939	Clarrie Bourton
May 1939	– March 1949	Bob Hewison
April 1949	– June 1950	Bob Wright
July 1950	– January 1958	Pat Beasley
January 1958	– March 1960	Peter Doherty
July 1960	– September 1967	Fred Ford
October 1967	– September 1980	Alan Dicks
October 1980	– January 1982	Bob Houghton
January 1982	– April 1982	Roy Hodgson
May 1982	– March 1988	Terry Cooper
March 1988	– September 1990	Joe Jordan
September 1990	– February 1992	Jimmy Lumsden
March 1992	– January 1993	Denis Smith
January 1993	– November 1994	Russell Osman
November 1994	– March 1997	Joe Jordan
March 1997		John Ward

Bristol City FC Supporters Club Player of the Year

1970/71	Gerry Sharpe
1971/72	Geoff Merrick
1972/73	John Emanuel
1973/74	Gerry Gow
1974/75	Gary Collier
1975/76	The Whole Team
1976/77	Norman Hunter
1977/78	Norman Hunter
1978/79	Gerry Gow
1979/80	Geoff Merrick
1980/81	Kevin Mabbutt
1981/82	No award
1982/83	Glyn Riley
1983/84	Howard Pritchard
1984/85	Alan Walsh
1985/86	Bobby Hutchinson
1986/87	Rob Newman
1987/88	Alan Walsh
1988/89	Keith Waugh
1989/90	Bob Taylor
1990/91	Andy Llewellyn
1991/92	Martin Scott
1992/93	Keith Welch
1993/94	Wayne Allison
1994/95	Matt Bryant
1995/96	Martin Kuhl
1996/97	Shaun Taylor

THE COMPLETE WHO'S WHO OF BRISTOL CITY FC FOOTBALL LEAGUE PLAYERS

Dave Affleck

Born: Coylton 26.7.1912
From: Notts County 5.34
To: Clapton Orient 7.35

	League	FAC	LC	MC	Total	
1934/35	3				3	(0)
Total	**3**				**3**	**(0)**

Paul Agostino

Born: Woodville, Australia 9.6.1975
From: Young Boys Berne 6.95 £50,000
To: Munich 1860 7.97

	League	FAC	LC	MC	Total	
1995/96	29+11(10)	4 (1)	2+1		35+12(11)	
1996/97	34+10 (9)	4 (5)	2+2 (2)	2	42+12(16)	
Total	**63+21(19)**	**4 (5)**	**6+2 (3)**	**4+1**	**77+24(27)**	

Peter Aitken

Born: Cardiff 30.6.1954
From: Bristol Rovers 11.80
To: York City 2.82

	League	FAC	LC	MC	Total	
1980/81	22 (1)	5			27	(1)
1981/82	19	5	4		28	(0)
Total	**41 (1)**	**5**	**4**		**55**	**(1)**

Mark Aizlewood

Born: Newport 1.10.1959
From: Bradford City 8.90 £125,000
To: Cardiff City 11.92

	League	FAC	LC	MC	Total	
1990/91	41+1 (2)	1	4	1	47+1	(2)
1991/92	34 (1)	4	1	0+1 (0)	39+1	(1)
1992/93	19+1	0+1		1	20+2	(0)
1993/94	5		4		9	(0)
Total	**99 (3)**	**5+1**	**5**	**6+1**	**115**	**(1)**

Bob Allen

Born: Shepton Mallet 5.12.1916
From: Notts County 11.46
To: Bridgwater Town 7.47

	League	FAC	LC	MC	Total	
1946/47	1	1			2	(0)
Total	**1**	**1**			**2**	**(0)**

Paul Allen

Born: Aveley 28.8.1962
From: Swindon Town 1.97
To: Milwall 6.97

	League	FAC	LC	MC	Total	
1996/97	13+1		1		14+1	
Total	**13+1**		**1**		**14+1**	

Peter Allen

Born: Bristol 8.10.1934
From: Soundwell 7.53

	League	FAC	LC	MC	Total	
1954/55	1				1	(0)
Total	**1**				**1**	**(0)**

Tom Allen

Born:
From:
To:

	League	FAC	LC	MC	Total	
1912/13	1	(1)			1	(1)
Total	**1**	**(1)**			**1**	**(1)**

Wayne Allison

Born: Huddersfield 16.10.1968
From: Watford 7.90 P/ex
To: Swindon Town 7.95 £475,000

	League	FAC	LC	MC	Total	
1990/91	18+19 (6)	1 (1)	0+3	1	20+22(7)	
1991/92	37+ 6(10)	2+1	2 (1)	1	42+7(11)	
1992/93	22+17 (4)	1	2+1 (1)	3+1 (2)	28+19(7)	
1993/94	35+ 4(15)	6 (5)	0+1	1+1 (1)	42+6(21)	
1994/95	37 (13)	3			40	(13)
Total	**149+46 (48)**	**13+1 (6)**	**4+5 (2)**	**6+2 (3)**	**172+54(59)**	

Charles Allwright

Born: Brentford 1.1.1886
From: Brentford
To: Swindon Town

	League	FAC	LC	MC	Total	
1919/20	11				11	(0)
Total	**11**				**11**	**(0)**

Ferguson Anderson

Born:
From: Shields Athletic
To:

	League	FAC	LC	MC	Total	
1911/12	7				7	(0)
Total	**7**				**7**	**(0)**

Bob Anderson

Born: Newcastle 9.11.1924
From: Bristol Rovers 4.54 £500
To: Retired 5.61

	League	FAC	LC	MC	Total	
1954/55	23				23	(0)
1955/56	22	1			23	(0)
1956/57	21				21	(0)
1957/58	35	2			37	(0)
1958/59	5				5	(0)
Total	**106**	**3**			**109**	**(0)**

Fred Andrews

Born: King's Norton 1.7.1886
From: Burton All Saints 1.24
To: Burton All Saints 9.24

	League	FAC	LC	MC	Total	
1923	1				1	(0)
Total	**1**				**1**	**(0)**

Archie Annan

Born: St Bernards 1879
From: Sheffield United 4.05
To: Burslem Port Vale 7.11

	League	FAC	LC	MC	Total	
1905/06	38	1			39	(0)
1906/07	38	2			40	(0)
1907/08	13	2			15	(0)
1908/09	26	10			36	(0)
1909/10	28	3			31	(0)
Total	**143**	**18**			**161**	**(0)**

Gordon Armstrong

Born: Newcastle 15.7.1967
From: Sunderland 8.95 Loan

	League	FAC	LC	MC	Total	
1995/96	6				6	(0)
Total	**6**				**6**	**(0)**

Dick Armstrong

Born: Newburn 31.8.1909
From: Nottingham Forest 5.35

	League	FAC	LC	MC	Total	
1935/36	36 (11)	1		2	39	(11)
1936/37	21 (5)	1		1	23	(5)
1937/38	23				23	(0)
1938/39	32 (2)	1		3	36	(2)
Total	**112 (18)**	**3**		**6**	**121**	**(18)**

Ray Atteveld

Born: Amsterdam, Holland 8.9.1966
From: Everton 3.92 £250,000
To: FC Waregem 11.93

	League	FAC	LC	MC	Total	
1991/92	4+3 (1)				4+3	(1)
1992/93	5+2		1		5+2	(0)
Total	**9+5 (1)**		**1**		**9+5**	**(1)**

John Atyeo

Born: Dilton Marsh 7.7.1932
From: Portsmouth 6.51
To: Retired 5.66

	League	FAC	LC	MC	Total	
1951/52	44 (12)	2 (2)			46	(14)
1952/53	33 (11)				33	(11)
1953/54	45 (22)	3 (3)			48	(25)
1954/55	46 (28)	1			47	(28)
1955/56	39 (30)	1 (1)			40	(31)
1956/57	37 (23)	3 (5)			40	(28)
1957/58	42 (23)	4 (2)			46	(25)
1958/59	40 (26)	3			43	(26)
1959/60	42 (16)	1 (1)			43	(17)
1960/61	37 (19)	5 (7)		3 (3)	45	(29)
1961/62	42 (26)	5 (3)	1	2 (1)	50	(30)
1962/63	30 (16)	3 (2)	1		34	(18)
1963/64	46 (21)	5 (4)		1 (2)	52	(27)
1964/65	38 (23)	4			42	(23)
1965/66	35 (19)	1			36	(19)
Total	**596 (315)**	**41 (30)**	**6 (5)**	**2 (1)**	**645**	**(351)**

Phil Bach

Born: Shropshire 1.1.1873
From: Middlesbrough 6.00
To: Re-instated amateur 1904

	League	FAC	LC	MC	Total	
1903/04	3				3	(0)
Total	**3**				**3**	**(0)**

Kevin Baddeley

Born: Swindon 12.3.1962
From: Apprentice 3.80
To: Swindon Town 6.81

	League	FAC	LC	MC	Total	
1980/81	1		1		2	(0)
Total	**1**		**1**		**2**	**(0)**

Jack Bailey

Born: Bristol 17.6.1921
From: BAC 12.44
To: Trowbridge Town 7.58

	League	FAC	LC	MC	Total	
1946/47	34	2			36	(0)
1947/48	42	3			45	(0)
1948/49	41	3			44	(0)
1949/50	14				14	(0)
1950/51	39	5			44	(0)
1951/52	43	2			45	(0)
1952/53	41	1			42	(0)
1953/54	39	3			42	(0)
1954/55	18				18	(0)
1955/56	6				6	(0)
1956/57	18	3			21	(0)
1957/58	12	3			15	(0)
Total	**347**	**25**			**372**	**(0)**

John Bailey

Born: Liverpool 1.4.1957
From: Newcastle United 9.88
To: Coaching Staff 7.91

	League	FAC	LC	MC	Total	
1988/89	35	6	5	2	48	(0)
1989/90	38 (1)	7	1	2	48	(1)
1990/91	6+1	1			7+1	(0)
Total	**79+1 (1)**	**14**	**6**	**4**	**103+1**	**(1)**

William Bailiff

Born: Ruabon 19.3.1882
From: Treharris 5.10
To: Treharris 10.11

	League	FAC	LC	MC	Total	
1910/11	7	1			8	(0)
Total	**7**	**1**			**8**	**(0)**

Joe Baillie

Born: Dumfries 26.2.1929
From: Wolverhampton Wand. 6.56
To: Leicester City 6.57

	League	FAC	LC	MC	Total	
1956/57	10				10	(0)
Total	**10**				**10**	**(0)**

David Bain

Born: Rutherglen 5.8.1900
From: Everton 11.28
To: Halifax Town 8.30

	League	FAC	LC	MC	Total	
1928/29	17 (1)	1			18	(1)
1929/30	33 (1)	1			34	(1)
Total	**50 (2)**	**2**			**52**	**(2)**

John Bain

Born: Glasgow 23.6.1957
From: Apprentice 7.74
To: Portland Timbers 2.79

	League	FAC	LC	MC	Total	
1976/77	2			0+3	2+3	(0)
1977/78	3+1			0+1	3+2	(0)
Total	**5+1**			**0+4**	**5+5**	**(0)**

Ian Baird

Born: Rotherham 1.4.1964
From: Hearts 6.93 £295,000
To: Plymouth Argyle 9.95 P/ex

	League	FAC	LC	MC	Total	
1993/94	16+3 (5)		2	1	19+3	(5)
1994/95	37 (6)	2 (1)	1		40	(7)
Total	**53+3 (11)**	**2 (1)**	**3**	**1**	**59+3**	**(12)**

Jimmy Baker

Born: Trethomas 5.5.1904
From: Coventry City 6.35
To: Colchester United 6.37

	League	FAC	LC	MC	Total	
1935/36	5				5	(0)
1936/37	5				5	(0)
Total	**10**				**10**	**(0)**

Chris Ball

Born: Leek 31.10.1906
From: Bristol Rovers 12.31
To: Walsall 2.32

	League	FAC	LC	MC	Total	
1931/32	3				3	(0)
Total	**3**				**3**	**(0)**

Henry Ball

Born: Bristol
From: Bristol City Wednesday 8.11

	League	FAC	LC	MC	Total	
1911/12	2 (1)	1			3	(1)
Total	**2 (1)**	**1**			**3**	**(1)**

Albert Banfield

Born: Bristol 5.5.1912
From: St Philips Marsh 7.33
To: York City 5.35

	League	FAC	LC	MC	Total	
1933/34	18 (4)			6 (2)	24	(6)
1934/35	20 (4)	4			24	(4)
Total	**38 (8)**	**4**		**6 (2)**	**48**	**(10)**

Laurie Banfield

Born: Paulton 11.11.1889
From: Paulton Rovers 7.11
To: Ilfracombe Town

	League	FAC	LC	MC	Total	
1911/12	1				1	(0)
1912/13	25	1			26	(0)
1913/14	28	2			30	(0)
1914/15	38	2			40	(0)
1919/20	40 (1)	5			45	(1)
1920/21	22 (1)				22	(1)
1921/22	42 (1)	2			44	(1)
1922/23	34 (2)	2			36	(2)
1923/24	28 (1)	4			32	(1)
1924/25	1				1	(0)
Total	**259 (6)**	**18**			**277**	**(6)**

Bert Banks

Born: Coventry 1.1.1874
From: Aston Villa 11.01
To: Watford 9.03

	League	FAC	LC	MC	Total	
1901/02	20 (9)				20	(9)
1902/03	22 (8)	2 (3)			24	(11)

Phil Barber

Born: Tring 10.6.1965
From: Millwall 7.95
To: Dover Athletic 9.96

	League	FAC	LC	MC	Total	
1995/96	3		2		5	(0)
Total	**3**		**2**		**5**	**(0)**

Stan Barber

Born: Wallsend 28.5.1908
From: Newcastle United 6.28
To: Exeter City 8.30

	League	FAC	LC	MC	Total	
1995/96	19 (1)				19	(1)
1929/30	4				4	(0)
Total	**23 (1)**				**23**	**(1)**

Dominic Barclay

Born: Bristol 5.9.1976
From: Trainee 7.93

	League	FAC	LC	MC	Total	
1993/94	2				2	(0)
1995/96	0+2				0+2	(0)
Total	**2+2**				**2+2**	**(0)**

Darren Barnard

Born: Rintein, Germany 30.11.1971
From: Chelsea 10.95 £75,000
To: Barnsley 8.97 £700,000

	League	FAC	LC	MC	Total	
1995/96	33+1 (4)	2		2	37+1	(4)
1996/97	44 (11)	4	4 (1)	2	54	(12)
Total	**77+1 (15)**	**6**	**4 (1)**	**4**	**91+1**	**(16)**

Charles Barnes

Born: Chesham 1879
From: Reading 6.02
To: Watford 8.04

	League	FAC	LC	MC	Total	
1902/03	12 (2)				12	(2)
1903/04	11 (3)				11	(3)
Total	**23 (6)**				**23**	**(6)**

Vic Barney

Born: Stepney 3.4.1922
From: Reading 10.48
To: Grimsby Town 6.49 £2,000

	League	FAC	LC	MC	Total	
1948/49	28 (4)	3 (1)			31	(5)
1948/49	28 (4)	3 (1)			31	(5)

Danny Bartley

Born: Paulton 3.10.1947
From: Apprentice 10.64
To: Swansea City 8.73 £10,000

	League	FAC	LC	MC	Total	
1965/66	8+1				8+1	(0)
1966/67	20	(2)	2		22	(2)
1967/68	12+1				12+1	(0)
1968/69	6+2		1		7+2	(0)
1969/70	16+1	(3)	1	1	18+1	(3)
1970/71	2+1				2+1	(0)
1971/72	16+1				16+1	(0)
1972/73	12+2	(1)	2		14+2	(1)
Total	**92**	**(6)**	**3**	**4**	**99**	**(6)**

Tom Batey

Born: Brancepeth 18.10.1894
From: Esh Winning 5.13
To: Durham City 1.19

	League	FAC	LC	MC	Total	
1914/15	7	(1)			7	(1)
Total	**7**	**(1)**			**7**	**(1)**

Bert Batten

Born: Bristol 14.5.1898
From: Paulton Rovers 7.20
To: Plymouth Argyle 5.21

	League	FAC	LC	MC	Total	
1920/21	7				7	(0)
Total	**7**				**7**	**(0)**

Billy Batty

Born: Killamarsh 13.7.1886
From: Sheffield United 4.10
To: Lincoln City 4.11

	League	FAC	LC	MC	Total	
1909/10	4				4	(0)
1910/11	1				1	(0)
Total	**5**				**5**	**(0)**

Cliff Beak

Born: Bristol 22.12.1902
From: Hanham Athletic 6.28

	League	FAC	LC	MC	Total	
1929/30	1				1	(0)
Total	**1**				**1**	**(0)**

George Beare

Born: Southampton 2.10.1885
From: Cardiff City 11.21
To: Cardiff City 9.22

	League	FAC	LC	MC	Total	
1921/22	14	(2)			14	(2)
Total	**14**	**(2)**			**14**	**(2)**

Albert 'Pat' Beasley

Born: Stourbridge 27.7.1913
From: Fulham 8.50
To: Manager

	League	FAC	LC	MC	Total	
1950/51	43	(3)	5		48	(3)
1951/52	23	(2)	2		25	(2)
Total	**66**	**(5)**	**7**		**73**	**(5)**

Walter Bennett

Born: Mexborough 1.1.1874
From: Sheffield United 4.05
To: Denaby United 7.07

	League	FAC	LC	MC	Total	
1904/05	3				3	(0)
1905/06	37	(20)	1		38	(20)
1906/07	8	(2)			8	(2)
Total	**48**	**(22)**	**1**		**49**	**(22)**

Walter Bennett

Born: Sheffield 17.4.1901
From: Gainsborough Trinity 5.28
To: Ballymena 6.30

	League	FAC	LC	MC	Total	
1928/29	14				14	(0)
1929/30	6				6	(0)
Total	**20**				**20**	**(0)**

Junior Bent

Born: Huddersfield 1.3.1970
From: Huddersfield Town 3.90 £30,000
To: Blackpool 8.97

	League	FAC	LC	MC	Total	
1989/90	15+5	(2)	0+1	3	1	19+6	(2)
1991/92	7+10	(2)	3+1(1)	0+1		10+12(3)
1992/93	13+7	(3)			1+2	14+9	(3)
1993/94	17+3	(2)	3+1			20+4	(2)
1994/95	40+1	(6)	3	(1)	2		45+1	(7)
1995/96	33+7	(2)	2	4	3	42+7	(2)
1996/97	17+5	(3)	2	1	2	22+5	(3)
Total	**142+38(20)**	**13+3(2)**	**10+1**	**7+2**	**172+44(22)**

Brian Bevan

Born: Exeter 20.3.1937
From: Bridgwater Town 2.56
To: Carlisle United 3.60

	League	FAC	LC	MC	Total	
1957/58	1				1	(0)
1959/60	1				1	(0)
Total	**2**				**2**	**(0)**

Roy Bicknell

Born: Doncaster 19.2.1926
From: Charlton Athletic 6.49
To: Gravesend & N. 6.51

	League	FAC	LC	MC	Total	
1949/50	17		1		18	(0)
1950/51	4				4	(0)
Total	**21**		**1**		**22**	**(0)**

Jack Billingham

Born: Daventry 12.1914
From: Northampton Town 7.37
To: Burnley 5.38

	League	FAC	LC	MC	Total	
1937/38	7			2		??	(?)
Total	**7**			**2**		**??**	**(?)**

Len Birks

Born: Stoke-on-Trent 6.10.1896
From: Plymouth Argyle 9.33
To: Yeovil & Potters 8.34

	League	FAC	LC	MC	Total	
1933/34	30		4		5	39	(0)
Total	**30**		**4**		**5**	**39**	**(0)**

Clayton Blackmore

Born: Neath 23.9.1964
From: Middlesbrough 11.96 Loan

	League	FAC	LC	MC	Total	
1996/97	5	(1)			5	(1)
Total	**5**	**(1)**			**5**	**(1)**

Herbert Blake

Born: Bristol 26.8.1894
From: Fishponds C. 5.14
To: Mid-Rhonnda 9.15

	League	FAC	LC	MC	Total	
1914/15	1				1	(0)
Total	**1**				**1**	**(0)**

Cecil Blakemore

Born: Stourbridge 8.12.1897
From: Crystal Palace 5.27
To: Brentford 5.29

	League	FAC	LC	MC	Total	
1927/28	19	(7)			19	(7)
1928/29	23	(13)			23	(13)
Total	**42**	**(20)**			**42**	**(20)**

Len Bond

Born: Ilminster 12.2.1954
From: Apprentice 9.71
To: Brentford 8.77 £8,000

	League	FAC	LC	MC	Total	
1970/71	1				1	(0)
1971/72	2				2	(0)
1972/73	10		2		12	(0)
1973/74	15		1	4	20	(0)
1976/77	2				2	(0)
Total	**30**		**3**	**4**	**37**	**(0)**

Llewellyn Booth

Born: Merthyr Tydfil 28.2.1912
From: Bangor City 7.36
To: Retired 5.46

	League	FAC	LC	MC	Total	
1936/37	19	(1)			19	(1)
1937/38	21	(6)	1	4	26	(6)
1938/39	23	(15)	1	1	25	(15)
1939/40	2				2	(0)
Total	**65**	**(22)**	**2**	**5**	**72**	**(22)**

Brian Borrows

Born: Liverpool 20.12.1960
From: Coventry City 9.93
To: Loan

	League	FAC	LC	MC	Total	
1993/94	6				6	(0)
Total	**6**				**6**	**(0)**

John Borthwick

Born: Poplar 1.1.1897
From:
To: Hartlepools United 7.22

	League	FAC	LC	MC	Total	
1921/22	1				1	(0)
Total	**1**				**1**	**(0)**

Tom Boucher

Born: West Bromwich 1.1.1873
From: Bristol Rovers 7.01
To: New Brompton 7.03

	League		FAC		LC		MC		Total	
1901/02	26	(8)	1						27	(8)
1902/03	25	(6)	1	(1)					26	(7)
Total	51	(14)	2	(1)					53	(15)

Clarrie Bourton

Born: Paulton 30.9.1908
From: Paulton Rovers 1.27
To: Blackburn Rovers 5.28
From: Plymouth Argyle 1.38
To: Retired 5.44

	League		FAC		LC		MC		Total	
1927/28	4	(1)	1						5	(1)
1937/38	19	(3)							19	(3)
1938/39	35	(10)					1		36	(10)
Total	58	(14)	1				1		60	(14)

Ted Bowen

Born: Goldthorpe 1.7.1903
From: Northampton Town 7.32

	League		FAC		LC		MC		Total	
1932/33	39	(28)	3	(4)			1	(1)	43	(33)
1933/34	16	(5)	2				1		19	(5)
Total	55	(33)	5	(4)			2		62	(38)

Archie Bown

Born: Highworth 1.1.1882
From: Swindon Town 7.19
To: Weymouth 8.22

	League		FAC		LC		MC		Total	
1919/20	4		1						5	(0)
1920/21	15	(4)	1						16	(4)
1921/22	16	(1)	2	(1)					18	(2)
Total	35	(5)	4	(1)					39	(6)

Steve Bowyer

Born: Northwich 12.10.1887
From: Liverpool 2.12
To: South Liverpool 7.13

	League		FAC		LC		MC		Total	
1911/12	13	(5)							13	(5)
1912/13	36	(9)	1						37	(9)
Total	49	(14)	1						50	(14)

Jack Boxley

Born: Cradley 31.5.1931
From: Stourbridge 10.50 £2,000
To: Coventry City 12.56
From: Coventry City 8.60
To: Chippenham Town 7.61

	League		FAC		LC		MC		Total	
1950/51	23	(2)							23	(2)
1951/52	16	(1)							16	(1)
1952/53	25	(4)	1						26	(4)
1953/54	41	(14)	3						44	(14)
1954/55	43	(11)	1						44	(11)
1955/56	40	(2)	1						41	(2)
1956/57	5								5	(0)
1960/61	12		1		1	(1)			14	(1)
Total	205	(34)	7		1	(1)			213	(35)

Danny Boxshall

Born: Bradford 2.4.1920
From: QPR 5.48
To: Bournemouth 7.50

	League		FAC		LC		MC		Total	
1948/48	28	(8)	3	(1)					31	(9)
1949/50	24	(2)							24	(2)
Total	52	(10)	3	(1)					55	(11)

John Boyd

Born: USA 10.9.1926
From: Gloucester City 12.50
To: Bath City 8.52

	League		FAC		LC		MC		Total	
1950/51	24	(6)							24	(6)
1951/52	7		1						8	(0)
Total	31	(6)	1						32	(6)

Terry Boyle

Born: Ammanford 29.10.1958
From: Crystal Palace 10.81 P/ex
To: Newport County 11.82

	League		FAC		LC		MC		Total	
1981/82	22+1		5		1				28+1	(0)
1982/83	14				5	(2)	2		21	(2)
Total	36+1		5		6	(2)	2		49+1	(2)

Tommy Brace

Born: Bristol 8.3.1908
From:
To:

	League		FAC		LC		MC		Total	
1929/30	1								1	(0)
Total	1								1	(0)

John Bradbury

Born: South Bank 1.1.1878
From: Barnsley 7.01
To: New Brompton 7.02

	League		FAC		LC		MC		Total	
1901/02	30	(4)	2						32	(4)
Total	30	(4)	2						32	(4)

Joe Bradford

Born: Peggs Green 22.1.1901
From: Birmingham 5.35
To: Retired 5.36

	League		FAC		LC		MC		Total	
1935/36	5	(1)							5	(1)
Total	5	(1)							5	(1)

Joe Brain

Born: Ebbw Vale 28.1.1910
From: Swansea Town 1.37
To: Watford 11.39

	League		FAC		LC		MC		Total	
1937/38	29	(8)	3	(1)			4	(2)	36	(11)
1938/39	3	(1)					2	(1)	5	(2)
Total	32	(9)	3	(1)			6	(3)	41	(13)

Tom Brand

Born: Scotland 1888
From: Motherwell 7.11

	League		FAC		LC		MC		Total	
1911/12	8								8	(0)
Total	8								8	(0)

Wayne Bray

Born: Bristol 17.11.1964
From: Apprentice 11.81
To: Weymouth 9.83

	League		FAC		LC		MC		Total	
1961/62	19	(2)							19	(2)
1962/63	9+1				2+1		1		12+2	(0)
Total	28+1	(2)			2+1		1		19	(2)

Jim Brennan

Born: Toronto 8.5.1977
From: Sora Lazio 10.94

	League		FAC		LC		MC		Total	
1996/97	7+1								7+1	(0)
Total	7+1								7+1	(0)

George Brewster

Born: Barlborough 19.10.1925
From: Retford Town 9.49
To: Gravesend & N. 6.51

	League		FAC		LC		MC		Total	
1949/50	6	(1)	1						7	(1)
1950/51	7	(2)							7	(2)
Total	13	(3)	1						14	(3)

Cyril Bridge

Born: Bristol 28.8.1909
From: St Philips Marsh 7.32

	League		FAC		LC		MC		Total	
1932/33	9		3						12	(0)
1934/35	27		7				1		35	(0)
1935/36	29						1		30	(0)
1936/37	29		1				2		32	(0)
1937/38	20		3				2		25	(0)
1938/39	41		1				2		44	(0)
Total	155		15				8		178	(0)

Alec Briggs

Born: Sheffield 21.6.1939
From: Soundwell 4.57
To: Retired 5.70

	League		FAC		LC		MC		Total	
1957/58	4								4	(0)
1959/60	4								4	(0)
1960/61	9								9	(0)
1961/62	46		5		1		1	(1)	53	(1)
1962/63	46		4		1				51	(0)
1963/64	38		5		1				44	(0)
1964/65	39		4		1				44	(0)
1965/66	40		1		1				42	(0)
1966/67	42		4		2				48	(0)
1967/68	39		5		1				45	(0)
1968/69	38+1		1		3				42+1	(0)
1969/70	4+1				3				7+1	(0)
Total	349+2		29		14		1	(1)	393+2	(1)

Ernie Brinton

Born: Bristol   26.5.1908
From: Avonmouth   2.30
To: Newport County   6.37

	League	FAC	LC	MC	Total
1929/30	7				7 (0)
1930/31	34 (1)				34 (1)
1931/32	39	3			42 (0)
1932/33	23	2		1	26 (0)
1933/34	39 (3)	3 (2)		7	49 (5)
1934/35	35 (3)	8			43 (3)
1935/36	40	1		3	44 (0)
1936/37	32	1		2	35 (0)
Total	249 (7)	18 (2)		13	280 (9)

Jack Brinton

Born: Avonmouth   11.7.1916
From: Newport County   8.35
To: Derby County   1.38

	League	FAC	LC	MC	Total
1935/36	2 (1)			1	3 (1)
1936/37	10			1	11 (0)
Total	12 (1)			2	14 (1)

Tommy Broad

Born: Stalybridge   31.7.1887
From: Oldham Athletic   5.12
To: Manchester City   3.19

	League	FAC	LC	MC	Total
1912/13	37 (3)	1			38 (3)
1913/14	38 (3)	2			40 (3)
1914/15	31 (2)	2			33 (2)
Total	106 (8)	5			111 (8)

Mike Brolly

Born: Galston   6.10.1954
From: Chelsea   6.74
To: Grimsby Town   9.76   £6,000

	League	FAC	LC	MC	Total
1974/75	13+2 (1)				13+2 (1)
1975/76	14+1 (1)	1 (1)	2	2	19+1 (2)
Total	27+3 (2)	1 (1)	2	2	32+3 (3)

Russel Bromage

Born: Stoke-on-Trent   9.11.1959
From: Port Vale   8.87
To: Brighton   8.90

	League	FAC	LC	MC	Total
1987/88	28+2	2	2	3	35+2 (0)
1988/89	13 (1)		3		16 (1)
1989/90	3				3 (0)
Total	44+2 (1)	2	5	3	54+2 (1)

Reg Brook

Born: Nottingham   1.7.1912
From: Southend United   6.37

	League	FAC	LC	MC	Total
1937/38	30 (1)			1	31 (1)
1938/39	41	1		2	44 (0)
Total	71 (1)	1		3	75 (1)

Cliff Brooksbank

Born: Halifax   1890
From: Exeter City   7.14

	League	FAC	LC	MC	Total
1914/15	10 (7)				10 (7)
Total	10 (7)				10 (7)

Ian Broomfield

Born: Bristol   17.12.1950
From: Apprentice   8.68
To: Stockport County   12.72

	League	FAC	LC	MC	Total
1968/69	1				1 (0)
1969/70	1				1 (0)
1970/71	10+2 (2)	1	3+2		14+4 (2)
1971/72	3				3 (0)
1972/73	3+1		0+1		3+2 (0)
Total	18+3 (2)	1	3+3		22+6 (2)

Joe Brough

Born: Burslem   10.5.1886
From: Liverpool   1.12
To: Burslem Port Vale   5.13

	League	FAC	LC	MC	Total
1911/12	8 (1)				8 (1)
1912/13	14 (10)				14 (10)
1912/13	22 (11)				22 (11)

Billy Brown

Born: South Inch, Dysart
From: Chelsea   11.13
To: Swansea Town   9.19

	League	FAC	LC	MC	Total
1913/14	24 (10)	2			26 (10)
1914/15	38 (13)	2			40 (13)
Total	62 (23)	4			66 (23)

Ian Brown

Born: Ipswich   11.9.1965
From: Chelmsford City
To: Northampton Town   12.94

	League	FAC	LC	MC	Total
1993/94	5+6 (1)	1		2	8+6 (1)
1994/95	0+1		0+2		0+3 (0)
Total	5+7 (1)	1	0+2	2	8+9 (1)

John Brown

Born: South Bank   1.1.1885
From: Middlesbrough   CS.08
To: Middlesbrough   CS.09

	League	FAC	LC	MC	Total
1908/09	3				3 (0)
Total	3				3 (0)

Tommy Brown

Born: Darlington   1.1.1896
From: Cardiff City   5.22
To: South Shields   6.23

	League	FAC	LC	MC	Total
1922/23	8				8 (0)
Total	8				8 (0)

Wayne Brown

Born: Southampton   14.1.1977
From: Trainee   7.95

	League	FAC	LC	MC	Total
1993/94	1				1 (0)
Total	1				1 (0)

David Bruton

Born: Dursley   31.10.1952
From: Apprentice   7.71
To: Swansea City   8.73   £10,000

	League	FAC	LC	MC	Total
1971/72	10+1	0+1			10+2 (0)
1972/73	6				6 (0)
Total	16+1	0+1			16+2 (0)

Matt Bryant

Born: Bristol   21.9.1970
From: Trainee   7.89
To:

	League	FAC	LC	MC	Total
1990/91	22 (1)				22 (1)
1991/92	43 (2)	4	2	1	50 (2)
1992/93	41 (1)	1	3	5	50 (1)
1993/94	27+1 (2)	3			30+1 (2)
1994/95	37 (3)	3	2		42 (3)
1995/96	31+1 (2)	1	2+1	3	37+2 (2)
Total	201+2 (11)	12	9+1	9	231+3 (11)

Richard Bryant

Born: Bristol   20.6.1963
From: Robinsons   12.85
To: Gloucester City   7.86

	League	FAC	LC	MC	Total
1985/86	2 (1)				2 (1)
Total	2 (1)				2 (1)

Bill Buckland

Born: Shipston-on-Stour   1.1.1900
From: Cinderford Town   7.24

	League	FAC	LC	MC	Total
1924/25	1				1 (0)
Total	1				1 (0)

Reg Bungay

Born: Reading   5.2.1911
From: Plymouth Argyle   7.35
To: Mansfield Town   7.36

	League	FAC	LC	MC	Total
1935/36	8 (3)				8 (3)
Total	8 (3)				8 (3)

Tommy Burden

Born: Andover   21.2.1924
From: Leeds United   10.54   £3,000
To: Glastonbury   5.61

	League	FAC	LC	MC	Total
1954/55	27 (8)				27 (8)
1955/56	41 (6)	1			42 (6)
1956/57	40 (2)	3			43 (2)
1957/58	38 (2)	4 (1)			42 (3)
1958/59	41 (1)	3			44 (1)
1959/60	30	1			32 (0)
1960/61	14 (1)				14 (1)
Total	227 (20)	12 (1)			42 (21)

Dave Burnside

Born: Bristol   10.12.1939
From: Plymouth Argyle   12.71
To: Colchester United   3.72

	League	FAC	LC	MC	Total
1971/72	1				1 (0)
Total	1				1 (0)

Les Burrows

Born: Exeter 1.1.1906
From: Taunton Town 4.29
To: Taunton Town 6.30

	League	FAC	LC	MC	Total	
1929/30	1				1	(0)
Total	1				1	(0)

Andy Burton

Born: Lochgelly 1.1.1884
From: Motherwell 7.05
To: Everton 7.11

	League	FAC	LC	MC	Total	
1905/06	37	(8)	1		38	(8)
1906/07	34	(13)	2		36	(13)
1907/08	32	(9)	2		34	(9)
1908/09	35	(8)	10	(2)	45	(10)
1909/10	33	(3)	3	(1)	36	(4)
1910/11	21	(4)	1		22	(4)
Total	192	(45)	19	(3)	211	(48)

Edwin Burton

Born: Dunston-on-Tyne 1893
From: Shildon Athletic 5.13
To: Killed in action 8.16

	League	FAC	LC	MC	Total	
1913/14	5	(1)			5	(1)
1914/15	13	(3)	1	(2)	14	(5)
Total	18	(4)	1	(2)	19	(6)

Terry Bush

Born: Ingoldisthorpe 29.1.1943
From: Juniors 2.60
To: Assistant-Secretary 7.70

	League	FAC	LC	MC	Total	
1960/61	2	(2)	1			3	(2)
1961/62	1			1		2	(0)
1962/63	2	(1)	1			3	(1)
1963/64	9	(1)				9	(1)
1964/65	37	(16)	4		1	42	(16)
1965/66	26+1	(8)	1	(1)	1	28+1	(9)
1966/67	21+1	(4)	2	(1)	1	24+1	(5)
1967/68	20+5	(2)	2		1	23+5	(2)
1968/69	7+4			1+1		8+5	(0)
1969/70	22+4	(9)	1		1	24+4	(9)
Total	147+15	(43)	12	(2)	5+1	2	166+16	(45)

Jock Butler

Born: Scotland 1889
From: Motherwell CS.11
To: Newport County CS.13

	League	FAC	LC	MC	Total	
1911/12	28	(11)	1		29	(11)
1912/13	15	(1)			15	(1)
Total	43	(12)	1		44	(12)

Gus Caesar

Born: Tottenham 5.3.1966
From: Cambridge United 9.91
To: Airdrie 1.92

	League	FAC	LC	MC	Total	
1991/92	9+1		1		2	12+1	(0)
Total	9+1		1		2	12+1	(0)

Percy Cainey

Born: Bristol 12.12.1914
From: Wesley Rangers 7.32
To: Bradford PA 5.36

	League	FAC	LC	MC	Total	
1932/33	12	(6)				12	(6)
1933/34	12	(1)	2	(1)	1	15	(2)
1934/35	31	(3)	9		1	41	(3)
1935/36	21	(2)	1		1	(1)	23	(3)
Total	76	(12)	12	(1)		3	(1)	91	(14)

Tommy Cairns

Born: Merryton 30.10.1890
From: Larkhall Thistle 7.11
To: Peebles Rovers 7.12

	League	FAC	LC	MC	Total	
1911/12	11	(1)			1	(0)
Total	11	(1)			1	(0)

Tony Caldwell

Born: Salford 21.3.1958
From: Bolton Wanderers 7.87
To: Grimsby Town 9.88 P/ex

	League	FAC	LC	MC	Total	
1987/88	8+8	(3)	2	(1)		1+2	11+10	(4)
1988/89	1			1		2	(0)
Total	9+8	(3)	2	(1)		2+2	13+10	(4)

Bob Caldwell

Born: South Kirkby 1.7.1909
From: Doncaster Rovers 5.36
To: Bristol Rovers 7.39

	League	FAC	LC	MC	Total	
1936/37	19	(1)			19	(1)
1937/38	3				3	(0)
1938/39	17	(2)	1		2	20	(2)
Total	39	(3)	1		2	42	(3)

Pat Callaghan

Born: Longbridge 1904
From: Aberdare Athletic 6.27
To: Aberdare Athletic 6.28

	League	FAC	LC	MC	Total	
1927/28	12	(1)			12	(1)
Total	12	(1)			12	(1)

Arthur Capes

Born: Burton-on-Trent 23.2.1875
From: Stoke 7.04
To: Swindon Town 7.05

	League	FAC	LC	MC	Total	
1904/05	29	(7)	5		34	(7)
Total	29	(7)	5		34	(7)

Louis Carey

Born: Bristol 22.1.1977
From: Trainee

	League	FAC	LC	MC	Total	
1995/96	22+1		2		1	25+1	(0)
1996/97	40+2		4	3		47+2	(0)
Total	62+3		6	3	1	72+3	(0)

Les Carter

Born: Farnborough 24.10.1960
From: Crystal Palace 2.82

	League	FAC	LC	MC	Total	
1981/82	16				16	(0)
Total	16				16	(0)

Tim Carter

Born: Bristol 5.10.1967
From: Sunderland 9.88 Loan

	League	FAC	LC	MC	Total	
1988/89	3				3	(0)
Total	3				3	(0)

Tommy Casey

Born: Camber Co. Down 11.3.1930
From: Portsmouth 3.59
To: Gloucester City 7.63 P/M

	League	FAC	LC	MC	Total	
1958/59	8				8	(0)
1959/60	25				25	(0)
1960/61	36	(5)	3		39	(5)
1961/62	40	(4)	5		2	47	(4)
1962/63	13		1		14	(0)
Total	122	(9)	9		2	133	(9)

Ray Cashley

Born: Bristol 23.10.1951
From: Juniors 9.70
To: Bristol Rovers 8.82

	League	FAC	LC	MC	Total	
1970/71	11		1		12	(0)
1971/72	29			1	30	(0)
1972/73	32		1	1	34	(0)
1973/74	27	(1)	5		2	34	(1)
1974/75	42		1	4		47	(0)
1975/76	42		1	2	3	48	(0)
1976/77	8			1	3	12	(0)
1977/78				0+1		0+1	(0)
1978/79	2			2		4	(0)
1979/80	14			1		15	(0)
1980/81	20			2	3	25	(0)
Total	227	(1)	9	11	14+1	261+1	(1)

Tommy Cavanagh

Born: Liverpool 29.6.1928
From: Doncaster Rovers 7.59
To: Carlisle United 6.60

	League	FAC	LC	MC	Total	
1959/60	24	(6)	1	(1)	25	(7)
Total	24	(6)	1	(1)	25	(7)

Peter Chambers

Born: Workington 1.1.1878
From: Bedminster 7.00
To: Swindon Town 7.06

	League	FAC	LC	MC	Total	
1901/02	28	(1)	2		30	(1)
1902/03	29		3		32	(0)
1903/04	33	(7)	3		36	(7)
1904/05	21	(2)	4		25	(2)
1905/06	20				21	(0)
Total	131	(10)	13		144	(10)

Ricky Chandler

Born: Bristol 26.9.1961
From: Apprentice 10.78
To: Bath City 7.83

	League	FAC	LC	MC	Total
1980/81	7+1				7+1 (0)
1981/82	30 (7)	3+1(1)			33+1 (8)
1982/83	26+3 (6)		3 (1)	3 (1)	32+3 (8)
Total	**63+4 (13)**	**3+1(1)**	**3 (1)**	**3 (1)**	**72+5(16)**

Bert Chapman

Born: Bristol 1871
From: Chatham 7.09
To: Maidstone 7.12

	League	FAC	LC	MC	Total
1907/08	1				1 (0)
1909/10	1				1 (0)
1910/11	2 (1)				2 (1)
1911/12	3				3 (0)
Total	**7 (1)**				**7 (1)**

Fred Chapple

Born: Treharris
From: Brentford 7.13
To: Douglas AFC 7.19

	League	FAC	LC	MC	Total
1913/14	16 (9)	2			18 (9)
1914/15	4 (1)				4 (1)
Total	**20 (10)**	**2**			**22 (10)**

Paul Cheesley

Born: Bristol 20.10.1953
From: Norwich City 12.73 £30,000
To: Shepton Mallet 7.78

	League	FAC	LC	MC	Total
1973/74	7+1 (2)	1			8+1 (2)
1974/75	13+2 (2)	1	2		16+2 (2)
1975/76	38 (15)		2 (1)	3	43 (15)
1976/77	3 (1)			3	6 (1)
Total	**61+3 (20)**	**2**	**4 (1)**	**6**	**73 (20)**

Percy Cherrett

Born: Christchurch 12.9.1899
From: Crystal Palace 5.27
To: Bournemouth 7.28

	League	FAC	LC	MC	Total
1927/28	25 (15)	1			26 (15)
Total	**25 (15)**	**1**			**26 (15)**

Ken Chilcott

Born: Rhondda 17.3.1920
From: Eastville United 10.37
To: Bridgwater Town 7.49

	League	FAC	LC	MC	Total
1937/38	1				1 (0)
1938/39	8 (1)				8 (1)
1946/47	31 (4)	2 (1)			33 (5)
1947/48	4 (1)				4 (1)
1948/49	2				2 (0)
Total	**46 (6)**	**2 (1)**			**48 (7)**

Clive Clack

Born: Cirencester 4.6.1900
From: Sunderland 5.23

	League	FAC	LC	MC	Total
1923/24	2				2 (0)
Total	**2**				**2 (0)**

Frank Clack

Born: Witney 30.3.1912
From: Brentford 5.47 £1,500
To: Guildford City 7.49

	League	FAC	LC	MC	Total
1946/47	1				1 (0)
1947/48	42	3			45 (0)
1948/49	24	3			27 (0)
Total	**67**	**6**			**73 (0)**

Brian Clark

Born: Bristol 13.1.1943
From: Juniors 3.60
To: Huddersfield Town 10.66

	League	FAC	LC	MC	Total
1960/61	1				1 (0)
1961/62	8 (2)				8 (2)
1962/63	42 (23)	4 (3)	1		47 (26)
1963/64	46 (18)	5 (2)	1		52 (20)
1964/65	46 (24)	4 (1)	1		51 (25)
1965/66	42 (15)	1	1		44 (15)
1966/67	10 (1)		2		12 (1)
Total	**195 (83)**	**14 (6)**	**6**		**215 (89)**

Don Clark

Born: Bristol 25.10.1917
From: North Bristol O.B. 5.37
To: Assistant-Secretary 6.51

	League	FAC	LC	MC	Total
1938/39	7				7 (0)
1946/47	37 (36)	2 (5)			39 (41)
1947/48	40 (22)	3 (3)			43 (25)
1948/49	27 (8)	3 (1)			30 (9)
1949/50	1				1 (0)
1951/52	5 (1)	3 (1)			8 (2)
Total	**117 (67)**	**11 (10)**			**128 (77)**

Willie Clark

Born: Airdrie 1880
From: Sunderland 10.10
To: Leicester Fosse 8.11

	League	FAC	LC	MC	Total
1910/11	24 (1)	1			25 (1)
Total	**24 (1)**	**1**			**25 (1)**

Malcolm Clarke

Born: Clydebank 20.6.1944
From: Cardiff City 7.69
To: Hartlepool 7.70

	League	FAC	LC	MC	Total
1969/70	2+1		1		3+1 (0)
Total	**2+1**		**1**		**3+1 (0)**

Harry Clay

Born: Kimberley 29.1.1981
From: Kimberley St. J. 11.01
To: Retired 5.13

	League	FAC	LC	MC	Total
1901/02	22				22 (0)
1902/03	34	3			37 (0)
1903/04	34	3			37 (0)
1904/05	34	5			39 (0)
1905/06	36	1			37 (0)
1906/07	8				8 (0)
1907/08	11				11 (0)
1908/09	37	10			47 (0)
1909/10	29				29 (0)
1910/11	28				28 (0)
1911/12	25				25 (0)
1912/13	12				12 (0)
Total	**310**	**22**			**332 (0)**

Rex Clayton

Born: Retford 4.1.1916
From: Manchester City 6.38
To: Lincoln City 7.39

	League	FAC	LC	MC	Total
1938/39	13 (3)		2		15 (3)
Total	**13 (3)**		**2**		**15 (3)**

John Clegg

Born: Sheffield 1.1.1890
From: 7.08
To: Barnsley 7.11

	League	FAC	LC	MC	Total
1908/09	1				1 (0)
1909/10	9	3			12 (0)
1910/11	3				3 (0)
Total	**13**	**3**			**16 (0)**

Roy Clipson

Born: Lincoln 18.4.1909
From: Bury 7.34
To: Dartford 10.35

	League	FAC	LC	MC	Total
1934/35	17	2		1	20 (0)
Total	**17**	**2**		**1**	**20 (0)**

Harry Cockerill

Born: Ryhope 14.1.1894
From: Mid-Rhondda 7.21
To: Reading 7.23

	League	FAC	LC	MC	Total
1921/22	3				3 (0)
1922/23	13				13 (0)
Total	**19**				**19 (0)**

Billy Coggins

Born: Bristol 16.9.1901
From: Bristol St George 9.25
To: Everton 3.30

	League	FAC	LC	MC	Total
1925/26	22				22 (0)
1926/27	42	3			45 (0)
1927/28	41	1			42 (0)
1928/29	40	1			41 (0)
1929/30	26	1			27 (0)
Total	**171**	**6**			**177 (0)**

Phil Coggins

Born: Bristol   10.7.1940
From: Dorset House BC   10.58
To: Bristol Rovers   7.60

	League	FAC	LC	MC	Total	
1959/60	4				4	(0)
Total	4				4	(0)

Andy Cole

Born: Nottingham   15.10.1971
From: Arsenal   3.92   Loan
From: Arsenal   7.92   £500,000
To: Newcastle United   3.93   £1,750,000

	League	FAC	LC	MC	Total	
1991/92	12	(8)			12	(8)
1992/93	29	(12)	1	3 (4) 4	(1) 37	(17)
Total	41	(20)	1	3 (4) 4	(1) 49	(25)

Gary Collier

Born: Bristol   4.2.1955
From: Apprentice   11.72
To: Coventry City   7.79   £325,000

	League	FAC	LC	MC	Total	
1972/73	3				3	(0)
1973/74	31		6	2	1+1 40+1	(0)
1974/75	41	(1)	1	4	46	(1)
1975/76	40	(1)	1	2	3 46	(1)
1976/77	42	(1)	1	1	3 47	(1)
1977/78	27		2	2	8 39	(0)
1978/79	9				9	(0)
Total	193	(3)	11	11	15+1 230	(3)

Ron 'Sammy' Collins

Born: Bristol   13.1.1923
From: Local   11.44
To: Torquay United   6.48

	League	FAC	LC	MC	Total	
1946/47	10	(2)			10	(2)
1947/48	4				4	(0)
Total	14	(2)			14	(2)

Roger Collinson

Born: Rawmarsh   5.12.1940
From: Doncaster Rovers   10.58
To: Stockport County   7.61

	League	FAC	LC	MC	Total	
1959/60	29	(1)	1		30	(1)
1960/61	21		3	2	26	(0)
Total	50	(1)	4	2	56	(1)

Duncan Colquhoun

Born: Glenfruin   24.7.1915
From: Blantyre Vic.   11.37
To: Southport   6.38

	League	FAC	LC	MC	Total	
1937/38	3			1 (1)	4	(1)
Total	3			1 (1)	4	(1)

Bill Compton

Born: Bedminster   5.4.1896
From: Bristol Motor Works   7.19
To: Exeter City   7.24

	League	FAC	LC	MC	Total	
1919/20	3				3	(0)
1921/22	8				8	(0)
1923/24	3				3	(0)
Total	14				14	(0)

Terry Compton

Born: Bristol   28.11.1931
From: Phildown Rovers   12.48
To: Salisbury   7.58

	League	FAC	LC	MC	Total	
1951/52	1				1	(0)
1952/53	1				1	(0)
1953/54	15				15	(0)
1955/56	4				4	(0)
1956/57	20				20	(0)
1957/58	3				3	(0)
Total	44				44	(0)

Fred Connelly

Born:
From: Rotherham M.   8.46

	League	FAC	LC	MC	Total	
1906/07	4	(2)			4	(2)
1907/08	9	(4)			9	(4)
Total	13	(6)			13	(6)

Jack Conner

Born: Renfrew   27.2.1896
From: Newport County   12.24
To: Millwall   6.25

	League	FAC	LC	MC	Total	
1924/25	16	(3)			16	(3)
Total	16	(3)			16	(3)

Jack Connor

Born: Maryport   25.7.1934
From: Huddersfield Town   10.60   P/ex
To: Coaching staff   6.71

	League	FAC	LC	MC	Total	
1960/61	28	(1)	5	2	35	(1)
1961/62	46	(5)	5 (1)	1	2 54	(6)
1962/63	29		4	1	34	(0)
1963/64	39		5	1	45	(0)
1964/65	43		4	1	48	(0)
1965/66	36		1	1	38	(0)
1966/67	42		4	2	48	(0)
1967/68	41	(1)	5 (1)		46	(2)
1968/69	42	(2)	1	5	48	(2)
1969/70	5+1	(1)	1		6+1	(1)
1970/71	3			2	5	(0)
Total	354+1	(10)	35 (2)	16	2 407+1	(12)

Joe Connor

Born: Lochee   14.7.1880
From: Walsall   7.01
To: Woolwich Arsenal   5.02

	League	FAC	LC	MC	Total	
1901/02	25	(8)	1 (1)		26	(9)
Total	25	(8)	1 (1)		26	(9)

Terry Connor

Born: Leeds   9.11.1962
From: Swansea City   9.91
To: Yeovil Town   7.93

	League	FAC	LC	MC	Total	
1991/92	9+2	(1)		1	10+2	(1)
1992/93	2+3		1	(1)	3+3	(1)
Total	11+5	(1)	1	(1) 1	13+5	(2)

Tony Cook

Born: Bristol   8.10.1929
From: Clifton St. Vincents   12.49
To: Worcester City   7.64

	League	FAC	LC	MC	Total	
1952/53	29	1			30	(0)
1953/54	38	3			41	(0)
1954/55	23	1			24	(0)
1955/56	20				20	(0)
1956/57	21				21	(0)
1957/58	7	2			9	(0)
1958/59	37	3			40	(0)
1959/60	42	1			43	(0)
1960/61	45	5	3		53	(0)
1961/62	40	5		2	47	(0)
1962/63	15	1			16	(0)
1963/64	3		1		4	(0)
Total	320	22	4	2	348	(0)

Charles Cook

Born: Cheltenham   28.1.1937
From: Gloucester City   2.57

	League	FAC	LC	MC	Total	
1956/57	1				1	(0)
1957/58	1				1	(0)
Total	2				2	(0)

W. Cook

Born:
From:
To:

	League	FAC	LC	MC	Total	
1911/12	3				3	(0)
Total	3				3	(0)

Walter Cookson

Born: Blackpool   1.1.1869
From: Nelson   7.01
To: Blackpool   7.02

	League	FAC	LC	MC	Total	
1901/02	16	(5)	2 (3)		18	(8)
Total	16	(5)	2 (3)		18	(8)

Frank Coombs

Born: East Ham   24.4.1925
From: Dartford   6.49
To: Southend United   6.50

	League	FAC	LC	MC	Total	
1949/50	24	1			25	(1)
Total	24	1			25	(1)

Terry Cooper

Born: Castleford 12.7.1944
From: Middlesbrough 7.78 £20,000
To: Bristol Rovers 8.79
From: Doncaster Rovers 5.82
To: Manager

	League	FAC	LC	MC	Total
1978/79	11		2		13 (0)
1982/83	37+1 (1)	1	3	0+2	41+3 (1)
1983/84	1+20	0+5		1	2+25(0)
1984/85	0+1				0+1 (0)
Total	**49+22 (1)**	**1+5**	**3**	**3+2**	**56+29(1)**

Levi Copestake

Born: Kiveton Park 1885
From: Blackpool 7.07
To: Exeter City 7.08
From: Exeter City 7.10

	League	FAC	LC	MC	Total
1907/08	2 (1)				2 (1)
1910/11	4				4 (0)
1911/12	29 (5)	1			30 (5)
1912/13	8				8 (0)
Total	**43 (6)**	**1**			**44 (6)**

Bill Corbett

Born: Wolverhampton 29.7.1920
From: Doncaster Rovers 6.48
To: Bath City 7.49

	League	FAC	LC	MC	Total
1948/49	1				1 (0)
Total	**1**				**1 (0)**

Fred Corbett

Born: West Ham 1.1.1881
From: Bristol Rovers 7.03
To: Bristol Rovers 4.05

	League	FAC	LC	MC	Total
1903/04	33 (13)	3 (1)			36 (14)
1904/05	16 (1)	1			17 (1)
Total	**49 (14)**	**4 (1)**			**53 (15)**

Peter Cormack

Born: Edinburgh 17.7.46
From: Liverpool 11.76 £50,000
To: Hibernian 2.80

	League	FAC	LC	MC	Total
1976/77	19+1 (6)	1			20+1 (6)
1977/78	25+1 (6)	1+1(1)	6 (2)		32+2 (7)
1978/79	14+3 (3)	2		3+1 (1)	19+3 (3)
1979/80	1+3		1	1+1	3+4 (0)
Total	**59+8 (15)**	**4+1(1)**	**1**	**10+2 (3)**	**65+10(16)**

Joe Cottle

Born: Bedminster 1.1.1886
From: Dolphins 7.05
To: Bristol Rovers 7.11

	League	FAC	LC	MC	Total
1905/06	33	1			34 (0)
1906/07	37	2			39 (0)
1907/08	36	2			38 (0)
1908/09	36	10			46 (0)
1909/10	38	3			41 (0)
1910/11	24	1			25 (0)
Total	**204**	**19**			**223 (0)**

Alf Cottrell

Born: Bristol 1.1.1913
From: Dockland Settlement 7.33
To: Northampton Town 7.35

	League	FAC	LC	MC	Total
1933/34	1			1	(0)
1934/35	3		1	4	(0)
Total	**4**		**1**	**5**	**(0)**

Ken Cousins

Born: Bristol 6.8.1922
From: Brislington 3.46
To: Bath City 7.48

	League	FAC	LC	MC	Total
1946/47	3			3	(0)
Total	**3**			**3**	**(0)**

John Cowell

Born: Blyth 9.6.1887
From: Rotherham Town 4.09
To: Sunderland 10.10

	League	FAC	LC	MC	Total
1908/09	1			1	(0)
1909/10	31 (20)	1		32	(20)
1910/11	5			5	(0)
Total	**37 (20)**	**1**		**38**	**(20)**

Eric Cox

Born:
From: Nunhead 7.32

	League	FAC	LC	MC	Total
1932/33	1			1	(0)
Total	**1**			**1**	**(0)**

Teddy Craig

Born: Stewarton 9.2.1903
From: Fulham 8.30
To: Halifax Town 8.32

	League	FAC	LC	MC	Total
1930/31	14 (1)			14	(1)
1931/32	33 (3)	3		36	(3)
Total	**47 (4)**	**3**		**50**	**(4)**

Alan Crawford

Born: Rotherham 30.10.1953
From: Chesterfield 8.82
To: Exeter City 7.85

	League	FAC	LC	MC	Total
1982/83	44+1 (7)	1	3	2	50+1 (7)
1983/84	31 (15)	3 (1)		2	36 (16)
1984/85	10+6 (4)		4 (1)	0+1	14+7 (5)
Total	**85+7 (26)**	**4 (1)**	**7 (1)**	**4+1**	**100+8(28)**

Chris Crowe

Born: Newcastle 11.6.1939
From: Nottingham Forest 1.67
To: Auburn (Aust) 5.69

	League	FAC	LC	MC	Total
1966/67	18 (6)	4 (2)		22	(8)
1967/68	38+1 (7)	4 (1)		42+1	(8)
1968/69	10		2	12	(0)
Total	**66+1 (13)**	**8 (3)**	**2**	**76+1(16)**	

Jim Crumley

Born: Dundee 17.7.1896
From: Swansea Town 8.23
To: Darlington 7.24

	League	FAC	LC	MC	Total
1923/24	2			2	(0)
Total	**2**			**2**	**(0)**

Jason Cundy

Born: Wimbledon 12.11.1969
From: Tottenham Hotspur 8.96 Loan

	League	FAC	LC	MC	Total
1996/97	6 (1)			6	(1)
Total	**6 (1)**			**6**	**(1)**

Edwin Cunningham

Born: Jarrow 20.9.1919
From: Luton Amateurs 5.39
To: Luton Town 7.47

	League	FAC	LC	MC	Total
1946/47	1			1	(0)
Total	**1**			**1**	**(0)**

Keith Curle

Born: Bristol 14.11.1963
From: Torquay United 3.84
To: Reading 10.87

	League	FAC	LC	MC	Total
1983/84	5+1				5+1 (0)
1984/85	37+3	2	1+1	4	44+4 (0)
1985/86	44 (1)	3	2	7	56 (1)
1987/88	24+4		4	8	36+4 (0)
1988/89	3				3 (0)
Total	**113+8 (1)**	**5**	**7+1**	**19**	**144+9 (1)**

Dermot Curtis

Born: Dublin 26.8.1932
From: Shelbourne 12.56 £5,000
To: Ipswich Town 9.58

	League	FAC	LC	MC	Total
1956/57	15 (13)	1 (1)			16 (14)
1957/58	11 (3)	2 (2)			13 (5)
Total	**26 (16)**	**3 (3)**			**29 (19)**

Mike Dale

Born:
From: Frome Town 7.10

	League	FAC	LC	MC	Total
1910/11	1				1 (0)
Total	**1**				**1 (0)**

Tom Darke

Born:
From: 7.04

	League	FAC	LC	MC	Total
1904/05	3 (2)				3 (2)
Total	**3 (2)**				**3 (2)**

Frank Davies

Born: Swansea 1.8.1903
From: Swansea Town 7.23
To: Charlton Athletic 10.26

	League	FAC	LC	MC	Total	
1923/24	24				24	(0)
1924/25	7				7	(0)
1925/26	23	1			24	(0)
Total	**54**	**1**			**55**	**(0)**

Jack Davies

Born: Denbigh 14.11.1916
From: Plymouth Argyle 5.48

	League	FAC	LC	MC	Total	
1948/49	30	(1)	3			33	(1)
Total	**30**	**(1)**	**3**			**33**	**(1)**

Richard Davies

Born: Quarrington Hill 1.1.1876
From: Bedminster 7.00
To: Bolton Wanderers 7.08

	League	FAC	LC	MC	Total	
1901/02	31	(2)	2			33	(2)
1902/03	5		1			6	(0)
Total	**36**	**(2)**	**3**			**39**	**(2)**

Ted Davies

Born: Bedminster 1.1.1892
From: Blackburn Rovers 5.25
To: Bath City 11.26

	League	FAC	LC	MC	Total	
1925/26	3				3	(0)
Total	**3**				**3**	**(0)**

Ken Davis

Born: Romsey 6.2.1933
From: Juniors 5.52
To: Minehead 1.54

	League	FAC	LC	MC	Total	
1952/53	1				1	(0)
Total	**1**				**1**	**(0)**

Richard Davis

Born: Plymouth 14.11.1993
From: Southampton 7.65
To: Barrow 3.69

	League	FAC	LC	MC	Total	
1967/68	6				6	(0)
1968/69	2				2	(0)
Total	**8**				**8**	**(0)**

W. Davis

Born:
From: 7.11

	League	FAC	LC	MC	Total	
1911/12	1				1	(0)
Total	**1**				**1**	**(0)**

Ted Dawson

Born: Chester-le-Street 16.1.1913
From: Manchester City 5.36
To: Gateshead 3.44

	League	FAC	LC	MC	Total	
1936/37	1				1	(0)
1937/38	39	3		3	45	(0)
1938/39	26	1		4	31	(0)
Total	**66**	**4**		**7**	**77**	**(0)**

Alf Dean

Born: West Bromwich 2.1.1877
From: Grimsby Town 4.02
To: Swindon Town 7.05

	League	FAC	LC	MC	Total	
1902/03	25	(10)	3	(1)		28	(11)
1903/04	32	(13)	3			35	(13)
1904/05	27	(12)	5	(1)		32	(13)
Total	**84**	**(35)**	**11**	**(2)**		**95**	**(37)**

Bill Demmery

Born: Kingswood 1877
From: Bristol East 7.02
To: Bristol Rovers 7.08

	League	FAC	LC	MC	Total	
1905/06	2				2	(0)
1906/07	30	2			32	(0)
1907/08	6				6	(0)
Total	**38**	**2**			**40**	**(0)**

Fred Dent

Born: Sheffield 24.1.1896
From: Mid-Rhondda 5.25
To: Exeter City 6.26

	League	FAC	LC	MC	Total	
1925/26	12	(1)				12	(1)
Total	**12**	**(1)**				**12**	**(1)**

Jantzen Derrick

Born: Bristol 10.1.1943
From: Juniors 1.60
To: Paris St. Germain 7.71

	League	FAC	LC	MC	Total	
1959/60	6		1			7	(0)
1960/61	32	(5)	4		2	38	(5)
1961/62	26	(4)	3	(3)	1	2	32	(7)
1962/63	35	(10)	4	(1)	1		40	(11)
1963/64	33	(4)	5		1		39	(4)
1964/65	11			1		12	(0)
1965/66	27+1	(1)	1		1		29+1	(1)
1966/67	33	(4)	4		1		38	(4)
1967/68	27+1	(2)	4		1		32+1	(2)
1968/69	16+3	(1)		1+1		17+4	(1)
1969/70	6+1			2		8+1	(0)
1970/71	1				1	(0)
Total	**253+6**	**(31)**	**26**	**(4)**	**12+1**	**2**	**293+7**	**(35)**

Peter Devine

Born: Blackburn 25.5.1960
From: Vancouver W. 7.81
To: Blackburn Rovers 9.82

	League	FAC	LC	MC	Total	
1981/82	19+2	(1)	3		3+1		25+3	(1)
Total	**19+2**	**(1)**	**3**		**3+1**		**25+3**	**(1)**

Jim Dickie

Born: Montrose 22.9.1903
From: New Brighton 12.28
To: Chester 8.30

	League	FAC	LC	MC	Total	
1928/29	25	(3)				25	(3)
1929/30	23	(1)				23	(1)
Total	**48**	**(4)**				**48**	**(4)**

Hyam Dimmer

Born: Scotstown 14.3.1914
From: Aldershot 5.47
To:

	League	FAC	LC	MC	Total	
1947/48	1				1	(0)
Total	**1**				**1**	**(0)**

Tommy Doherty

Born: Bristol
From: Trainee

	League	FAC	LC	MC	Total	
1996/97		0+1				0+1	(0)
Total		**0+1**				**0+1**	**(0)**

Eamonn Dolan

Born: Dagenham 20.9.1967
From: West Ham 2.89 Loan

	League	FAC	LC	MC	Total	
1988/89	3				3	(0)
Total	**3**				**3**	**(0)**

Bill Dolman

Born: Bloxwich 30.8.1906
From: Chesterfield 5.34
To: Luton Town 3.36

	League	FAC	LC	MC	Total	
1934/35	41	9			50	(0)
1935/36	20	1		2	23	(0)
Total	**61**	**10**		**2**	**73**	**(0)**

John Donaldson

Born: Glasgow 1.1.1909
From: Kilsyth Rangers 7.31
To:

	League	FAC	LC	MC	Total	
1931/32	4				4	(0)
Total	**4**				**4**	**(0)**

Louie Donowa

Born: Ipswich 24.9.1964
From: Ipswich Town 8.90 £55,000
To: Birmingham City 8.91 £60,000

	League	FAC	LC	MC	Total	
1990/91	11+13	(3)	0+1		1		12+14	(3)
Total	**11+13**	**(3)**	**0+1**		**1**		**12+14**	**(3)**

Billy Down

Born: Bristol 8.11.1963
From: Apprentice 10.81
To: Bristol Manor Farm 7.82

	League	FAC	LC	MC	Total	
1981/82	1				1	(0)
Total	**1**				**1**	**(0)**

David Down

Born: Bristol 7.7.1948
From: Apprentice 9.65
To: Bradford PA 10.67

	League	FAC	LC	MC	Total
1966/67	5 (3)	2 (1)	1 (1)		8 (5)
1967/68	1+1				1+1 (0)
Total	**6+1 (3)**	**2 (1)**	**1 (1)**		**9+1 (5)**

Ian Doyle

Born: Torquay 27.2.1959
From: Barnstaple Town 12.78
To: Gloucester City 7.81

	League	FAC	LC	MC	Total
1979/80	1+1	0+1		0+1	1+3 (0)
1980/81	1		1	0+2	2+2 (0)
Total	**2+1**	**0+1**	**1**	**0+3**	**3+5 (0)**

Walter Dransfield

Born: Sheffield 1901
From: Worksop 12.27
To: Merthyr Town 7.28

	League	FAC	LC	MC	Total
1927/28	2				2 (0)
Total	**2**				**2 (0)**

Jimmy Drinnan

Born: Harthill 28.5.1906
From: Larkhall Thistle 7.23
To: Aberaman Ath. 7.24

	League	FAC	LC	MC	Total
1923/24	2	1			3 (0)
Total	**2**	**1**			**3 (0)**

Bob Drummond

Born: Dalmeny 1.1.1898
From: Pembroke Dock 7.27
To: Bournemouth 7.27

	League	FAC	LC	MC	Total
1926/27	2 (1)	1			3 (1)
Total	**2 (1)**	**1**			**3 (1)**

Chuck Drury

Born: Darlaston 4.7.1937
From: WBA 8.64 £7,500
To: Bradford PA 3.68

	League	FAC	LC	MC	Total
1964/65	16 (1)				16 (1)
1965/66	28 (1)	1	1		30 (1)
1966/67	7				7 (0)
Total	**51 (2)**	**1**	**1**		**53 (2)**

Jack Dryden

Born: Broomhill 21.8.1908
From: Sheffield United 7.36
To: Burnley 6.38

	League	FAC	LC	MC	Total
1936/37	35 (4)	1		1	37 (4)
1937/38	28 (9)	3		2 (2)	33 (11)
Total	**63 (13)**	**4**		**3 (2)**	**70 (15)**

Richard Dryden

Born: Stroud 14.6.1969
From: Birmingham City 12.94 £200,000
To: Southampton 8.96 £150,000

	League	FAC	LC	MC	Total
1994/95	15+4 (1)	0+1			15+5 (1)
1995/96	17+1 (1)	1	4	2	24+1 (1)
Total	**32+5 (2)**	**1+1**	**4**	**2**	**39+6 (2)**

Brian Drysdale

Born: Wingate 24.2.1943
From: Hartlepool 5.69 £10,000
To: Oxford United 7.77

	League	FAC	LC	MC	Total
1969/70	42	1	5		48 (0)
1970/71	42	1	9		52 (0)
1971/72	42 (1)	1	1		44 (1)
1972/73	34 (1)	3	1		38 (1)
1973/74	32+2	6	4	1	43+2 (0)
1974/75	38	1	4		43 (1)
1975/76	39	1	2	3 (1)	45 (1)
1976/77	11		1	3	15 (0)
Total	**280+2 (3)**	**14**	**27**	**7 (1)**	**328 (4)**

Ernie Dunn

Born: 1909
From: Trowbridge Town 6.32

	League	FAC	LC	MC	Total
1932/33	19 (1)			1	20 (1)
1933/34	8				8 (0)
Total	**27 (1)**			**1**	**28 (1)**

Joe Durrell

Born: Stepney 15.3.1953
From: West Ham 7.73
To: Gillingham 11.75

	League	FAC	LC	MC	Total
1973/74	2+2	1			3+2 (0)
1974/75	1+3	1			2+3 (0)
Total	**3+5**	**2**			**5+5 (0)**

Reg Dyer

Born: Bristol 18.4.1900
From: Ashton City 10.21
To: Fulham 5.25

	League	FAC	LC	MC	Total
1921/22	1				1 (0)
1922/23	17	1			18 (0)
1923/24	17				17 (0)
1924/25	14	2			16 (0)
Total	**49**	**3**			**52 (0)**

Sieb Dykstra

Born: Kerkrade, Holland 20.10.1966
From: QPR 9.95 Loan

	League	FAC	LC	MC	Total
1995/96	8			2	10 (0)
Total	**8**			**2**	**10 (0)**

Bill Dymond

Born: Exeter 13.2.1920
From: Exeter City 9.45
To: Exeter City 6.47

	League	FAC	LC	MC	Total
1946/47	8 (1)				8 (1)
Total	**8 (1)**				**8 (1)**

Jackie Dziekanowski

Born: Warsaw, Poland 30.9.1962
From: Celtic 1.92 £250,000
To: Legia Warsaw 9.93

	League	FAC	LC	MC	Total
1991/92	16+1 (4)	2 (2)			18+1 (6)
1992/93	24+2 (3)		3+1	5+1	32+2 (3)
Total	**40+3 (7)**	**2 (2)**	**3+1**	**5+1**	**50+3 (9)**

Jason Eaton

Born: Bristol 29.1.1969
From: Trowbridge Town 3.89 £1,000
To: Gloucester City 11.90

	League	FAC	LC	MC	Total
1988/89	0+2				0+2 (0)
1990/91	6+5 (1)	0+1	1+1		7+7 (1)
Total	**6+7 (1)**	**0+1**	**1+1**		**7+9 (1)**

Jon Economou

Born: Holloway 25.10.1961
From: Apprentice 10.79
To: Devizes Town 8.84

	League	FAC	LC	MC	Total
1981/82	17+2 (1)				17+2 (1)
1982/83	34 (2)	1	3	3	41 (2)
1983/84	11+1	2	1	1	15+1 (0)
Total	**62+3 (3)**	**3**	**4**	**4**	**73 (3)**

John Eddolls

Born: Bristol 19.8.1919
From: Peasedown M.W. 9.45
To: Bristol Rovers 8.48

	League	FAC	LC	MC	Total
1946/47	6	1			7 (0)
Total	**6**	**1**			**7 (0)**

Albert Edwards

Born:
From: Aston Villa 10.12
To: Newport County 7.13

	League	FAC	LC	MC	Total
1912/13	4				4 (0)
Total	**4**				**4 (0)**

Cliff Edwards

Born: Chase Terrace 8.3.1921
From: WBA 6.48
To: Gravesend & N. 7.50 P/M

	League	FAC	LC	MC	Total
1948/49	14				14 (0)
1949/50	19 (3)	1			20 (3)
Total	**33 (3)**	**1**			**34 (3)**

Rob Edwards

Born: Kendal 1.7.1973
From: Carlisle United 3.91 £135,000
To:

	League	FAC	LC	MC	Total
1991/92	12+8	2	1+1		15+9 (0)
1992/93	14+4	2	3	5 (1)	24+4 (1)
1993/94	31+8 (2)	6		1	38+8 (2)
1994/95	29+1	0+2	2		31+3 (0)
1995/96	18+1	2	2	3 (1)	25+1 (1)
1996/97	31	2+1	4	1	38+1 (0)
Total	**135+22 (2)**	**14+3**	**12+1**	**10 (2)**	**171+26 (4)**

Alec Eisentrager

Born: Germany 20.7.1927
From: Trowbridge Town 8.49
To: Merthyr Tydfil 7.58

	League		FAC	LC	MC	Total	
1949/50	37	(11)	1			38	(11)
1950/51	42	(5)	5			47	(5)
1951/52	37	(7)	2			39	(7)
1952/53	38	(12)	1			39	(12)
1953/54	19	(3)				19	(3)
1954/55	10	(2)				10	(2)
1955/56	32	(16)				32	(16)
1957/58	10					10	(0)
1958/59	8	(1)	4			12	(1)
Total	233	(57)	13			246	(57)

Sid Elliott

Born: Sunderland 1.1.1908
From: Chelsea 7.30
To: Notts County 3.32

	League		FAC		LC	MC	Total	
1930/31	25	(15)	1				26	(15)
1931/32	25	(9)	3	(4)			28	(13)
Total	50	(24)	4	(4)			54	(28)

John Emanuel

Born: Swansea 19.4.1948
From: Ferndale 5.71
To: Newport County 6.76

	League		FAC	LC	MC	Total	
1971/72	33	(2)		1		34	(2)
1972/73	33+1	(5)	3			36+1	(5)
1973/74	24+2	(2)	0+2	1	2	27+4	(2)
1974/75	31	(1)		3		34	(1)
1975/76	3+1					3+1	(0)
Total	124+4	(10)	3+2	5	2	134+6	(10)

Terry Emery

Born: Bristol 8.9.1936
From: Local 2.57

	League		FAC	LC	MC	Total	
1956/57	1					1	(0)
1957/58	10		2			12	(0)
Total	11		2			13	(0)

Gary Emmanuel

Born: Swansea 1.2.1954
From: Newport County 8.85 N/C
To: Swansea City 8.85

	League	FAC	LC	MC	Total	
1985/86	2		1		3	(0)
1985/86	2		1		3	(0)

Bobby Etheridge

Born: Gloucester 25.3.1934
From: Gloucester City 9.56
To: Cheltenham Town 7.65 P/M

	League		FAC		LC		MC		Total	
1956/57	21	(6)	3	(1)					24	(7)
1957/58	31	(7)							31	(7)
1958/59	41	(13)	3						44	(13)
1959/60	27	(2)	1						28	(2)
1960/61	38	(3)	5		3				46	(3)
1961/62	46	(5)	5	(1)	1		2		54	(6)
1962/63	45	(6)	4	(2)	1	(1)			50	(9)
1963/64	10				1				11	(0)
Total	259	(42)	21	(4)	6	(1)	2		288	(47)

Gordon Eveleigh

Born: Lymington 26.7.1922
From: Guildford City 5.48
To: Guildford City 6.49

	League	FAC	LC	MC	Total	
1948/49	2				2	(0)
1948/49	2				2	(0)

Stephen Fagan

Born: Attercliffe 28.10.1886
From: Plymouth Argyle 7.10
To: Stockport County 7.12

	League	FAC	LC	MC	Total	
1910/11	18				18	(0)
1911/12	16				16	(0)
Total	34				34	(0)

Albert Fairclough

Born: St Helens 4.10.1891
From: Southend United 3.21
To: Derby County 7.24

	League		FAC		LC	MC	Total	
1920/21	8	(5)					8	(5)
1921/22	38	(12)	1				39	(12)
1922/23	31	(19)	2	(3)			33	(22)
1923/24	14	(8)					14	(8)
Total	91	(44)	3	(3)			94	(47)

Frank Farr

Born: Bristol 1909
From: Local 7.31
To: Bath City 7.34

	League	FAC	LC	MC	Total	
1931/32	1				1	(0)
1933/34	8				8	(0)
Total	9				9	(0)

Keith Fear

Born: Bristol 8.5.1952
From: Juniors 6.69
To: Plymouth Argyle 2.78

	League		FAC		LC		MC	Total	
1970/71	10+2	(2)						10+2	(2)
1971/72	5+4	(1)			1			6+4	(1)
1972/73	21+3	(7)	1					22+3	(7)
1973/74	32+3	(8)	4+1	(1)	2+2	(1)	2	40+6	(10)
1974/75	29+2	(8)	1		3			33+2	(8)
1975/76	13+2		1					14+2	(0)
1976/77	17+9	(6)	1	(1)				18+9	(7)
Total	127+25	(34)	8+1	(2)	6+2	(1)	2	143+28	(35)

Freddie Fenton

Born: Gainsborough 1.1.1878
From: WBA 7.04
To: Swindon Town 7.07

	League		FAC	LC	MC	Total	
1904/05	21	(1)	1			22	(1)
1905/06	13					13	(0)
1906/07	2					2	(0)
Total	36	(1)	1			37	(1)

Alex Ferguson

Born: Gainsborough 4.8.1904
From: Newport County 5.46
To: Swindon Town 9.47

	League	FAC	LC	MC	Total	
1946/47	32	1			33	(0)
Total	32	1			33	(0)

Iain Ferguson

Born: Newarthill 4.8.1962
From: Hearts 3.90 Loan

	League		FAC	LC	MC	Total	
1989/90	8+3	(2)				8+3	(2)
Total	8+3	(2)				8+3	(2)

Ivor Fish

Born: Cardiff 1.1.1913
From: GWR Institute 3.34

	League		FAC		LC	MC	Total	
1934/35	1						1	(0)
1935/36	6	(1)				1	7	(1)
Total	7	(1)				1	8	(1)

Albert Fisher

Born: Glasgow 1.6.1879
From: Aston Villa 7.03
To: Brighton 8.05

	League		FAC		LC	MC	Total	
1903/04	24	(8)	3	(1)			27	(9)
1904/05	26	(13)	5				31	(13)
Total	50	(21)	8	(1)			58	(22)

Paul Fitzpatrick

Born: Liverpool 5.10.1965
From: Bolton Wanderers 8.86
To: Carlisle United 10.88

	League		FAC	LC		MC		Total	
1986/87	18+1	(2)	4	1+1		4+1		27+3	(2)
1987/88	22+1	(5)	1	2		2		27+1	(5)
1988/89	0+1							0+1	(0)
Total	40+3	(7)	5	3+1		6+1		54+5	(7)

Tony Fitzpatrick

Born: Glasgow 3.3.1956
From: St. Mirren 8.79 £225,000
To: St. Mirren 8.81 £150,000

	League		FAC	LC	MC	Total	
1979/80	41		2	6	8	57	(0)
1980/81	34	(1)	4	1	2	41	(1)
Total	75	(1)	6	7	10	98	(1)

Mark Flatts

Born: Haringey 14.10.1972
From: Arsenal 3.95 Loan

	League	FAC	LC	MC	Total	
1994/95	4+2				4+2	(0)
1994/95	4+2				4+2	(0)

Robert Fleck

Born: Glasgow 11.8.1965
From: Chelsea 1.95 Loan

	League		FAC	LC	MC	Total	
1994/95	10	(1)				10	(1)
Total	10	(1)				10	(1)

Jack Flynn

Born: 1.1.1875
From: Walsall 7.01
To: Reading 7.03

	League	FAC	LC	MC	Total
1901/02	31 (1)	1			32 (1)
Total	**31 (1)**	**1**			**32 (1)**

Johnny Forbes

Born: Scotland 1892
From: Dundee Violet 7.11

	League	FAC	LC	MC	Total
1911/12	27 (5)	1			28 (5)
Total	**27 (5)**	**1**			**28 (5)**

Tony Ford

Born: Thornbury 26.11.1944
From: Apprentice 11.61
To: Bristol Rovers 12.69 £4,000

	League	FAC	LC	MC	Total
1961/62	8		2		10 (0)
1962/63	2				2 (0)
1963/64	14				14 (0)
1964/65	46 (5)	4 (1)	1		51 (6)
1965/66	40 (2)	1	1		42 (2)
1966/67	40 (3)	4	2 (1)		46 (4)
1967/68	8+1				8+1 (0)
1968/69	5				5 (0)
1969/70	7				7 (0)
Total	**170+1 (10)**	**9 (1)**	**4 (1)**	**2**	**185 (12)**

Allan Foster

Born: Rawmarsh
From: Rotherham Town CS09
To: Watford CS11

	League	FAC	LC	MC	Total
1909/10	7 (1)				7 (1)
1910/11	6				6 (0)
Total	**13 (1)**				**13 (1)**

Jackie Foster

Born: Sunderland 21.3.1903
From: Grimsby Town 6.26
To: Brentford 5.29

	League	FAC	LC	MC	Total
1926/27	1	3 (1)			4 (1)
1927/28	29 (3)				29 (3)
1928/29	17 (1)	1			18 (1)
Total	**47 (4)**	**4 (1)**			**51 (5)**

Jason Fowler

Born: Bristol 20.8.1974
From: Trainee 7.93
To: Cardiff City 7.96

	League	FAC	LC	MC	Total
1992/93	0+1		0+1		0+2 (0)
1993/94	0+1			1	1+1 (0)
1994/95	10+3		0+1		10+4 (0)
1995/96	6+4			1	7+4 (0)
Total	**16+9**		**1+1**	**1+1**	**18+11(0)**

Ray Fox

Born: Bristol 20.1.1921
From: St. Adhelm's 7.38
To: Bath City 7.50

	League	FAC	LC	MC	Total
1946/47	12		0+1		12+1 (0)
1947/48	6				6 (0)
1948/49	5				5 (0)
Total	**23**		**0+1**		**23+1 (0)**

Tom Foy

Born: Croydon 1.1.1911
From: Scarborough 3.34
To: Barrow 6.35

	League	FAC	LC	MC	Total
1933/34	6 (1)				6 (1)
1934/35	4 (1)				4 (1)
Total	**10 (2)**				**10 (2)**

Don Freeman

Born: Dartford 29.8.1921
From: Charlton Athletic 5.49
To: Watford 11.50

	League	FAC	LC	MC	Total
1949/50	8				8 (0)
Total	**8**				**8 (0)**

Tom Fuge

Born: Bristol
From: Llanelli 7.13

	League	FAC	LC	MC	Total
1913/14	6 (3)				6 (3)
Total	**6 (3)**				**6 (3)**

Ernie Gadsby

Born: New Whittington 1.1.1889
From: Barnsley 7.10
To: Castleford Town 7.11

	League	FAC	LC	MC	Total
1910/11	10 (1)	1			11 (1)
Total	**10 (1)**	**1**			**11 (1)**

Tom Gale

Born: Falkirk
From: Rotherham M. 7.06
To: Grimsby Town 7.08

	League	FAC	LC	MC	Total
1906/07	1				1 (0)
1907/08	2				2 (0)
Total	**3**				**3 (0)**

Frank Gallacher

Born: Paisley 1.1.1913
From: Barnsley 3.38

	League	FAC	LC	MC	Total
1937/38	12 (4)				12 (4)
1938/39	10 (1)	1		3 (1)	14 (2)
Total	**22 (5)**	**1**		**3 (1)**	**26 (6)**

John Galley

Born: Clowne 7.5.1944
From: Rotherham United 12.67 £25,000
To: Nottingham Forest 12.72 £30,000

	League	FAC	LC	MC	Total
1967/68	21 (16)	5 (2)			26 (18)
1968/69	39 (19)	1 (1)	3 (2)		43 (22)
1969/70	20 (9)		4 (1)		24 (10)
1970/71	35 (12)		7		42 (12)
1971/72	37 (22)	1	1		39 (22)
1972/73	20 (6)		1 (1)		21 (7)
Total	**172 (84)**	**7 (3)**	**16 (4)**		**195 (91)**

Steve Galliers

Born: Preston 21.8.1957
From: Wimbledon 2.87 £37,500
To: Maidstone United 7.89 £20,000

	League	FAC	LC	MC	Total
1986/87	9				9 (0)
1987/88	35 (6)	2		2	39 (6)
1988/89	30+3	4+1	9	3	46+4 (0)
Total	**74+3 (6)**	**6+1**	**9**	**5**	**94+4 (6)**

Bert Gane

Born: Kingswood 1.2.1886
From: Bradford City 7.14
To: Douglas AFC 7.20

	League	FAC	LC	MC	Total
1914/15	1				1 (0)
1919/20	1				1 (0)
Total	**2**				**2 (0)**

Andrew Gara

Born: Ireland 1.1.1875
From: Nottingham Forest 10.02
To: Ashton Town 7.04

	League	FAC	LC	MC	Total
1902/03	18 (6)	3			21 (6)
Total	**18 (6)**	**3**			**21 (6)**

Chris Garland

Born: Bristol 24.4.1949
From: Apprentice 5.66
To: Chelsea 9.71 £100,000
From: Leicester City 12.76 £110,000
To: Yeovil Town 2.83

	League	FAC	LC	MC	Total
1966/67	1				1 (0)
1967/68	29+1 (8)	3+1(1)			32+2 (9)
1968/69	31 (6)	1	3 (2)		35 (8)
1969/70	39 (6)	1	5		45 (6)
1970/71	38 (8)	1	8 (3)		47 (11)
1971/72	4 (3)				4 (3)
1976/77	20+1 (7)				20+1 (7)
1977/78	2			2	4 (0)
1978/79	4+1 (1)		0+1	4 (2)	8+2 (3)
1979/80	10		2 (2)	3 (1)	15 (3)
1980/81	10+5 (1)	1	1	2	14+5 (1)
1981/82	1+1 (1)	1			2+1 (1)
1982/83	7+2 (1)				7+2 (1)
Total	**196+11(42)**	**10+1(3)**	**17+1 (5)**	**11 (3)**	**234+13(53)**

Graham Garland

Born: Barton Regis   1.1.1896
From: Kingswood   7.27

	League	FAC	LC	MC	Total	
1927/28	1				1	(0)
1928/29	5	(2)			5	(2)
1929/30	1				1	(0)
Total	**7**	**(2)**			**7**	**(2)**

Mark Gavin

Born: Baillieston   10.12.1963
From: Hearts   10.88   £35,000
To: Watford   8.90   P/ex
From: Watford   12.91   £60,000
To: Exeter City   2.94

	League	FAC	LC	MC	Total	
1988/89	26+3	(3)	6	6	3	41+3 (3)
1989/90	36+4	(3)	7 (1)	2	3 (1)	48+4 (5)
1991/92	12+2	(1)	3	6	3	24+2 (1)
1992/93	16+3	(1)	1	0+1	3	20+4 (1)
1993/94	6+2				1	7+2 (0)
Total	**96+14**	**(8)**	**17 (1)**	**14+1**	**13 (1)**	**140+15(10)**

Pat Gechern

Born: Musselburgh, Scotland   1899
From:
To:

	League	FAC	LC	MC	Total	
1911/12	4	(1)			4	(1)
Total	**4**	**(1)**			**4**	**(1)**

James Geddes

Born: Stane Shotts   1902
From: Albion Rovers   6.26
To: Morton   6.29

	League	FAC	LC	MC	Total	
1926/27	3	3			6	(0)
1927/28	2	(1)			2	(1)
Total	**5**	**(1)**	**3**		**8**	**(1)**

Mike Gibson

Born: Derby   15.7.1939
From: Shrewbury Town   4.63
To: Gillingham   7.72

	League	FAC	LC	MC	Total	
1962/63	2				2	(0)
1963/64	39	5			44	(0)
1964/65	46	4	1		51	(0)
1965/66	42	1	1		44	(0)
1966/67	42	4	2		48	(0)
1967/68	40	5	1		46	(0)
1968/69	41	1	3		45	(0)
1969/70	38	1	5		44	(0)
1970/71	30		9		39	(0)
1971/72	11	1			12	(0)
Total	**331**	**22**	**22**		**375**	**(0)**

Harry Gildea

Born: Broxburn   1.1.1890
From: Grimsby Town   7.10
To: Lochgelly United   7.11

	League	FAC	LC	MC	Total	
1910/11	1				1	(0)
Total	**1**				**1**	**(0)**

John Giles

Born: Bristol   7.11.1947
From: Apprentice   6.65
To: Exeter City   5.69

	League	FAC	LC	MC	Total	
1966/67	3	(1)			3	(1)
Total	**3**	**(1)**			**3**	**(1)**

Cyril Gilhespy

Born: Fencehouses   18.2.1896
From: Liverpool   5.25
To: Blackburn Rovers   6.29

	League	FAC	LC	MC	Total	
1925/26	35	(6)			35	(6)
1926/27	40	(8)			40	(8)
1927/28	14	(7)	1		15	(7)
1928/29	28	(4)			28	(4)
Total	**117**	**(25)**	**1**		**118**	**(25)**

Donnie Gillies

Born: Glencoe   20.6.1951
From: Morton   3.73   £30,000
To: Bristol Rovers   6.80   £50,000

	League	FAC	LC	MC	Total	
1972/73	11	(2)				11	(2)
1973/74	28+8	(6)	6 (1)	3+1	0+2	37+11(7)
1974/75	28+1	(9)		3 (1)		31+1(10)
1975/76	22+3	(1)		0+2	1+1	23+6 (1)
1976/77	37+1	(3)	1	1	2	41+1 (3)
1977/78	24+3	(4)	1+1		7 (1)	32+4 (5)
1978/79	27	(1)	2	1	1+1	31+1 (1)
1979/80	7+1			0+1	4+1 (1)	11+3 (1)
Total	**184+17(26)**		**10+1(1)**	**8+4 (1)**	**15+5 (2)**	**217+27(30)**

Sammy Gilligan

Born: Dundee   1.1.1882
From: Celtic   5.04
To: Liverpool   5.10

	League	FAC	LC	MC	Total	
1904/05	30	(14)	5 (1)			35	(15)
1905/06	37	(20)	1			38	(20)
1906/07	37	(15)	2 (3)			39	(18)
1907/08	33	(16)	2			35	(16)
1908/09	29	(10)	10 (3)			39	(13)
1909/10	22	(3)	3 (2)			25	(5)
Total	**188**	**(78)**	**23 (9)**			**211**	**(87)**

Alf Gilson

Born: Lichfield   1.6.1879
From: Brentford   6.03

	League	FAC	LC	MC	Total	
1903/04	29		3		32	(0)
1904/05	18	(1)	2		20	(1)
Total	**47**	**(1)**	**5**		**52**	**(1)**

Ernie Glenn

Born: Redditch   12.4.1902
From: Willenhall Town   5.23
To: Retired   7.31

	League	FAC	LC	MC	Total	
1923/24	24	4			28	(0)
1924/25	35				35	(0)
1925/26	33	1			34	(0)
1926/27	37	3			40	(0)
1927/28	41	1			42	(0)
1928/29	41	1			42	(0)
1929/30	39	1			40	(0)
1930/31	26	1			27	(0)
Total	**276**	**12**			**288**	**(0)**

Shaun Goater

Born: Bermuda   25.2.1970
From: Rotherham United   7.96   £175,000

	League	FAC	LC	MC	Total	
1996/97	39+3	(23)	3	4 (1)	2 (1)	48+3(25)
Total	**39+3**	**(23)**	**3**	**4 (1)**	**2 (1)**	**48+3(25)**

Robert Goddard

Born: Bristol   22.11.1896
From: Charles Hill   7.21
To: Reading   8.25

	League	FAC	LC	MC	Total	
1921/22	7				7	(0)
1922/23	4				4	(0)
1923/24	10				10	(0)
Total	**21**				**21**	**(0)**

Les Golledge

Born: Chipping Sodbury   3.8.1911
From: Kingswood   7.30
To: Bristol Rovers   6.35

	League	FAC	LC	MC	Total	
1931/32	9	(2)			9	(2)
1932/33	7	1			8	(0)
1933/34	8	(1)	1	1	(1)	10	(2)
1934/35	1				1	(0)
Total	**25**	**(3)**	**2**	**1**	**(1)**	**28**	**(4)**

Michael Good

Born: Airdrie   1.7.1875
From: Preston North End   7.02
To: Reading   7.03

	League	FAC	LC	MC	Total	
1902/03	32	(5)	3		35	(5)
Total	**32**	**(5)**	**3**		**35**	**(5)**

Ray Gooding

Born: Hartlepool   16.2.1959
From: Coventry City   3.82   Loan

	League	FAC	LC	MC	Total	
1981/82	3				3	(0)
Total	**3**				**3**	**(0)**

Greg Goodridge

Born: Barbados   10.2.1975
From: QPR   8.96   £50,000

	League	FAC	LC	MC	Total	
1996/97	19+9	(6)	3+1(1)	2	0+2	24+12(7)
Total	**19+9**	**(6)**	**3+1(1)**	**2**	**0+2**	**24+12(7)**

Colin Gordon
Born: Stourbridge 17.1.1963
From: Reading 3.88 Loan

	League	FAC	LC	MC	Total
1967/68	8 (4)	2			10 (4)
Total	8 (4)	2			10 (4)

Bobby Gould
Born: Coventry 12.6.1946
From: WBA 12.72 £70,000
To: West Ham 11.73 £70,000

	League	FAC	LC	MC	Total
1972/73	19 (8)	3 (2)			22 (10)
1973/74	16 (7)		4 (2)	2 (2)	22 (11)
Total	35 (15)	3 (2)	4 (2)	2 (2)	44 (21)

Charlie Gould
Born: Bristol
From:
To:

	League	FAC	LC	MC	Total
1911/12	26	1			27 (0)
1912/13	1				1 (0)
Total	27	1			28 (0)

Gerry Gow
Born: Glasgow 29.5.1952
From: Juniors 6.69
To: Manchester City 10.80 £175,000

	League	FAC	LC	MC	Total
1969/70	1				1 (0)
1970/71	37+1 (5)	1	6+2		44+3 (5)
1971/72	39 (9)	1	1		41 (9)
1972/73	42 (12)	3 (1)	1		46 (13)
1973/74	41 (1)	5	4	2	52 (1)
1974/75	22+2 (1)		4 (1)		26+2 (3)
1975/76	42 (5)	1	2	3	48 (5)
1976/77	27+3 (1)		1	1+1	29+4 (1)
1977/78	37+1 (4)	2	2	8	49+1 (4)
1978/79	38 (5)	2 (1)		2	42 (6)
1979/80	31 (4)	2	4 (1)	4	41 (5)
1980/81	11		2	2+1 (2)	15+1 (2)
Total	368+7 (48)	17 (2)	27+2 (2)	22+2 (2)	434+11(54)

Malcolm Graham
Born: Wakefield 26.1.1934
From: Barnsley 5.59 P/ex
To: Leyton Orient 6.60 £5,250

	League	FAC	LC	MC	Total
1959/60	14 (8)				14 (8)
Total	14 (8)				14 (8)

Alex Gray
Born: Glasgow 1.1.1899
From: Kilmarnock 5.26
To: Queen of the South 7.27

	League	FAC	LC	MC	Total
1926/27	8 (3)	3			11 (3)
Total	8 (3)	3			11 (3)

Harry Green
Born: Sheffield 1.1.1908
From: Leeds United 5.34
To: York City 6.35

	League	FAC	LC	MC	Total
1934/35	12 (1)			1	13 (1)
Total	12 (1)			1	13 (1)

Kevin Griffin
Born: Plymouth 5.10.1953
From: Apprentice 9.71
To: Bath City 7.75

	League	FAC	LC	MC	Total
1971/72	1+1				1+1 (0)
1973/74	0+2	1			1+2 (0)
1974/75	4	0+1			4+1 (0)
Total	5+3	1+1			6+4 (0)

Ivor Guy
Born: Bristol 27.2.1926
From: Hambrook Villa 8.44
To: Bath City 8.57

	League	FAC	LC	MC	Total
1946/47	32	1			33 (0)
1947/48	38 (1)	3			41 (1)
1948/49	36 (1)	3			39 (1)
1949/50	28	1			29 (0)
1950/51	46	5 (1)			51 (1)
1951/52	36	2			38 (0)
1952/53	37	1			38 (0)
1953/54	46	3			49 (0)
1954/55	45	1			46 (0)
1955/56	39	1			40 (0)
1956/57	21	1			22 (0)
Total	404 (2)	22 (1)			426 (3)

Stan Guy
Born:
From: Liverpool 7.36

	League	FAC	LC	MC	Total
1936/37	1				1 (0)
Total	1				1 (0)

Billy Hales
Born: Bristol
From: Local 7.03
To: Bristol Rovers 5.04

	League	FAC	LC	MC	Total
1903/04	1				1 (0)
Total	1				1 (0)

Bertie Hall
Born: Newburn 1.4.1903
From: Norwich City 5.32

	League	FAC	LC	MC	Total
1932/33	2	1			3 (0)
Total	2	1			3 (0)

Colin Hall
Born: Wolverhampton 2.2.1948
From: Bradford City 7.72
To: Chelmsford City 7.73

	League	FAC	LC	MC	Total
1972/73	0+1	0+1			0+2 (0)
Total	0+1	0+1			0+2 (0)

George Hall
Born: Worksop 5.9.1912
From: Newport County 5.37

	League	FAC	LC	MC	Total
1937/38	12	3	3		18 (0)
1938/39	1				1 (0)
Total	13	3	3		19 (0)

Bruce Halliday
Born: Sunderland 3.1.1961
From: Bury 8.83
To: Hereford United 6.85

	League	FAC	LC	MC	Total
1983/84	41	5	2	1	49 (0)
1984/85	11+1	2 (1)	1	0+1	14+2 (1)
Total	52+1	7 (1)	3	1+1	63+2 (1)

John Hampshire
Born: Goldthorpe 5.10.1913
From: Manchester City 4.36
To: Bath City 7.38

	League	FAC	LC	MC	Total
1935/36	2				2 (0)
1936/37	16		1		17 (0)
1937/38	3		2		5 (0)
Total	21		3		24 (0)

Gary Hamson
Born: Nottingham 24.8.1959
From: Leeds United 7.86
To: Port Vale 12.86

	League	FAC	LC	MC	Total
1986/87	12 (2)	1	3	1	17 (2)
Total	12 (2)	1	3	1	17 (2)

Pat Hanlin
Born: West Calder
From: Everton 7.05

	League	FAC	LC	MC	Total
1905/06	14				14 (0)
1906/07	36 (3)	2			38 (3)
1907/08	34	2			36 (0)
1908/09	22	1			23 (0)
1909/10	24				24 (0)
1910/11	32	1			33 (0)
Total	162 (3)	6			168 (3)

Vegard Hansen
Born: Drammen, Norway 8.8.1969
From: Stromsgodset 11.94 £105,000
To: Stromsgodset 3.96

	League	FAC	LC	MC	Total
1994/95	29	3			32 (0)
1995/96	7+1		4	1	12+1 (0)
Total	36+1	3	4	1	44+1 (0)

Steve Harding
Born: Bristol 23.7.1956
From: Apprentice 7.74
To: Bristol Rovers 6.77

	League	FAC	LC	MC	Total
1975/76	2				2 (0)
Total	2				2 (0)

Bob 'Brook' Hardy
Born: South Bank 16.6.1885
From: South Bank 5.08

	League	FAC	LC	MC	Total
1908/09	26 (4)	8 (2)			34 (6)
1909/10	28 (5)	3			31 (5)
1910/11	20 (4)				20 (4)
Total	74 (13)	11 (2)			85 (15)

Mick Harford

Born: Sunderland 12.2.1959
From: Newcastle United 8.81 £160,000
To: Birmingham City 3.82 £100,000

	League		FAC		LC		MC	Total	
1961/62	30	(11)	5	(2)	5	(1)		40	(14)
Total	**30**	**(11)**	**5**	**(2)**	**5**	**(1)**		**40**	**(14)**

Andrew Hargett

Born: Bristol
From: Army 7.03
To: Bath City 7.05

	League		FAC	LC	MC	Total	
1903/04	15	(3)				15	(3)
1904/05	4					4	(0)
Total	**19**	**(3)**				**19**	**(3)**

NOTE: Confusion exists in regard to appearances in 1904/05 as George Hargett was also on City's books at that time. Some sources indicate that George made 3 appearances and Andrew 1 during that campaign.

Jack Hargreaves

Born: Rotherham 1.5.1915
From: Leeds United 5.42
To: Yeovil Town 7.47

	League		FAC		LC	MC	Total	
1946/47	26	(9)	2	(2)			28	(11)
Total	**26**	**(9)**	**2**	**(2)**			**28**	**(11)**

David Harle

Born: Denaby 15.8.1963
From: Leeds United 3.86
To: Scunthorpe United 11.86

	League		FAC		LC	MC	Total	
1985/86	8				4		12	(0)
1986/87	15	(2)	1		3		19	(2)
Total	**23**	**(2)**	**1**		**3**	**4**	**31**	**(2)**

Marvin Harriott

Born: Dulwich 20.4.1974
From: Barnsley 12.93 Free
To: Fortuna Cologne 7.95 Free

	League	FAC	LC	MC	Total	
1993/94	17				17	(0)
1994/95	19		1		20	(0)
Total	**36**		**1**		**37**	**(0)**

Joshua 'Jack' Harris

Born: Glasgow 5.11.1891
From: Burnley 5.12
To: Leeds United 7.22

	League		FAC	LC	MC	Total	
1912/13	32	(2)	1			33	(2)
1913/14	31	(5)	2			33	(5)
1914/15	35	(9)	2			37	(9)
1919/20	35	(5)	5	(2)		40	(7)
1920/21	42	(2)	1			43	(2)
1921/22	30	(3)	2			32	(3)
Total	**205**	**(26)**	**13**	**(2)**		**218**	**(28)**

Walter Harris

Born: Plymouth 11.7.1904
From: Scotswood 6.29
To: Loughborough 7.30

	League		FAC	LC	MC	Total	
1912/13	26	(15)				26	(15)
Total	**26**	**(15)**				**26**	**(15)**

Fred Harrison

Born: Winchester 2.7.1880
From:
To:

	League		FAC	LC	MC	Total	
1913/14	15	(5)				15	(5)
Total	**15**	**(5)**				**15**	**(5)**

Gerry Harrison

Born: Lambeth 15.4.1972
From: Watford 6.91
To: Huddersfield Town 3.94

	League		FAC	LC		MC	Total	
1991/92	0+4					1	1+4	(0)
1992/93	24+9	(1)	1	1+2		4+1	30+12	(1)
1993/94	1						1	(0)
Total	**25+13**	**(1)**	**1**	**1+2**		**5+1**	**32+16**	**(1)**

Ted Harston

Born: Monk Bretton 27.2.1907
From: Reading 5.34
To: Mansfield Town 10.35

	League		FAC		LC		MC	Total	
1934/35	22	(15)	8	(3)	1	(1)		31	(19)
1935/36	6		(2)					6	(2)
Total	**28**	**(17)**	**8**	**(3)**	**1**	**(1)**		**37**	**(21)**

Adam Hart

Born: Scotland
From: Port Glasgow 6.22

	League	FAC	LC	MC	Total	
1922/23	2				2	(0)
Total	**2**				**2**	**(0)**

Jimmy Harvey

Born: Lurgan 2.5.1958
From: Hereford United 3.87
To: Tranmere Rovers 10.87

	League	FAC	LC	MC	Total	
1986/87	2				2	(0)
1987/88	0+1				0+1	(0)
Total	**2+1**				**2+1**	**(0)**

Bert Hawkins

Born: Bristol 29.9.1923
From: Bristol Rovers 5.49
To: Bath City 6.50

	League		FAC	LC	MC	Total	
1949/50	8	(4)				8	(4)
Total	**8**	**(4)**				**8**	**(4)**

Nigel Hawkins

Born: Bristol 7.9.1968
From: Trainee 2.87
To: Blackpool 10.89

	League		FAC	LC		MC	Total	
1987/88	1						1	(0)
1988/89	7+10	(2)	1	2+2		1	11+12	(2)
Total	**8+10**	**(2)**	**1**	**2+2**		**1**	**12+12**	**(2)**

Fred Hawley

Born: Derby 28.7.1890
From: Swindon Town 3.23
To: Brighton 8.25

	League		FAC	LC	MC	Total	
1922/23	10					10	(0)
1923/24	26	(1)	4			30	(1)
1924/25	37		2			39	(0)
Total	**73**	**(1)**	**6**			**79**	**(1)**

Alan Hay

Born: Dunfermline 28.11.1958
From: Bolton Wanderers 7.78
To: York City 8.82

	League		FAC		LC		MC	Total	
1979/80	3+1				2+1		5	10+2	(0)
1980/81	36	(1)	4		1+1		2+1	43+2	(1)
1981/82	33+1				2			35+1	(0)
Total	**72+2**	**(1)**	**4**		**5+2**		**7+1**	**88+5**	**(1)**

Jack Haycox

Born: Cheltenham 1.1.1910
From: Newport County 5.36
To: Torquay United 2.38

	League		FAC		LC	MC		Total	
1936/37	24	(17)			1	(1)		25	(18)
1937/38	19	(8)	3	(2)		4	(2)	26	(12)
Total	**43**	**(25)**	**3**	**(2)**		**5**	**(3)**	**51**	**(30)**

Jimmy Heale

Born: Bristol 19.9.1914
From: South Bristol Central 7.31
To: Manchester City 1.34

	League		FAC		LC	MC	Total	
1931/32	9		3				12	(0)
1932/33	2	(1)					2	(1)
1933/34	15	(7)	4	(2)			19	(9)
Total	**26**	**(8)**	**7**	**(2)**			**33**	**(10)**

Tom Henry

Born: South Bank
From: South Bank 7.13

	League	FAC	LC	MC	Total	
1913/14	2				2	(0)
1914/15	1				1	(0)
Total	**3**				**3**	**(0)**

Matt Hewlett

Born: Bristol 25.2.1976
From: Trainee

	League		FAC	LC		MC	Total	
1993/94	11+1			2			13+1	(0)
1994/95	0+1						0+1	(0)
1995/96	27	(2)		0+1			27+1	(2)
1996/97	33+3	(2)	2+1	(2) 3+1		2	40+5	(4)
Total	**71+5**	**(4)**	**2+1**	**(2) 5+2**		**2**	**80+8**	**(6)**

Billy Hick

Born: West Pelton 13.2.1903
From: Southend United 5.28
To: Exeter City 1.29

	League	FAC	LC	MC	Total	
1928/29	10	(1)			1	11	(1)
Total	10	(1)			1	11	(1)

Jack Hick

Born: Birmingham 1.1.1912
From: Birmingham 8.34
To: Ipswich Town 7.39

	League	FAC	LC	MC	Total	
1934/35	11			1	12	(0)
1935/36	20	1		2	23	(0)
1936/37	28	1			29	(0)
1937/38	12	3		4	19	(0)
1938/39	12			1	13	(0)
Total	83	5		8	96	(0)

Alastair Hill

Born: Glasgow 25.4.1934
From: Dundee 11.59
To: Stirling Albion 3.60

	League	FAC	LC	MC	Total	
1959/60	3		1		4	(0)
Total	3		1		4	(0)

Brian Hill

Born: Bedworth 31.7.1941
From: Coventry City 3.71 Loan

	League	FAC	LC	MC	Total	
1970/71	7				7	(0)
Total	7				7	(0)

Frank Hilton

Born: Barnsley 1.1.1884
From: Doncaster St. John's 7.05

	League	FAC	LC	MC	Total	
1905/06	26	(5)	1			27	(5)
1906/07	32	(4)	2			34	(4)
1907/08	30	(5)	2	(1)		32	(6)
1908/09	27	(7)	4			31	(7)
1909/10	1				1	(0)
Total	116	(21)	9	(1)		125	(22)

Wally Hinshelwood

Born: Battersea 27.10.1929
From: Reading 2.56 £15,000
To: Millwall 6.60 £1,100

	League	FAC	LC	MC	Total	
1955/56	10	(1)				10	(1)
1956/57	40	(7)	3	(1)		43	(8)
1957/58	38	(3)	4	(2)		42	(5)
1958/59	40	(3)				40	(3)
1959/60	20	(2)				20	(2)
Total	148	(16)	7	(3)		155	(19)

Martyn Hirst

Born: Batley 26.10.1961
From: Bath City 10.83
To: Weymouth 1.86

	League	FAC	LC	MC	Total	
1983/84	22+2	(1)	4	(1)		1	27+2	(2)
1984/85	13+3	1	3	1	18+3	(0)
1985/86	1				1	(0)
Total	36+5	(1)	5	(1)	3	2	46+5	(2)

Jack Hodge

Born: Plymouth
From: Plymouth Argyle 7.34
To: Luton Town 3.36

	League	FAC	LC	MC	Total	
1934/35	32	(5)	9	(4)			41	(9)
1935/36	30	(3)	1		2	33	(3)
Total	62	(8)	10	(4)		2	74	(12)

Syd Homer

Born: Bloxwich 14.1.1903
From: Bristol Rovers 11.29
To: Worcester City 8.34

	League	FAC	LC	MC	Total	
1929/30	28	(4)	1			29	(4)
1930/31	36	(4)				36	(4)
1931/32	38	(4)				38	(4)
1932/33	42	(5)	3		1	(1)	46	(6)
1933/34	35	(1)	3		7	45	(1)
Total	179	(18)	7		8	(1)	194	(19)

Chris Honor

Born: Bristol 5.6.1968
From: Apprentice 7.85
To: Airdrie 8.91 £20,000

	League	FAC	LC	MC	Total	
1985/86	1				1	(0)
1986/87	1+1				1+1	(0)
1987/88	14+3	1		1	16+3	(0)
1988/89	24+2	3+1		4+1	29+4	(0)
1989/90	4+10	(1)		1		5+10	(1)
Total	44+16	(1)	4+1	1	5+1	52+18	(1)

Mike Hooper

Born: Bristol 10.2.1964
From: Mangotsfield United 11.83
To: Wrexham 2.85

	League	FAC	LC	MC	Total	
1984/85	1	1			2	(0)
Total	1	1			2	(0)

Peter Hooper

Born: Teignmouth 2.2.1933
From: Cardiff City 7.63 £11,000
To: Worcester City 7.66

	League	FAC	LC	MC	Total	
1963/64	38	(12)	5	(2)	1		44	(14)
1964/65	7	(1)	1	1	(1)		9	(2)
1965/66	9	(1)				9	(1)
Total	54	(14)	6	(2)	2	(1)		62	(17)

Idris 'Dai' Hopkins

Born: Merthyr Tydfil 11.10.1907
From: Brentford 5.47
To: Sleipner 5.48

	League	FAC	LC	MC	Total	
1963/64	24	3			27	(0)
Total	24	3			27	(0)

Gordon Hopkinson

Born: Sheffield 19.6.1933
From: Doncaster Rovers 7.48
To: Cheltenham Town 7.61

	League	FAC	LC	MC	Total	
1958/59	34	(1)	3			37	(1)
1959/60	12	(1)				12	(1)
1960/61	21		2	1		24	(0)
Total	67	(2)	5	1		73	(2)

Dean Horrix

Born: Taplow 21.11.1961
From: Millwall 3.90
To: Deceased 3.90

	League	FAC	LC	MC	Total	
1989/90	3				3	(0)
Total	3				3	(0)

Jim Hosie

Born: Glasgow 1.1.1876
From: Stockport County 7.03

	League	FAC	LC	MC	Total	
1903/04	32	(5)	3	(2)			35	(7)
1904/05	21	(5)	3			24	(5)
Total	53	(10)	6	(2)			59	(12)

Tommy Howarth

Born: Bury 15.4.1890
From: Army 1.14
To: Leeds United 3.21

	League	FAC	LC	MC	Total	
1913/14	6	(2)				6	(2)
1919/20	36	(14)	5	(5)			52	(19)
1920/21	10	(1)				20	(1)
Total	52	(17)	5	(5)			78	(22)

Ted Howling

Born: Stockton 1.1.1885
From: South Bank 5.13
To: Bradford PA 7.15

	League	FAC	LC	MC	Total	
1913/14	18				18	(0)
1914/15	37	2			39	(0)
Total	55	2			57	(0)

George Howson

Born: Bolton
From: Little Hulton 7.25
To: New Brighton 5.27

	League	FAC	LC	MC	Total	
1925/26	3				3	(0)
Total	3				3	(0)

Jamie Howland

Born: Sheffield 23.1.1966
From: Sheffield United 3.94 Loan

	League	FAC	LC	MC	Total	
1993/94	6				6	(0)
Total	6				6	(0)

Clarence Hughes

Born:
From:
To:

	League	FAC	LC	MC	Total	
1914/15	2				2	(0)
1919/20	3				3	(0)
Total	5				5	(0)

Dick Hughes

Born: Sunderland 2.8.1902
From: Sunderland 9.20
To: Exeter City 8.32

	League	FAC	LC	MC	Total	
1920/21	5				5	(0)
1921/22	36	1			37	(0)
1922/23	29	1			30	(0)
1923/24	15				15	(0)
1924/25	34	2			36	(0)
1925/26	36	1			37	(0)
1926/27	26	3			29	(0)
1927/28	3				3	(0)
1928/29	22				22	(0)
1929/30	18	1			19	(0)
1930/31	19				19	(0)
1931/32	25	3			28	(0)
Total	268	12			280	(0)

James Hughes

Born: Cuddington
From: Birmingham 5.34

	League	FAC	LC	MC	Total	
1934/35	10				10	(0)
Total	10				10	(0)

Joe Hughes

Born: Perth
From: Porth Athletic 7.21

	League	FAC	LC	MC	Total	
1921/22	3				3	(0)
Total	3				3	(0)

Mark Hughes

Born: Port Talbot 3.2.1962
From: Swansea City 2.85
To: Tranmere Rovers 9.85 £3,000

	League	FAC	LC	MC	Total	
1984/85	19+1			3	22+1	(0)
1985/86	2		1		3	(0)
Total	21+1		1	3	25+1	(0)

Glenn Humphries

Born: Hull 11.8.1964
From: Doncaster Rovers 10.87 £20,000
To: Scunthorpe United 3.91 £50,000

	League	FAC	LC	MC	Total	
1987/88	24	2			26	(0)
1988/89	20+2	3	3	2	28+2	(0)
1989/90	36+1	7		2	45+1	(0)
1990/91	1+1				1+1	(0)
Total	81+4	12	3	4	100+4	(0)

Mark Humphries

Born: Glasgow 23.12.1971
From: Leeds United 10.94
To: Raith Rovers 12.95

	League	FAC	LC	MC	Total	
1994/95	4				4	(0)
Total	4				4	(0)

Bert Humpish

Born: Bury 3.4.1902
From: Arsenal 12.30
To: Stockport County 8.32

	League	FAC	LC	MC	Total	
1930/31	8	1			9	(0)
1931/32	28	(1)	3		31	(1)
Total	36	(1)	4		40	(1)

Ernie Hunt

Born: Swindon 17.3.1943
From: Coventry City 12.73 £8,000
To: Atherstone Town 11.74

	League	FAC	LC	MC	Total	
1973/74	9+2	(2)	4		13+2	(2)
1974/75	0+1				0+1	(0)
Total	9+3	(2)	4		13+3	(2)

Norman Hunter

Born: Eighton Banks 29.10.1943
From: Leeds United 10.76 £40,000
To: Barnsley 6.79 P/C

	League	FAC	LC	MC	Total	
1976/77	31		1		32	(0)
1977/78	38	(3)		1	4	43	(3)
1978/79	39	(1)	2	1	5	(1) 47	(2)
Total	108	(4)	3	2	9	(1)122	(5)

Bobby Hutchinson

Born: Glasgow 19.6.1953
From: Tranmere Rovers 7.84
To: Walsall 2.87 £10,000

	League	FAC	LC	MC	Total	
1984/85	29+2	(4)		1	4	34+2	(4)
1985/86	42	(5)	3	2	(1) 7	(1) 54	(7)
1986/87	18+1	(1)	3	(1) 4	2	27+1	(2)
Total	89+3	(10)	6	(1) 7	13	(1)115+3	(13)

Billy Ingham

Born: 1.1.1882
From: Aberdare 7.05

	League	FAC	LC	MC	Total	
1905/06	1				1	(0)
Total	1				1	(0)

Sam Irving

Born: Belfast 20.8.1894
From: Shildon Athletic 12.13
To: Dundee 7.19

	League	FAC	LC	MC	Total	
1913/14	14	(3)			14	(3)
1914/15	4	(1)			4	(1)
Total	18	(4)			18	(4)

Norman Jackson

Born: Bradford 6.7.1925
From: Sheffield Wednesday 6.54
To: Oldham Athletic 6.56

	League	FAC	LC	MC	Total	
1954/55	7	1			8	(0)
1955/56	1				1	(0)
Total	8	1			9	(0)

Frank Jacobs

Born: Bristol 22.4.1940
From: Juniors 5.58
To: Cheltenham Town 7.61

	League	FAC	LC	MC	Total	
1959/60	4				4	(0)
1960/61	1		1		2	(0)
Total	5		1		6	(0)

Trevor Jacobs

Born: Bristol 28.11.1946
From: Juniors 7.65
To: Bristol Rovers 5.73 Free

	League	FAC	LC	MC	Total	
1966/67	2				2	(0)
1967/68	21	(1)	3	1	25	(1)
1968/69	37		1	3	41	(0)
1969/70	31	(2)	1	2	34	(2)
1970/71	21		4		25	(0)
1971/72	15+1				15+1	(0)
1972/73	3				3	(0)
Total	130+1	(3)	5	10	145	(3)

Pertti Jantunen

Born: Lahti, Finland 25.6.1952
From: Eskilstuna 3.79 £50,000

	League	FAC	LC	MC	Total	
1978/79	0+1				0+1	(0)
1979/80	7	(1)	3	(1) 5	15	(2)
Total	7+1	(1)	3	(1) 5	15+1	(2)

Mervin Jarvis

Born: Bristol 20.10.1924
From: Douglas AFC 5.48
To:

	League	FAC	LC	MC	Total	
1948/49	4				4	(0)
Total	4				4	(0)

Jimmy Jay

Born: Bristol
From: Bristol East 7.01
To: Brentford 7.03

	League	FAC	LC	MC	Total	
1901/02	11	(1)	1		12	(1)
1902/03	10	(3)			10	(3)
Total	21	(4)	1		22	(4)

Eddie Jenkins

Born: Cardiff 16.7.1909
From: Cardiff City 6.34
To: Newport County 7.35

	League	FAC	LC	MC	Total	
1934/35	10				10	(0)
Total	10				10	(0)

Wally Jennings

Born: Bristol 1.4.1909
From: South Bristol Cent. 7.28
To: Cardiff City 6.34

	League	FAC	LC	MC	Total	
1929/30	7				7	(0)
1930/31	21				21	(0)
1931/32	26				26	(0)
1932/33	1				1	(0)
1933/34	35	4		4	43	(0)
Total	90	4		4	98	(0)

Arthur Johnson

Born: Atherstone 1.1.1904
From: Birmingham 5.28
To: Coventry City 7.31

	League	FAC	LC	MC	Total	
1928/29	12	1			13	(0)
1929/30	33	(7)	1		34	(7)
1930/31	15				15	(0)
Total	60	(7)	2		62	(7)

Joe Johnson

Born: Grimsby 4.4.1911
From: Scunthorpe United 5.31
To: Stoke City 4.32

	League	FAC	LC	MC	Total	
1931/32	7				7	(0)
Total	7				7	(0)

Peter Johnson

Born: Harrogate 5.10.1958
From: Newcastle United 9.82 Loan

	League	FAC	LC	MC	Total	
1982/83	20	1	(1)		21	(1)
Total	20	1	(1)		21	(1)

Steve Johnson

Born: Liverpool 23.6.1957
From: Wigan Athletic 3.85
To: Scunthorpe United 7.86

	League	FAC	LC	MC	Total	
1984/85	6+2	(3)			6+2	(3)
1985/86	8+5		1+1	2	11+6	(0)
Total	14+7	(3)	1+1	2	17+8	(3)

Andy Jones

Born: Wrexham 9.1.1963
From: Charlton Athletic 11.89 Loan

	League	FAC	LC	MC	Total	
1989/90	2+2	(1)		1	(1)	3+2	(2)
Total	2+2	(1)		1	(1)	3+2	(2)

Billy Jones

Born: Brighton 6.3.1876
From: Loughborough 7.97
To: Tottenham Hotspur 7.05

	League	FAC	LC	MC	Total	
1901/02	34	2	(1)		36	(1)
1902/03	32	(2)	3		35	(2)
1903/04	32	(4)	3		35	(4)
1904/05	32	(3)	5	(1)	37	(4)
1905/06	18		1		19	(0)
Total	148	(9)	14	(2)	162	(11)

Edwin Jones

Born: Tyldesley 1.1.1891
From: Atherton 2.10
To: Weymouth 7.23

	League	FAC	LC	MC	Total	
1910/11	3				3	(0)
1911/12	31	1			32	(0)
1912/13	25	(4)			25	(4)
1913/14	9				9	(0)
1914/15	1				1	(0)
1919/20	10				10	(0)
1920/21	20	1			21	(0)
1921/22	6				6	(0)
1922/23	2				2	(0)
Total	107	(4)	2		109	(4)

Ernie Jones

Born: Bristol 12.5.1919
From: Victoria Athletic 2.38
To: Wells City 7.48

	League	FAC	LC	MC	Total	
1946/47	22	(1)	2		24	(1)
1947/48	5				5	(0)
Total	27	(1)	2		29	(1)

Ernie Jones

Born: Cwmbwrla 12.11.1920
From: Southampton 11.51 P/C
To: Rhyl 4.54 P/M

	League	FAC	LC	MC	Total	
1951/52	22	(3)	1		23	(3)
1952/53	17	(3)	1		18	(3)
1953/54	11	(1)			11	(1)
Total	50	(7)	2		52	(7)

John Jones

Born: Wolverhampton 1.1.1887
From: Wellington Town 7.13
To: Wolves 8.19

	League	FAC	LC	MC	Total	
1913/14	1				1	(0)
1914/15	18	2			20	(0)
Total	19	2			20	(0)

Mark Jones

Born: Bristol 2.12.1965
From: Apprentice 6.82
To: Weston-Super-Mare 6.83

	League	FAC	LC	MC	Total	
1982/83	0+1				0+1	(0)
Total	0+1				0+1	(0)

Steve Jones

Born:
From: Aberdare 7.01

	League	FAC	LC	MC	Total	
1901/02	5	(2)	2	(2)	7	(4)
Total	5	(2)	2	(2)	7	(4)

Tommy Jones

Born: Cardiff
From: Army 8.19
To: Southend United 6.21

	League	FAC	LC	MC	Total	
1919/20	4				4	(0)
1920/21	6				6	(0)
Total	10				10	(0)

Joe Jordan

Born: Carluke 15.12.1951
From: Southampton 2.87
To: Manager

	League	FAC	LC	MC	Total	
1986/87	19	(3)		5	(4)	24	(7)
1987/88	17+11	(4)	1	2	0+1	20+11	(4)
1988/89	2+7	(1)	0+1	5+1		7+9	(1)
1989/90	0+1					0+1	(0)
Total	38+19	(8)	1+1	7+1	5+1	(4)	51+21	(12)

Abdul Kamara

Born: Southampton 10.2.1974
From: Southampton 7.93
To: Gillingham 11.94

	League	FAC	LC	MC	Total	
1993/94	0+1				0+1	(0)
Total	0+1				0+1	(0)

Sid Kearney

Born: Liverpool 28.3.1917
From: Accrington Stanley 1.47
To: Street 8.50

	League	FAC	LC	MC	Total	
1946/47	16	(2)			16	(2)
1947/48	26	(3)			26	(3)
1948/49	15				15	(0)
1949/50	8				8	(0)
Total	65	(5)			65	(5)

John Kearns

Born: Nuneaton 1.4.1880
From: Aston Villa 7.12

	League	FAC	LC	MC	Total	
1912/13	36	1			37	(0)
1913/14	37	(1)	2		39	(1)
1914/15	20				20	(0)
Total	93	(1)	3		96	(1)

Albert Keating

Born: Swillington Common 20.6.1902
From: Newcastle United 11.25
To: Blackburn Rovers 5.28
From: Cardiff City 11.32
To: North Shields 7.33

	League	FAC	LC	MC	Total	
1925/26	19	(8)	1		20	(8)
1926/27	35	(23)			35	(23)
1927/28	25	(16)	1		26	(16)
1932/33	21	(6)	2	(1)	23	(7)
Total	100	(53)	4	(1)	104	(54)

Jimmy Keen

Born: Walker 25.11.1897
From: Walker Celtic 7.20
To: Newcastle United 5.22 £100

	League	FAC	LC	MC	Total	
1920/21	1				1	(0)
1921/22	8	(1)	2		10	(1)
Total	9	(1)	2		11	(1)

Bobby Kellard

Born: Edmonton 1.3.1943
From: Portsmouth 7.68
To: Leicester City 8.70 £50,000

	League	FAC	LC	MC	Total
1968/69	42 (3)	1	3		46 (3)
1969/70	35 (3)		3 (2)		38 (5)
Total	77 (6)	1	6 (2)		84 (8)

Errington Kelly

Born: Sandy Bay, St Vincent 8.4.1958
From: Lincoln City 2.83
To: Coventry City 8.83

	League	FAC	LC	MC	Total
1982/82	4+1 (1)				4+1 (1)
Total	4+1 (1)				4+1 (1)

Lawrie Kelly

Born: Bellshill 19.11.1911
From: Southend United 6.36
To: Aldershot 5.37

	League	FAC	LC	MC	Total
1936/37	1				1 (0)
Total	1				1 (0)

Nyrere Kelly

Born: Meriden 14.2.1966
From: Juniors 9.82
To: R.C. Warwick 7.83

	League	FAC	LC	MC	Total
1982/83	2+4 (1)		0+1		2+5 (1)
Total	2+4 (1)		0+1		2+5 (1)

Roger Kenyon

Born: Blackpool 4.1.1949
From: Vancouver W. 10.79
To: Vancouver W. 2.80

	League	FAC	LC	MC	Total
1979/80	4		1	1	6 (0)
Total	4		1	1	6 (0)

John Kerr

Born: Birkenhead 23.11.1959
From: Tranmere Rovers 8.83
To: Stockport County 1.84

	League	FAC	LC	MC	Total
1983/84	13+1 (4)	2	2		17 (4)
Total	13+1 (4)	2	2		17 (4)

Herbert Kirby

Born: Barry 23.3.1903
From: Barry 11.24
To: Charlton Athletic 1.26

	League	FAC	LC	MC	Total
1924/25	5				5 (0)
Total	5				5 (0)

Harry 'Jazzo' Kirk

Born: Dillington 22.4.1899
From: Sherwood R 3.20
To: Plymouth Argyle 7.21

	League	FAC	LC	MC	Total
1919/20	6 (2)				6 (2)
1920/21	11 (5)				11 (5)
Total	11 (5)				11 (5)

Robert Kirk

Born: Clydebank 22.2.1899
From: Albion Rovers 7.24
To: Exeter City 7.27

	League	FAC	LC	MC	Total
1924/25	22 (1)				22 (1)
1925/26	30 (4)				30 (4)
1926/27	2				2 (0)
Total	54 (5)				54 (5)

Phil Kite

Born: Bristol 26.10.1962
From: Cardiff City 8.94
To: Bristol Rovers 7.96

	League	FAC	LC	MC	Total
1994/95	2				2 (0)
1995/96	3+1		2+1		5+2 (0)
Total	5+1		2+1		7+2 (0)

William Knox

Born: Douglas Water
From: Luton Town 8.32
To: Stockport County 7.33

	League	FAC	LC	MC	Total
1932/33	19 (1)				19 (1)
Total	19 (1)				19 (1)

Bjorn Kristensen

Born: Malling, Denmark 10.10.1963
From: Newcastle United 11.92 Loan

	League	FAC	LC	MC	Total
1992/93	4				4 (0)
Total	4				4 (0)

Martin Kuhl

Born: Frimley 10.1.1965
From: Derby County 12.94 £330,000
To:

	League	FAC	LC	MC	Total
1994/95	17 (1)	2			19 (1)
1995/96	46 (6)	2	4	3	55 (6)
1996/97	22+9	4 (2)	2+2		28+11(2)
Total	85+9 (7)	8 (2)	6+2	3	102+11(9)

John Kurila

Born: Glasgow 10.4.1941
From: Hamilton Steelers 8.63
To: Northampton Town 11.63

	League	FAC	LC	MC	Total
1963/64	6				6 (0)
Total	6				6 (0)

Fred Laidman

Born: Durham 20.6.1913
From: Everton 6.38
To: Darlington 7.39

	League	FAC	LC	MC	Total
1938/39	10 (1)		2		12 (1)
Total	10 (1)		2		12 (1)

Jim Lamberton

Born:
From:
To:

	League	FAC	LC	MC	Total
1902/03	3				3 (0)
Total	3				3 (0)

Francis Lanceley

Born: Bristol 16.9.1908
From: Bath City 9.32

	League	FAC	LC	MC	Total
1932/33	5				5 (0)
Total	5				5 (0)

Jack Landells

Born: Gateshead 11.11.1904
From: West Ham 7.34
To: Carlisle United 6.35

	League	FAC	LC	MC	Total
1934/35	21 (2)	9 (2)			30 (4)
Total	21 (2)	9 (2)			30 (4)

Billy Lane

Born: Tottenham 23.10.1904
From: Watford 1.36 £200
To: Clapton Orient 7.37

	League	FAC	LC	MC	Total
1935/36	20 (9)				20 (9)
1936/37	10 (2)			1	11 (2)
Total	30 (11)			1	31 (11)

Kevin Langan

Born: Jersey 7.4.78
From: Trainee 7.95

	League	FAC	LC	MC	Total
1996/97			1		1 (0)
Total			1		1 (0)

Frank Latham

Born: Bristol
From: Bristol Rovers 7.08
To:

	League	FAC	LC	MC	Total
1908/09	1				1 (0)
Total	1				1 (0)

George Lawrence

Born: Basford 10.3.1889
From: Derby County 9.24
To: Lincoln City 8.25

	League	FAC	LC	MC	Total
1924/25	14				14 (0)
Total	14				14 (0)

Andy Leaning

Born: York 18.5.1963
From: Sheffield United 9.88
To: Lincoln City 3.94

	League	FAC	LC	MC	Total
1988/89	6		2		8 (0)
1989/90	19	2	2	1	24 (0)
1990/91	29	1	1		31 (0)
1991/92	20	4		1	25 (0)
1992/93	1				1 (0)
Total	75	7	5	2	89 (0)

Ian Leigh

Born: Ilfracombe 11.6.1962
From: AFC Bournemouth 1.85 Loan

	League	FAC	LC	MC	Total
1984/85	1				1 (0)
Total	1				1 (0)

Walter Leigh

Born: Yardley 1.11.1874
From: Grimsby Town 7.02
To: New Brampton 7.03

	League	FAC	LC	MC	Total
1902/03	30 (5)	3 (1)			33 (6)
Total	30 (5)	3 (1)			33 (6)

George Lewis

Born: Chasetown 1.1.1876
From: Notts County 7.02
To: Stourbridge 7.03

	League	FAC	LC	MC	Total
1902/03	30 (1)	3			33 (1)
Total	30 (1)	3			33 (1)

Glyn Lewis

Born: Abertillery 3.7.1921
From: Crystal Palace 7.48
To: Llanelli 7.50

	League	FAC	LC	MC	Total
1948/49	18				18 (0)
Total	18				18 (0)

Andy Llewellyn

Born: Bristol 26.2.1966
From: Apprentice 2.84
To: Yeovil Town 7.50

	League	FAC	LC	MC	Total
1982/83	5+2			2	7+2 (0)
1983/84				0+1	0+1 (0)
1984/85	22		2	2	26 (0)
1985/86	38 (1)	3	2	4+1	47+1 (1)
1986/87	31	2	4	5	42 (0)
1987/88	36+6 (1)	1	2		39+6 (1)
1988/89	13+3 (1)	1	4	2	20+3 (1)
1989/90	46	7	2	3	58 (0)
1990/91	42	1	4	1	48 (0)
1991/92	37	3	2	1	43 (0)
1992/93	12	1			13 (0)
1993/94	15	2			17 (0)
Total	297+11 (3)	23	20	20+2	360+13(3)

Leo Loftus

Born: Ferryhill 24.1.1906
From: Nottingham Forest 6.32
To: Gillingham 8.35

	League	FAC	LC	MC	Total
1932/33	29 (14)	3 (3)		1	33 (17)
1933/34	39 (11)	4		2	45 (11)
1934/35	25 (4)	3 (2)			28 (6)
Total	93 (29)	10 (5)		3	106 (34)

Alec Logan

Born: Barrhead 1.2.1880
From: Aston Villa 11.10

	League	FAC	LC	MC	Total
1910/11	20 (7)				20 (7)
1911/12	17 (2)				17 (2)
Total	37 (9)				37 (9)

Colin Loss

Born: Brentwood 15.8.1973
From: Gresley Rovers 3.94
To: Merthyr Tydfil 6.95

	League	FAC	LC	MC	Total
1994/95	3+2		1		4+2 (0)
Total	3+2		1		4+2 (0)

Gordon Low

Born: Aberdeen 11.7.1940
From: Huddersfield Town 3.61
To: Stockport County 7.68

	League	FAC	LC	MC	Total
1960/61	7				7 (0)
1961/62	10 (1)		1		11 (1)
1962/63	17		1		18 (0)
1963/64	32 (2)	5 (1)			37 (3)
1964/65	46 (1)	4	1		51 (1)
1965/66	42 (2)	1 (1)	1		44 (3)
1966/67	41 (6)	4	2		47 (6)
1967/68	8+2		1		9+2 (0)
Total	203+2 (12)	15 (2)	6		224+2(14)

George Lowrie

Born: Tonypandy 19.12.1919
From: Newcastle United 9.49 £10,000
To: Coventry City 2.52 £2,750

	League	FAC	LC	MC	Total
1949/50	26 (8)	1			27 (8)
1950/51	16 (11)				16 (11)
1951/52	6 (2)	1			7 (2)
Total	48 (21)	2			50 (21)

Mike Lyons

Born: Bristol 31.1.1932
From: Winterbourne 6.50
To: Bristol Rovers 7.53

	League	FAC	LC	MC	Total
1950/51	1				1 (0)
1951/52	1				1 (0)
Total	2				2 (0)

Derrick Lythgoe

Born: Bolton 5.5.1933
From: Norwich City 8.62
To: King's Lynn 7.64

	League	FAC	LC	MC	Total
1962/63	6 (1)				6 (1)
1963/64	7 (1)				7 (1)
Total	13 (2)				13 (2)

Kevin Mabbutt

Born: Bristol 5.12.1958
From: Apprentice 1.76
To: Crystal Palace 10.81 P/ex

	League	FAC	LC	MC	Total
1977/78	16+10 (4)	2 (2)	1 (1)	6+1 (5)	25+11(12)
1977/78	26+1 (9)			2	28+1 (9)
1978/79	21+6 (6)	1	5 (2)	7 (3)	34+6(11)
1980/81	38 (9)	5 (5)	2	3	48 (14)
1981/82	11 (1)		4		15 (1)
Total	112+17(29)	8 (7)	12 (3)	18+1 (8)	150+18(47)

Rod McAree

Born: Dungannon 19.8.1974
From: Liverpool 7.94
To: Dungannon 7.95

	League	FAC	LC	MC	Total
1994/95	6		2		8 (0)
Total	6		2		8 (0)

Aidan McCaffrey

Born: Newcastle 30.8.1957
From: Bristol Rovers 2.82 Loan

	League	FAC	LC	MC	Total
1981/82	6 (1)				6 (1)
Total	6 (1)				6 (1)

Peter McCall

Born: West Ham 11.9.1936
From: King's Lynn 4.55
To: Oldham Athletic 5.62

	League	FAC	LC	MC	Total
1957/58	7				7 (0)
1958/59	38 (1)	3			41 (1)
1959/60	20	1			21 (0)
1960/61	11	1	1		13 (0)
1961/62	2				2 (0)
Total	78 (1)	5	1		84 (1)

Johnny McCann

Born: Govan 23.7.1934
From: Barnsley 5.59
To: Huddersfield Town 10.60 P/ex

	League	FAC	LC	MC	Total
1959/60	26				26 (0)
1960/61	4				4 (0)
Total	30				30 (0)

John McCarthy

Born: Cork 22.1.1922
From: Cork 7.49

	League	FAC	LC	MC	Total
1949/50	3				3 (0)
Total	3				3 (0)

Steve McClaren

Born: Fulford 3.5.1961
From: Derby County 2.88 £50,000
To: Oxford United 8.89 P/Ex

	League	FAC	LC	MC	Total
1987/88	16 (1)				16 (1)
1988/89	44+1 (1)	4	9 (1)	2+1	59+2 (2)
Total	60+1 (2)	4	9 (1)	2+1	75+2 (3)

Scott McGarvey

Born: Glasgow 22.4.1963
From: Grimsby Town 9.88 P/Ex
To: Oldham Athletic 5.89

	League	FAC	LC	MC	Total
1988/89	20+6 (9)	6 (1)		2+1 (1)	28+7(11)
Total	20+6 (9)	6 (1)		2+1 (1)	28+7(11)

Tom McGovern

Born: Glasgow
From: Clydebank 6.24
To: Merthyr Town 6.25

	League	FAC	LC	MC	Total
1924/25	3 (1)				3 (1)
Total	3 (1)				3 (1)

Francis McGurk

Born: Eddlewood 15.1.1909
From: Birmingham 6.35
To: Whittaker Eng 7.36

	League	FAC	LC	MC	Total
1935/36	3		1		4 (0)
Total	3		1		4 (0)

Hugh McIlmoyle

Born: Cambuslang 29.1.1940
From: Wolverhampton W. 3.67 £27,000
To: Carlisle United 9.67 £22,000

	League	FAC	LC	MC	Total
1966/67	12 (2)				12 (2)
1967/68	8 (2)		1		9 (2)
Total	12 (4)				12 (2)

Jim McIntyre

Born: Dumbarton 24.5.1972
From: Duntocher BC 10.91
To: Airdrie 9.93

	League	FAC	LC	MC	Total
1991/92	1				1 (0)
1992/93			0+1		0+1 (0)
Total	1		0+1		1+1 (0)

Henry McKop

Born: Zimbabwe 8.7.1967
From: Bonner SC 7.93
To: Shelbourne 7.95

	League	FAC	LC	MC	Total
1993/94	2+2				2+2 (0)
1994/95	0+1				0+1 (0)
Total	2+3				2+3 (0)

John McLean

Born: Port Glasgow 22.5.1872
From: Grimsby Town 5.98
To: Bristol Rovers 7.02

	League	FAC	LC	MC	Total
1901/02	34 (1)	2			36 (1)
Total	34 (1)	2			36 (1)

John McLean

Born: Clydebank 29.10.1896
From: Vale of Leven 6.25
To: Taunton United 6.26

	League	FAC	LC	MC	Total
1925/26	1				1 (0)
Total	1				1 (0)

Alan McLeary

Born: Lambeth 6.10.1964
From: Charlton Athletic 7.95
To: Millwall 2.97

	League	FAC	LC	MC	Total
1995/96	30+1		2		32+1 (0)
1996/97	1+2		3		4+2 (0)
Total	31+3		5		36+3 (0)

Andrew McMutrie

Born: Dreghorn 30.10.1906
From: Motherwell 5.29

	League	FAC	LC	MC	Total
1929/30	10 (1)				10 (1)
Total	10 (1)				10 (1)

Brian McNeill

Born: Newcastle 1.4.1956
From: Apprentice 4.74
To: Plymouth Argyle 12.78

	League	FAC	LC	MC	Total
1975/76	0+2				0+2 (0)
1976/77	0+1				0+1 (0)
Total	0+3				0+3 (0)

John MacPhail

Born: Dundee 7.12.1955
From: York City 7.86 £15,000
To: Sunderland 7.87

	League	FAC	LC	MC	Total
1986/87	26 (1)	5		6	37 (1)
Total	26 (1)	5		6	37 (1)

Mike Mahoney

Born: Bristol 25.10.1950
From: Apprentice 8.68
To: Torquay United 8.70 £5,000

	League	FAC	LC	MC	Total
1968/69	1			1	1 (0)
1969/70	3				3 (0)
Total	4				4 (0)

Jimmy Mann

Born: Goole 15.12.1952
From: Leeds United 5.74
To: Barnsley 2.82

	League	FAC	LC	MC	Total
1974/75	29+1 (6)	1	1		31+1 (6)
1975/76	30+6 (7)	1	2	2+1 (3)	35+7(10)
1976/77	25+5 (1)		1	3 (2)	29+5 (3)
1977/78	26+5 (1)		1	7+1 (2)	35+6 (3)
1978/79	23+5 (1)	0+1	1	4 (2)	28+6 (3)
1979/80	28+1 (3)	1 (1)	3	5	37+1 (4)
1980/81	22+3 (6)	1+1(1)	1 (1)	1+1	25+5 (8)
1981/82	22 (6)	5 (2)	5 (1)		32 (9)
Total	205+26(31)	10+2(4)	15	(2)22+3 (9)	252+31(46)

Harry Mardon

Born: Cardiff 8.6.1914
From: Bournemouth 11.38

	League	FAC	LC	MC	Total
1938/39	13 (3)	1 (1)		1 (2)	15 (6)
Total	13 (3)	1 (1)		1 (2)	15 (6)

Paul Mardon

Born: Bristol 14.9.1969
From: Trainee 1.88
To: Birmingham City 8.91 £65,000

	League	FAC	LC	MC	Total
1987/88	8		1		9 (0)
1988/89	13+7	3+2 (1)			16+9 (1)
1989/90	2+5	0+1			2+6 (0)
1990/91	6+1				6+1 (0)
Total	29+13	3+3 (1)	1		33+16(1)

George Marks

Born: Amesbury 9.4.1915
From: Blackburn Rovers 8.48
To: Reading 10.48

	League	FAC	LC	MC	Total
1948/49	9				9 (0)
Total	9				9 (0)

Reuben Marr

Born: Doncaster 1.1.1884
From: Mexborough Town 7.06

	League	FAC	LC	MC	Total
1906/07	30 (2)	1			31 (2)
1907/08	24	1			25 (0)
1908/09	18	9			27 (0)
1909/10	25 (3)	3			28 (3)
1910/11	30 (2)				30 (2)
1911/12	33 (3)	1			34 (3)
1912/13	9 (1)				9 (1)
1919/20	9	1			10 (0)
Total	178 (11)	16			194 (11)

Tom Marrison

Born: Rotherham 1.1.1885
From: Oldham Athletic 7.12

	League	FAC	LC	MC	Total
1912/13	13 (1)	1			14 (1)
Total	13 (1)	1			14 (1)

Gary Marshall

Born: Bristol 20.4.1964
From: Shepton Mallet 7.83
To: Carlisle United 7.88

	League	FAC	LC	MC	Total
1983/84	0+1				0+1 (0)
1984/85	3+2 (2)				3+2 (2)
1985/86	14+5 (2)		1+1	2+1	17+7 (2)
1986/87	18+6 (2)	3+2(2)	0+2	3+2	24+12(4)
1987/88	13+6 (1)	0+2	2	1+1	16+9 (2)
Total	48+22 (7)	3+2(2)	3+3	6+4	60+31(9)

Julian Marshall

Born: Swansea 6.7.1957
From: Hereford United 8.80
To: Blackburn Rovers 2.82

	League	FAC	LC	MC	Total
1980/81	26	5		0+1	31+1 (0)
1981/82	3		1		4 (0)
Total	29	5	1	0+1	35+1 (0)

Dave Martin

Born: East Ham 25.4.1963
From: Southend United 7.93
To: Gillingham 7.95

	League	FAC	LC	MC	Total
1993/94	33+1 (1)	6		2	41+1 (1)
1994/95	3+1				3+1 (0)
Total	**36+2 (1)**	**6**		**2**	**44+2 (1)**

Jimmy Martin

Born: Stoke-on-Trent 2.12.1896
From: Aberdare Athletic 5.26
To: Blackpool 2.28

	League	FAC	LC	MC	Total
1926/27	23 (11)	2 (1)			25 (12)
1927/28	17 (5)	1 (1)			18 (6)
Total	**40 (16)**	**3 (2)**			**43 (18)**

Craig Maskell

Born: Aldershot 10.4.1968
From: Southampton 12.95 Loan

	League	FAC	LC	MC	Total
1995/96	5 (1)				5 (1)
Total	**5 (1)**				**5 (1)**

S. R. Mason

Born:
From:
To:

	League	FAC	LC	MC	Total
1910/11	3	1			4 (0)
Total	**3**	**1**			**4 (0)**

Graham Masters

Born: Bristol 13.8.1931
From: Dorset House OB 8.48
To: Glastonbury 7.54

	League	FAC	LC	MC	Total
1951/52	9 (1)	1			10 (1)
Total	**9 (1)**	**1**			**10 (1)**

Alf Matthews

Born: Bristol 28.4.1901
From: Parson Street OB 12.20
To: Exeter City 6.22

	League	FAC	LC	MC	Total
1921/22	1				1 (0)
Total	**1**				**1 (0)**

Billy Matthews

Born: Plas Bennion 4.4.1897
From: Liverpool 3.22
To: Wrexham 11.23

	League	FAC	LC	MC	Total
1921/22	12				12 (0)
1922/23	29 (1)	2			31 (1)
1923/24	1				1 (0)
Total	**42 (1)**	**2**			**44 (1)**

Billy Maxwell

Born: Arbroath 21.9.1876
From: Millwall 7.05
To: Leopold 7.09

	League	FAC	LC	MC	Total
1905/06	38 (25)	1 (1)			39 (26)
1906/07	37 (17)	2 (2)			39 (19)
1907/08	34 (13)	2			36 (13)
1908/09	11 (3)				11 (3)
Total	**120 (58)**	**5 (3)**			**125 (61)**

Andy May

Born: Bury 26.2.1964
From: Huddersfield Town 8.90 £90,000
To: Millwall 6.92 P/ex

	League	FAC	LC	MC	Total
1990/91	44+1 (3)	1	4	1 (1)	50+1 (4)
1991/92	44+1 (1)	3 (1)	1	1	49+1 (2)
Total	**88+2 (4)**	**4 (1)**	**5**	**2 (1)**	**99+2 (6)**

Billy Mays

Born: Ynyshir 12.3.1902
From: Watts Town 9.23
To: Plymouth Argyle 6.26

	League	FAC	LC	MC	Total
1923/24	12 (1)				12 (1)
1924/25	5 (1)				5 (1)
1925/26	2 (2)				2 (2)
Total	**19 (4)**				**19 (4)**

Geert Meijer

Born: Amsterdam, Holland 15.3.1951
From: Ajax 3.79 £80,000
To: Sparta Rotterdam 2.80 £50,000

	League	FAC	LC	MC	Total
1978/79	9 (2)				9 (2)
1979/80	3+3		1+1	5	9+4 (0)
Total	**12+3 (2)**		**1+1**	**5**	**18+4 (2)**

Mickey Mellon

Born: Paisley 18.3.1972
From: Hearts 4.89
To: WBA 2.93 £75,000

	League	FAC	LC	MC	Total
1989/90	7+2		0+1		7+3 (0)
1991/92	12+4				12+4 (0)
1992/93	7+3 (1)	1	3	4+2	15+5 (1)
Total	**26+9 (1)**	**1**	**3+1**	**4+2**	**34+12(1)**

Billy Menmuir

Born: Glasgow 3.2.1952
From: Sandyhills YMCA 6.69
To: Hearts 9.71

	League	FAC	LC	MC	Total
1969/70	1				1 (0)
1970/71	0+1				0+1 (0)
Total	**1+1**				**1+1 (0)**

Arthur Mercer

Born: St Helens 1.1.1903
From: Connahs Quay 7.30
To: Chester 10.31

	League	FAC	LC	MC	Total
1930/31	30 (8)	1			31 (8)
1931/32	1				1 (0)
Total	**31 (8)**	**1**			**32 (8)**

Geoff Merrick

Born: Bristol 29.4.1951
From: Apprentice 8.68
To: Yeovil Town 2.82

	League	FAC	LC	MC	Total
1967/68	1				1 (0)
1968/69	2				2 (0)
1969/70	3+1		1		4+1 (0)
1970/71	13+4	0+1	4		17+4 (0)
1971/72	42	1	1		44 (0)
1972/73	41 (3)	3	1		45 (3)
1973/74	40	5 (2)	4	2	51 (2)
1974/75	42 (3)	1	4 (1)		47 (4)
1975/76	42 (2)	1	2	3	48 (2)
1976/77	39 (1)	1	1	3	44 (1)
1977/78	37	2	2	7	48 (0)
1979/80	39 (1)	2	6	4	51 (1)
1980/81	17+1		2	1	20+1 (0)
1981/82	3		2		5 (0)
Total	**361+6 (10)**	**16+1(2)**	**30**	**(1)20**	**427+6(13)**

Barry Meyer

Born: Bournemouth 21.8.1932
From: Newport County 9.61
To: Hereford United 7.63

	League	FAC	LC	MC	Total
1961/62	5 (1)				5 (1)
1962/63	6 (7)				6 (7)
Total	**11 (8)**				**11 (8)**

Andy Mickleweight

Born: Birmingham 31.10.1931
From: Bristol Rovers 5.53
To: Swindon Town 9.55

	League	FAC	LC	MC	Total
1953/54	38 (16)	3 (3)			41 (19)
1954/55	3 (1)				3 (1)
Total	**41 (17)**	**3 (3)**			**44 (20)**

Paul Miller

Born: Bisley 31.1.1968
From: Wimbledon 1.90 Loan

	League	FAC	LC	MC	Total
1989/90	0+3			2	2+3 (0)
Total	**0+3**			**2**	**2+3 (0)**

Ralph Milne

Born: Dundee 13.5.1961
From: Charlton Athletic 1.88 £60,000
To: Manchester United 11.88 £170,000

	League	FAC	LC	MC	Total
1987/88	19 (4)			2	21 (4)
1988/89	10+1 (2)		3+1 (3)		13+2 (5)
Total	**29+1 (6)**		**3+1 (3)**	**2**	**34+2 (9)**

Paul Milsom

Born: Bristol 5.10.1974
From: Trainee 7.93
To: Cardiff City 3.95

	League	FAC	LC	MC	Total
1993/94	1+2			2	3+2 (0)
Total	**1+2**			**2**	**3+2 (0)**

Arthur Milton

Born: Bristol 10.3.1928
From: Arsenal 2.55 £4,000
To: Gloucester CCC 5.55

	League	FAC	LC	MC	Total
1954/55	14 (3)		2		16 (3)
Total	14 (3)		2		16 (3)

Brian Mitchell

Born: Stonehaven 16.7.1963
From: Bradford City 7.92
To: Hull City 8.93

	League	FAC	LC	MC	Total
1992/93	15+1	4	4		23+1 (0)
Total	15+1	4	4		23+1 (0)

Ken Mitchelson

Born: Edmonton 16.5.1928
From: Charlton Athletic 5.49
To: Bath City 7.54

	League	FAC	LC	MC	Total
1949/50	19	1			20 (0)
1952/53	9				9 (0)
Total	28	1			29 (0)

Walter Moles

Born: Tottenham 1.1.1878
From: Tottenham Hotspur 7.01

	League	FAC	LC	MC	Total
1901/02	6				6 (0)
Total	6				6 (0)

Jan Moller

Born: Malmo, Sweden 17.9.1953
From: Malmo 12.80 £120,000
To: Toronto Blizzard 3.82 £85,000

	League	FAC	LC	MC	Total
1980/81	17	3			20 (0)
1981/82	31	5	5		41 (0)
Total	48	8	5		61 (0)

Bill Molloy

Born: Gateshead 2.4.1900
From: Swansea Town 9.33
To:

	League	FAC	LC	MC	Total
1933/34	7 (2)		6 (3)	13	(5)
Total	7 (2)		6 (3)	13	(5)

John Mooney

Born: Glasgow 1.1.1898
From: Glasgow Perthshire 6.21
To: Cowdenbeath 7.23

	League	FAC	LC	MC	Total
1921/22	1				1 (0)
1922/23	1				1 (0)
Total	2				2 (0)

Gordon Moore

Born: Greenock 27.6.1968
From: Juniors 6.85
To:

	League	FAC	LC	MC	Total
1985/86	0+1				0+1 (0)
Total	0+1				0+1 (0)

Cliff Morgan

Born: Bristol 26.9.1913
From: Bristol Boys 9.30
To: Coaching staff 6.49

	League	FAC	LC	MC	Total
1931/32	7 (2)				7 (2)
1932/33	3 (1)				3 (1)
1933/34	14	1		6	21 (0)
1934/35	29 (1)	5			34 (1)
1935/36	34	1		3	38 (0)
1936/37	32 (1)	1		1	34 (1)
1937/38	41 (2)	3		1	45 (2)
1938/39	19			2 (1)	21 (1)
1939/40	3				3 (0)
1946/47	32 (2)	2			34 (2)
1947/48	19	3			22 (0)
1948/49	15 (2)	3			18 (2)
Total	248 (11)	19		13 (1)	280 (12)

Jerry Morgan

Born: Bristol 1.1.1892
From: Fishponds C. 7.12
To: Caerphilly 7.13

	League	FAC	LC	MC	Total
1912/13	2				2 (0)
Total	2				2 (0)

Jock Morgan

Born: Penicuik 18.8.1899
From: Doncaster Rovers 7.30
To: Barrow 6.31

	League	FAC	LC	MC	Total
1930/31	1				1 (0)
Total	1				1 (0)

Monty Morgan

Born: Mountain Ash 1.5.1910
From: Plymouth Argyle 7.38

	League	FAC	LC	MC	Total
1938/39	2		3 (2)	5	(2)
Total	2		3 (2)	5	(2)

Nicky Morgan

Born: East Ham 30.10.1959
From: Stoke City 3.90
To: Exeter City 2.94

	League	FAC	LC	MC	Total
1989/90	7 (4)				7 (4)
1990/91	43+1 (13)		4 (4)		47+1 (17)
1991/92	15+4 (3)	2	2 (2)		19+4 (5)
1992/93	10 (3)				10 (3)
1993/94				1	1 (0)
Total	75+5 (23)	2	6 (6)	1	84+5 (29)

Sid Morgan

Born: Bristol 1.8.1926
From: AG Farmers 12.47
To: Millwall 3.58

	League	FAC	LC	MC	Total
1948/49	9				9 (0)
1949/50	18				18 (0)
1950/51	26	2			28 (0)
1952/53	10				10 (0)
1953/54	8				8 (0)
Total	71	2			73 (0)

Trevor Morgan

Born: Forest Gate 30.9.1956
From: AFC Bournemouth 3.84 £10,000
To: Exeter City 11.84 P/Ex
From: Bristol Rovers 1.86
To: Bolton Wanderers 6.87

	League	FAC	LC	MC	Total
1983/84	15 (5)				15 (5)
1984/85	17 (3)	1	4 (3)		22 (6)
1986/87	19 (7)				19 (7)
Total	51 (15)	1	4 (3)		22 (6)

Jack Morris

Born: Liscard 11.2.1978
From: Notts County 7.03
To: New Brompton 7.04

	League	FAC	LC	MC	Total
1903/04	29 (11)	3 (1)			32 (12)
Total	29 (11)	3 (1)			32 (12)

James Morton

Born: Leith
From: Barnsley 4.14

	League	FAC	LC	MC	Total
1913/14	4 (1)				4 (1)
1914/15	8 (6)				8 (6)
Total	12 (7)				12 (7)

Horace Moseley

Born: Lewisham 19.7.1912
From: Millwall 8.34
To: Dartford 7.35

	League	FAC	LC	MC	Total
1934/35	4		1		5 (0)
Total	4		1		5 (0)

Arthur Moss

Born: Crewe 14.11.1887
From: Aston Villa 7.12
To: Runcorn

	League	FAC	LC	MC	Total
1912/13	18	1			19 (0)
1913/14	33	2			35 (0)
1914/15	34	2			36 (0)
Total	85	5			90 (0)

Con Moulson

Born: Fethard 3.9.1902
From: Grimsby Town 5.31
To: Lincoln City 4.32

	League	FAC	LC	MC	Total
1931/32	11 (1)				11 (1)
Total	11 (1)				11 (1)

David Moyes

Born: Glasgow 25.4.1963
From: Cambridge United 10.85 £10,000
To: Shrewsbury Town 10.87 £25,000

	League	FAC	LC	MC	Total
1985/86	27 (2)			7	34 (2)
1986/87	41 (3)	5	4	8 (4)	58 (7)
1987/88	15 (1)		2		17 (1)
Total	83 (6)	5	6	15 (4)	109 (10)

James Mullen

Born: Larne 10.1.1921
From: Crystal Palace 2.49
To: Barrow 9.50

	League	FAC	LC	MC	Total	
1948/49	16	(2)		7	23	(2)
1949/50	1				1	(0)
Total	**17**	**(2)**		**7**	**24**	**(2)**

Stuart Munro

Born: Falkirk 15.9.1962
From: Blackburn Rovers 2.93
To: Falkirk 11.95

	League	FAC	LC	MC	Total	
1992/93	16			7	23	(0)
1993/94	43+1	6	2	1 (1)	52+1	(1)
1994/95	29+2	3	1		33+2	(0)
1995/96	3		2	0+1	5+1	(0)
Total	**91+3**	**9**	**5**	**8+1 (1)**	**113+4**	**(1)**

Billy Munroe

Born: Dublin 28.11.1933
From: Ards 12.57
To: Scunthorpe United 7.58

	League	FAC	LC	MC	Total	
1957/58	1				1	(0)
Total	**1**				**1**	**(0)**

David Murray

Born: Wynberg, SA 1.1.1902
From: Everton 10.26
To: Bristol Rovers 11.28

	League	FAC	LC	MC	Total	
1926/27	1				1	(0)
1927/28	15				15	(0)
Total	**16**				**16**	**(0)**

Russell Musker

Born: Teignmouth 10.7.1962
From: Apprentice 8.79
To: Gillingham 11.83 £7,500

	League	FAC	LC	MC	Total	
1980/81	4				4	(0)
1981/82	32+1	3	4		39+1	(0)
1982/83	6	(1)	1	3	10	(1)
1983/84	2+1			1	3+1	(0)
Total	**44+2**	**(1)**	**3**	**5**	**4**	**56+2 (1)**

Stuart Naylor

Born: Wetherby 6.12.1962
From: West Bromwich Albion 8.96

	League	FAC	LC	MC	Total	
1996/97	35	4	4	1	44	(0)
Total	**35**	**4**	**4**	**1**	**44**	**(0)**

Dick Neal

Born: Fencehouses 14.1.1906
From: Southampton 5.37
To: Accrington Stanley 6.38

	League	FAC	LC	MC	Total	
1937/38	6	2		1 (1)	9	(1)
Total	**6**	**2**		**1 (1)**	**9**	**(1)**

Reg Neal

Born: Blackpool 1914
From: Yeovil & Petters United 6.36
To: Gillingham 6.37

	League	FAC	LC	MC	Total	
1936/37	9		1		10	(0)
Total	**9**		**1**		**10**	**(0)**

Tom Neate

Born: Chippenham 22.12.00
From: Chippenham Town 7.24
To: Chippenham Town 7.25

	League	FAC	LC	MC	Total	
1924/25	2		1		3	(0)
Total	**2**		**1**		**3**	**(0)**

Bert Neesam

Born: Brompton, Yorkshire 2.6.1892
From: Grange Town A 9.13
To: Bath City 7.28

	League	FAC	LC	MC	Total	
1913/14	1				1	(0)
1914/15	19	(10)	2		21	(10)
1919/20	35	(6)	4	(1)	39	(7)
1920/21	36		1		37	(0)
1921/22	41		2		43	(0)
1922/23	31	(1)	2		33	(1)
1923/24	10				10	(0)
1924/25	30		2		32	(0)
1925/26	26	(1)			26	(1)
1926/27	40		3		43	(0)
1927/28	12				12	(0)
Total	**281**	**(18)**	**16**	**(1)**	**297**	**(19)**

Billy Nesbitt

Born: Portsmouth, Lancs 22.11.1891
From: Burnley 5.23
To: Clapton Orient 7.24

	League	FAC	LC	MC	Total	
1923/24	26	4			30	(0)
Total	**26**	**4**			**30**	**(0)**

Steve Neville

Born: Walthamstow 18.9.1957
From: Exeter City 11.84 P/ex
To: Exeter City 7.88 £10,000

	League	FAC	LC	MC	Total	
1984/85	26+2	(8)		4	30+2	(8)
1985/86	46	(19)	3 (3)	2	7 (3)	58 (25)
1986/87	19+1	(8)	4 (2)	2 (1)	2	27+1(11)
1987/88	37+3	(5)	0+1	0+2	2	39+6 (5)
Total	**128+6**	**(40)**	**7+1(5)**	**4+2 (1)**	**15**	**(3) 154+9(49)**

George Newlands

Born: Campbeltown 14.1.1906
From: Shotts B'field 7.27
To: Distillery 11.32

	League	FAC	LC	MC	Total	
1927/28	1				1	(0)
1928/29	2				2	(0)
1929/30	16				16	(0)
1930/31	29				29	(0)
1931/32	42	3			45	(0)
Total	**90**	**3**			**93**	**(0)**

Rob Newman

Born: Bradford-on-Avon 13.12.1963
From: Apprentice 10.81
To: Norwich City 7.91 £600,000

	League	FAC	LC	MC	Total	
1981/82	15+6	(3)				15+6 (3)
1982/83	42+1	(3)	1	4 (1)	3	50+1 (4)
1983/84	29+1	(1)	2	2	1	34+1 (1)
1984/85	34	(3)		4	3	41 (3)
1985/86	37+2	(3)	3	1	6	47+2 (3)
1986/87	43+2	(6)	5	2+1	8 (2)	58+3 (8)
1987/88	44	(11)	2	2	3	51 (11)
1988/89	46	(6)	6 (1)	9 (1)	3	64 (8)
1989/90	46	(8)	7 (1)	2	3	58 (9)
1990/91	46	(8)	1	4	1 (1)	52 (9)
Total	**382+12(52)**	**27**	**(2) 30+1 (2)31**		**(3) 470+13(59)**	

Billy Nichol

Born: Newcastle .1.1887
From: Celtic 7.12

	League	FAC	LC	MC	Total	
1912/13	3				3	(0)
Total	**3**				**3**	**(0)**

Alan Nicholls

Born: Plymouth 10.2.1963
From: Apprentice 2.80
To: Retired 5.84

	League	FAC	LC	MC	Total	
1980/81	4	(1)				4	(1)
1981/82	27	(1)	1			28	(1)
1982/83	39	(3)	1	2	2	44	(3)
Total	**70**	**(5)**	**2**	**2**	**2**	**76**	**(5)**

Ron Nicholls

Born: Sharpness 4.12.1933
From: Cardiff City 7.61
To: Cheltenham Town 7.65

	League	FAC	LC	MC	Total	
1961/62	6		1		7	(0)
1962/63	29	3	1		33	(0)
1963/64	4				4	(0)
Total	**39**	**3**	**2**		**44**	**(0)**

Harry Nicholson

Born: Wetherall 25.1.1932
From: Leyton Orient 7.60
To: Poole Town 7.61

	League	FAC	LC	MC	Total	
1960/61	1				1	(0)
Total	**1**				**1**	**(0)**

John Nicholson

Born: Ayr 8.3.1888
From: Glasgow Ashfield 7.11
To: Glasgow Rangers 7.21

	League	FAC	LC	MC	Total	
1911/12	37	1			38	(0)
1912/13	33	1			34	(0)
1913/14	31	1			32	(0)
1914/15	33	(1)	2		35	(1)
1919/20	29	(2)	4		33	(2)
1920/21	34	(1)	1		35	(1)
Total	**197**	**(4)**	**10**		**207**	**(4)**

John Nixon

Born: Bathgate 1885
From: Hibernian 7.07

	League	FAC	LC	MC	Total	
1907/08	7				7	(0)
Total	**7**				**7**	**(0)**

David Noake

Born: Dorchester 9.6.1940
From: Luton Town 6.61
To: Trowbridge Town 7.62

	League	FAC	LC	MC	Total	
1961/62	11 (3)	2			13	(3)
Total	**11 (3)**	**2**			**13**	**(3)**

Billy Noble

Born: Edinburgh 1.1.1898
From: Cumnock Juniors 7.20

	League	FAC	LC	MC	Total	
1920/21	6				6	(0)
Total	**6**				**6**	**(0)**

Ray Norris

Born: Bristol 15.7.1922
From: Bedminster Down 5.47
To: Gloucester City 7.48

	League	FAC	LC	MC	Total	
1947/48	3				3	(0)
Total	**3**				**3**	**(0)**

Kevin Nugent

Born: Edmonton 10.4.1969
From: Plymouth Argyle 9.95 £75,000
To: Cardiff City 7.97

	League	FAC	LC	MC	Total	
1995/96	29+5 (8)	2			31+5	(8)
1996/97	19+17 (6)	1+2(1)	1+2	0+1	21+22	(7)
Total	**48+22(14)**	**3+2(1)**	**1+2**	**0+1**	**52+27**	**(15)**

Paddy O'Brien

Born: Glasgow 1.1.1875
From: Woolwich Arsenal 7.97
To: Swindon Town 7.02

	League	FAC	LC	MC	Total	
1901/02	8 (7)				8	(7)
Total	**8 (7)**				**8**	**(7)**

Dennis Oram

Born: Bristol 14.1.1920
From: St Pancras 8.46

	League	FAC	LC	MC	Total	
1946/47	3				3	(0)
Total	**3**				**3**	**(0)**

Albert Osborne

Born: Bristol 1886
From: Bristol Rovers 8.10

	League	FAC	LC	MC	Total	
1910/11	1				1	(0)
1911/12	1				1	(0)
Total	**2**				**2**	**(0)**

Harry Osman

Born: Bentworth 29.1.1911
From: Millwall 10.47
To: Dartford 8.48

	League	FAC	LC	MC	Total	
1947/48	18 (1)	3			21	(1)
Total	**18 (1)**	**3**			**21**	**(1)**

Russell Osman

Born: Repton 14.2.1959
From: Southampton 10.91 £60,000
To: Sudbury Town 1.95

	League	FAC	LC	MC	Total	
1991/92	30+1 (2)	4			34+1	(2)
1992/93	33+1	1	1	2	37+1	(0)
1993/94	4+1 (1)		0+2	1	5+3	(1)
Total	**67+3 (3)**	**5**	**1+2**	**3**	**78+5**	**(3)**

Gordon Owen

Born: Barnsley 14.6.1959
From: Barnsley 8.86 £30,000
To: Mansfield Town 1.88 £35,000

	League	FAC	LC	MC	Total	
1986/87	34+1 (5)	2 (2)	4	6	46+1	(7)
1987/88	17+1 (6)	1	2 (2)	1	21+1	(8)
Total	**51+2 (11)**	**3 (2)**	**6 (2)**	**7**	**67+2**	**(15)**

Ernie 'Ginger' Owers

Born: Bromley 21.10.1889
From: Darlington 3.12
To: Clyde 3.13

	League	FAC	LC	MC	Total	
1911/12	8 (3)				8	(3)
1912/13	23 (13)	1			24	(13)
Total	**31 (16)**	**1**			**32**	**(16)**

Gary Owers

Born: Newcastle 3.10.1968
From: Sunderland 12.94 P/ex

	League	FAC	LC	MC	Total	
1994/95	21 (2)	3			24	(2)
1995/96	34+3 (2)	1	2	3	40+3	(2)
1996/97	46 (4)	4	4 (1)	2 (1)	56	(6)
Total	**101+3 (8)**	**8**	**6 (1)**	**5 (1)**	**120+3**	**(10)**

W Padfield

Born: Paulton
From:
To:

	League	FAC	LC	MC	Total	
1910/11	4				4	(0)
Total	**4**				**4**	**(0)**

Geoff Palmer

Born: Barnsley 12.11.1940
From: Doncaster Rovers 8.58
To: Gloucester City 7.62

	League	FAC	LC	MC	Total	
1961/62	1				1	(0)
Total	**1**				**1**	**(0)**

John Palmer

Born: Bristol 1.7.1958
From: Weston-Super-Mare 3.83
To: Weston-Super-Mare 7.84

	League	FAC	LC	MC	Total	
1982/83	2+6				2+6	(0)
Total	**2+6**				**2+6**	**(0)**

Simon Panes

Born: Almondsbury 22.2.1960
From: Melksham Town 8.82
To: Mangotsfield United 7.83

	League	FAC	LC	MC	Total	
1982/83	2+2				2+2	(0)
Total	**2+2**				**2+2**	**(0)**

Albert Parker

Born: Eccles
From: Manchester United 5.32
To: Carlisle United 7.34

	League	FAC	LC	MC	Total	
1932/33	41 (1)	3			44	(1)
1933/34	13			5	18	(0)
Total	**54 (1)**	**3**		**5**	**62**	**(1)**

Gilbert Parker

Born: Eccles
From: 6.31
To:

	League	FAC	LC	MC	Total	
1931/32	3				3	(0)
Total	**3**				**3**	**(0)**

Gordon Parr

Born: Bristol
From: Juniors 2.57
To: Waterford 7.72

	League	FAC	LC	MC	Total	
1957/58	2				2	(0)
1962/63	16	2	1		19	(0)
1963/64	38 (2)	5			43	(2)
1964/65	21 (1)		1		22	(1)
1965/66	17+1 (1)				17+1	(1)
1966/67	38	4	1		43	(0)
1967/68	36	5	1		42	(0)
1968/69	42	1	3		46	(0)
1969/70	38	1	5		44	(0)
1970/71	31+2	1	8		40+2	(0)
1971/72	2+3				2+3	(0)
Total	**281+6 (4)**	**19**	**20**		**320+6**	**(4)**

George Parris

Born: Ilford 11.9.1964
From: Birmingham City 12.94 Loan

	League	FAC	LC	MC	Total	
1994/95	6				6	(0)
Total	**6**				**6**	**(0)**

Scott Partridge

Born: Grimsby 13.10.1974
From: Bradford City 2.94
To: Cardiff City 2.97

	League	FAC	LC	MC	Total
1993/94	7+2 (4)				7+2 (4)
1994/95	14+19 (2)	0+3	1		15+22(2)
1995/96	3+6 (1)	0+1	2+1		5+8 (1)
1996/97	0+6		0+1 (1)		0+7 (1)
Total	**24+33 (7)**	**0+4**	**3+2 (1)**		**27+39(8)**

Scott Paterson

Born: Aberdeen 13.5.1972
From: Liverpool

	League	FAC	LC	MC	Total
1994/95	2+1		1		3+1 (0)
1995/96	16+2 (1)	1	1	1	19+2 (1)
1996/97	15+4	1		1	17+4 (0)
Total	**33+7 (1)**	**2**	**2**	**2**	**39+7 (1)**

Johnny Paul

Born: Glasgow 29.1.1904
From: Port Glasgow 8.22
To: Taunton Town 11.30

	League	FAC	LC	MC	Total
1922/23	6 (1)	1 (1)			7 (2)
1923/24	31 (1)				31 (1)
1924/25	36 (11)	1			37 (11)
1925/26	29 (8)	1			30 (8)
1926/27	18 (12)	3 (1)			21 (13)
1927/28	33 (3)	1			34 (3)
1928/29	40 (8)	1			41 (8)
1929/30	13 (5)	1			14 (5)
Total	**206 (49)**	**9 (2)**			**215 (51)**

Ernie Peacock

Born: Bristol 11.2.1924
From: Notts County 10.46
To: Weymouth 6.59

	League	FAC	LC	MC	Total
1946/47	16 (1)				16 (1)
1947/48	6				6 (0)
1948/49	8				8 (0)
1949/50	16 (1)				16 (1)
1950/51	44 (1)	5 (1)			49 (2)
1951/52	34				34 (0)
1952/53	46 (1)				46 (1)
1953/54	32 (1)	1			33 (1)
1954/55	44	1			45 (0)
1955/56	40 (1)	1			41 (1)
1956/57	19 (1)	3			22 (1)
1957/58	30	2			32 (0)
1958/59	8				8 (0)
Total	**343 (7)**	**13 (1)**			**356 (9)**

Jim Pearce

Born: Chirk
From: Army 8.34
To: Rochdale 5.39

	League	FAC	LC	MC	Total
1934/35	29 (1)	9			38 (1)
1935/36	40	1		3	44 (0)
1936/37	24	1		1	26 (0)
1937/38	37 (1)	3		2	42 (1)
1938/39	18			2	20 (0)
Total	**148 (2)**	**14**		**8**	**170 (2)**

Horace Pearson

Born: Tamworth 6.4.1907
From: Newport County 9.38

	League	FAC	LC	MC	Total
1938/39	16		1		17 (0)
Total	**16**		**1**		**17 (0)**

John Pender

Born: Luton 19.11.1963
From: Charlton Athletic 10.87 £55,000
To: Burnley 9.90 £70,000

	League	FAC	LC	MC	Total
1987/88	28 (2)	2		2	32 (2)
1988/89	45 (1)	6	9	3	63 (1)
1989/90	10	2		2	14 (0)
Total	**83 (3)**	**10**	**9**	**7**	**109 (3)**

Tom Penman

Born: 1887
From: Crook Town 7.08

	League	FAC	LC	MC	Total
1908/09	1				1 (0)
Total	**1**				**1 (0)**

Tom Penn

Born: Heath Common 11.10.1901
From: Altofts Colliery 7.25
To: Darlington 7.27

	League	FAC	LC	MC	Total
1925/26	6				6 (0)
Total	**6**				**6 (0)**

Glenn Pennyfather

Born: Billericay 11.2.1963
From: Ipswich Town 2.93 £80,000
To: Canvey Island 4.94

	League	FAC	LC	MC	Total
1992/93	14 (1)				14 (1)
1993/94	7+5	2+1		1	10+6 (0)
Total	**21+5 (1)**	**2+1**		**1**	**24+6 (1)**

Hubert Perry

Born: Manchester 1.1.1911
From: Bridgwater Town 5.29
To: Bath City 2.31

	League	FAC	LC	MC	Total
1929/30	1				1 (0)
Total	**1**				**1 (0)**

Frank Peters

Born: Birmingham 26.2.1910
From: Swindon Town 5.36

	League	FAC	LC	MC	Total
1936/37	40 (9)	1		2	43 (9)
1937/38	35 (5)	3		3	41 (5)
1938/39	38 (8)	1			39 (8)
Total	**113 (22)**	**5**		**5**	**123 (22)**

Roger 'Lou' Peters

Born: Cheltenham 5.3.1944
From: Apprentice 3.61
To: Bournemouth 6.68 £5,000

	League	FAC	LC	MC	Total
1960/61	1				1 (0)
1961/62	13 (1)		1		14 (1)
1962/63	19 (3)	2		1	22 (3)
1964/65	40 (6)	3		1	44 (6)
1965/66	35 (6)	1		1	37 (6)
1966/67	28 (9)	4 (2)	1		33 (11)
1967/68	22	3		1	26 (0)
Total	**158 (25)**	**13 (2)**	**6**		**177 (27)**

Forbes Phillipson-Masters

Born: Bournemouth 14.11.1955
From: Plymouth Argyle 11.82
To: Yeovil Town 8.85

	League	FAC	LC	MC	Total
1982/83	25 (2)				25 (2)
1984/85	25 (1)	2	4	1	32 (1)
Total	**50 (3)**	**2**	**4**	**1**	**57 (3)**

John Picken

Born: Hurlford 1.1.1880
From: Burnley 10.13

	League	FAC	LC	MC	Total
1913/14	27 (7)	2 (1)			29 (8)
1914/15	24 (6)	1			25 (6)
Total	**51 (13)**	**3 (1)**			**54 (14)**

Tommy Pickett

Born: Merthyr Tydfil 5.2.1909
From: QPR 6.32
To: Yeovil & Petters 7.33

	League	FAC	LC	MC	Total
1932/33	6	3			9 (0)
Total	**6**	**3**			**9 (0)**

Dwayne Plummer

Born: Bristol 12.5.1978
From: Trainee 9.95

	League	FAC	LC	MC	Total
1995/96	1+10		2+1	0+1	3+12 (0)
1996/97	0+2				0+2 (0)
Total	**1+12**		**2+1**	**0+1**	**3+14(0)**

Bill Pocock

Born: Bristol 24.2.1884
From: St Francis 6.19
To: St Johnstone 7.26

	League	FAC	LC	MC	Total
1919/20	39 (10)	5			44 (10)
1920/21	40 (14)	1			41 (14)
1921/22	40 (3)	2			42 (3)
1922/23	40 (7)	2			42 (7)
1923/24	40 (5)	4 (1)			44 (6)
1924/25	18 (2)	2			20 (2)
1925/26	21 (5)	1			22 (5)
Total	**238 (46)**	**17 (1)**			**255 (47)**

Alex Pool

Born: Annan 1.1.1901
From: Blackburn Rovers 5.25
To: Exeter City 7.26

	League	FAC	LC	MC	Total	
1925/26	12				12	(0)
Total	12				12	(0)

Alonzo Poulton

Born: Wolverhampton 28.3.1890
From:
To:

	League		FAC	LC	MC	Total	
1921/22	20	(5)				20	(5)
1922/23	8	(4)				8	(4)
Total	28	(9)				28	(9)

Derek Presley

Born: Warminster 8.3.1930
From: Warminster Town 3.50
To: Bristol Rovers 5.52

	League	FAC	LC	MC	Total	
1950/51	4				4	(0)
1951/52	5				5	(0)
Total	9				9	(0)

Alf Price

Born:
From:
To:

	League	FAC	LC	MC	Total	
1904/05	3				3	(0)
Total	3				3	(0)

John Price

Born: New Washington
From:
To:

	League	FAC	LC	MC	Total	
1923/24	3				3	(0)
Total	3				3	(0)

Howard Pritchard

Born: Cardiff 18.10.1958
From: Apprentice 8.76
To: Swindon Town 8.81
From: Swindon Town 8.83
To: Gillingham 8.86

	League		FAC		LC		MC		Total	
1978/79	1				1				2	(0)
1979/80	15+1		2	(2)			3	(1)	20+1	(3)
1980/81	15+6	(2)	3+1		1		1+1		20+8	(2)
1983/84	46	(10)	5	(3)	2		1		54	(13)
1984/85	39	(6)	2		4		3		48	(6)
1985/86	32+2	(6)	3		1		5+2	(1)	41+4	(7)
Total	148+9	(24)	15+1	(5)	9		13+3	(2)	185+13	(31)

Mark Prudhoe

Born: Washington 8.11.1963
From: Walsall 11.87 Loan

	League	FAC	LC	MC	Total	
1987/88	3		2		5	(0)
Total	3		2		5	(0)

John Pugsley

Born: Grangetown 1.4.1900
From: Grimsby Town 5.27
To: Charlton Town 5.28

	League	FAC	LC	MC	Total	
1927/28	16	1			17	(0)
Total	16	1			17	(0)

Bob Pullan

Born: Darlington 19.2.1898
From: Dawdon 7.20
To: Exeter City 7.24

	League		FAC	LC	MC	Total	
1921/22	1					1	(0)
1922/23	10	(1)				10	(1)
1923/24	7		3			10	(0)
Total	18	(1)	3			21	(1)

David Pyle

Born: Trowbridge 12.12.1936
From: Bristol Rovers 7.62
To: Trowbridge Town 7.63

	League	FAC	LC	MC	Total	
1962/63	8				8	(0)
Total	8				8	(0)

Johnny Quigley

Born: Glasgow 28.6.1935
From: Huddersfield Town 10.66 P/ex
To: Mansfield Town 7.68 £3,000

	League		FAC	LC	MC	Total	
1966/67	25	(5)	4			29	(5)
1967/68	41	(2)	5			46	(2)
Total	66	(7)	9			75	(7)

Mike Quinlan

Born: Barnsley 4.12.1941
From: Doncaster Rovers 3.59
To: Welton Rovers 7.61

	League	FAC	LC	MC	Total	
1960/61	2				2	(0)
Total	2				2	(0)

Tom Radford

Born: Bristol
From: Salisbury C. 7.08
To: Treharris 12.11

	League	FAC	LC	MC	Total	
1908/09	1				1	(0)
Total	1				1	(0)

Ian Rae

Born: Grangemouth 19.1.1933
From: Falkirk 10.57

	League	FAC	LC	MC	Total	
1957/58	12	1			13	(0)
Total	12	1			13	(0)

Jock Rae

Born: Blackmill, Argyllshire 1.1.1912
From: Partick Thistle 7.37
To: B.A.C. 7.39

	League	FAC	LC	MC	Total	
1937/38	2				2	(0)
Total	2				2	(0)

Jimmy Randall

Born: Guide Post 12.12.1904
From: Derby County 5.35
To: Ashington 7.36

	League	FAC	LC	MC	Total	
1935/36	19				19	(0)
Total	19				19	(0)

Arthur Rankin

Born: Glasgow 30.4.1904
From: Dykehead 8.26
To: Charlton Athletic 7.29

	League		FAC		LC	MC	Total	
1926/27	41	(9)	3				44	(9)
1927/28	28	(3)	1				29	(3)
1928/29	1						1	(0)
Total	70	(1)	4				74	(12)

Dickie Reader

Born: Derby 30.6.1894
From: Derby County 6.14
To: Luton Town 6.22

	League		FAC		LC	MC	Total	
1914/15	1						1	(0)
1919/20	28	(3)	5				33	(3)
1920/21	13	(1)					13	(1)
1921/22	9						9	(0)
Total	51	(4)	5				56	(4)

Gordon Reed

Born: Spennymoor 1.5.1913
From: Everton 4.32
To: Newport County 2.34

	League		FAC		LC		MC	Total	
1931/32	2	(1)						3	(1)
1932/33	3							3	(0)
1933/34	7	(3)	2	(2)				9	(5)
Total	12	(4)	2	(2)				15	(6)

John Rees

Born: Ebbw Vale 1.10.1909
From: Ebbw Vale 7.30
To: Southampton 7.31

	League	FAC	LC	MC	Total	
1930/31	1				1	(0)
Total	1				1	(0)

Duggie Regan

Born: Stoke-under-Ham 3.6.1922
From: Exeter City 12.52
To: Weymouth 7.56

	League		FAC	LC	MC	Total	
1952/53	21	(7)				21	(7)
1953/54	12	(4)	3			15	(4)
1954/55	3					3	(0)
1955/56	3					3	(0)
Total	39	(11)	3			42	(11)

Jimmy Regan

Born: Hemsworth 7.12.1927
From: Rotherham United 6.53
To: Coventry City 3.56

	League		FAC	LC	MC	Total	
1953/54	25	(1)	2			27	(1)
1954/55	22		1			23	(0)
1955/56	4					4	(0)
Total	51	(1)	3			54	(1)

Nicky Reid

Born: Urmston 30.10.1960
From: Blackburn Rovers 9.92 Loan

	League	FAC	LC	MC	Total
1992/93	3+1		1		4+1 (0)
Total	3+1		1		4+1 (0)

David Rennie

Born: Edinburgh 29.8.1964
From: Leeds United 7.89
To: Birmingham City 2.92

	League	FAC	LC	MC	Total
1989/90	45 (4)	7	2	3	57 (4)
1990/91	29+3 (2)	1	4	1	35+3 (2)
1991/92	27 (2)	1	2	1	31 (2)
Total	101+3 (8)	9	8	5	123+3 (8)

Glyn Riley

Born: Barnsley 24.7.1958
From: Barnsley 8.82
To: Aldershot 10.87

	League	FAC	LC	MC	Total
1982/83	43+1 (16)	1	4	3	51+1(16)
1983/84	42 (16)	4 (1)	2 (1)		48 (18)
1984/85	44 (18)	2 (1)	4 (2)	4 (1)	54 (22)
1985/86	33+8 (10)	3 (1)	1	6+1 (5)	43+9(16)
1986/87	22+6 (1)	3 (1)	3 (1)	7 (2)	35+6 (5)
Total	184+15(61)	13 (4)	14 (4)	20+1 (8)	231+16(77)

Joe Riley

Born: Sheffield 1.1.1908
From: Bristol Rovers 5.33
To: Bournemouth 5.35

	League	FAC	LC	MC	Total
1933/34	34 (13)	4 (2)		7 (3)	45 (18)
1934/35	25 (8)	7			32 (8)
Total	59 (21)	11 (2)		7 (3)	77 (26)

Willis Rippon

Born: Beighton 15.5.1886
From: Kilnhurst Town 7.07
To: Woolwich Arsenal 7.10

	League	FAC	LC	MC	Total
1907/08	7 (2)				7 (2)
1908/09	23 (7)	8 (5)			31 (12)
1909/10	6 (4)	1 (1)			7 (5)
Total	36 (13)	9 (6)			45 (19)

Steve Ritchie

Born: Glasgow 17.2.1954
From: Apprentice 9.71
To: Morton 7.73

	League	FAC	LC	MC	Total
1972/73	1				1 (0)
Total	1				1 (0)

Tom Ritchie

Born: Edinburgh 2.01.1952
From: Bridgend Thistle 7.69
To: Sunderland 1.81
From: Sunderland 6.82
To: Yeovil Town 12.84

	League	FAC	LC	MC	Total
1972/73	24+7 (4)	0+1	1		25+8 (4)
1973/74	39 (6)	6	4	2 (1)	51 (7)
1974/75	32+1 (4)	1	3+1		36+2 (4)
1975/76	42 (18)	1	2	3 (1)	48 (19)
1976/77	30+1 (7)	1	1	3 (2)	35+1 (9)
1977/78	41 (11)	2 (1)	2	9 (4)	54 (16)
1978/79	39+1 (9)	2 (1)	1 (1)	5 (3)	47+1(14)
1979/80	35+3 (13)	1	5 (1)	6 (5)	47+3(19)
1980/81	27 (5)	3 (3)	2 (1)	3 (1)	35 (10)
1982/83	37 (12)	1	3 (1)	3 (1)	44 (14)
1983/84	45 (12)	5 (2)	2	1 (1)	53 (15)
1984/85	10+1 (1)	1+1	1		12+2 (1)
Total	401+14(102)	24+2(7)	27+1 (4)	35 (19)	487+17(132)

Dennis Roberts

Born: Bretton 5.2.1918
From: Notts County 5.38
To: Retired 5.54

	League	FAC	LC	MC	Total
1938/39	24	1		2	27 (0)
1946/47	42	2			44 (0)
1947/48	38	3			41 (0)
1948/49	41	3			44 (0)
1949/50	39	1			40 (0)
1950/51	41	5			46 (0)
1951/52	46 (1)	2			48 (1)
1952/53	17 (1)				17 (1)
1953/54	15				15 (0)
Total	303 (2)	17		2	322 (2)

Bill Roberts

Born: Bargoed 12.7.1908
From: Tottenham Hotspur 9.33
To: Newport County 7.38

	League	FAC	LC	MC	Total
1933/34	35 (1)	4		8	47 (1)
1934/35	29	9			38 (0)
1935/36	35	1		3	39 (0)
1936/47	36 (6)	1		2	39 (6)
Total	135 (7)	15		13	173 (7)

Jim Robertson

Born: Perth 1873
From: New Brampton 7.01
To: Accrington Stanley 7.02

	League	FAC	LC	MC	Total
1901/02	12	2			12 (2)
Total	12	2			12 (2)

Liam Robinson

Born: Bradford 29.12.1965
From: Bury 8.93
To: Burnley 7.94

	League	FAC	LC	MC	Total
1993/94	31+10 (4)	6	2 (1)	1	40+10(5)
Total	31+10 (4)	6	2 (1)	1	40+10(5)

Cuthbert Robson

Born: High Wheatley 19.10.1900
From: Connahs Quay 5.30
To: Chester 10.31

	League	FAC	LC	MC	Total
1930/31	23 (2)	1			24 (2)
1931/32	2				2 (0)
Total	25 (2)	1			26 (2)

Arnold Rodgers

Born: Wickersley 5.12.1923
From: Huddersfield Town 10.49
To: Shrewsbury Town 6.56

	League	FAC	LC	MC	Total
1949/50	28 (18)	1			29 (18)
1950/51	39 (20)	5 (3)			44 (23)
1951/52	36 (12)	1 (1)			37 (13)
1952/53	33 (26)	1			34 (26)
1953/54	23 (14)				23 (14)
1954/55	26 (13)	1 (1)			27 (14)
1955/56	10 (3)				10 (3)
Total	195 (106)	9 (5)			204 (111)

David Rodgers

Born: Bristol 28.2.1952
From: Juniors 7.69
To: Torquay United 2.82

	League	FAC	LC	MC	Total
1970/71	7	1	2 (1)		10 (1)
1971/72	8 (1)				8 (1)
1972/73	34 (1)	3	1		38 (1)
1973/74	26+2 (1)	3+1	2	2	33+3 (1)
1974/75	5				5 (0)
1976/77	1				1 (0)
1977/78	15 (1)		1		16 (1)
1978/79	36 (5)	2 (1)	1	5	44 (6)
1979/80	26 (6)	2	1	1	30 (6)
1980/81	14	4	3		21 (0)
1981/82	18	3	5 (1)		26 (1)
Total	190+2 (15)	18+1(1)	16 (2)	8	232 (18)

Jimmy Rogers

Born: Wednesbury 31.12.1929
From: Wolves 5.50
To: Coventry City 12.56
From: Coventry City 12.58
To: Cinderford Town 7.62

	League	FAC	LC	MC	Total
1950/51	8 (2)	2 (2)			10 (4)
1951/52	22 (10)				22 (10)
1952/53	18 (4)				18 (4)
1953/54	13 (3)	3			16 (3)
1954/55	44 (25)	1			45 (25)
1955/56	34 (25)	1			35 (25)
1956/57	16 (5)				16 (5)
1958/59	9				9 (0)
1959/60	31 (16)	1			32 (16)
1960/61	37 (8)	3 (3)	1		41 (11)
1961/62	38 (4)	5 (1)		1	44 (5)
Total	270 (102)	16 (6)	1	1	288 (108)

Lee Rogers

Born: Bristol 8.4.1967
From: Apprentice 12.84
To: Exeter City 6.88

	League	FAC	LC	MC	Total	
1984/85	6		2		8	(0)
1985/86	21	3	1		25	(0)
1986/87	3			1	4	(0)
Total	30	3	3	1	37	(0)

Dickie Rooks

Born: Sunderland 29.4.1940
From: Middlesbrough 6.69
To: Willington 7.72 P/C

	League	FAC	LC	MC	Total	
1969/70	38	(1)		5	(1)	43	(2)
1970/71	34	(2)	1	6		41	(2)
1971/72	24	(1)	1	1		26	(1)
Total	96	(4)	2	12	(1)	110	(5)

Leslie Rose

Born: Bristol 25.9.1890
From: Clifton St. Vincents
To: St. Pancras

	League	FAC	LC	MC	Total	
1913/14	4				4	(0)
Total	4				4	(0)

Leroy Rosenior

Born: Clapton 24.3.1964
From: West Ham 3.92
To: Fleet Town 7.95

	League	FAC	LC	MC	Total	
1991/92	5+3	(5)				5+3	(5)
1992/93	29+9	(7)	0+1	3	(1) 4	(1)	36+10(9)
1993/94	1+4		1+1		1	(1)	3+5 (0)
Total	35+16	(7)	1+2	3	(1) 5	(2)	44+18(14)

Shaun Rouse

Born: Great Yarmouth 28.2.1972
From: Glasgow Rangers 6.92
To: Weston-super-Mare 7.93

	League	FAC	LC	MC	Total	
1992/93				0+2	0+2	(0)
Total				0+2	0+2	(0)

Alfie Rowles

Born: Bristol 6.5.1916
From: Weston-Super-Mare 7.37
To: Retired - Injury 5.39

	League	FAC	LC	MC	Total	
1937/38	15	(18)				15	(18)
1938/39	9	(2)		1		10	(2)
Total	24	(20)		1		25	(20)

Joe Royle

Born: Liverpool 8.4.1949
From: Manchester City 11.37 £90,000
To: Norwich City 8.80 £60,000

	League	FAC	LC	MC	Total	
1977/78	26	(6)	2			28	(6)
1978/79	40	(7)	2	1	4	(1)	47	(8)
1979/80	34+1	(3)		5+1 (2)	2+2	41+4	(5)
Total	100+1	(16)	4	6+1 (2)	6+2(1)	116+4(19)

Tommy Rudkin

Born: Peterborough 17.6.1919
From: Southampton 5.49
To: Hastings United 6.51

	League	FAC	LC	MC	Total	
1949/50	27	(3)				27	(3)
1950/51	7	(1)	3			10	(1)
Total	34	(4)	3			37	(4)

Alec Russell

Born: Bristol 17.4.1925
From: Local 11.47
To: Bridgwater Town 7.49

	League	FAC	LC	MC	Total	
1947/48	2				2	(0)
1948/49	1				1	(0)
Total	3				3	(0)

John 'Buck' Ryan

Born: Alloa 16.10.1930
From: Newcastle United 7.60
To: Poole Town 3.61

	League	FAC	LC	MC	Total	
1960/61	3	1			4	(0)
Total	3	1			4	(0)

Charlie Sargeant

Born: Cornsay 2.2.1909
From: Norwich City 6.31
To: Hull City 5.32

	League	FAC	LC	MC	Total	
1931/32	27	(10)				27	(10)
Total	27	(10)				27	(10)

Ray Savino

Born: Norwich 16.11.1938
From: Norwich City 7.62
To: Kings Lynn 3.68

	League	FAC	LC	MC	Total	
1962/63	15	(1)				15	(1)
1963/64	8				8	(0)
1964/65	34	(1)	4	(1)		38	(2)
1965/66	8				8	(0)
1966/67	7		1		8	(0)
1967/68	3				3	(0)
Total	75	(2)	4	(1) 1		80	(3)

Ken Scattergood

Born: Bradford 6.4.1912
From: Sheffield United 8.33
To: Stoke City 5.34

	League	FAC	LC	MC	Total	
1933/34	39	(1)	4		8	51	(1)
Total	39	(1)	4		8	51	(1)

Martin Scott

Born: Sheffield 7.1.1968
From: Rotherham United 12.90 £200,000
To: Sunderland 12.94 £450,000

	League	FAC	LC	MC	Total	
1990/91	27	(1)				27	(1)
1991/92	46	(3)	4	2	1	53	(3)
1992/93	35	(3)	1	4	(1) 6	(1)	46	(5)
1993/94	45	(5)	6	2	1	54	(5)
1994/95	18	(2)		2		20	(2)
Total	171	(14)	11	10	(1) 8	(1)200	(16)

Tom Scott

Born: Newcastle 6.4.1904
From: Liverpool 10.28
To: Preston North End 6.30

	League	FAC	LC	MC	Total	
1928/29	22	(6)				22	(6)
1929/30	13				13	(0)
Total	22	(6)				22	(6)

Aubrey Scriven

Born: Cleobury Mortimer 7.7.1904
From: Bradford City 5.32
To: Worcester City 7.34

	League	FAC	LC	MC	Total	
1932/33	30	(8)	3		1	(1) 34	(9)
1933/34	24	(4)	2	(1)		7	(3) 33	(8)
Total	54	(12)	5	(1)		8	(4) 67	(17)

David Seal

Born: Penrith, Australia 26.1.1972
From: Aalst 6.94
To: Northampton Town 8.97

	League	FAC	LC	MC	Total	
1994/95	5+4		0+1			5+5	(0)
1995/96	19+11(10)	1	4	(3)	2+1	(1)	26+12(14)
1996/97	0+12		0+1		0+13(0)
Total	24+27(10)	1+1	4+1	(3)	2+1	(1)	31+30(14)

Frank Searle

Born: Hednesford 30.1.1906
From: Willenhall Town 12.26
To: Charlton Athletic 7.28

	League	FAC	LC	MC	Total	
1927/28	1				1	(0)
Total	1				1	(0)

Mark Shail

Born: Sweden 15.10.1963
From: Yeovil Town 3.93 £45,000

	League	FAC	LC	MC	Total	
1992/93	3+1					3+1	(0)
1993/94	35+1	(2)	6	(1)	2	1	44+1	(3)
1994/95	37+1	(2)	3	2		42+1	(2)
1995/96	9+3		2	1+1	1	13+4	(0)
1996/97	10+1				10+1	(0)
Total	94+7	(4)	11	(1)	5+1	2	112+8	(5)

Arthur Sharp

Born: Nottingham 14.11.1910
From: Carlisle United 6.32
To: Aldershot 5.33

	League	FAC	LC	MC	Total	
1932/33	28	(9)			1	29	(9)
Total	28	(9)			1	29	(9)

Gerry Sharpe

Born: Gloucester 17.3.1946
From: Apprentice 3.64
To: Youth Coach 7.71

	League	FAC	LC	MC	Total	
1964/65	13	(6)	3	(2)		16	(8)
1965/66	18+1	(6)		1		19+1	(6)
1966/67	25	(8)		2		27	(8)
1967/68	5+1	(1)	1			6+1	(1)
1968/69	36	(10)	1		1	38	(10)
1969/70	28+2	(10)	1		4	(1)	33+2(11)
1970/71	24	(7)	1		9	(3)	34	(10)
Total	149+4	(48)	7	(2) 17	(4)	173+4(54)

John Shaw

Born: Stirling 4.2.1954
From: Leeds United 5.74
To: Exeter City 7.85

	League	FAC	LC	MC	Total	
1976/77	32	1			33	(0)
1977/78	42	2	2	9	55	(0)
1978/79	40	2	1	3	46	(0)
1979/80	28	2	6	8	44	(0)
1980/81	5	2			7	(0)
1981/82	15				15	(0)
1982/83	46	1	4	3	54	(0)
1983/84	46	5	2		53	(0)
1984/85	41	1	4	4	50	(0)
Total	295	16	19	27	357	(0)

Ben Shearman

Born: Lincoln 1.6.1884
From: Rotherham Town 4.09
To: West Bromwich Albion 6.11

	League		FAC	LC	MC	Total	
1909/10	35	(2)	3			38	(2)
1910/11	25	(2)	1			26	(2)
Total	25	(2)	1			26	(2)

Gary Shelton

Born: Nottingham 21.3.1958
From: Oxford United 8.89 P/Ex
To: Chester City 7.94

	League		FAC	LC	MC		Total	
1989/90	43	(9)	6	1	2	(1)	52	(10)
1990/91	43	(8)	1	4	1		49	(8)
1991/92	18+1	(3)	1	1	1		21+1	(3)
1992/93	42	(4)	1	4	4	(2)	51	(6)
1993/94	3			2	1		6	(0)
Total	149+1	(24)	9	12	9	(3)	179+1	(27)

Tony Shepherd

Born: Glasgow 16.11.1966
From: Celtic 12.88 Loan

	League	FAC	LC	MC	Total	
1988/89	2+1	1	1	1	5+1	(0)
Total	2+1	1	1	1	5+1	(0)

David Sherlaw

Born: Penicuik 17.9.1901
From: Bathgate 5.25
To: Charlton Athletic 7.26

	League		FAC	LC	MC	Total	
1925/26	20	(6)	1			21	(6)
1925/26	20	(6)	1			21	(6)

George Showell

Born: Bilston 9.2.1934
From: Wolves 5.65
To: Wrexham 11.66

	League	FAC	LC	MC	Total	
1965/66	9+3				9+3	(0)
Total	9+3				9+3	(0)

Carl Shutt

Born: Sheffield 10.10.1961
From: Sheffield Wednesday 10.87 £55,000
To: Leeds United 3.89 P/Ex

	League		FAC	LC		MC		Total	
1987/88	18+4	(9)	2			3	(2)	23+4	(11)
1988/89	21+3	(1)		5+1	(4)	5+2 (4)	3	34+6	(9)
Total	21+3	(1)		5+1	(4)	5+2 (4)	3	34+6	(9)

Fitzroy Simpson

Born: Bradford-on-Avon 26.2.1970
From: Manchester City 9.94 Loan

	League	FAC	LC	MC	Total	
1994/95	4				4	(0)
Total	4				4	(0)

Ronnie Sinclair

Born: Stirling 19.11.1964
From: Leeds United 9.89
To: Stoke City 11.91

	League	FAC	LC	MC	Total	
1989/90	27	5		2	34	(0)
1990/91	17		3	1	21	(0)
Total	44	5	3	3	55	(0)

Alan Skirton

Born: Bath 23.1.1939
From: Blackpool 11.68 £15,000
To: Torquay United 7.71

	League		FAC		LC		MC		Total	
1968/69	21	(3)	1	(1)					22	(4)
1969/70	34+1	(7)	1	(1)	5				40+1	(8)
1970/71	20+2	(4)			8	(2)			28+2	(6)
Total	75+3	(14)	2	(2)	13	(2)			90+3	(18)

Allan Sliman

Born: Busby 27.2.1906
From: Arthurlie 9.28
To: Chesterfield 3.32

	League		FAC	LC	MC	Total	
1928/29	26					26	(0)
1929/30	40	(1)	1			41	(1)
1930/31	40		1			41	(0)
1931/32	30		3			33	(0)
Total	136	(1)	5			141	(1)

Andy Smailes

Born: Radcliffe, Northumb. 25.5.1896
From: Wednesday 10.23
To: Rotherham United 8.29

	League		FAC		LC	MC	Total	
1923/24	30	(7)	4	(1)			34	(8)
1924/25	42	(3)	2				44	(3)
1925/26	24	(2)	1				25	(2)
1926/27	32	(2)					32	(2)
1927/28	20						20	(0)
1928/29	14						14	(0)
Total	162	(14)	7	(1)			169	(15)

David Smith

Born: Sidcup 25.6.1961
From: Gillingham 8.89
To: Plymouth Argyle 12.91 £200,000

	League		FAC	LC		MC	Total	
1989/90	45	(4)	7	2	(1)	2+1	56+1	(5)
1990/91	32+2	(5)	1	4	(1)	0+1	37+3	(6)
1991/92	17+1	(1)		2	(2)		19+1	(3)
Total	94+3	(10)	8	8	(4)	2+2	112+4	(14)

Dave Smith

Born: Dundee 22.9.1933
From: Brighton 6.62
To: Burnley 6.63

	League	FAC	LC	MC	Total	
1962/63	3				3	(0)
Total	3				3	(0)

David Smith

Born: Bristol 5.10.1934
From: Juniors 4.53
To: Millwall 9.59

	League		FAC	LC	MC	Total	
1955/56	3					3	(0)
1956/57	15	(1)				15	(1)
1957/58	1		2			3	(0)
1958/59	2					2	(0)
Total	21	(1)	2			23	(1)

Gary Smith

Born: Trowbridge 12.11.1962
From: Apprentice 11.79
To: Bath City 7.81

	League	FAC	LC	MC	Total	
1980/81	7+7				7+7	(0)
Total	7+7				7+7	(0)

George Smith

Born: Connahs Quay
From: Gainsborough Trinity 7.05
To: Crystal Palace 7.07

	League		FAC	LC	MC	Total	
1906/07	11	(2)				11	(2)
Total	11	(2)				11	(2)

Harry Smith

Born: Wolverhampton 10.10.1932
From: Torquay United 7.61
To: Dorchester Town 7.62

	League	FAC	LC	MC	Total	
1961/62	1				1	(0)
Total	1				1	(0)

Jack Smith

Born: Bristol
From: Victoria Albion 7.21
To: Plymouth Argyle 2.24

	League		FAC	LC	MC	Total	
1921/22	10	(3)				10	(3)
1922/23	11	(9)				11	(9)
1923/24	6					6	(0)
Total	27	(12)				27	(12)

Mark Smith

Born: Redruth 21.9.1963
From: Apprentice 9.81
To: Exmouth Town 7.82

	League	FAC	LC	MC	Total	
1981/82	1+4				1+4	(0)
Total	1+4				1+4	(0)

Nigel Smith

Born: Bath 12.1.1966
From: Apprentice 1.84
To: Cheltenham Town 7.85

	League	FAC	LC	MC	Total	
1982/83	2				2	(0)
Total	2				2	(0)

Reg Smith

Born: Westbury
From: Trowbridge Town   3.35

	League		FAC		LC		MC	Total	
1935/36	6	(1)			1	(1)		7	(2)
1936/37	1							1	(0)
Total	**7**	**(1)**			**1**	**(1)**		**8**	**(2)**

George Sommerville

Born: Dalziel
From: Burnley   8.32
To: Burton Town   7.34

	League	FAC	LC	MC	Total	
1932/33	31		1		32	(0)
1933/34	3				3	(0)
Total	**34**		**1**		**35**	**(0)**

Lemmo Southway

Born: Bristol   22.7.1893
From: Local   7.13
To: Exeter City   7.22

	League	FAC	LC	MC	Total	
1919/20	13				13	(0)
1920/21	8				8	(0)
1921/22	6	1			7	(0)
Total	**6**	**1**			**7**	**(0)**

Bill Spalding

Born: Glasgow   24.11.1926
From: Ballymena   1.50
To: Bideford   7.51

	League	FAC	LC	MC	Total	
1949/50	9				9	(0)
1950/51	1	2			3	(0)
Total	**10**	**2**			**12**	**(0)**

Arthur Spear

Born: Bristol   1883
From: Local   7.04

	League		FAC	LC	MC	Total	
1904/05	12					12	(0)
1905/06	24	(1)				24	(1)
1906/07	15		1			16	(0)
1907/08	23		1			24	(0)
1908/09	33		10			43	(0)
1909/10	26		3			29	(0)
1910/11	3					3	(0)
Total	**136**	**(1)**	**15**			**151**	**(1)**

Gordon Spiring

Born: Bristol   1918
From: Local   7.37
To: Glastonbury   7.48

	League		FAC	LC	MC	Total	
1938/39	4	(1)				4	(1)
Total	**4**	**(1)**				**4**	**(1)**

Peter Spiring

Born: Glastonbury   13.12.1950
From: Juniors   6.68
To: Liverpool   3.73   £60,000

	League		FAC		LC		MC	Total	
1969/70	4				0+1			4+1	(0)
1970/71	6				1			7	(0)
1971/72	28+3	(9)	1	(1)	0+1			29+4	(10)
1972/73	21+2	(7)	3		1			25+2	(7)
Total	**59+5**	**(16)**	**4**	**(1)**	**2+2**			**65+7**	**(17)**

Steve Stacey

Born: Bristol   27.8.1944
From: Ipswich Town   9.70
To: Exeter City   9.71

	League	FAC	LC	MC	Total	
1970/71	9		1		10	(0)
Total	**9**		**1**		**10**	**(0)**

Fred Staniforth

Born: Kilnhurst   1.1.1884
From: Mexborough Town   7.06
To: Grimsby Town   7.11

	League		FAC	LC		MC	Total	
1906/07	24	(3)	2				26	(3)
1907/08	35	(4)	2				37	(4)
1908/09	34	(4)	10				44	(4)
1909/10	22	(3)	1	(1)			23	(4)
1910/11	19						19	(0)
Total	**134**	**(14)**	**15**	**(1)**			**149**	**(15)**

Garry Stanley

Born: Burton-on-Trent   4.3.1954
From: Wichita Wings   8.88
To: Gosport Borough   7.89

	League		FAC		LC	MC		Total	
1988/89	8+2		2+2		1	0+2		11+6	(0)
Total	**8+2**		**2+2**		**1**	**0+2**		**11+6**	**(0)**

Phil Starbuck

Born: Nottingham   24.11.1968
From: Sheffield United   9.95   Loan

	League		FAC	LC	MC	Total	
1995/96	5	(1)		1		6	(1)
Total	**5**	**(1)**		**1**		**6**	**(1)**

Cecil Steeds

Born: Bristol   11.1.1929
From: Juniors   3.47
To: Bristol Rovers   5.52

	League	FAC	LC	MC	Total	
1949/50	4				4	(0)
1951/52	5				5	(0)
Total	**9**				**9**	**(0)**

Dick Steel

Born: Ferryhill   13.3.1930
From: Ferryhill Athletic   6.53
To: York City   7.56

	League	FAC	LC	MC	Total	
1953/54	1				1	(0)
1955/56	2				2	(0)
Total	**3**				**3**	**(0)**

Charles Stevens

Born:
From:
To:

	League	FAC	LC	MC	Total	
1905/06	1				1	(0)
Total	**1**				**1**	**(0)**

Paul Stevens

Born: Bristol   4.4.1960
From: Apprentice   4.78
To: Bath City   7.85

	League		FAC		LC	MC	Total	
1977/78	1						1	(0)
1980/81	14		1				15	(0)
1981/82	46	(1)	5		5		56	(1)
1982/83	10		1		2	3	16	(0)
1983/84	45+1	(2)	5		1	1	52+1	(2)
1984/85	30				4	3	37	(0)
Total	**146+1**	**(3)**	**12**		**12**	**7**	**177+1**	**(3)**

Arthur Stevenson

Born: Padiham   1906
From: Sheffield United   5.30

	League		FAC	LC	MC	Total	
1930/31	5	(1)				5	(1)
Total	**5**	**(1)**				**5**	**(1)**

Bill Stolz

Born: Bristol   20.11.1875
From: Bedminster St. F.   7.04
To: Bedminster St. F.   7.05

	League	FAC	LC	MC	Total	
1904/05	1				1	(0)
Total	**1**				**1**	**(0)**

Fred Stone

Born: Bristol   5.7.1925
From: Warmley   6.47
To: Chippenham Town   7.53

	League		FAC	LC	MC	Total	
1947/48	4	(1)				4	(1)
1948/49	15	(1)				15	(1)
1949/50	23	(1)				23	(1)
1950/51	7					7	(0)
1951/52	12					12	(0)
1952/53	3					3	(0)
Total	**64**	**(3)**				**64**	**(3)**

Kenny Stroud

Born: Fulham   1.12.1953
From: Newport County   10.83
To: Bath City   9.85

	League		FAC		LC	MC	Total	
1983/84	34	(3)	4				38	(3)
1984/85	34+1	(1)	2			4	40+1	(1)
Total	**68+1**	**(1)**	**6**			**4**	**78+1**	**(4)**

Con Sullivan

Born: Bristol   22.8.1928
From: Horfield O.B.   5.49
To: Arsenal   2.54

	League	FAC	LC	MC	Total	
1950/51	20	3			23	(0)
1951/52	46	2			48	(0)
1952/53	7				7	(0)
Total	**73**	**5**			**78**	**(0)**

Charles Sutherland

Born: Lanark
From: Millwall 8.22
To: Merthyr Town 5.26

	League		FAC	LC	MC	Total	
1922/23	36	(9)	1			37	(9)
1923/24	22	(1)	1			23	(1)
1924/25	34	(11)	2			36	(11)
1925/26	11	(2)				11	(2)
Total	103	(23)	4			107	(23)

Gerry Sweeney

Born: Glasgow 10.7.1945
From: Morton 8.71 £22,000
To: Trowbridge Town 2.82

	League		FAC		LC		MC		Total	
1971/72	33+4	(3)	1		1				35+4	(3)
1972/73	40+1	(2)	3	(1)	1				44+1	(3)
1973/74	42	(3)	5		4	(1)	2		53	(4)
1974/75	42	(6)	1		4	(2)			47	(8)
1975/76	32+2	(5)	1		2		3	(1)	38+2	(6)
1976/77	42	(32)	1		1		3		47	(32)
1977/78	38	(1)	2		2		9	(1)	51	(2)
1978/79	42		2		1		5		50	(0)
1979/80	40+1		1		6	(1)	9		56+1	(1)
1980/81	38		5		2		2		47	(0)
1981/82	8+2		1		3				12+2	(0)
Total	397+10	(52)	23	(1)	27	(4)	33	(2)	480+10	(59)

Frank Sweet

Born: Bristol 1903
From: St. Michael's 7.10

	League		FAC	LC	MC	Total	
1910/11	2	(1)				2	(1)
1911/12	2					2	(0)
Total	4	(1)				4	(1)

Trevor Tainton

Born: Bristol 8.6.1948
From: Apprentice 9.65
To: Torquay United 2.82

	League		FAC		LC		MC		Total	
1967/68	4								4	(0)
1968/69	3+3								3+3	(0)
1969/70	25+4	(1)	1		3				29+4	(1)
1970/71	26+8	(1)	1		5+3				32+11	(1)
1971/72	41+1	(5)	1		1				43+1	(5)
1972/73	34+4	(2)	3	(1)	1				38+4	(3)
1973/74	42	(5)	6	(1)	4		2		54	(6)
1974/75	38	(1)	1		4				43	(1)
1975/76	42		1		2		3		48	(0)
1976/77	37+2	(2)	1		1		3	(1)	42+2	(3)
1977/78	36+2	(3)	2		2		9	(1)	49+2	(4)
1978/79	37	(1)	2		1		5	(1)	45	(2)
1979/80	34+5		2		6		9		51+5	(0)
1980/81	40+1	(2)	5		2		3		50+1	(2)
1981/82	19	(1)	5	(1)	3				27	(2)
Total	448+30	(24)	31	(3)	35+3		34	(3)	548+33	(30)

Alex Tait

Born: Bedlington 28.11.1933
From: Newcastle United 6.60 £5,000
To: Doncaster Rovers 6.64

	League		FAC		LC	MC	Total	
1960/61	35	(15)	4	(1)	3		42	(16)
1961/62	34	(13)	5	(5)	1	1	41	(18)
1962/63	37	(10)	2				39	(10)
1963/64	11					1	12	(0)
Total	117	(38)	11	(6)	4	2	134	(18)

Albert Talbot-Lewis

Born: Bedminster 20.1.1877
From: Leicester Fosse 7.07
To: Retired 5.08

	League	FAC	LC	MC	Total	
1907/08	21	2			23	(0)
Total	21	2			23	(0)

Micky Tanner

Born: Bristol 28.10.1964
From: Lawrence W.H. 7.85
To: Bath City 7.88

	League		FAC	LC		MC		Total	
1985/86	2							2	(0)
1986/87	4+1	(1)	1			1+1	(1)	6+2	(1)
1987/88	10+2			2	(1)	1		13+2	(1)
Total	16+3	(1)	1	2	(1)	2+1	(1)	21+4	(2)

Ron Tasker

Born:
From:
To:

	League	FAC	LC	MC	Total	
1913/14	1				1	(0)
Total	1				1	(0)

Archie Taylor

Born: Dunscroft 7.11.1939
From: Doncaster Rovers 5.58
To: Barnsley 7.61

	League		FAC	LC	MC	Total	
1959/60	2	(1)				2	(1)
1960/61	10	(1)				10	(1)
Total	12	(2)				12	(2)

Bob Taylor

Born: Horden 3.2.1967
From: Leeds United 3.89 P/Ex
To: West Bromwich Albion 1.92 £300,000

	League		FAC		LC		MC		Total	
1988/89	12	(8)							12	(8)
1989/90	37	(27)	7	(5)	2	(2)	1		47	(34)
1990/91	34+5	(11)	1		4		1		40+5	(11)
1991/92	13+5	(4)	1+1		0+1		1+1	(1)	15+7	(5)
Total	96+10	(50)	9+1	(5)	6+1	(2)	3+1	(1)	47	(34)

Jock Taylor

Born: Cowdenbeath 17.8.1909
From: Raith Rovers 7.27
To: Halifax Town 5.34

	League	FAC	LC	MC	Total	
1927/28	2				2	(0)
1928/29	21	1			22	(0)
1929/30	33	1			34	(0)
1930/31	23	1			24	(0)
1931/32	33	3			36	(0)
1932/33	27	3			30	(0)
1933/34	9			2	11	(0)
Total	148	9		2	159	(0)

Shaun Taylor

Born: Plymouth 26.2.1963
From: Swindon Town 9.96 £50,000

	League		FAC	LC	MC	Total	
1996/97	29	(1)	3		2	34	(1)
Total	29	(1)	3		2	34	(1)

Jim Terris

Born: Chippenham 25.7.1933
From: Chippenham Town 10.55
To: Carlisle United 4.59

	League	FAC	LC	MC	Total	
1956/57	1				1	(0)
1957/58	3		1		4	(0)
Total	4		1		5	(0)

Cyril Terry

Born: Bloxwich 1.8.1909
From: Manchester City 6.31
To: Yeovil & Petters 7.32

	League	FAC	LC	MC	Total	
1931/32	5				5	(0)
Total	5				5	(0)

Harry Thickett

Born: Hexthorpe 1.1.1873
From: Sheffield United 5.04
To: Manager

	League	FAC	LC	MC	Total	
1904/05	14	4			18	(0)
Total	14	4			18	(0)

Bill Thomas

Born: Derby 18.11.1918
From: BAC 3.44
To: Stonehouse 7.50

	League		FAC		LC	MC	Total	
1946/47	35	(14)	2	(1)			37	(15)
1947/48	30	(2)	3				33	(2)
1948/49	6	(1)					6	(1)
1949/50	6	(1)					6	(1)
Total	77	(18)	5	(1)			82	(19)

Sid Thomas

Born: Machynlleth 12.11.1919
From: Fulham 6.50
To: Retired – Illness 5.51

	League		FAC	LC	MC	Total	
1950/51	13	(1)				13	(1)
Total	13	(1)				13	(1)

David Thompson

Born: Ashington 20.11.1968
From: Millwall 6.92
To: Brentford 2.94

	League	FAC	LC	MC	Total	
1992/93	17		4	4+1	25+1	(0)
Total	17		4	4+1	25+1	(0)

John Thompson

Born: Redcar 22.7.1892
From: Sheffield United 11.20
To: Retired 5.22

	League		FAC	LC	MC	Total	
1920/21	26	(1)	1			27	(1)
1921/22	3					3	(0)
Total	29	(1)	1			30	(1)

Steve Thompson

Born: Plymouth 12.1.1963
From: Juniors 7.81
To: Torquay United 2.83

	League	FAC	LC	MC	Total	
1981/82	0+1	(1)			0+1	(1)
1982/83	10+1				10+1	(0)
Total	10+2	(1)			10+2	(1)

Dan Thomson

Born: Dundee 10.8.1891
From: St. Johnstone 7.25
To: Bournemouth 7.26

	League	FAC	LC	MC	Total	
1925/26	6				6	(0)
Total	6				6	(0)

Cliff Thorley

Born: West Melton 12.11.1913
From: Cheltenham Town 3.38
To: Retired 3.39

	League	FAC	LC	MC	Total	
1937/38	11	(3)			11	(3)
1938/39	3			1	4	(0)
Total	14	(3)		1	15	(3)

Mike Thresher

Born: Cullompton 9.3.1931
From: Chard Town 1.54
To: Bath City 7.65

	League	FAC	LC	MC	Total	
1954/55	22				22	(0)
1955/56	35	1			36	(0)
1956/57	36	2			38	(0)
1957/58	41	3			44	(0)
1958/59	41	3			44	(0)
1959/60	40	1			41	(0)
1960/61	41	5	3		49	(0)
1961/62	37	5	1	1	44	(0)
1962/63	41	4	1		46	(0)
1963/64	38	(1)	5	1	44	(1)
1964/65	7				7	(0)
Total	379	(1)	29	6	1	415	(1)

Bert Tindill

Born: South Hiendley 31.12.1926
From: Doncaster Rovers 2.58 £8,000
To: Barnsley 5.59 P/Ex

	League	FAC	LC	MC	Total	
1957/58	14	(10)			14	(10)
1958/59	42	(19)	3	(2)	45	(21)
Total	56	(29)	3	(2)	59	(31)

Brian Tinnion

Born: Stanley 23.2.1968
From: Bradford City 3.93 £180,000

	League	FAC	LC	MC	Total	
1992/93	11	(2)			11	(2)
1993/94	40+1	(5)	6	(2)	2	48+1	(7)
1994/95	33+2	(2)	3	(1)	2	38+2	(3)
1995/96	27+3	(3)	0+1		1+1	28+5	(3)
1996/97	30+2	(1)	4	4	2	40+2	(1)
Total	141+8	(13)	13+1	(3)	8	3+1	165+10	(16)

Michael Toman

Born: Whitehaven 15.12.1913
From: Preston North End 5.38

	League	FAC	LC	MC	Total	
1938/39	2			2	4	(0)
Total	2			2	4	(0)

Jim Tomlinson

Born: Horwich 17.5.1910
From: Bolton White H. 7.34

	League	FAC	LC	MC	Total	
1934/35	1				1	(0)
Total	1				1	(0)

David Tong

Born: Blackpool 21.9.1955
From: Cardiff City 10.85
To: Cambridge United 8.86

	League	FAC	LC	MC	Total	
1985/86	19	3		2	24	(0)
Total	19	3		2	24	(0)

Sam Tonner

Born: Dunfermline 10.8.1894
From: Clapton Orient 7.25
To: Crystal Palace 7.26

	League	FAC	LC	MC	Total	
1925/26	6	(1)			6	(1)
Total	6	(1)			6	(1)

Alex Torrance

Born: Glasgow 29.9.1901
From: Renfrew Juniors 6.21
To: Bath City 7.28

	League	FAC	LC	MC	Total	
1921/22	30	(2)	1		31	(2)
1922/23	35	(2)	2		37	(2)
1923/24	38	(4)	4		42	(4)
1924/25	16		1		17	(0)
1925/26	32	(1)	1		33	(1)
1926/27	11	(1)			11	(1)
1927/28	5				5	(0)
Total	167	(10)	9		176	(10)

Bill Tovey

Born: Bristol 18.1.1931
From: Juniors 12.48
To: Retired 5.53

	League	FAC	LC	MC	Total	
1948/49	4				4	(0)
1951/52	17	(1)	2		19	(1)
1952/53	36	(1)	1		37	(1)
Total	36	(1)	1		37	(1)

Ron Tovey

Born: Bristol 24.9.1930
From: Southmead Sports 1.53
To: Chippenham Town 7.54

	League	FAC	LC	MC	Total	
1952/53	6	(3)			6	(3)
1952/53	6				6	(0)
Total	12	(3)			12	(3)

Frank Townrow

Born: West Ham 1.11.1902
From: Dundee 6.30
To: Bristol Rovers 6.31

	League	FAC	LC	MC	Total	
1930/31	22	(5)			22	(5)
Total	22	(5)			22	(5)

Len Townsend

Born: Brentford 31.8.1917
From: Brentford 6.47
To: Millwall 7.49

	League	FAC	LC	MC	Total	
1947/48	39	(31)	3	(3)	42	(34)
1948/49	35	(14)	3	(2)	38	(16)
Total	74	(45)	6	(5)	80	(50)

Charles Treasure

Born: Farrington Gurney 1.9.1896
From: Paulton Rovers 7.19
To: Halifax Town 6.22

	League	FAC	LC	MC	Total	
1919/20	33	5			38	(0)
1920/21	29	1			30	(0)
1921/22	1				1	(0)
Total	63	6			69	(0)

Billy Tuft

Born: Wolverhampton 1.1.1874
From: Walsall 7.01

	League	FAC	LC	MC	Total	
1901/02	34	2			36	(0)
1902/03	33	3			36	(0)
1903/04	32	3			35	(0)
1904/05	33	5			38	(0)
1905/06	5				5	(0)
Total	137	13			150	(0)

Arthur Turner

Born:
From: Plymouth Argyle 5.32
To: York City 5.34

	League	FAC	LC	MC	Total	
1932/33	12		1		13	(0)
1933/34	4		1		5	(0)
1934/35	1				1	(0)
Total	17		2		19	(0)

Harold Turner

Born: Whitwell 1.1.1913
From: Chesterfield 6.35
To: Retired 9.36

	League	FAC	LC	MC	Total	
1935/36	6		1	(1)	7	(1)
Total	6		1	(1)	7	(1)

John Turner

Born: Wednesbury 1.1.1915
From: Chester 10.37
To: Clapton Orient 7.39

	League	FAC	LC	MC	Total	
1937/38	22		1		23	(0)
1938/39	1		2		3	(0)
Total	23		3		26	(0)

Robbie Turner

Born: Littlethorpe 18.9.1966
From: Wimbledon 1.89
To: Plymouth Argyle 7.90 £150,000

	League		FAC		LC	MC	Total	
1988/89	19	(6)					19	(6)
1989/90	26+7	(8)	7	(3)		2	35+7	(11)
Total	**45+7**	**(14)**	**7**	**(3)**		**2**	**54+7**	**(17)**

Graham Underhill

Born: Bristol 10.4.1968
From: Apprentice 4.86
To: Chippenham Town 7.87

	League	FAC	LC	MC	Total	
1985/86	1				1	(0)
Total	**1**				**1**	**(0)**

Frank Vallis

Born: Bristol 5.5.1896
From: Horfield United 7.19
To: Merthyr Town 6.26

	League	FAC	LC	MC	Total	
1919/20	42	5			47	(0)
1920/21	42	1			43	(0)
1921/22	22	2			24	(0)
1922/23	38	2			40	(0)
1923/24	30	4			34	(0)
1924/25	28	2			30	(0)
1925/26	17	1			18	(0)
Total	**219**	**17**			**236**	**(0)**

Gilbert Vallis

Born: Bristol 1.1.1898
From: Horfield United 11.19
To: Bridgend 7.20

	League	FAC	LC	MC	Total	
1919/20	6				6	(0)
Total	**6**				**6**	**(0)**

Henry Vallis

Born: Bristol
From: Dundee 7.21

	League	FAC	LC	MC	Total	
1921/22	10				10	(0)
Total	**10**				**10**	**(0)**

John Vaughan

Born: Isleworth 26.6.1964
From: West Ham 3.86 Loan
From: Fulham 1.88 Loan

	League	FAC	LC	MC	Total	
1985/86	2				2	(0)
1987/88	3				3	(0)
Total	**5**				**5**	**(0)**

Percy Vials

Born: Market Harborough 31.1.1908
From: Market Harborough 10.28
To: Middlesbrough 5.32

	League		FAC	LC		MC	Total	
1928/29	27	(13)					27	(13)
1929/30	20	(9)	1				21	(9)
1930/31	18	(12)	1	(1)			19	(13)
1931/32	8	(2)	3				11	(2)
Total	**73**	**(36)**	**5**	**(1)**			**78**	**(37)**

Ernie Vickerstaffe

Born: Hanley
From: Eastville A. 7.01
To: Leicester O.B. 7.02

	League	FAC	LC	MC	Total	
1901/02	1				1	(0)
Total	**1**				**1**	**(0)**

Derek Virgin

Born: Bristol 10.2.1934
From: Ilminster Town 8.53
To: Bath City 6.61

	League		FAC	LC	MC	Total	
1955/56	2		1			3	(0)
1957/58	1					1	(0)
1958/59	4	(2)				4	(2)
1959/60	8	(1)				8	(1)
1960/61	6	(1)	1			7	(1)
Total	**21**	**(4)**	**2**			**23**	**(4)**

H. E. Wadley

Born:
From:
To:

	League	FAC	LC	MC	Total	
1904/05	1				1	(0)
Total	**1**				**1**	**(0)**

Walter Wadsworth

Born: Bootle 1.10.1890
From: Liverpool 5.26
To: Flint Town 6.28

	League		FAC	LC	MC	Total	
1926/27	40					40	(0)
1927/28	27	(1)	1			28	(1)
Total	**67**	**(1)**	**1**			**68**	**(1)**

Billy Walker

Born: New Cumnock 5.5.1893
From: Merthyr Town 10.22
To: Wednesday 10.23

	League		FAC		LC	MC	Total	
1922/23	32	(7)	2	(1)			34	(8)
1923/24	5						5	(0)
Total	**32**	**(7)**	**2**	**(1)**			**34**	**(8)**

George Walker

Born: Sunderland 30.5.1934
From: Chippenham Town 5.56
To: Carlisle United 3.59

	League		FAC	LC	MC	Total	
1956/57	2	(1)				2	(1)
1957/58	12	(4)	2			14	(4)
1958/59	1					1	(0)
Total	**15**	**(5)**	**2**			**17**	**(5)**

George Wallis

Born: Sawley 1.1.1910
From: Birmingham 8.34
To: Bath City 8.37

	League		FAC	LC	MC	Total	
1934/35	17	(3)	1			18	(3)
1935/36	12	(6)	1		1	14	(6)
1936/37	13	(5)			1	14	(5)
Total	**42**	**(14)**	**2**		**2**	**46**	**(14)**

Alan Walsh

Born: Hartlepool 9.12.1956
From: Darlington 8.84 £18,000
To: Besiktas 7.89

	League		FAC		LC		MC		Total	
1984/85	45	(20)	2		4	(2)	4	(4)	55	(26)
1985/86	44	(18)	3	(1)	2		7	(2)	56	(21)
1986/87	41	(16)	5	(1)	4	(2)	8	(2)	58	(21)
1987/88	39+3	(12)	2		2		3	(1)	46+3	(13)
1988/89	46	(11)	6	(1)	9	(4)	3		64	(16)
Total	**215+3**	**(77)**	**18**	**(3)**	**21**	**(8)**	**25**	**(9)**	**279**	**(97)**

Jack Walsh

Born: Blackburn 11.2.1901
From: Aberdare Athletic 12.26
To: Millwall 3.32

	League		FAC	LC	MC	Total	
1926/27	21					21	(0)
1927/28	38		1			39	(0)
1928/29	20		1			21	(0)
1929/30	26	(1)				26	(1)
1930/31	38		1			39	(0)
1931/32	21					21	(0)
Total	**164**	**(1)**	**3**			**167**	**(1)**

Tot Walsh

Born: Bolton 12.2.1900
From: Bolton Wanderers 1.24
To: Crystal Palace 5.28

	League		FAC		LC	MC	Total	
1923/24	17	(2)	3	(2)			20	(4)
1924/25	38	(20)	2	(1)			40	(21)
1925/26	33	(25)	1				34	(25)
1926/27	39	(32)	2				41	(32)
1927/28	15	(9)					15	(9)
Total	**142**	**(88)**	**8**	**(3)**			**150**	**(91)**

Tommy Ware

Born: Bristol
From: Local 7.11
To: Killed in Action 6.15

	League	FAC	LC	MC	Total	
1911/12	5	1			6	(0)
1912/13	26	1			27	(0)
1913/14	20	2			22	(0)
Total	**20**	**2**			**22**	**(0)**

Ken Waterhouse

Born: Ormskirk 23.1.1930
From: Rotherham United 4.63
To: Darlington 8.64

	League		FAC	LC	MC	Total	
1962/63	10	(1)				10	(1)
1963/64	6			1		7	(0)
Total	**16**	**(1)**		**1**		**17**	**(1)**

Cyril Watkin

Born: Stoke-on-Trent 27.7.1926
From: Stoke City 7.52
To: Leek Town 3.54

	League	FAC	LC	MC	Total	
1952/53	3				3	(0)
Total	**3**				**3**	**(0)**

Johnny Watkins

Born: Bristol 9.4.1933
From: Clifton St. Vincent 6.51
To: Cardiff City 6.59 £2,500

	League	FAC	LC	MC	Total
1953/54	2				2 (0)
1954/55	23	(5)	3		26 (5)
1957/58	40	(9)	2	(1)	42 (10)
1958/59	30	(5)	3	(1)	33 (6)
Total	95	(19)	8	(2)	103 (21)

Barry Watling

Born: Walthamstow 16.7.1946
From: Leyton Orient 7.65
To: Notts County 7.69

	League	FAC	LC	MC	Total
1967/68	1				1 (0)
1968/69	1				1 (0)
Total	2				2 (0)

Kevin Watson

Born: Hackney 3.1.1974
From: Tottenham Hotspur 12.94 Loan

	League	FAC	LC	MC	Total
1994/95	1+1				1+1 (0)
Total	1+1				1+1 (0)

Keith Waugh

Born: Sunderland 27.10.1956
From: Sheffield United 12.84 Loan
From: Sheffield United 7.85
To: Coventry City 8.89

	League	FAC	LC	MC	Total
1984/85	3				3 (0)
1985/86	44	3	3	7	57 (0)
1986/87	46	5	4	8	63 (0)
1987/88	40	1	2	1	44 (0)
1988/89	37	6	7		53 (0)
Total	37	6	7	3	53 (0)

Bob Weaver

Born: Ponkey 1.1.1912
From: Luton Town 5.33

	League	FAC	LC	MC	Total
1933/34	3				3 (0)
Total	3				3 (0)

George Webber

Born: Bristol
From:
To:

	League	FAC	LC	MC	Total
1934/35	1				1 (0)
Total	1				1 (0)

Billy Wedlock

Born: Bedminster 28.10.1888
From: Aberdare Athletic 7.05
To: Retired 5.21

	League	FAC	LC	MC	Total
1905/06	38	(2)	1		39 (2)
1906/07	34	(2)	2		36 (2)
1907/08	34	(2)	2		36 (2)
1908/09	32	(1)	10		42 (1)
1909/10	35	(1)	3		38 (1)
1910/11	34	(3)	1		35 (3)
1911/12	35	(3)	1		36 (3)
1912/13	23	(1)			23 (1)
1913/14	30	(1)	2		32 (1)
1914/15	32	(1)	2		34 (1)
1919/20	30		5		35 (0)
1920/21	5				5 (0)
Total	362	(17)	29		391 (17)

Keith Welch

Born: Bolton 3.10.1968
From: Rochdale 8.91 £200,000

	League	FAC	LC	MC	Total
1991/92	26	2			28 (0)
1992/93	45	1	4	6	56 (0)
1993/94	45	6	2	2	55 (0)
1994/95	44	3	2		49 (0)
1995/96	35	2	2	1	40 (0)
1996/97	11		1		12 (0)
Total	206	14	10	10	240 (0)

Arnie White

Born: Bristol 25.07.1924
From: Soundwell 3.47
To: Millwall 8.51

	League	FAC	LC	MC	Total
1946/47	8				8 (0)
1947/48	6	(2)			6 (2)
1948/49	15				15 (0)
1949/50	32	(4)	1		33 (4)
1950/51	21	(6)			21 (6)
Total	82	(12)	1		83 (12)

Bill White

Born: Altrincham 26.7.1907
From: Newport County 5.35
To: Lincoln City 12.36

	League	FAC	LC	MC	Total
1935/36	35	(8)	1	3 (2)	39 (10)
1936/37	15	(7)	1		16 (7)
Total	50	(15)	2	3 (2)	55 (17)

Jack White

Born: Doncaster 17.3.1924
From: Aldershot 10.52
To: Cambridge City 4.58

	League	FAC	LC	MC	Total
1952/53	33	(4)	1		34 (4)
1953/54	40	(3)	3		43 (3)
1954/55	46	(2)	1		47 (2)
1955/56	41	(1)	1		42 (1)
1956/57	36	(1)	3		39 (1)
1957/58	20		2		22 (0)
Total	216	(11)	11		227 (11)

Clive Whitehead

Born: Birmingham 24.11.1955
From: Northfield Juniors 8.73
To: West Bromwich Albion 11.81 £100,000

	League	FAC	LC	MC	Total
1973/74	9+3	(2)	2 (1)	0+1	11+4 (3)
1974/75	10+4		1+3 (1)		11+7 (1)
1975/76	19+3	(4)		1	20+3 (4)
1976/77	41	1	1	3	46 (0)
1977/78	31+2	(2)	2	6 (1)	39+2 (3)
1978/79	22+8	(2)	2 1	2+2 (1)	27+10(3)
1979/80	40	2 (2)	5	6	53 (2)
1980/81	31	3	2	3	39 (0)
1981/82	6		2		8 (0)
Total	209+20(10)	8 (2)	16+3 (2)21+3 (2)		254+26(16)

Dave Whitelaw

Born: Calder 1.1.1910
From: Calder United 7.30
To: Southend United 7.31

	League	FAC	LC	MC	Total
1930/31	12	1			13 (0)
Total	12	1			13 (0)

Jonah Wilcox

Born: Coleford 19.1.1894
From: Abertillery 7.19
To: Bradford PA 9.22

	League	FAC	LC	MC	Total
1919/20	8	(2)			8 (2)
1920/21	38	(14)	1		39 (14)
1921/22	13	(4)	2		15 (4)
Total	59	(20)	3		62 (20)

Adrian Williams

Born: Bristol 4.8.1943
From: Apprentice 7.60
To: Exeter City 7.63

	League	FAC	LC	MC	Total
1960/61	4	1 (3)	2 (1)		7 (4)
Total	4	1 (3)	2 (1)		7 (4)

Alan Williams

Born: Bristol 3.6.1938
From: Juniors 9.55
To: Oldham Athletic 6.61 £1,000

	League	FAC	LC	MC	Total
1956/57	11				11 (0)
1957/58	34	2			36 (0)
1958/59	39	(1)	3		42 (1)
1959/60	39	(1)			39 (1)
1960/61	11	1			12 (0)
Total	134	(2)	6		140 (2)

Bertie Williams

Born: Merthyr Tydfil 4.3.1907
From: Merthyr Town 7.27
To: Sheffield United 1.32

	League	FAC	LC	MC	Total
1927/28	14	(4)			14 (4)
1928/29	8	1			9 (0)
1929/30	36	(16)	1 (1)		37 (17)
1930/31	22	(3)	1		23 (3)
1931/32	23	(3)	3 (2)		26 (5)
Total	103	(26)	6 (3)		109 (29)

Bobby 'Shadow' Williams

Born: Bristol 17.2.1940
From: Juniors 5.58
To: Rotherham United 3.65 £10,000

	League		FAC		LC	MC		Total	
1958/59	2	(1)						2	(1)
1959/60	9	(4)						9	(4)
1960/61	36	(7)	4	(2)	2			42	(9)
1961/62	45	(21)	5	(1)	1	2	(1)	53	(23)
1962/63	38	(19)	4	(1)	1			43	(20)
1963/64	41	(20)	5	(1)	1			47	(21)
1964/65	16	(4)	1		1			18	(4)
Total	**187**	**(76)**	**19**	**(5)**	**6**	**2**	**(1)**	**214**	**(82)**

Brian Williams

Born: Salford 5.11.1955
From: Bristol Rovers 7.85
To: Shrewbury Town 7.87

	League		FAC		LC	MC	Total	
1985/86	36	(1)	0+1		2	7	45+1	(1)
1986/87	41	(2)	5		2	8	56	(2)
Total	**77**	**(3)**	**5+1**		**4**	**15**	**101+1**	**(3)**

Cyril Williams

Born: Bristol 17.11.1921
From: Juniors 5.39
To: West Bromwich Albion 6.48 P/ex
From: West Bromwich Albion 8.51 £4,500
To: Chippenham Town 7.58 P/M

	League		FAC		LC	MC	Total	
1946/47	41	(17)	2	(1)			43	(18)
1947/48	37	(10)	3	(3)			40	(13)
1951/52	39	(6)	1				40	(6)
1952/53	42	(17)	1				43	(17)
1953/54	39	(4)	3	(1)			42	(5)
1954/55	39	(4)	1				40	(4)
1955/56	34	(3)	1				35	(3)
1956/57	22	(8)	2				24	(8)
1957/58	3						3	(0)
Total	**296**	**(69)**	**14**	**(5)**			**310**	**(74)**

Gary Williams

Born: Bristol 8.6.1963
From: Apprentice 8.80
To: Portsmouth

	League		FAC		LC	MC	Total	
1980/81	1						1	(0)
1981/82	33	(1)	5		1		39	(1)
1982/83	35+1		1		3		39+1	(0)
1983/84	30		5		2	0+1	37+1	(0)
Total	**99**	**(1)**	**11**		**6**	**0+1**	**116+2**	**(1)**

Paul Williams

Born: Newton Abbot 20.2.1964
From: Ottery St Mary 3.83
To: Saltash United 7.84

	League		FAC	LC	MC	Total	
1982/83	11	(1)				11	(1)
1983/84	5+3		1	0+2	1	7+5	(0)
Total	**16+3**	**(1)**	**1**	**0+2**	**1**	**8+5**	**(1)**

Sid Williams

Born: Bristol 21.12.1919
From: Eastville United 7.37
To: Stonehouse 6.52

	League		FAC	LC		MC	Total	
1946/47	13	(3)					13	(3)
1947/48	26	(2)					26	(2)
1948/49	13	(1)	3				16	(1)
1949/50	17	(3)					17	(3)
1950/51	25	(2)	5	(1)			30	(3)
1951/52	4						4	(0)
Total	**98**	**(11)**	**8**	**(1)**			**106**	**(12)**

Tommy Williams

Born: Easington 23.5.1899
From: Bristol Rovers 6.28
To: Merthyr Town 2.29

	League		FAC	LC	MC	Total	
1928/29	8	(4)				8	(4)
Total	**8**	**(4)**				**8**	**(4)**

George Willshaw

Born: Hackney 18.10.19.12
From: Southend United 7.38
To: Clapton Orient 7.39

	League		FAC	LC	MC		Total	
1938/39	34	(9)	1		2	(1)	37	(10)
Total	**34**	**(9)**	**1**		**2**	**(1)**	**37**	**(10)**

Bob Wilson

Born: Birmingham 23.5.1943
From: Cardiff City 10.69 Loan

	League	FAC	LC	MC	Total	
1969/70	1				1	(0)
Total	**1**				**1**	**(0)**

Jimmy Wilson

Born: Garforth 1.1.1909
From: Bradford PA 8.34
To: Bristol Rovers 6.38

	League	FAC	LC	MC	Total	
1934/35	1		1		2	(0)
1935/36	22		1		23	(0)
1936/37	41	1		2	44	(0)
1937/38	3			2	5	(0)
Total	**67**	**1**		**6**	**74**	**(0)**

John Wilson

Born: Leadgate 8.3.1897
From: Manchester United 5.32

	League	FAC	LC	MC	Total	
1932/33	18	3			21	(0)
Total	**18**	**3**			**21**	**(0)**

Les Wilson

Born: Manchester 10.7.1947
From: Wolves 3.71 Loan
From: Wolves 11.71 £15,000
To: Norwich City 9.73

	League		FAC	LC	MC	Total	
1970/71	10					10	(0)
1971/72	11	(1)	1			12	(1)
1972/73	21+1			1		22+1	(0)
Total	**42+1**	**(1)**	**1**	**1**		**44+1**	**(1)**

Peter Wilson

Born: Scotland
From:
To:

	League	FAC	LC	MC	Total	
1911/12	10				10	(0)
Total	**10**				**10**	**(0)**

Paul Wimbleton

Born: Havant 13.11.1964
From: Cardiff City 5.89
To: Shrewsbury Town 1.90

	League		FAC		LC		MC		Total	
1969/70	10+6	(2)	1	(1)	2	(1)	0+1		13+7	(4)
Total	**10+6**	**(2)**	**1**	**(1)**	**2**	**(1)**	**0+1**		**13+7**	**(4)**

Ken Wimshurst

Born: South Shields 23.3.1938
From: Southampton 10.67 £15,000
To: Assistant Coach 7.72

	League		FAC		LC	MC	Total	
1967/68	29	(3)	5				34	(3)
1968/69	40+1	(1)	1		3		44+1	(1)
1969/70	18+2						18+2	(0)
1970/71	34	(3)	1		7	(1)	42	(4)
1971/72	25	(2)	1		1		27	(2)
Total	**146+3**	**(9)**	**8**		**11**	**(1)**	**165**	**(10)**

Graham Withey

Born: Bristol 11.6.1960
From: Bath City 9.86
To: Cheltenham Town 7.87

	League	FAC	LC	MC	Total	
1986/87	1+1	1	0+1		2+2	(0)
Total	**1+1**	**1**	**0+1**		**2+2**	**(0)**

Dickie Wombwell

Born: Nottingham 1.1.1877
From: Derby County 7.02
To: Manchester United 3.05

	League		FAC		LC	MC	Total	
1902/03	34	(11)	3	(2)			37	(13)
1903/04	34	(5)	3	(1)			37	(6)
1904/05	24	(3)	5				29	(3)
Total	**92**	**(19)**	**11**	**(3)**			**103**	**(22)**

Eddie Woods

Born: Ton Pentre 29.7.1951
From: Ferndale 9.71
To: Newport County 9.74

	League	FAC	LC	MC	Total	
1972/73	1+1				1+1	(0)
Total	**1+1**				**1+1**	**(0)**

Tommy Woods

Born: Atherton
From: Plymouth Argyle   6.37

	League	FAC	LC	MC	Total	
1937/38	7		2		9	(0)
Total	**7**		**2**		**9**	**(0)**

Charles Worlock

Born: Bristol   24.2.1895
From: St. Philips Marsh   8.22
To: Bradford PA   5.25

	League	FAC	LC	MC	Total	
1922/23	35	(3)	2		37	(3)
1923/24	14				14	(0)
1924/25	24	(6)	2		26	(6)
Total	**73**	**(9)**	**4**		**77**	**(9)**

Jack Wren

Born: St. Werburghs   30.1.1894
From: Millwall   7.19
To: Notts County   8.22

	League	FAC	LC	MC	Total	
1919/20	37	(1)	5		42	(1)
1920/21	38		1		39	(0)
1921/22	29		2		31	(0)
Total	**104**	**(1)**	**8**		**112**	**(1)**

Mike Wyatt

Born: Bristol   12.9.1974
From: Trainee   7.92
To: Bath City   7.95

	League	FAC	LC	MC	Total	
1993/94	8+2		2	1	11+2	(0)
1994/95	1+2				1+2	(0)
Total	**9+4**		**2**	**1**	**12+4**	**(0)**

Bob Young

Born: Guard Bridge   1.1.1886
From: Dundee Violet   7.07

	League	FAC	LC	MC	Total	
1907/08	24				24	(0)
1908/09	21				21	(0)
1909/10	14				14	(0)
1910/11	36	1			37	(0)
1911/12	27	1			28	(0)
1912/13	22	1			23	(0)
1913/14	17	1			18	(0)
1914/15	6				6	(0)
1919/20	1				1	(0)
Total	**168**	**4**			**172**	**(0)**

KEY	
FAC . . . . FA Cup games played
LC . . . . League Cup games played
MC . . . . Miscellaneous Cup games

Ex-City players pictured at the official opening of the Carling Atyeo Stand on October 10th, 1994, left to right: Bobby Williams, Alan Williams, Jimmy Rogers, Mike Thresher, Lou Peters, Alec Tait, Andy Micklewright, Johnny Watkins, Gordon Parr, Wally Hinshelwood, Mike Gibson, Don Clark, Tony Ford, Alec Eisentrager, Jantzen Derrick, Dermot Curtis, Tony Cook, Geoff Bradford (ex-Bristol Rovers), Tommy Burden, Terry Bush, Jack Boxley, Roy Bentley and physio Les Bardsley.